Monasticism in North-Western Europe, 800–1200

About the volume:

This is a full-scale integrated synthesis of the origins, spread and effects of monasticism in Scandinavia, and along the shores of the Baltic and the North Sea, against the background of the struggle between Christian and non-Christian traditions.

Beginning with a review of the geography and communications by land and, especially, by sea, of the region, Tore Nyberg goes on to describe early monasticism among the Frisians, Saxons and the Danes, then in Norway and Sweden, Saxony, Slesvig and Ribe, and finally in Pomerania and the southern Baltic littoral up to AD 1200.

Throughout the book the author stresses the place of abbeys and convents within their local surroundings, as centres of conversion, recruitment and redistribution of wealth. He traces the intellectual, literary and liturgical connections between monastic centres and neighbouring cathedral towns and royal strongholds, and the means by which orders or congregations maintained discipline from the centre. He also describes the leaders who emerged from convent, abbey or congregation to command local and regional political and cultural life, and the ways in which monastic centres influenced popular devotion.

The book throws new light on subjects such as the survival of paganism and the development of Christian kingship, and demonstrates that early Scandinavian church history has greater coherence than has hitherto been suggested.

About the editor:

Tore Nyberg has been responsible for research and teaching in medieval history at the Institute of History and Western Civilization at the University of Southern Denmark, Odense, since 1970.

Monasticism in North-Western Europe, 800–1200

TORE NYBERG

Routledge
Taylor & Francis Group
LONDON AND NEW YORK

First published 2000 by Ashgate Publishing

Reissued 2018 by Routledge
2 Park Square, Milton Park, Abingdon, Oxon OX14 4RN
711 Third Avenue, New York, NY 10017, USA

Routledge is an imprint of the Taylor & Francis Group, an informa business

Typeset in Sabon by Manton Typesetters, Louth, Lincolnshire, UK.

A Library of Congress record exists under LC control number: 00026602

ISBN 13: 978-1-138-72142-5 (hbk)
ISBN 13: 978-1-138-72141-8 (pbk)
ISBN 13: 978-1-315-19454-7 (ebk)

Contents

List of figures

Preface

My first expression of gratitude must go to the three initiators of monastic studies who attempted, and for the first time presented to the public, an overall picture of monasticism in their respective countries. They represented by their efforts the conscientious, but only recently awakened, scholarly ambitions of their times in Scandinavia. Andreas Rhyzelius (1677–1761), who ended his life as Bishop of Linköping, published his *Monasteriologia* on Swedish monastic history in 1740 (Rhyzelius, 1740). The book on Danish monasticism which the later bishop, Jacob Brøgger Daugaard (1796–1861), published in 1830 was his prize essay at the Royal Society of Sciences and Letters in Copenhagen (Daugaard, 1830). In Norway it was the Director of the Royal Archives in Christiania, Christian Christoph Andreas Lange (1810–61), who created the pioneer work on Norwegian monasticism which appeared in Christiania in 1847 and, in a second edition, in 1856 (Lange, 1847). The list can be extended by adding the names of some scholars of our century who trod in the footsteps of these heroic pioneers: university teachers like the Copenhagen church historian Hal Koch (1904–63) (Koch, 1936) and scholars of the Cistercian Order like the Catholic parish priest Eduard Ortved (1855–1930) (Ortved, 1927; 1933). Lauritz Weibull (1873–1960), the great admirer of Archbishop Eskil, and Niels Skyum-Nielsen (1921–82), representatives of the 'school of historical criticism', focused upon how to understand marginal Scandinavian monasticism in the framework of medieval European church and society. One of their followers was the enthusiastic Scanian promotor of Premonstratensian studies, Curt Wallin (1908–92). In Sweden the devotion to monasticism inspired Hilding Johansson, the Lund scholar who was at home in Skara and Lidköping in western Sweden, to undertake fundamental Cistercian studies which also took into account liturgical sources.

My debt of gratitude towards Niels Skyum-Nielsen is also very personal: I had the privilege of his friendship. The writings of Åke Hyenstrand and Peter Sawyer on Scandinavian society and religion at the time of the conversion to Christianity brought further inspiration. Then came the fundamental scholarly contributions of Brian Patrick McGuire, now of Roskilde, on the Cistercians in Denmark and of James France on the Cistercians in Scandinavia. Erik Cinthio, Lund, published collected studies on monasticism in Scania, Øyvind Lunde presented his results on monasteries in medieval Trondheim and elsewhere in Norway, and Jens Vellev, Aarhus, went on publishing new results from excavations and further studies on Scandinavian monasticism in his yearbook *Hikuin*, and they are joined by a number of outstanding scholars in history and archaeology whose contributions to the history of particular sites are found in the references.

The corollary of the national and regional studies was the international perspective to which above all Kaspar Elm contributed, his Ordensstudien conferences and publications bringing together students of all types of religious life in Berlin in the 1970s and 1980s. Furthermore, the new Centre Européen de Recherches sur les Congrégations et Ordres Religieux (CERCOR) in St Etienne, France, founded by the late Professor Pierre-Roger Gaussin, has meant a tremendous step forward in encouraging studies on all aspects of religious life. I am above all grateful to have been allowed to participate in this community of scholars on monasticism initiated by Professor Gaussin, with its conferences and publications.

It seemed appropriate to go beyond the frontiers of Scandinavia proper and, by including Frisia and the northernmost dioceses of Germany, to make North-Western Europe the geographical scope of this book. In this connection I am deeply indebted to Johannes Adriaan Mol, Leeuwarden, who from the perspective of the Fryske Akademy has shared with me his broad perspective upon, and detailed knowledge of, Frisian monasticism.

Last but not least I thank the Institute of History and Western Civilization and the Centre for History at the University of Southern Denmark, Odense, for providing the scholarly environment and resources for the research which led to this book.

Tore Nyberg
Odense, 1999

List of abbreviations

CER	'Cronica Ecclesiae Ripensis'
CR	'Chronicon Roskildense'
DBL	*Dansk Biografisk Leksikon*
DD	*Diplomatarium Danicum*
DK	*Danmarks Kirker*
DMA	*Danmarks middelalderlige annaler*
DS	*Diplomatarium Suecanum*
LDat	'Liber daticus Lundensis'
MGH DD	*Monumenta Germaniae Historica, Diplomata regum*
MGH SS	*Monumenta Germaniae Historica, Scriptores*
NBL	*Norsk Biografisk Leksikon*
NL	*Necrologium Lundense*
SBL	*Svenskt biografiskt lexikon*
SE	*Series Episcoporum*
SM	*Scriptores minores*
VSD	*Vitae Sanctorum Danorum*

Introduction

'Monasticism in North-Western Europe in the period from *c.* 800 to *c.* 1200' demands a definition of terms. As a notion, 'monasticism' is related to *monachus*, *monasticus*, *monasterium*, Latin words connected to 'someone living alone', Greek *monos*. A 'monk' is someone living 'alone' by force of a religious motivation. In the period we are dealing with here, however, monks are no longer physically alone, as they were in the initial stages of the desert fathers in Egypt in the third and fourth centuries AD. The first millenium had made monasticism communitarian, cenobitic, and in that form, it reached North-Western Europe with the Christian mission of the seventh to tenth centuries. The same is true for nuns – parallel to the male form, we speak of a nun as *monacha* or *monialis*.

In North-Western Europe, Christianity has been the only movement offering a programme for the way of life of a person living 'alone' and for communities consisting of such persons. The programme was made up of a number of *logia*, sayings, of the founder of this religion and some of his followers, handed down together with a certain 'vulgate' interpretation linked to these sayings. Impulses inspiring to monasticism did not reach North-Western Europe directly from the Bible, however, but mostly through the intermediary of monastic rules, above all the Rule of St Benedict. Basic features are the individual's renouncing of physical reproduction on the basis of, for example, Matthew 19:11–12, and his or her renouncing of the right to dispose of property as exposed, for example, in Matthew 19:16–22, Mark 10:17–22 and Luke 18:18–23. The conclusion was the same in all versions: 'If you want to be perfect' or 'You still lack one thing': 'Go, sell what you have, give it to the poor, and you will have a treasure in heaven; then come and follow me.' Furthermore, the notion of obedience was developing, meaning to 'follow' or 'listen' to the giver of advice for a perfect life in community. A fixed code of general behaviour identified as monastic was already widely accepted when Christianity arrived in North-Western Europe. It had got its 'Benedictine' form in the Carolingian period when Benedict of Aniane placed Benedict of Nursia's Rule in the very centre of Western monasticism.

The region introduced here as 'North-Western Europe' is defined by it being exposed only to the form of monasticism which was mediated by the Carolingian empire. It comprises only areas situated outside the *limes* of the Roman Empire, since inside the *limes* older traditions still exerted their influence upon religious life. Only maritime regions (except Scotland) will be considered, all Scandinavia including the coasts of the Baltic being considered as maritime.

The time frame *c.* 800 to *c.* 1200 has been chosen because it is the period when Christianity slowly progressed northwards and eastwards outside the *limes*. The Frisians were already Christians by *c.* 800, the Saxons had just been violently incorporated into the Carolingian empire. Christian mission to Scandinavia started with the missionaries St Willibrord from Echternach before 800 and St Ansgar from Corvey around 830. By *c.* 1000 Denmark, Norway and Iceland had adopted Christianity, and by *c.* 1100 all the Scandinavian kingdoms were Christian, at least officially, whereas Christianity did not make great progress in the Slav principalities of present-day Mecklenburg and Pomerania, in former Prussia, in Livonia, Estonia and Finland before *c.* 1150. The thirteenth century marks the arrival of the Mendicants, who gave the growing urban population a new model for religious life which falls outside the scope of this book.

Monasteries are institutions whose existence presuppose a material basis and an authority to guarantee their permanent existence. We deal with founders – royal, noble, ecclesiastical – as well as with public authorities securing and protecting the monasteries as institutions – public assemblies, kings, bishops. Before a society with some affinity to European political structures of the tenth and eleventh centuries had been established in North-Western Europe, monasteries could not exist, even if a religious motivation for monastic life was there.

The community, which produces founder and protector, is made up of parents, sisters, brothers, cousins, uncles and friends of those who enter monastic life. They are those whom monks and nuns pray for and whose names they keep in their necrologies and memorial books. Thus, besides charters and chronicles, books of divine service and memorial books constitute an important source material for this study.

The mental world of monks and nuns also comprises neighbouring religious institutions. These may be those of the hierarchical church – bishop, cathedral clergy – or other institutions belonging to the 'monastic order' in the wider sense of this word. The use of the phrase 'monastic order' or 'religious order' has been widely debated elsewhere and will only be briefly touched on here. 'Benedictine', 'Augustinian' and other similar terms will not be used to distinguish between different branches or strings of monasticism, but to repeat the main characteristic of monasticism as such in the period we deal with (Benedictine) and to remind the reader of the existence of affinitive movements (Augustinian).

A 'missionary frontier' was present in more or less all aspects of Christian life during the period under consideration. Differentiation and conflicting interests inside monasticism, as they can be studied in France and elsewhere at the same time, may have been externally transferred to North-Western Europe but cannot be said to have grown out of any intrinsic necessity here. Such conflicts, then, may be disregarded and the continuity of monastic life as a world of its own may be taken for granted.

In another sense, however, society and the mental horizon of the peoples of North-Western Europe in this period was characterized by change. First we have the terrific change of leaving one set of religious practices in order to adopt another. In dealing with monasticism, we have to deal with the change of behaviour of the individual when leaving his half-Christian worldly life to enter the monastery. Then, changes occur in the competition between religious orders, for example when a monastery is being transferred from one observance to another, or when a new monastery is being built close to an existing one, thereby changing its place in society.

A comparative perspective is necessary in dealing with monasticism in North-Western Europe in this period. Comparisons within the different regions of North-Western Europe will turn out to be just as essential as comparisons between developments in this area and other parts of Western Christendom.

To investigate the growth of monasticism in maritime North-Western Europe until the arrival of the Mendicants on the background of politics, church and society also implies establishing a chronology, related partly to political and economic trends in society and to developments of monasticism in England and continental Europe. Waves of monastic foundations and recruitment to established monasteries will have to be identified and discussed. Was there at any time a monastic 'breakthrough' among the inhabitants of a certain region? Are there indications of monasteries and convents being attractive to different layers of society for different reasons at different times? Were monasteries in this period a bulwork against paganism?

Monasticism must have contributed in creating a new type of man out of the material which North-Western Europe had formed during a long development of maritime culture. What came out of this cultural encounter in the period until the arrival of the Mendicants lies hidden under many layers of later events. The following study can only hope to uncover a few aspects of these early expressions of religious conviction. What in part might look like a history of institutions, may nevertheless contribute to our understanding of the men and women who were engaged in creating new forms of human existence in the first Christian centuries of North-Western Europe by donating part of their fortune, using their authority, or themselves entering monasteries in order to practise there the basic norms of Christianity in the strict forms of monastic life.

CHAPTER ONE

The monastic geography of North-Western Europe

I The regions

Already in Carolingian times, the Germanic languages spoken in North-Western Europe were separated into the north Germanic – the Scandinavian – languages, and the south Germanic, which developed into Frisian and the different forms of Low (and High) German. One of the most important cultural and political barriers, therefore, is the one between the continental Saxons and Frisians, on the one side, and the Danes on the other: the Danevirke. This frontier between the Scandinavian and the Teutonic tribes was valid throughout the period treated in this book. It is useful as well for the scholarly treatment of monasticism. Monastic impulses that circulated inside the Carolingian empire reached all peoples belonging to the empire, and inspired monastic foundations there long before any Scandinavian group was ready even to accept Christianity.

Saxony

The Saxons or 'Old Saxons', as they were still called in Wulfstan's account from the ninth century, to distinguish them from those Saxons who had emigrated to Britain in the fifth and sixth century, inhabited most of the land from beyond the Rhine *limes* to Elbe in the north. Two large rivers flowing northwards through the land of the Saxons unified and simultaneously divided it in elongated south–north sections: the Ems and the Weser with its tributary the Aller.

The Saxons were not a seafaring people, which the Frisians were, who increasingly specialized in sea transport and commerce, expanding eastwards along the coast as far as the land of Danes. Settlement was dense in Upper Saxony and progressively thinner in Lower Saxony towards the marshy coast to the north. In 804, Charlemagne and Archbishop Hildebald of Cologne organized the Saxon mission by establishing four bishoprics: Münster for those living west of the Ems; Osnabrück for the land east of the Ems around its tributary, the river Hase; Bremen for the main Saxon settlement area around the estuary of the Weser;

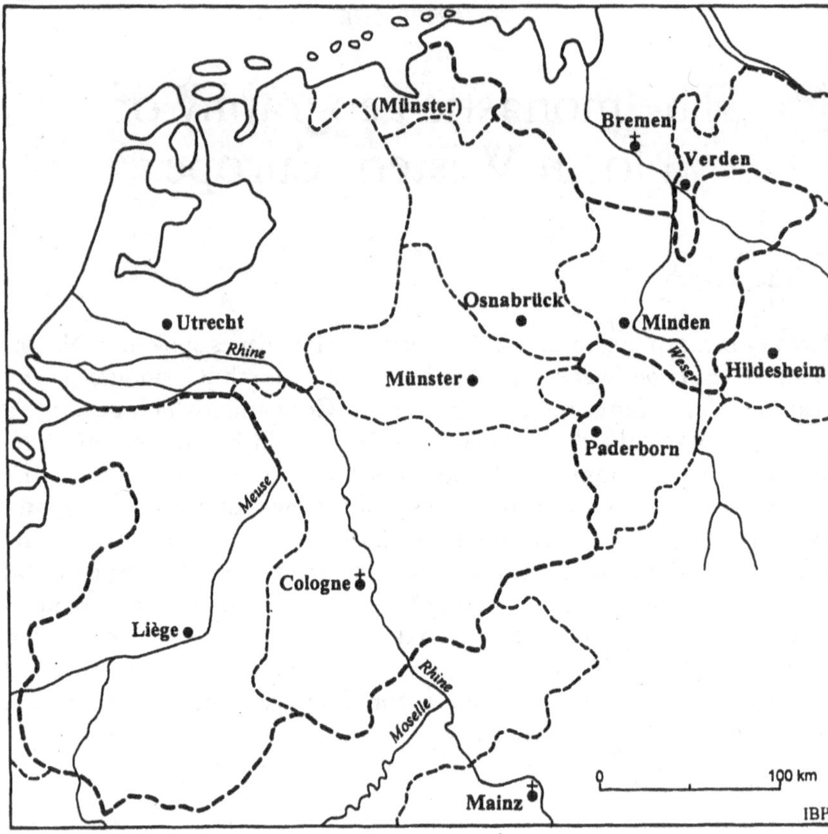

--- Boundary of the Church Province of Cologne   --- Boundary of diocese

Archiepiscopal see   • Episcopal see

1.1 Diocesan boundaries in continental North-Western Europe: the church province of Cologne with neighbouring dioceses. (Drawn by Inger Bjerg Poulsen, after Platelle [1993].)

and Minden further up the Weser. Besides the area around the upper course of the Ems, Münster was also given the administration of the Frisian coastland (see Figure 1.1).

East of Bremen, the missionaries from Cologne met those sent there by the Archbishop of Mainz. An episcopal see under Mainz had been in existence at Paderborn south of Minden since 804, and the ecclesiastical province of Mainz came to take care of religious matters as far as the Elbe and its western affluent, the river Fulda, by means of several suffragan bishoprics: Bardowic, which Louis the Pious *c.* 815 ordered to be moved to Verden, near where the Aller joined the Weser, one in Hildesheim east of Minden, to be followed by Halberstadt further east in 827.

The men who changed the role of Saxony in the context of the Christian mission were Emperor Louis the Pious and the monk Ansgar of Corvey, for whom an episcopal see was established in Hamburg in 831, only to be plundered by Viking raids in 845. In compensation, Ansgar became Bishop of Bremen and this diocese was removed from the supremacy of the Archbishop of Cologne and made into the missionary archbishopric of Hamburg-Bremen (Seegrün 1967; 1976; Wavra 1991). Hereby a German maritime region was created, with significant consequences for Scandinavia's meeting with Christianity and with continental European culture. The archbishopric of Hamburg-Bremen lacked suffragan bishops and split in half: the area around Bremen and the Weser estuary, and the area beyond the Elbe, the Transalbingia, with the Danevirke as its northern frontier, and the *limes Saxoniae* as its eastern frontier, the 'Saxon *limes*' – a term created in analogy to the *limes* of the Roman Empire. It separated Transalbingia from the region of the Slavic Obodrites. Its task was exclusively the propagation of the Christian faith among the neighbouring non-German peoples.

The Ottonian duchy of Saxony thus counted no less than one independent archbishopric and seven well-established episcopal sees within its territory. To provide these mighty sees with faithful and loyal bishops was a main concern of the Ottonian and Salian kings and emperors. Monasteries grew up in collaboration with, and very often directly inspired by, these bishops, who were active within the framework of the so-called 'Ottonian-Salian Imperial Church System'. After the investiture contest, Saxon principalities became Denmark's mighty neighbours, partners and competitors, for example under Duke Henry the Lion (died 1195).

Frisia

The situation of the Frisians was very different. A people without a state but with a common law, they managed to survive thanks to their choosing to live on the *geest* – an inland belt of dry and sandy soil parallel to the coast – and the marshland, where no one else wanted to live, and to carry out sea-borne commerce from their coastal refuges (Kletler, 1924). The see of Utrecht had been founded for the Frisians in 695, with Willibrord as its first bishop (died 739). Utrecht administered the Christian mission in all the coastal land as far as the Ems estuary, which was under the bishops of Münster.

Unlike the Saxons, the Frisians found themselves in ecclesiastically weak areas on the outskirts of established dioceses: Utrecht, Münster,

Bremen. Monasticism among the Frisians, therefore, once it emerged, turned out to display a character very different from patterns prevalent in Saxony. Powerful and influential families dominated even more than in Saxony, yet without getting involved in the investiture conflict as was the case with the Saxons.

The southern coast of the Baltic Sea

To the east of the 'Saxon *limes*', various Slav tribes became involved in Carolingian and Danish politics and warfare at the time when Saxony became Christian. Under the name of Vends, their attacks upon the isles of the Danes were recorded by Danish historians like Saxo and Svend Aggesen, as well as the Danish victory over them at Lyrskov Hede near Slesvig[1] in 1043. The closest neighbours of Saxony along the coast, the Obodrites, lived as far east as Rügen, followed by the Wilzians between Rügen and the river Oder. The lands between the rivers Oder and Vistula were inhabited by the Pomeranians, the land east of the Vistula by the Prussians (Pruzzi).

German eastward migration and Christian mission had long made its impact upon this region where Christian principalities came into being in the course of the twelfth century. The decisive blow to the last non-Christian cult centre, Arkona on the island of Rügen, came through conquest by the Danes in 1169.

In the 1160s, the diocesan boundaries of the region were defined: under Duke Henry the Lion, the missionary see of Oldenburg was moved to recently founded Lübeck, the land of the Obodrites was given two episcopal sees, Ratzeburg and Schwerin, and the three bishops were made suffragans of the archbishop of Hamburg-Bremen. Rügen was incorporated in the Danish diocese of Roskilde. The Wilzian lands and Pomerania were brought together into the diocese of Kammin or Kamień, which the Pope, because of competing German and Polish claims, decided in 1174 to keep outside existing church provinces – the German Archbishop of Magdeburg here competed with the Polish primate, the Archbishop of Gniezno. Kammin became exempt, in other words directly subordinated to the Pope. Only the eastern part of Pomerania, known as Pommerelia, which politically belonged to Poland, was part of a Polish diocese, Włocławek (*diocesis Wladislaviensis*, German Leslau). The eastern Christian frontier lay at the river Vistula in our period – the Prussians were not yet baptized.

Under the pressure of German princes and colonists the transformation of Slav agricultural society caused many Slav groups to flee further east to escape Germanization. Poland became the only Slav kingdom in this region to be organized upon principles originating in Western Europe. However, this kingdom displayed an inland culture from the start. As in the case of the Ems and the Weser, the inland population did not show any tendency to move towards the sea and earn their living there. Germanized Vends and Pomeranians organized themselves along the coast as feudal principalities, stimulated urbanization and paved the way for the Hanseatic League.

Jutland

A Danish kingdom, the centre of which is not known with certainty, had erected the wall called Danevirke in the eighth century. To the north of the Danevirke is the Cimbrian peninsula: Jutland, land of the Jutes. Politically capable of dealing directly with Carolingian Europe, Jutland was united by at least the middle of the tenth century under the Jelling kings. In contrast to the west coast with its few trading sites – Ribe, the present-day Ringkøbing area, the western estuary of the Limfjorden, and, on the island of Vendel to the north of Limfjorden, the area of Børglum and Hjørring – the east coast offered many more openings: the eastern end of Limfjorden with Aalborg; the estuary of Gudenåen, Jutland's biggest river, with the town of Randers; Aarhus, walled in from the tenth century; further settlements in the bottom of the bays of today's Horsens, Vejle, Kolding and Haderslev; and, finally, Hedeby, which the Germans refer to as Haithabu, walled by the eighth century.

Zealand (Sjælland)

Jutland's political unity is normally taken to be the starting-point for Danish power extending eastwards to the isles: to Funen, Langeland and Femern, to Lolland and Falster, and to Zealand; from there, finally, to the southern part of the Scandinavian peninsula: Scania and Halland. Three regions emerged out of this movement, as evidenced by the three provincial laws of Jutland, Zealand and Scania. The highly maritime Danish kingdom received its Christianity partly from the South – its earliest three dioceses in Jutland 948 and that on Funen before 988 rested on imperial initiative – partly from the West; Cnut the Great installed the first bishops in Zealand and Scania around 1020. Funen and Zealand opened up to the North by the harbours of Odense and Roskilde, the two episcopal sees, and were part of an internal Danish maritime system between the coastal areas of eastern Jutland and of Halland, with the island of Samsø as a link in the middle. Roskilde became a centre of royal power after Swein Forkbeard was buried there in 1014.

Scania

The Zealand and Scania bishoprics were instituted at the same time, but their further history pushed them apart. Very early the regional construction of Danish power gave the diocese for Scania-Halland, based at Lund, a character of its own, marked by its position as the archbishopric for all Scandinavia between 1104 and 1153, for Denmark and Sweden between 1153 and 1164, and from that time for Denmark alone. Blekinge, the coastal area to the east of Scania, may have been Swedish in the pre-Christian period, according to Adam of Bremen; in the twelfth century at the latest it was part of Denmark and of the archdiocese of Lund.

Scania with Halland and Blekinge, its two adjacent strips of coastal land, was by nature split into a rich western and southern coastal zone, well adapted to agriculture and coastal trade, and a less inhabited inland zone in the north-east, where the land rose and was inhospitable to the type of agriculture normally preferred by the Danes. Lund, founded by Cnut the Great *c.* 1020 lies in the coastal zone, and it is no wonder that after a generation the need was felt for another ecclesiastical centre facing inland. This is how Dalby came into being as a diocesan centre for some years in the 1060s.

Västergötland-Värmland, 'Western Götaland' and 'the Land of the Wermilani'

Between the two huge lakes, Lake Vätter and Lake Väner, a very old settlement area filled the plain which partly descended towards the north, partly towards the south-west, with rivers running out into the Kattegat through Halland. The inland orientation towards the huge lake in the north brought the people into close contact with the less densely populated area to the north of the lake, the people which Adam of Bremen calls Wermilani. Missionaries arrived here very early, since this area, contrary to the adjacent region to the east, offered a more comfortable passage overland from the Viken area in Norway to the Danish territory of the archbishops of Lund. The first Christian king, Olof Skötkonung, created the episcopal see of Skara here *c.* 1020. The river valleys running south to west did carry some cultural impulses between the Danes and the Swedes of Västergötland but, seen from the central settlement area south of Lake Väner, these valleys were outskirts and not very densely populated.

The diocese of Skara, consisting of all the land around Lake Väner but, turning its back to maritime Halland as well as to Lake Vätter and the people to the east of that lake, was quickly identified as a region of its own by the missionaries who as early as the eleventh century saw the chance here to establish a model for a Christian kingdom among the Swedes. Early impulses, possibly from Byzantium, created some unique patterns in this region, for example of decorated memorial slabs with the tree of life as their main motif, which is only known from this diocese, but which continued to be used for at least two centuries; an exact dating is not possible.

Småland-Östergötland, 'the Small Lands' and 'East Götaland'

The huge forests to the north of Scania created an effective barrier between Danes and Swedes. To the north of the highlands, most of which constitute Småland, are lands more suitable for farming, the plains of 'East Götaland' to the east of Lake Vätter – but never on such a scale as the Danes could enjoy, much further to the south. The maritime character of early settlement is evident; although the coast, dotted with rocky islands, was ideal for piracy, travel by sea was preferred to travel by land, as we can see from the voyages of Ansgar in the ninth century. In the eleventh century, too, foreign missionaries recognized the potential of this region for trade and cultural development.

Three important islands played the role of staging posts for Christian penetration into the interior of Scandinavia and the eastern part of the Baltic Sea: Öland in the South-East, Gotland between Sweden and Livonia, and Åland between the Mälar region and Finland. The missionary diocese created somewhere here *c.* 1060 under the famous Birka name soon merged in the diocese of Linköping. Not until the twelfth century do we find further collaboration between the church and a Swedish kingdom, that of King Sverker (died 1156).

Folklanden, 'the Folk Lands', around Lake Mälar

A number of Swedish tribes were grouped around the twisting Lake Mälar. One of these tribes, in the area called Attundaland on the northern shore of Lake Mälar ('The Land of Eight Units') adopted Christianity in the early eleventh century; their conversion is evidenced by numerous runic inscriptions. Their northern neighbours, however, those of Tiundaland ('The Land of Ten Units') seem to have hesitated, while the people of Fjädrundaland ('The Land of Four Units'), the Västmänningar to their west, and the Södermänningar south of the lake followed suit. With the consent of some of the rulers in this area, missionaries created an ecclesiastical centre in Sigtuna in Attundaland on the northern shore of Lake Mälar *c.* 1060. In spite of further diocesan division – two more episcopal sees, Västerås for the Västmänningar and Strängnäs for the Södermänningar, were planned *c.* 1100 – the region retained its unity, and soon took the lead among the Swedish regions by becoming the centre of royal power and, from 1164, by being the home of the archbishopric of Sweden, Uppsala. The archdiocese itself consisted to a great extent of a fourth region, which is not treated here since no monasteries were ever founded there: Norrland, denoting all the remaining coastal and inland areas in the North with a Swedish population along the Baltic Sea. A land which rose gradually from the sea, the working of the ice in the last glacial period was now reversed.

Viken, 'the Bay', the first region of 'the Way to the North', Norway

Seen from the interests of coastal trade around the North Sea and Kattegat, the Swedes appeared to be an inland people. Even in the eleventh and twelfth centuries, a ship sailing north along the coast of Halland probably never touched upon any Swedish settlement as it left Danish waters and proceeded along the Norwegian coast, the Bohuslän of today. Entering Viken, 'the Bay', it had access to a rich and densely populated agricultural area along the coast and in the valleys. Two Norwegian kings, Olav Tryggvesson (died 995) and Olav Haraldsson (died 1030), encouraged missionaries to work in the region, building churches and baptizing. Christianization in its deeper sense was a rather slow process, however, to judge from Adam of Bremen's comments that the Norwegians used far more sorcery and superstitious practices than Danes and Swedes (*Adam*, 1917, IV, ch. 32). Wandering missionary bishops gave way to the episcopal see of Oslo to provide the religious organization of the region.

The Viken region stood under the strong influence of impulses from Denmark and thereby from some of the religious centres of continental Europe known to the Danes. Administrative units known in Jutland as 'sysler' are found in Viken but not in other Norwegian regions. On several occasions when there was civil war, the influential families in Viken were in touch with the Danes against powerful warlords from other Norwegian regions. Four provincial laws underline the regional structure of early Christian Norway. One, the Borgartingslov, covered the Viken area on both sides of the bay: Vestfold, Østfold and present-day Bohuslän; it was named after the meeting place of the Thing,

(Sarps)Borg in Østfold. Inland, in the Opplandene, 'the lands higher up', the Eidsivatingslov was valid, named after the Eidsiva Thing. Shortly before 1153, a diocese of its own, Hamar, was created for this area.

Vestlandet

The long Norwegian coast from the southern agricultural district of Agder in the south to Møre and Romsdal in the north shares the same climate and geographical characteristics: mild winters thanks to the Gulf Stream, innumerable deep bays enabling access from the sea, narrow stretches of arable land. Here, a society of seafaring warriors and farmers could survive, although under cramped conditions. The first bishopric of the region, on the very exposed island of Selja, was centrally placed, but with the rise of a stronger royal power in the course of the eleventh century, Bergen became the central place and episcopal see of the region. It kept its key role within this region, united by its common law, the Gulatingslov, although around 1115 the southern part with some inland districts was made into the separate diocese of Stavanger.

Trøndelag

Thanks to the combination of a high northern latitude with the warmth of the Gulf Stream, a dense settlement area came into being in protected pockets further north. The farmers living around the Nidelv had their assembly at the Frosta Thing, from where their provincial law took the name Frostatingslov. Above all the tomb of the first Christian king, St Olav, helped create an urban settlement in Nidaros, the *os*, or 'mouth', of the river Nid. The bishop who established his see here under the protection of strong kings or warlords, supported by the tomb of the holy martyr king, became the most influential of the Norwegian bishops, since the unity of the Norwegian kingdom was imposed from here. In 1153, Nidaros became the see of Norway's archbishop, who then had four mainland suffragans and two on the Atlantic islands, besides his authority over the Faeroe islands, the two bishoprics of Iceland, and the Norse colonists in Greenland. Nidaros developed into a main contact area for the inhabitants of the long coast further north with its population of fishermen and hunters, where monasticism never gained access.

Contrary to the extension of the archdiocese, which coincided with the present-day Norwegian border with Sweden, but covered all the rest of the Norwegian coast to the north, for long periods the Norwegian

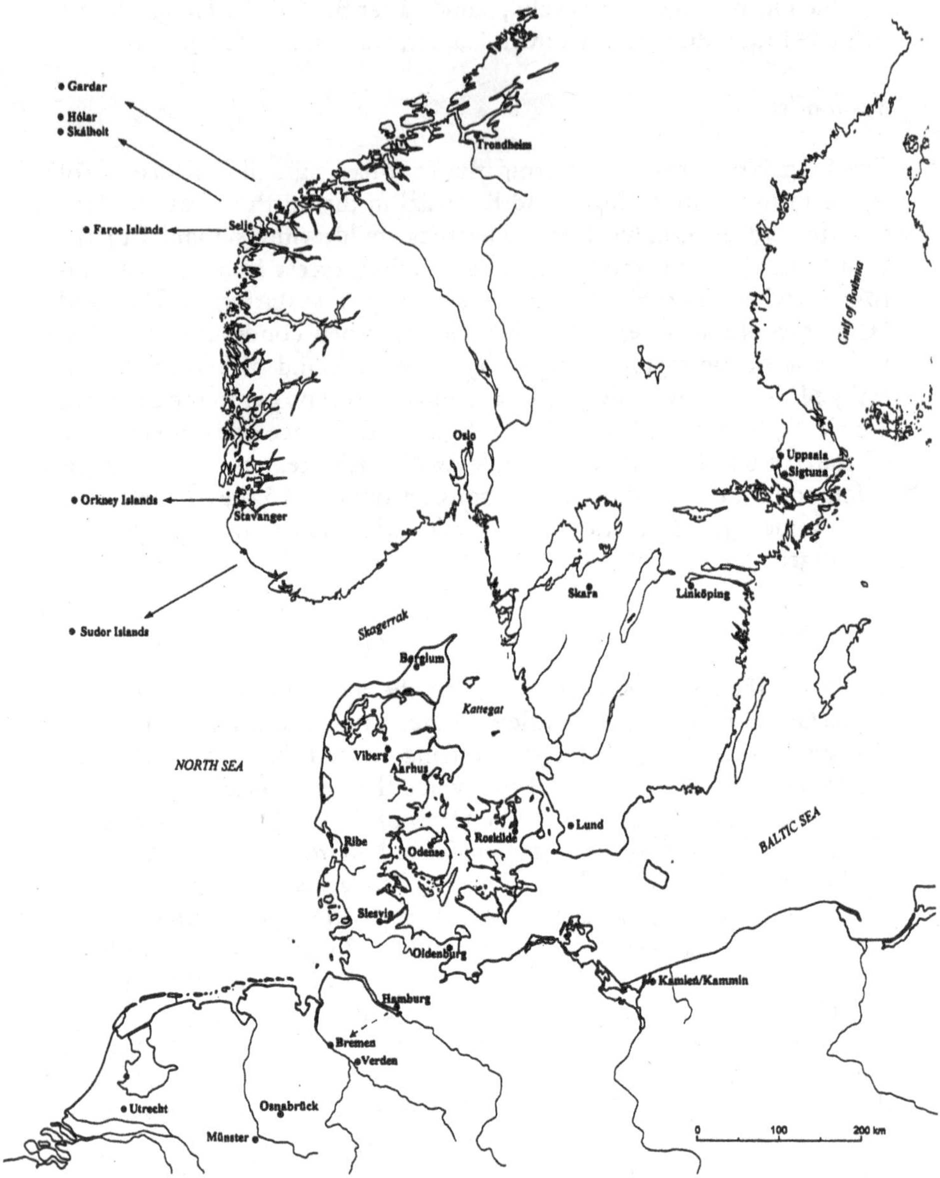

Map I Episcopal sees in North-Western Europe, *c.* 1130. (Drawn by Inger Bjerg Poulsen.)

kings held supremacy over Jämtland, Trøndelag's eastern neighbouring province around Storsjön beyond the mountain ridge. Even Härjedalen and the two northern parishes of what today is the Swedish province of Dalarna were claimed by the kings of Norway. Such a hinterland provided Trøndelag with resources making the unification of Norway possible from there.

Iceland and Greenland

Christian Iceland began in the year 1000 when the Allthing decided that Christianity should be the official religion of all Iceland. The background for this decision is the colonization of Iceland by Norse settlers *c.* 870, coming from Norway probably by way of Norse colonies in and around the British Isles. Some colonists proceeded to Greenland and even to places on the North American continent. It is only thanks to the Gulf Stream that the volcanic island of Iceland can offer conditions suitable to man. The settlers developed a pastoral society with a constitution characterized by common decisions in all important matters.

Christianity stimulated the Icelanders' love of travelling and caused gifted young men from influential families to seek centres of learning in England and in continental Europe. Iceland received its first bishop in 1056; he established himself in Skálholt. Because of communication problems – Skálholt was easily accessible only from the western, southern and eastern quarters of the island – a second episcopal see was established in 1106 in Hólar for the northern quarter. The colonists in Greenland likewise got their own episcopal see of Gardar. Its first bishop seems to have been Eirikr in the second decade of the twelfth century.

II Communications

The previous section provided a description of those regions of North-Western Europe into which the monastic life was introduced in the middle ages. The far north was omitted because it lacked monasteries; none the less, it has to be considered because of its role in the communications system.

Sea routes

Two important sea routes follow the Scandinavian peninsula: one along its western, another along its eastern shore.

The crucial evidence for the western route is the report of a certain Ohthere, who left northern Norway loaded with exotic products. He followed Norway's long coast until the land became Danish – Halland to his left, Jutland to his right – passing north of Zealand through Storebælt, probably between Funen and Langeland, to arrive south of Ærø at Hedeby. Since he later arrived in England with his goods, we know about his journey from his own report incorporated into King Alfred's (died 899) translation of Orosius (Jørgensen 1985; Ottar og Wulfstan 1983). The different segments of this sea route are crucial to the understanding of how Christianity spread.

Early evidence for the eastern route is the undated itinerary (Gallén, 1993) in the manuscript of the Danish land register, the so-called 'Kong Valdemars Jordebog', of places and landmarks which the sailor has to pass on his way from the eastern tip of Blekinge to Reval in Estonia. The route runs west of the island of Öland, follows the coast up to the archipelago outside Lake Mälar, skirts the southern edge of the Åland archipelago, follows the coast of Finland eastwards and finally crosses the Finnish Bay southwards from where Hangö stands today. Likewise, in the southern Baltic, commerce followed the coast. This tendency of communication routes to follow coastlines helps to explain why the peoples along the south-eastern shore of the Baltic, for example the Lithuanians, did not sail to Scandinavia, and why direct contacts the other way were rare. Adam of Bremen's assertion that Jumne in the Oder estuary was situated 'opposite to' Birka has been a riddle to many scholars, who believe that Birka was localized in the Mälar region. A possible explanation is that Birka has been erroneously localized too far to the north. If, instead, Birka is placed somewhere along the coast between the Lake Mälar estuary and Blekinge, in Linköping or the area of Köpingsvik in Öland for example (Nyberg, 1991), it would be more reasonable to say that it lay 'opposite to' Jumne; the sailor would take the southward route along the coast and cross the open sea from the south-eastern tip of Blekinge, passing Bornholm on the way.

One important sea route used by the Frisians is the one along the west coast of Jutland. It was probably along this route that early missionaries came to Denmark. The Frisians had a strong position in Bremen and Hamburg, and Frisian merchants may have been the intermediaries for many lines of communication between centres in Jutland like Ribe and Hjørring, and the nearest ecclesiastical centres of Saxony.

East of the peninsula, the sea route from Hedeby to Scandinavia overshadowed all others. From the eleventh century, however, Slesvig became the ecclesiastical centre, thereby reducing the role of Hedeby. This new situation ultimately led to the foundation of German Lübeck in 1157, from then on the starting-point of all important sea routes into the Baltic Sea.

Land routes

Evidence for land routes in Scandinavia is limited. For Jutland there is early evidence of the existence of *hærvejen*, a 'road of warriors' going south–north through the peninsula as far as the area of Viberg/Viborg, Jutland's Thing. The land routes from Scania to neighbouring Swedish provinces to the north followed the inhabited areas along the coast of Halland and the valley of one of the rivers flowing down from Västergötland to the sea through Halland (see Map I). The most important land routes in Norway are the parallel valleys of Gudbrandsdalen and Østerdalen, both ascending from south to north over the pass leading to Trøndelag. Land routes were also essential for communication between Norwegian and Swedish settlements on either side of the dividing mountain chain. The most important land routes between Swedish lands are those cutting through the forest areas of Tiveden and Kolmården.

Note

1. The Scandinavian form Slesvig will be used here instead of the German form Schleswig.

CHAPTER TWO

Early monasticism among Frisians and Saxons

I The Frisians

The Frisians, a people of cattle-breeders and seafarers, settled on elevated pieces of land called *terpen*, suited to three to five families and their cattle. Hundreds of such *terpen* secured Frisian life from floods. On the marshy coastal land the inhabitants were familiar with sailing and fishing, exchanging goods, buying and selling. Further inland, on the sandy soils, agriculture was nearer at hand.

The Carolingian empire did not use the same violent methods against the Frisians as it did against the Saxons, for example that of resettlement of whole tribes in other regions of the empire. The Frisians were left undisturbed in their natural surroundings without attaining a political form. That they were not an independent unit in the eyes of the men of the Carolingian empire can be seen by the way diocesan boundaries were imposed upon them. The diocese of Utrecht was reconstructed after heavy Norse attacks under the Lotharingian Bishop Balderic (918–75) (*Series Episcoporum* [*SE*] *V: I*, pp. 168, 183f.). Meanwhile, however, a new diocese had been founded in Bremen on the river Weser by St Willehad in 787. Both sides of the estuary of the Weser with its Frisian population fell under his jurisdiction. In 805, between the Utrecht and Bremen jurisdictions, St Liudger, first Bishop of Münster, was given both shores of the estuary of the river Ems with its Frisian population for his diocese. This coastal part was separated from the rest of the diocese of Münster by that of Osnabrück (see Fig. 1.1). By an eastward migration of Frisians, believed to have taken place in the tenth and eleventh centuries (cf. Kletler, 1924, pp. 150–67), some of them settled on the islands along the shores of the Danes, so that from 948 they came under the Danish diocese of Slesvig.

To mention the successive Frisian subunits from west to east (Lambert, 1985, pp. 87–90) means following the shifting types of Frisian monasticism: Westergo with Staveren, Ostergo around Dokkum, Hunsingo until the river Hunse, Fivelgo between the rivers Hunse and Fivel, the Reiderland on both sides of the southern part of the Ems estuary, Emsgo, and Federgo, finally, among the Eastern Frisians in

'Ostfriesland', the Brokmerland and the principality of Jever, partly under the counts of Oldenburg in Saxony and/or the archbishops of Hamburg-Bremen.

The early inclusion of the Frisians into Carolingian Europe on the fringe of newly established bishoprics meant that they were not of primary importance to any single ecclesiastical body, possibly with the exception of the northern region of the diocese of Münster, which came to be organized as the archdeaconry. Looked at from the horizon of the bishops of the three dioceses of Utrecht, Münster and Bremen, the Frisians represented just one section of their pastoral engagements and duties, and they provided just one, and by no means the most important, share of their income.

This basic feature is of principal importance to the development of monasticism among the Frisians. A nucleus of monastic community life existed in Staveren as early as the ninth century. But to the bishops of Utrecht, other centres of monastic life were more essential. Old abbeys of importance in Carolingian and Ottonian Europe were situated in more central areas of continental Europe. Perhaps also the feelings of hatred and resentment resulting from the Frankish occupation of Frisian lands made it impossible for church authorities of the Carolingian empire to find an echo among the Frisians for a monastic development. A number of centrally placed European monasteries: Fulda, Werden, Prüm, Corvey, St Amand in Doornik and St Paul in Utrecht, owned extended property in Frisian lands without this giving rise to any daughter foundation for centuries in these areas – in accordance with the typical system of property administration of the period (Bleiber, 1965). Monastic culture was far away, concentrated in a few, illustrious institutions and surrounded by awe and respect. The absence of monastic community life in the Frisian areas until well into the twelfth century, then, although mission had converted the Frisians to Christianity centuries earlier, can perfectly well be explained by this general structure of continental European monasticism in Carolingian and Ottonian times.

II The Saxons

The Saxons of the coastland

To the Saxons, an inland people living around the upper course of the rivers Weser and Elbe, the sea was not a high priority. The Frisians were already there. Following a recent summary (Wavra, 1991) of scholarly discussions, it is nevertheless clear that for Saxon expansion northwards the river Elbe was of absolutely central importance. In its lower course and around the estuary, the stage was set for either a friendly or hostile confrontation between the Saxons, the seafaring Frisians, and Scandinavians looking south for armed or commercial expeditions. In its upper course, the confrontation with Slavic peoples became dramatic in the tenth century, compared to the comparatively peaceful situation further north near the Baltic coast, where a forest belt through present-day Holsten,[1] the 'Saxon *limes*', separated the Saxons from the Slavic Obodrites, with whom the Carolingians as well as the Danish kings entered into various kinds of alliances.

Charlemagne's campaigns in the area of Bardowic and Lüneburg between 780 and 799 (Wavra, 1991, p. 207) paved the way for a concentrated missionary effort along the Elbe. Inevitably the Elbe came to play a very central role in Saxon politics now that it was the cornerstone of an empire. The Saxons living 'on the other side of the Elbe', *trans Albiam*, became the Transalbingians or the Nordalbingians, and the Eider was stabilized as the southern frontier of the Danish realm. To the north of the Eider, the Danevirke, a long earth and brick wall from east to west across the foot of Jutland provided a vivid expression of the Danish decision to defend their realm against the Saxons in case of aggression. From the Saxon and Carolingian point of view, all Transalbingia was border territory, to be administered and defended from centres around the Elbe.

This situation might help to explain why all three diocesan centres founded as a result of the Carolingian expansion northwards are situated on the right bank of the two Saxon rivers: Bremen and Verden on the Weser, Hamburg on the Elbe, administering regions extending north and north-east.

The diocese of Bremen

For the diocese of Bremen, we owe to the Franconian priest Adam, who arrived in Bremen *c.* 1067 to serve under Archbishop Adalbert, a fairly intimate knowledge of religious community life in this diocese prior to 1072, the earliest date at which he could have finished his great work, *Gesta Hammaburgensis ecclesiae pontificum* (*Adam*, 1917).

In 787, the region where the Anglo-Saxon missionary, St Willehad, was active on the lower Elbe under the authority of the archbishops of Cologne had been elevated to the diocese of Bremen, where Willehad consecrated the first church, dedicated to St Peter, shortly before his death on 8 November 789. His disciple, Willeric, took over the admininistration and was consecrated bishop not later than 805; he died in 838 and was in turn followed by Leuderic, who died in August 845. One of the main problems of the history of Christian mission in northern Europe is the union of the diocese of Bremen with the missionary diocese of Hamburg, which took place in different stages between 845 and 864 under the Corvey monk and missionary, St Ansgar, as bishop. During this process, the diocese of Bremen was removed from the supervision of the archbishops of Cologne.

Adam, in describing the origin of religious community life in this diocese, sometimes mentions a *claustrum*, he speaks of *monasteria* and *cenobia* inhabited by servants of God, male as well as female, enumerates them and assigns them to the archbishop who founded or consecrated them. These different terms are used indiscriminately and are generally interpreted as denoting communities of the type which from the eleventh century onwards were called secular.

Adam states (I, ch. 30) that Ansgar, when he was not travelling, cared for *congregationum suarum* (his communities). The first two, he says, were Ramelsloh and Bremen for men – the men in Bremen *habitu quidem usi canonico regula vivebant monastica* (lived according to monastic rule, although they used the dress of canons). The third was Bassum, *congregatio sanctarum virginum* (a community of holy virgins), and finally there were hospitals, of which the Bremen one is the most prominent and mentioned as the fourth *congregatio* in his list. In the section on Archbishop Rimbert's time in office (865–88, I, ch. 43) Adams sums up: 'his predecessor founded four *cenobia*, to them he added the lonely Bücken as the fifth one'. The hospital in Bremen, then, could easily be termed a *cenobium* by Adam. Next step was when Archbishop Adaldag (937–88) is said to have added a sixth and a seventh community (*Adam*, II, ch. 13): to the five *cenobia* now came Heeslingen for women and Reepsholt 'in Frisia' for men. However, Adam uses the term *monasterium* in speaking of the mission among the Slavs east of the Elbe (II, ch. 26): *monasteria etiam virorum ac mulierum Deo servientium constructa sunt plurima* (there were also founded many communities for men and women who served God). He speaks of the son af a Slavic prince who had gone to school in the *monasterium* in Lüneburg (II, ch. 66), which, however, in the same chapter also is being called a *cenobium*. Even the cathedral community of Bremen is in one place (Adam, skolion[2] no. 57) called a *monasterium*, and the same word is found in the description of the community founded by Bishop Eilbert of Farria (Adam, IV, ch. 3).

There is no doubt that forms of community life such as those indicated here by Adam were spread over the whole of Western Christianity. We are not always able to trace them, although they very often appear in the sources of the eleventh and twelfth centuries on the occasion of their adopting one of the monastic rules. However, out of the seven foundations mentioned by Adam only Heeslingen, situated far inland south of the Elbe estuary on Bremen's border with the diocese of Verden, later adopted a monastic rule: as Benedictine nuns they moved to Zeven in 1141.

Other communities mentioned by Adam without being assigned to an episcopal founder are Wildeshausen, called a *prepositura* 'church or monastery headed by a provost' on the river Hunte adjoining the diocese of Osnabrück (III, ch. 59), and Harsefeld near the Elbe (ibid.), which Adam perhaps also wants to subsume under the heading of a *prepositura*. Harsefeld adopted the Benedictine rule after 1100 (*Germania Benedictina VI*, 1979, pp. 137f.; Streich, 1986, p. 69). Bassum, Bücken and the Frisian Reepsholt remained communities without vows, and the famous monastery in Rastede did not yet exist in Adam's time.

The list makes evident, that the development of monasticism in the diocese of Bremen was just as slow as in Frisian lands.

The diocese of Verden

A little further up the Weser from Bremen, the episcopal see of Verden was in existence at the latest in 815, when a charter mentions a certain Spatto as bishop and abbot (Streich, 1986, p. 124). Spatto appears to have been Abbot of Amorbach, south of the Main not far from Mainz, an abbey which may have undertaken the mission in the land between the Weser and the Elbe – one reason why this diocese came to belong to the church province of Mainz, while Bremen adhered to the archbishops of Cologne.

To the missionaries working in the diocese of Verden, the Elbe constituted a long border area to the Slavic peoples across the river. From the Slavic side, however, there was also easy access overland for merchants from the Baltic area who may have wanted to exchange valuable goods from the north for salt, for example. It is symptomatic that Bardowic, just north of Lüneburg, which was known for its salt production, seems to have been the earliest centre of mission in this area on the Saxon side of the Elbe. Bardowic was an excellent commercial crossroad in times of peaceful exchange, but its position must have been too exposed to Slavic raids in times of confrontation. Whatever the reasons, we probably – with Drögereit 1978 – have to reckon with a withdrawal of the episcopal administration from Bardowic to Verden on the safer right shore of the Aller, a tributary of the Weser.

Apparently the Ilmenau valley from south to north with Lüneburg and Bardowic was the primary line of communication through the diocese, leading directly to the region of the Hammaburg. Monastic impulses from the South led to the foundation of St Michael's in Lüneburg, which existed as a male community from 954 and adopted the Benedictine rule under Abbot Livezo from St Pantaleon in Cologne between 973 and 992 (*Germania Benedictina VI*, 1979, pp. 325f.; Streich 1986, p. 91), and of Oldenstadt near Uelzen, a community of religious women which is believed to have existed from the 960s and which adopted the Benedictine rule in 1006 (*Germania Benedictina VI*, p. 389; Streich, 1986, p. 105).

Inasmuch as the development of Christian institutions was so rich in the eastern part of the diocese, one must interpret the move of the episcopal see from Bardowic westwards to Verden as an act of defence in the face of hostile attacks. The area across the Elbe opposite to Bardowic-Lüneburg was certainly less well adapted for a diocesan centre around 815, since the 'Saxon *limes*' from the north met the Elbe further downstream, so that the corresponding area to the north of the Elbe was chosen for the Hammaburg (Lobbedey, 1977), constructed some time around 820 according to plans worked out by Emperor Louis the Pious (Wavra, 1991, pp. 208–18). With the Hammaburg as the seat of a bishop, the Verden diocese was squeezed in between the dioceses of Minden, Hildesheim and Halberstadt on the southern side, and that of Bremen and the new missionary diocese of Hamburg on the northern side. Verden's clergy was thus shielded from a direct confrontation with missionary activities other than those over the Elbe frontier to the East.

Concomitantly, however, Bardowic developed into a commercial centre. At least some Scandinavians, namely the traders from the island of Gotland in the Baltic, regularly frequented Bardowic, where they were interested in buying salt and metalwork, as demonstrated by finds in Gotland (Yrwing, 1978, p. 106 with notes 8 and 9). Passing Oldenburg in Holsten, they had to pass the Saxon frontier at Artlenburg and pay customs there. About 70 Bohemian coins found in Gotland, together with Bavarian, Hungarian and Arabic ones, must have reached the island in the course of the tenth and eleventh centuries.

With Bardowic as a meeting place for Gotlandic and Saxon merchants, one must not ignore the possibility that impulses from the Archangel St Michael's monastery in Lüneburg may have given Gotlanders an insight into the monastic interpretation of Christianity as early as the beginning of the eleventh century, the period when, according to Sven-Erik Pernler (1977), Christianity was thoroughly adopted on the whole island. Gotland is curiously absent from the world horizon of Adam of Bremen, which may be partly due to the fact that distant Bremen, not Hamburg, was the residence of the archbishop he served, and that commerce was not normally a subject to write about in dealing with the great deeds of archbishops. But it may also illustrate the preoccupation of medieval churchmen with their own diocese and region; after all, Hamburg-Bremen was an archbishopric, while its southern neighbours in the Verden diocese were just suffragans to other archbishops.

The missionary diocese of Hamburg

Hamburg was the third maritime diocese of Saxony prior to Adam's time. In order to create the diocese of Hamburg for Ansgar in the 820s, the Bishop of Verden had been forced to give up the Hammaburg area as well as Stormarn and Holsten formerly belonging to his jurisdiction. After the long process of negotiations following the devastating Viking attack on the Hammaburg in 845, city and region were finally, by papal decree of 31 May 864, united to the diocese of Bremen. Bremen was taken out of the jurisdiction of the archbishops of Cologne.

Ansgar died in 865. His pupil and biographer Rimbert (died 888) followed him in office at the head of an archdiocese without suffragans. Hamburg was part of the name of the diocese, but it was administered as a unit from Bremen, where St Peter's was the cathedral.

In Nordalbingia, a small monastic community is said to have existed in Ansgar's time in Welenao (*Vita Anskarii*, 1884 chs 13–14), which has been identified with a place near Itzehoe in Holsten, but no continuation of this monastic *cella* can be traced (Freytag, 1977, p. 147). There is scattered evidence that before the attack of 845, Ansgar established a community in Hamburg itself, which supposedly was transferred to nearby Ramelsloh in the diocese of Verden, retaining its status as a propriety monastery (*Eigenkloster*) of the archbishops (Streich, 1986, p. 112).

A real change in the prospects for monastic growth, however, was brought about by Charlemagne's successor, the German kingdom of Otto I who, after his victory over the Hungarians in 955, assumed the title of an emperor in 962 with the help of the young Pope John XII. Otto I, having the Carolingian collaboration of kingdom and church as a model, counted upon help and assistance from his bishops for his moves towards the east as well as the north. Around 946/47, three dioceses for Jutland were planned and established by decree of Archbishop Adaldag of Hamburg-Bremen, who by this move would receive his first three suffragans. Horst Fuhrmann proposed in 1964 that Diethard of Hildesheim and Bernhard of Halberstadt assisted in the consecration of the bishops for these three dioceses of Jutland: Liafdag *Ripeensis*, Horath *Sleoswicensis*, Reginbrand *Arhuswensis*, to quote the spelling these unfamiliar names of new diocesan centres got in the council charter (*SE VI: II*, pp. 38 with notes 9 and 12, p. 64 with notes 7a and 12, and p. 96 with notes 13 and 26).

Later in the same year, the diocese of Brandenburg and probably also that of Havelberg were established. The move in two directions could not have been possible without the king. The decision to go beyond the existing borders with new initiatives opens up a new epoch, which ultimately brought monasticism to these areas of expansion.

According to Helmut Beumann and Jürgen Petersohn, who analysed the expansion plans of Otto I, the primary concept of 948 was simple: the Archbishop of Hamburg-Bremen was to care for the spread of Christianity among all the northern peoples, whereas the mission to all Slavic peoples was to be confided to an archbishopric which was yet to be instituted. Otto's victory over the Hungarians on the Lech on 10 August 955 enabled him finally to solemnly proclaim, in 968, the erection of the archbishopric of Magdeburg on the Elbe.

However, the realization of the plan would imply that some of the coastal areas inhabited by the Obodrites – Wagrians around Oldenburg, Polabians around Ratzeburg – would have to be taken out of the sphere of influence of Hamburg-Bremen, whose archbishops had already begun organizing the church there and tried to prove from earlier papal documents that this was their legal right and duty. After negotiations between the king and the prelates (the Archbishop of Mainz had hoped to continue the expansion of his church province eastwards from the diocese of Verden over the Elbe) the matter had to be postponed until the king's Italian matters were settled and he could ask for the Pope's approval. Archbishop Adaldag did not want to give up his jurisdiction over the Obodrites, and perhaps he let a second bishop of the newly erected see of Slesvig, Marko, administer the church in their lands. When Magdeburg finally was erected, the Hamburg-Bremen options were fulfilled: the Obodrites were the only Slav people to remain in the province of Hamburg-Bremen, and Archbishop Adaldag could consecrate his first Bishop of Oldenburg for the Obodrites, Egward (Petersohn, in *SE V: II*, p. 58). Such is, in short, the summary of these events, in spite of the extremely demanding task of penetrating a number of forgeries of papal charters circumscribing the realm allotted to the archbishops of Hamburg-Bremen (cf. Wavra, 1991).

The conclusion for the area covered by the original missionary diocese of Hamburg is the same as for Bremen, since both regions were administered as one diocese: in the ninth and tenth centuries, religious community life did not yet take on the forms of monasticism here but remained limited to forms of common life among the clergy. According to Adam, these clerical communities, the most important of which was probably that of the cathedral clergy of St Peter's in Bremen (Streich, 1986, p. 48), only to a limited degree corresponded to the norms of monastic observance prevalent in these centuries. Adam remarks, that St Peter's in Bremen 'nearly up to our times' *regula vivebant monastica* (lived very much like monks), (*Adam*, I, ch. 30), an expression which upon closer inspection does not necessarily imply more than that they lived communally, shared common revenues (*mensa*) and did not marry.

Notes

1. The Scandinavian form Holsten will be used here instead of the German form Holstein.
2. Skolion is the term used in scholarship on Adam of Bremen for 'gloss'.

CHAPTER THREE

The archbishops' options

The Slav option

Thanks to Archbishop Adaldag of Hamburg-Bremen, political intrigues got their final solution in the agreement of 968, by which an archdiocese of Magdeburg with five suffragan dioceses was created and Hamburg-Bremen was allowed to continue its work among the Obodrites. Adam of Bremen uses the opportunity (II, ch. 17–23) to insert a description of the Slavs, since the Obodrites now had their own episcopal see, Oldenburg. He gives us some unique information on those Slav peoples who were not yet Christianized (cf. Petersohn, 1979).

According to Adam, the Obodrites are divided into the Wagrians with their central settlement, their *civitas*, in Oldenburg; the Obodrites proper or Reregians with Magnopolis, Mecklenburg; and the Polabians with Ratzeburg as a central place. These three peoples identified themselves as one ethnic group and also acted accordingly, being involved under one prince in Danish as well as in Carolingian and Ottonian negotiations and treaties (cf. Hoffmann, 1986).

The next groups mentioned by Adam never succeeded in the same way. Under the name of Liutizi they were loosely linked together in a tribal union offering strong resistance against Christianity during the rebellions of the following period. When finally Christianity carried the victory, there was, as Petersohn (1979) says, no place for the Liutizians to establish an ecclesiastical or political entity. The western Liutizian groups sided with the Obodrites, the eastern ones with the Pomeranians, and they lost whatever unity they may have had.

One reason for the difference between the Obodrites and the Liutizi can be found in the existence of a commercial centre in their midst: Jumne at the mouth of the Oder, the Jomsborg of Scandinavian sources, enthusiastically described by Adam as one of the biggest 'cities' and centres of commerce in Europe – though it is clear that he never visited the place; he openly admits that it is based upon hearsay. It was a place with trading links to Ostrogard Ruzzie – Novgorod in Russia – *cuius metropolis civitas est Chiue, aemula sceptri Constantinopolitani, clarissimum decus Greciae* (the capital of which is Kiev, competitor to Constantinople's reign, the shining honour to Greece). It adhered to foreign gods, and Saxons who had access to the place for the sake of business were not allowed to show their Christian faith in public.

Adam goes no further east than a little beyond the river Peene, the border of the diocese of the Obodrites. He only mentions in passing the third Slavic group, the Pomeranians, living beyond the Oder along the coast where they stuck strongly to their own identity, especially in confrontation with what soon became the kingdom of Poland. The eastern Liutizian tribes found shelter in the Pomeranian diocese of Kammin on both sides of the Oder estuary.

So this was now the Slavic field of Hamburg-Bremen's missionary efforts, the fourth suffragan bishopric of the ageing Archbishop Adaldag, administered by Egward, Latinized Evagrius. Compared to the immense and unknown world in the north, this region was limited in size, its outer border was already fixed by imperial decree. Nevertheless, Adam in his attempt to grasp the spirit of Adaldag's epoch before the first great rebellion against Christian mission in 983, states that 'churches were built everywhere in Sclavania, several *monasteria* for God-serving men as well as women were constructed' (*Adam*, II, ch. 26). Supplementary information by the priest Helmold from Bosau is trustworthy, when he describes the situation around 960 when Oldenburg was administered by Bishop Marko of Slesvig (Helmold von Bosau, 1973, ch. 12): Oldenburg already had a community of priests at the cathedral, he says, and the Mecklenburg area also included a nuns' convent. The first Slav rebellion of 983 – or rather the decades of war it inaugurated, (cf. Petersohn, 1979, pp. 22f.) – annihilated these efforts and there is hardly any evidence of continuity until Christian community life was taken up again in Helmold's times. In Adam's times, a hundred years after this first rebellion, its chronology was confused and its events were partly mixed up with later periods of war.

The Danish option

To Archbishop Adaldag, while considering the future policy of his missionary work, it must have carried a certain weight that the mission to the north, contrary to the Slav option, had a strong asset: the memory of a great predecessor, Ansgar. This monk enjoyed the reputation of having founded two churches among the Danes, Slesvig and Ribe. The two settlements were chosen by Otto I and his bishops in 946/47 as episcopal sees, apparently destined by them to become veritable 'cities', if they did not already regard them as such. Urban history and archaeology have uncovered some aspects of the importance of the two areas of urbanization towards the end of the tenth century.

Hedeby/Haithabu excavations have not yet brought to light anything like a Christian church within the walls of the eighth century. The closest one gets to a spot well adapted to theories of an early church from Ansgar's times south of the river Schlei is Haddeby some 800 metres north of the wall. North of the Schlei estuary, however, was a Christian settlement: Slesvig. A Christian centre, perhaps even Ansgar's church, must have already existed somewhere around the estuary of the Schlei in the tenth century, not least upon the testimony of an Arabian merchant from about 965 (Radtke, 1984). Hedeby and Slesvig seem to have coexisted for a certain period of time around the year 1000 until the settlement in the circular wall was finally deserted around 1020 (Hoffmann, 1980; Radtke, 1984; 1995). As the see of a bishop, Slesvig must have had a congregation of Christians, a church and a clergy when on 26 June 965 Otto I issued his privilege of freedom from imperial tax to the three episcopal sees of Jutland (*MGH DD*, I, no. 294).

Ribe excavations (1981–90, cf. Nielsen, 1985) have sensationally dated the origin of this commercial and craft centre well into the seventh and eighth centuries. There is no doubt that Adaldag, like Ansgar, regarded Ribe as a *civitas* in the Roman mediterranean sense, a centre of commerce with a permanent settlement and the residence of a bishop. It is one of the important discoveries of Danish archaeologists in the last decades that a Christian settlement around a church south of the river, on the spot where the cathedral now stands, originated next to the old settlement on the northern shore of the river. This led to a shift of urban centre from the northern bank with its old St Peter's church to the area around the present cathedral, without a break in continuity of settlement.

Moreover, whereas Slavonia had just one ecclesiastical centre, Jutland had three, the third being Aarhus/Århus, where no connection to Ansgar was recorded. There must have been Christians there, since it was made an episcopal see in 948 and was privileged in 965, like Slesvig and Ribe. There is positive evidence from archaeology, that the first known church in Aarhus was situated outside the wall. Compared to the situation among the Slavs, with the trading town of Jumne outside the influence of the Christian faith, Jutland must have appeared as the best option for Archbishop Adaldag in choosing where to concentrate missionary efforts. Not even the records of Christian communities in the Slav countries can in his eyes have outweighed the positive signs from the Danish mission and the prospects of winning a strong kingdom and a royal family for Christianity.

Danish government and two early abbeys

A so-called Swedish dynasty had seized power among the Danes in 895 but had soon been replaced by the kings of the Jelling dynasty (Randsborg, 1980; Skovgaard-Petersen, 1977). In order to evaluate correctly the first evidence of monasticism in Southern Jutland, the chronology of the Jelling kings' attitude to Christianity needs some corrections. In a recent analysis, Bent Østergård (1994) has criticized scholarly research for having put too much trust in the unique information of Widukind in his Saxon chronicle from around 968, that the first Saxon king, Henry I (918–36), after his victory over the Danes in 934, also baptized a Danish king by name of Chnuba. He points out that the Corvey annals, Widukind's source, does not say anything about the baptism of a Danish king as a consequence of Henry's victory, and that none of the later historians who quote the notice on the baptism of a Danish king in 934 knows the name of this king.

Chnuba must be identical with King Gnupa, known from a runic inscription. His existence is therefore historically well attested: not so the dates of his reign, however. Adam's account of the first kings of the Jelling dynasty is confused by the many personal names he uses for them and by the way he mocks them: a certain Hardegon, Harthacnut Vurm, just Vurm or Worm, then Gorm which sounds similar to a 'wurm', led him astray so that historians did not believe in his chronology, argues Østergård. He pleads to dismiss Widukind's notice that Gnupa was alive in 934 and was baptized, and places Gnupa in connection with the German attack upon Denmark *c.* 917 instead.

It is undeniable that the baptism of a Danish king in 934, had it really taken place, would have found quite another echo all around among the historians of the time. The confusion in the oldest authority of all later historians, Adam, did not contribute to clarification. So many events would have been concentrated in the few years 934–36, had Gnupa still been alive that late, argues Østergård. Separating Adam's different pieces of evidence from their stiff mockery, then, Østergård leaves much more time for the Jelling dynasty to seize power and contemplate its stand towards Christianity. With this interpretation, the baptism of Harald Blueteeth in the early 960s appears much more reasonable and predictable: the dynasty had had much more time to consider the matter of religion than the earlier chronology would admit. Furthermore the body of a king found in the Jelling burial and thought to be King Gorm does not show an old man, as was to be expected had Gorm been the first Jelling king, but a man of about 40. Adam then must have made the mistake of making Gorm the cruel persecutor of the Christians, which in fact, says Østergard, Harthacnut Orm had been, whereas Gorm must have been an intermediate figure, not too opposed to the new religion. With Østergård I would advocate the following series of Danish kings of the tenth century:

Swedish kings over the Danes:	
Olov	895
His sons Gurd and Gnupa	until *c.* 917
Gnupa's son Sigtrygg	*c.* 917
Jelling kings:	
Harthacnut Orm, the son of a Sven	*c.* 918–*c.* 948
Gorm	*c.* 948–*c.* 958
Harald Bluetooth	*c.* 958–87
Swein Forkbeard	987–1014

Placing the take-over of the Jelling kings already in the early years of the German King Henry I (919–36) and the Hamburg-Bremen Archbishop Unni (918–36), and assuming that the first king of the new dynasty, the enemy of the Saxons and the persecutor of the Christians as mentioned by Adam, was not Gorm but Harthacnut Orm, makes the conversion of Denmark a more lengthy process. King Henry's attack in 934 after years of confrontation would make more sense that way, enabling Archbishop Unni able to make his first visitation journey to the North, which ultimately carried him to Birka. There he died in 936 and there his body was buried with the exception of the head, which was taken to Bremen and buried in the cathedral (*Der Bremer Dom*, 1979). The erection of the three Jutish dioceses would also make more sense if Harthacnut Orm was dead in 948 and Gorm, as a transitional and more flexible figure, made the prospects of Christian expansion look brighter.

We could also take into account that a certain Odinkar, a member of an influential Danish family, according to Adam (II, ch. 49) stemming from royal ancestors, had taken up studies in Bremen and was baptized there by Archbishop Adaldag (who died in 988). Adam calls him *Odinkar iunior* and *filius Toki ducis Winlandensis* 'son of Toki, the earl of Vendel', the then island north of the Limfjord – to distinguish him from his uncle, *Odinkar senior*, one of the early missionaries who worked without the limitations of diocesan boundaries (*Adam*, II, ch. 26, 36).

The younger Odinkar's early career took place against the background of the worst crisis in the northern mission. Saxon troops under Otto II won a victory over the Danes in 973, but ten years later, in 983, the great rebellion against the Saxons broke out and made the residence of Christian bishops impossible in Slesvig as well as in Oldenburg. King

Harald's conversion would be no obstacle to him keeping at a distance from Saxon power.

With such a long preparation period for the Christianization of Denmark, postulated here on the basis of written records, new consideration can be given to the foundation date of two early monasteries in South Jutland: St Michael's Benedictine abbey on the outskirts of Slesvig, and Our Lady's Benedictine abbey in Seem near Ribe for both monks and nuns. Could both or one of them have been initiated still in Otto II's times, before the Slav-Danish rebellion of 983?

With its circular church St Michael's flourished in the middle of the eleventh century (Radtke, in Lafrenz, 1985). The dedication to St Michael was common in the earliest missionary period. There are strong links between the exiled bishop of Slesvig, Ekkihard, who died 1026, and St Michael's Benedictine abbey in Hildesheim, which would point to a foundation in the first decades of the eleventh century under his guidance.[1] But Ekkihard ended his life on the river Eider without succeeding in resuming episcopal residence in Slesvig, which had been interrupted since the 983 rebellion (Radtke, in *SE VI: II*, p. 104). The initiative for a foundation could have been there already before 983, for example under Marko's successor, a Bishop Adaldag of whom nothing but the name has been handed down, or under the exiled non-resident bishops Folcbert and Poppo until about the year 1000 (Radtke, in *SE VI: II*, p. 101–3).

For Our Lady's at Seem, the first guess is *Odinkar iunior* mentioned above, whom Adaldag's successor Libentius/Liawizo (988–1013) had ordained Bishop of Ribe not later than 1005 – in that year he took part in a synod in Dortmund. He outlived Libentius's successors Unwan (1013–29), Libentius II (1029–32), Hermann (1032–35) and Becelin/Alebrand (1035–43) and died in 1043. He probably administered the diocese of Aarhus as well after the death (at an unknown date) of its first bishop, Reginbrand. It would be a reasonable guess that he also administered the diocese of Odense to which imperial officials had to give their immunity by a charter issued in Wildeshausen on 18 March 988, and for which no name of a proper bishop upon its erection has been handed down (*MGH DD*, II, no. 41; *SE VI: II*, p. 57).

There is no evidence to link the younger Odinkar in his long time in office as bishop of Ribe with any known religious community. But since his time in office fully covered the reign of Cnut the Great (1018–35), some early scholars as well as Father A. Eilermann OSB of Gerleve (*Germania Benedictina VI*, 1979, p. 459), on the basis of Adam of Bremen (skolion no. 25) made him a transmitter of Benedictine monasticism from England to Denmark. If one believes this to be correct,

Seem would undoubtedly be one of the most plausible candidates for such early Anglo-Saxon Benedictine foundations in Denmark. However, Peter Sawyer has doubted the English connection attributed by Adam to the younger Odinkar – the two Odinkars should have been mixed up (Gelting, in *SE VI: II*, p. 68 n. 53). The evidence for an Anglo-Saxon background for the younger Odinkar's role in Ribe, therefore, is very uncertain.

Instead, a handful of relics found in the altar of the church of Seem points in another direction. Two small parchment strips in a script of the eleventh century indicate 'Relics of St Gereon and his associates', the martyrs of antiquity whose relics were kept in the abbey church of St Gereon in Cologne, and a stone by which St Stephen had been stoned. A set of 13 relics in a script of the twelfth century written by one and the same hand mentions an *os*, a 'bone', of each of the apostles St Bartolomew, St John the Baptist, St Stephen the First Martyr, St Pancras, St George, St Agapitus, the Frisian missionary St Willibrord, and the Bishop of Hildesheim, St Godehard (Gotthard) (1022–38), who was canonized in 1131. Further relics are a hair of St Mary Magdalene, *de articulis dextri pedis sancti Martini* (fragments of St Martin's right foot) and, without further specification, 'From the Cantiani', martyrs from Aquileja (Gad, 1974; Vellev, 1974). Tue Gad concludes that this collection does not contain anything that reminds us of England and that there are no exotic relics among them, deriving from the Holy Land or the like; they could have been acquired anywhere in a well-equipped German cathedral or monastery, says Gad. St Willibrord was buried at Echternach, St Godehard points exclusively to Hildesheim. In the diocesan calendars, the 13 saints represented here are found in this combination only in Hamburg, Bremen, Minden and Paderborn. Gad believes that the script belongs to the twelfth century and that the relics, therefore, may have been brought to Denmark not much later than 1131, the year Bishop Godehard of Hildesheim was canonized.

Against this background one may ask: why should the monks in Seem at an early stage, probably in the eleventh century, have acquired relics of St Gereon in Cologne and, shortly after 1131, the collection including St Willibrord of Echternach and St Godehard of Hildesheim, if these regions had not been part of their normal communication system, very probably tracing the footsteps of the original founders? One might even ponder if Bishop Godehard, a Benedictine monk who had formerly been Abbot of Hersfeld and Niederaltaich and had died 1038, may not have patronized the foundation of Seem in his lifetime, or if the pioneer monks of Seem came later from St Michael's in Hildesheim, bringing the veneration for St Godehard with them. The relic find makes it hard to argue in favour of an Anglo-Saxon origin for Our Lady's abbey of Seem.

There is no evidence whatsoever, then, to support the theory that any Benedictine monks Cnut the Great might have brought to Denmark from England ever settled in Seem outside Ribe or, for that matter, in St Michael's outside Slesvig. A German background must be assumed for both these foundations. A great deal of evidence indicates a foundation date of both in the first decades of the eleventh century, Bishop Godehard's and the younger Odinkar's times, which is also that of Bishop Ekkihard (until 1026) and his successor Bishop Rodulf (1026–47) of Slesvig.

That any of the two foundations should go back to the time before 983 is therefore purely hypothetical. Even if we allow the Jelling dynasty to have come to power a little earlier than scholars have assumed so far, the 983 rebellion changed the situation, because it must have given new force to the resistance against Christianity from the side of Harthacnut Orm as late as the 940s. The earliest manifestations of monasticism on the Jutish peninsula, then, located in the immediate neighbourhood of the only two functioning Jutish episcopal sees, cannot with any reasonable certainty be traced further back than to the second or third decade of the eleventh century. Both communities must be assumed to have come into being with the help of monks from German mother houses and in close collaboration with the bishops in office for the two sees during the first three decades of the eleventh century. In both cases, the introduction of monastic community life may be interpreted as an episcopal measure to strengthen the spiritual structure of their dioceses, now that Christianity was no longer in danger thanks to the Danish-English condominium under Cnut (1018–35) and his son Harthacnut (1035–42) and thanks to the Danish-Norwegian kingdom of the Christian king St Olav's son Magnus the Good (1042–47), who won a decisive battle against Slavic warriors near Slesvig in 1043 (Hoffmann, 1986, p. 21; Radtke, 1992), the year in which Odinkar died.

The bishops of both sees collaborated with the secular power to the benefit of their church. According to the 'Cronica Ecclesiae Ripensis' (CER), Odinkar of Ribe received half of the income from Ribe for his see from Cnut the Great who is said to have been his *avunculus* 'uncle'. Rudolf of Slesvig was the host when Magnus the Good met Archbishop Becelin in Slesvig after the king's victory over the Slavs in 1043.

A marriage link created on that occasion between the Saxon Duke Bernhard and the Danish King Magnus secured peace: Magnus's half-sister, Ulvhild, his father St Olav's only legitimate child from marriage with princess Åstrid of Sweden, was betrothed to Ordulf, Bernhard's son. The marriage is said later to have been celebrated in St Clement's church in Nidaros in front of St Olav's shrine (Jonas Jansen, in *Norsk Biografisk Leksikon* [*NBL*], 1975, XVII). Ordulf is duly commemorated among the Benedictines of St Michael's in Lüneburg: the chronicle (*MGH SS*, XXIII, p. 395, under the year 1025) states that Ordulf, who succeeded his father as duke in 1062 and died in 1074, was buried in the middle of St Michael's abbey church, where also his son Magnus (1074–1106) and his daughter-in-law, the duchess and Hungarian Princess Sofia, were buried *iuxta patrem et matrem* (alongside his father and mother). It is significant that the series of ducal burials in the abbey church began with Ulvhild, the daughter of St Olav, who died 1071 before her husband. Henry the Lion, among other princes, was descended from this Saxon-Norwegian marriage of Ordulf and Ulvhild. So there was undoubtedly a link between St Michael's in Lüneburg and what was going on in Slesvig at an early stage of the re-established diocese after 1026.

Thus, although initiatives with regard to St Michael's in Slesvig could theoretically have been taken by some of the early bishops of Slesvig or by Ekkihard while still in exile before 1026, existing evidence points at contacts relevant to possible monastic connections for the time after 1026. For Seem, the younger Odinkar may have profited from connections to German Benedictine circles presumably in Hildesheim under Bishop Godehard for a foundation close to his see of Ribe. The *terminus ante quem* for both abbeys, however, must be set much later, and might very well not be the same for the two, as will be discussed in a following chapter.

Note

1. He took part in the consecration of the crypt in September, 1015, of the abbey church in September, 1022, and in the dedication of a chapel to St Martin in November, 1022, just before Bishop Bernward took the monastic habit there as an expression of his monastic turn of mind (Vita Bernwardi, *Monumentia Germaniae Historica, Scriptores* [*MGH SS*] IV, p. 780).

CHAPTER FOUR

Eleventh-century monasticism: Eastern Denmark

I The period 1020–1100

Swein Forkbeard, who died in 1014, had defeated and occupied England. His son Cnut won a victory over Edmund Ironside, while Cnut's brother, Harthacnut, reigned for a while in Denmark. From 1018 to 1035, Cnut was king of England and Denmark in union. His 17 years in power was an important epoch in the history of both countries – Adam felt that Cnut had reigned *per multos annos* (for many years) (II, ch. 55).

The two countries were not comparable. Even the way of imagining them as entities stretching north–south more or less parallel to each other is misleading – geographically, but above all culturally. There was no such thing as a short-cut passage over the North Sea from, for example, Ribe to Newcastle, which are roughly on the same latitude. Danes travelling to England went south to the Frisian coast, from which they could cross to London, Ipswich, Yarmouth or Hull. The Danes in Viking times were relatively uninterested in Scotland, although a fleet setting sail directly west from the mouth of Limfjorden north of mainland Jutland would find the Firth of Forth, Dundee and Aberdeen.

The Norwegians were in a different position. The Shetlands and the Orkneys were right on their way, directly west of the rich agrarian coastland of Agder and Hordaland. Norwegians would approach the British Isles from the north, following the western coasts of Scotland southwards until they reached Ireland. They would not take the route round the Danish coast, 'Jutland Side' as the famous chapter 32 of *Knytlinga Saga* (1986, p. 60) renders it, unless they had the intention of uniting their forces with those of the Danes in a common enterprise.

The 80 years of Danish–English symbiosis and its aftermath, together with the corresponding English influence on Scandinavia, *c.* 1020 to *c.* 1100, saw some very important changes in cultural relations. Around 1020, England with its partly Roman background was a thoroughly Christian country in a kind of Roman and Anglo-Saxon synthesis, where bishoprics and monasteries had been reorganized and acquired new vitality during the preceding half century, influencing the immigrant Danish population. At the same time, three Scandinavian kingdoms were governed by kings who had taken baptism and adopted Christianity as the official cult of their respective realms, but where vast layers of the population still did not profess the new faith, certainly not wholeheartedly, and in many cases persevered in the practice of the old cult. The Norwegian settlers of one colonial Scandinavian region, Iceland, had decided in common to adopt Christianity and the conditions were the same: private worship of the old gods was still allowed or tolerated on the farms.

Around 1100, things looked very different. Now, Anglo-Saxon England had been overlaid by a layer of Romance Norman culture with French as its daily language. Anglo-Saxon England was persecuted in its own homeland. William, the great warrior who seized the kingdom, kept power firmly in his own hands until his death in 1087, handing it over to his son William, who died in 1100. During the last quarter of the century hope slowly waned that a change would ever come and Anglo-Saxon England again be free of the invaders. The English had to adjust to other Christian habits and let other *oratores* intercede for them to God.

The Scandinavians, instead, had entered upon a slow process of 'Scandinavizing' the impulses Christian mission had brought to them. Missionaries were ready to pay a high price in return for royal assistance in eradicating the old cults, at least in public, as is well testified by Adam, when in the 1070s he told the story of how it all had come about in Denmark and Norway but was yet to be achieved in Sweden.

The Norwegians, after three generations of Christian influence since the first Scandinavian martyr-king, St Olav, fell in battle in 1030, were now under King Olav Kyrre (1066–93) prepared to address God in the forms of the new cult. Denmark, after 100 years of Christian kings, got its martyr-king, Cnut, in 1086; the next 15 years saw the rise of his cult, favoured by his brother Erik (1095–1103).

During the last two decades of the eleventh century, the Swedes apparently began to realize; much against their will, that the great sacrificial gatherings of January or February to be performed periodically by the king could no longer be carried out undisturbed. Adam of Bremen described them as being celebrated every ninth year in Uppsala, a place he located near Sigtuna and Birka. His account is based on hearsay and discussions have lasted long about the real shape of these sacrifices. A list of sacrificial gatherings based on what we today might call an eight-year cycle has been proposed (Henriksson, 1995) with the argument that what Adam (IV, ch. 26) meant by his statement that the sacrifices recurred in a nine-year cycle was based upon the old way of counting by which both end years are counted. According to Henriksson, adherents of the old cult were able to celebrate their sacrifice in 1052, 1060, 1068, 1076 and 1084 without the Christians being able to impede it – the last of these years during the violent reign of a certain Sven, who seized power in time for the sacrifice of 1084 but was killed in 1087 by the Christian King Inge whom he had replaced in 1084. From a quite different angle Adam's description has recently been linked to events of the Investiture Contest and to letters written by Pope Gregory VII to Scandinavian rulers in 1076 (Janson, 1998). The argument is, that Adam, who adhered to the Imperial side in the conflict, polemized against King Edmund/Emund and Bishop Osmund in Uppsala who probably favoured the Gregorian side, and that monks called in from reformed abbeys in Lotharingia to found a monastic community in Uppsala were the intended targets for Adam's polemics against paganism.

In the course of these 80 years, the Christian mission in Scandinavia created a basic church organization and laid the basis for the local cult through a network of wooden churches spread over the areas of settlement. In certain places the mission may have propagated a monastic way of life parallel to that of lay Christians. In a very few places stone churches were built (Krins, 1968); if they were meant for monastic communities, they may have underlined the importance of monasticism to the average population.

The foundation of Christian institutions in Scandinavia is unthinkable without the support of royal power. It is therefore generally agreed among scholars today that it was in the interest of church officials at all levels (cf. Breengaard, 1982) to support a royalty imbued with a sacred character, although the sacred could no longer be reached by help of myths of divine ancestors. It was, however, possible to make the sacred incarnate by a means well known to the Christian tradition: combining the sacred with the personal sanctity won by martyrdom. In the case of St Olav 1030 and his cult from the following decade onwards, this combination with its Anglo-Saxon background occurred for the first time in Scandinavia (Hoffmann, 1975; Nyberg, 1995/96). The second time was the case of St Cnut, 1086, and his cult, approved by papal letter and by the elevation of the relics in 1100. Thus the kings are key figures if one wants to understand how the diocesan as well as the monastic institutions could be established, presented and propagated in this early phase of Scandinavian Christendom up to *c.* 1100.

II Zealand and the diocese of Roskilde

We have encountered the first two Scandinavian bishoprics so far: Slesvig and Ribe, and have tried to place the monastic foundation of each of the two in its earliest possible context. The next step must be to follow those bishoprics that originated under the impact of the Anglo-Saxon mission.

Adam tells us (II, ch. 55) that King Cnut, as he returned victorious from England (*c.* 1020),

> brought numerous bishops from England to Denmark, among whom he placed Bernhard in Scania, Gerbrand in Zealand, and Reginbert in Funen. Our archbishop Unwan was highly aggrieved at that and is said to have taken Gerbrand into custody on his way back from England, [since] he heard that he had been ordained by the English archbishop, Aelnod [1020–38]. But he did penitence, as he was required to, and promised with due submission to be faithful to the Hamburg see, and was afterwards taken into the closest confidence of the archbishop. At his intervention, the archbishop even sent messengers to King Cnut, offering gifts and congratulating him on his achievements in England, while criticizing him for his unlawful nomination of the bishops he had sent from England. The king gratiously accepted this and later entered into an agreement with the archbishop, that henceforth he would undertake everything according to the judgement of the archbishop. This the [present] king of the Danes [Svend Estridsen, 1047–74] told me about his uncle, and he did not even conceal Bishop Gerbrand being taken in custody.

Adam knew the geography of Denmark and probably had a clear concept of Zealand, Gerbrand's diocese; he may have sailed all around it, passing eastwards along its northern shore (Jørgensen and Nyberg, 1992). His frequent references to information afforded personally by the king, Svend Estridsen, makes reasonable a guess that the king cultivated Adam's friendship in order to have him make known Christianity's progress in his realm. Roskilde had already developed into what in eleventh-century ecclesiastical circles was called a *civitas*: there (in 1014), in its Holy Trinity church built by the king himself, Swein Forkbeard was buried (II, ch. 28), there was the *sedes regia Danorum* (the royal residence of the Danes) (IV, ch. 5), there King Cnut's sister, Estrid, lived with her husband Ulf, until Ulf had to leave Denmark for Sweden towards the end of the 1020s because of tensions with his brother-in-law (Balle, 1983).

In the archives Adam found a letter which Archbishop Adalbert around 1065 had addressed to Bishop W. of Roskilde concerning a synod in Slesvig, which he quoted (III, ch. 76). Evidently the diocese at that time was named after the episcopal see. On the other hand, Adam often refers to Seland and bishops 'of Zealand', so we must conclude that the period *c.* 1020–70 before Adam wrote was a period of consolidation for the diocese when the name of the episcopal see had not yet replaced an older way of using the island's name for the diocese.

During this period, diocesan structures and a network of parish churches came into being in the diocese of Roskilde. Gerbrand's death, after Archbishop Unwan's, in 1029, gave Unwan's successor, Libentius II, the chance to nominate one Avoco whose period of office is unknown. Avoco was a German cleric. The next bishop, Wilhelmus (Wilhelm), ordained by Archbishop Adalbert (1043–72) prior to the reform of diocesan boundaries *c.* 1060, was apparently a confident of King Svend Estridsen, who dominates this epoch not least by force of his long reign, which lasted for at least 27 years, 1047–74.

A community of clerics around the bishop may have existed in Roskilde since the 1020s (Arhnung, 1937, pp. 4–7). Bishop Wilhelm inaugurated the construction of a stone cathedral on the high ground a little removed from the harbour area with its two old churches, St Clement, later called St Jørgensbjerg church, and St Ib (James). He died 8 May in a year not earlier than 1067, but probably prior to the king (*SE VI: II*, p. 82, n. 95) who died in 1074 or possibly in 1076.

There are no indications that Bishop Wilhelm, who started his career as the king's scribe, promoted monastic life. More interesting is the repeated mention of *monasterium* and *monasteria* in connection with Svend the Norwegian, Sveno Noricus as his name is Latinized, who became Wilhelm's successor between 1067 and 1074 and died in 1088. The 'Roskilde Chronicle', composed *c.* 1140, says expressly that he founded a *monasterium* in Ringsted in honour of Our Lady and *aliud* 'another one' in Slagelse (*Scriptores minores* [*SM*], I, p. 23). Saxo Grammaticus, without doubt a cleric of the Roskilde diocese who received his education in the second half of the twelfth century, interpreted this (Saxo Lib. 12, I, 5) to mean that Svend the Norwegian founded St Michael's in Slagelse. However, Saxo does not speak about a religious community there. His remark does in fact not deal with *monasteria* but with *Mariae sacraria*, which explains why in one sentence he gives Bishop Svend the merit of having founded three institutions: two Marian foundations, 'one *in urbe* (= in Roskilde), the other in Ringsted', then 'the third' or 'a third one, St Michael's in Slagelse'. In Saxo's own time, around 1200, Our Lady's in Roskilde was a community of Cistercian nuns, Our Lady's in Ringsted was a flourishing Benedictine abbey for monks. Consequently, these two 'Marian sanctuaries' are stressed in Saxo's text. Since the 'Roskilde Chronicle', in dealing with the prebends

Bishop Svend instituted for the cathedral clergy in Roskilde, uses the term *claustrum lapideum* for the building where the canons had their living, terminology is consistent: there is a *claustrum* for the canons in Roskilde but a *monasterium* for the monks in Ringsted. Saxo merely confirms, in other words, what the 'Roskilde Chronicle' had already stated.

St Michael's in Slagelse has been thoroughly excavated (Olsen, 1972). Foundations of a wooden church under the floor of a stone church, which originally had a *Westwerk* with two towers, similar to that of Gandersheim, confirm that an early construction here from the first half of the eleventh century was replaced by the stone church. The parish church of Slagelse, St Peter's, an impressive construction from the twelfth century, gives some hint of a possible plan behind the dedication of the two churches. St Michael the Archangel, who weighs the good and bad deeds of man at the hour of individual judgement after death, would aptly protect the perfect striving of the elected ones in monastic life, here just as in Hildesheim, Lüneburg, Slesvig and other places, while St Peter would represent the ordinary pastoral work of the *Ecclesia docens* and the catechumenate for baptism in the footsteps of the apostles, especially the prince of apostles, the Bishop of Rome, the successor of Peter.

Nowhere does Saxo state, however, that there was a *monasterium* at St Michael's in Slagelse. Saxo may represent a Roskilde tradition that kept the memory of what might have been planned in the eleventh century as a monastic foundation in Slagelse but did not succeed, and which had already ceased to exist by *c.* 1140 when the 'Roskilde Chronicle' was composed. The conclusion must be that under Bishop Svend the Norwegian, i.e. at the latest in 1088, in the diocese of Roskilde, the monastic inspiration led to the establishment of at least two, possibly three houses: one for men in Ringsted, perhaps a second for men in Slagelse, and a third for women in Roskilde.

Danish political history in Bishop Svend's period was dramatic. Bishop Svend, apparently still nominated by King Svend Estridsen, governed the diocese under Svend's sons and successors, Harald Hen (1074–80) and Cnut (1080–86), who reorganized the kingdom and was killed in Odense, the victim of a rebellion. The two were probably half-brothers; the names of King Svend's many consorts have not been handed down to posterity. Bishop Svend of course witnessed the king's great donation to the cathedral of Lund of 21 May, 1085, but lived to see the king's violent death and succession of the next brother, Oluf (1086–95), a man of quite another character than Cnut.

Slagelse on the western fringe of Zealand and Ringsted more in the middle of the island were both centres of comparable size and importance in the establishment of a Danish royal administration under Svend Estridsen, Harald and Cnut.[1] There was nothing on the eastern shore of the island to compare with them. The model of medium-sized churches with communities of clerics leading a regular life or at least a life in common, using a common building to sleep in and taking their meals together, was new in England at the time, as it was in many other countries. It is a reasonable assumption that an effective bishop of the eleventh century made efforts to inaugurate monastic life in both Ringsted and Slagelse. Both must have been weak, since Ringsted needed a renewal in 1135, and the Slagelse community, if it ever materialized, must have ceased to exist *c.* 1140, when the 'Roskilde Chronicle' was composed.

There is, on the other hand, no reason to believe that the Ringsted foundation was a failure. Scholars who disregard the existence of a monastic community in Ringsted prior to 1135 forget that many communities of these early periods have left very few sources to later generations, although we know that they did exist. As the analysis of the events of 1135 will show, some details in the procedure of the royal benevolence shown to Ringsted abbey would be very difficult to explain, had the monastery not existed without interruption since Bishop Svend founded it.

No charters have been handed down to show in detail how these regulars were organized during the first decades after their foundation in the 1080s and from whence they draw their resources for the needs of daily life. Since all sources speak of the bishop as founder, it looks as if the kings – Svend Estridsen, Harald, Cnut – were not major benefactors to the two or three communities. No doubt, however, Bishop Svend secured royal acceptance and authorization for his foundation.

In conclusion, to establish monastic communities with intercessory prayer as one of their principal tasks – all in accordance with medieval concepts of society, that is, that those who fight and those who pray are equally important – would strengthen a diocese on its way to becoming stabilized. Bishop Svend, who undoubtedly enjoyed Svend Estridsen's support in everything, in this respect would share some of the king's basic attitudes, as we know them from Adam: a strong feeling for the sacrifices and renounciations necessary to establish the Christian faith and for the many martyrs the new faith claimed. Between the 1040s and the 1080s this bishop, Norwegian by birth, must have adopted the idea of religious institutions specializing in abstinence, contemplation and intercessory prayer for all the diocese – and for all the reign, in so far as Zealand in this epoch gradually became the centre of royal power in Denmark. By 1088, the community of monks in Ringsted and the community of nuns in Roskilde must have been in existence.

III The two Scania dioceses

For the southern province of the Scandinavian peninsula and the long coast stretching northwest of Scania, called Halland, King Swein Forkbeard had nominated an Anglo-Saxon missionary, Gotebald, as a missionary bishop as early as *c.* 1000. Gotebald had earlier been preaching in Sweden and Norway, says Adam (II, ch. 41; *SE VI: II*, p. 13). It is not known if he had received the approval of Archbishop Libentius I/Liawizo (988–1013) when he got his task from the king, or was even known to him, since this archbishop's influence in the north was very limited as a consequence of the Danish and Slav rebellions of 983 (*SE V: II*, p. 24). The king may have relied upon the English ecclesiastical authorities from where Gotebald must have received his ordination.

King Cnut the Great continued this mission by placing one Bishop Bernard at the head of the church in Scania (*SE VI: II*, p. 13). Since it is known that Cnut founded the city of Lund on a site which previously probably either was the meeting place of the provincial Thing community (Blomqvist, 1951, pp. 18–23, 38) or a royal demesne from Svend Forkbeard's time (Andrén, 1980), it is possible that Bishop Bernhard took up residence in Lund and even contributed to the beginnings of urban developments in the 1020s. Andrén has compared Lund's earliest street layout with English examples of the same period (Andrén, 1980, p. 84). However, little is known of Bishop Bernhard, and Adam states that after him, Scania was looked after by Bishops Gerbrand and Avoco from Zealand.

Scania was the region where Svend Estridsen enjoyed support at the time of tension between him and King Magnus the Good in the 1040s. Once he had been accepted as king by the Danes – in 1047, after Magnus had died young in a riding accident – he left the area. After some battles with Harald Hardrada of Norway, the 1050s were the period of consolidation for King Svend Estridsen, to whom Zealand was more central than Scania. He entered into negotiations with Archbishop Adalbert of Hamburg-Bremen (1043–72), the superior of all his bishops, with whom an agreement on a new distribution of dioceses was made (*c.* 1060) (*SE VI: II*, pp. 69, 117). The immediate cause of the change was the death of Bishop Wal, who had administered other parts of Jutland together with his own diocese, Ribe. The calculation was that it would be easier to change the borders now, before a new Bishop of Ribe, agreeable to the king, was found, who might then be consecrated by the archbishop. New borders would create new dioceses in northern Jutland, where the pastoral situation must have seemed unsatisfactory to the archbishop. In view of the casual way in which the king had employed bishops ordained in England, it must have seemed essential to Archbishop Adalbert to settle the new nominations in agreement with the king.

In that connection, a new diocese was established in Scania, apparently to serve the inland areas of the province, so different from the agrarian coastal regions which according to Adam were assigned to a reduced diocese of Lund. The new episcopal see was Dalby, a royal demesne some 10 km east of Lund, where Svend Estridsen had begun building a stone house for himself and a church in stone (Cinthio, 1989) (see Figure 4.1). A fervent clergyman, Egino, possibly of German origin, was appointed first Bishop of Dalby (*SE VI: II*, p. 36). During the first half of the 1060s, when the Christians in Sweden suffered persecution, Egino travelled by inland routes to the diocese of Skara in Västergötland and participated in the destruction of idols and images from the old faith, says Adam. He also preached among the *Pleicani*, the Blekingar, which may possibly have contributed to the later integration of their province into Denmark.

As the result of a compromise, so its seems, the king in return must have got the archbishop's consent to the appointment of his uncle Henry, former Bishop of the Orkneys and a follower of Cnut the Great, as first bishop of the now reduced diocese of Lund. Unlike Egino, this man not only represented the Anglo-Saxon line in the Danish mission, but according to Adam (IV, ch. 8), he was not even interested in his task, a friend of eating and drinking who died without honour some time shortly after the Norman conquest of England (*SE VI: II*, p. 14). Since dividing Scania into two dioceses had been unsuccessful, Dalby was simply abolished. Egino left Dalby and for the last years of his life he was given the restored diocese of Lund, where he died in 1072.

One of his important acts as Bishop of Lund was the decision to found a *praepositura fratrum regulariter viventium* (community of regular canons) at his former see Dalby (*Adam*, IV, ch. 9). The church was handed over to the community which may have come into being in the following decades. Cinthio believes that constructions thought to be part of a royal manor were donated to the community by one of the subsequent kings – probably Erik the Good (1095–1103) or Niels (1104–34) – at the beginning of the twelfth century as religious life started to flourish (Cinthio 1947; 1983; Krins, 1968, pp. 27–33).

The decision to establish a monastic community in Dalby did not materialize at once, however. Cinthio (1989) is careful not to fix any date too far back in time for the introduction of the statutes of regular

4.1 The entrance to the crypt of the church of the Austin priory of Dalby, Scania. (Photograph: Antikvarisk-topografiska arkivet, Stockholm.)

canons in Dalby. The three oldest entries of deceased canons of Dalby in 'Liber daticus Lundensis' (LDat), dated palaeographically to the period *c.* 1130–70 and taken over from the *Necrologium Lundense* (*NL*) as it existed in 1123, inform us of the anniversary of *Alwinus presbiter et canonicus regularis Dabbuensis* (26 July), *Joharus Dabuensis canonicus* (30 July) and *Lothen Dalbyensis canonicus et decanus* (13 September). If these and only these three canons died in the period *c.* 1130–70 – the number of deceased canons of Dalby increases in the following decades – the community may have adopted the statutes and taken the vows of regular canons some time around the second decade of the twelfth century and not earlier. There is every reason to believe that the list of names of deceased canons in Dalby is complete, since in 1136, a formal agreement of mutual commemoration of all deceased members of the cathedral chapter of St Lawrence, the Benedictines of All Saints in Lund, and the canons in Dalby was made and written into the *Necrologium* (*NL*, pp. 127–9).

What, then, was the content of Egino's decision mentioned by Adam? It may have hinted at a serious plan to establish monastic life in Dalby, which Adam may have been informed of around the time he was writing – Egino died in the same year as Archbishop Adalbert, 1072, and Adam, who probably had finished his *Gesta* by then, had to dedicate his work to the next archbishop, Liemar. Another possibility is that Egino's idea, as known to Adam, aimed at a community of secular canons living 'nearly like monks', according to Adam's way of putting it in another case. The 'canonical movement' of the regular canons of St Augustine had not yet reached Scandinavia.

Scania: Lund cathedral chapter and the Benedictines of All Saints

The form of community life observed by the cathedral canons of Lund was investigated first in 1923 when Lauritz Weibull edited statutes and obituary lists from the manuscript (Lund University Library, Mh 6), *Necrologium Lundense* (1923), and more recently in 1978 in the re-edition of the statutes edited by Erik Buus as *Consuetudines Lundenses* (1978).

The statutes for the cathedral chapter of Lund are clearly a derivation of the Aachen statutes for canonical life in the form adopted by the communities of Marbach and St Ruf near Avignon. During the eleventh century, before the clear distinction between secular and regular canons had been more or less forced upon the 'canonical movement' by the highest church authorities (Weinfurter, 1975), even the secular canons referred to St Augustine as a spiritual guarantee for the old tradition of this movement. With the growing monastic inspiration working inside the canonical movement under the influence of the ideas of Pope Gregory VII, many canonical communities decided to place themselves under the 'yoke' of public vows in the more perfect observance of their rule. The Rule of St Augustine entered into this development as a distinction between secular and regular canons: either you observe the Rule of St Augustine and, in addition, the statutes of your particular canonical tradition, or you leave the Rule of St Augustine aside and continue your life according to canonical statutes without taking public vows of poverty and of obedience. Even the general ideal of clerical celibacy could be applied differently as long as a canon had not made a public vow in relation to which his relations to women could be brought forth as a public scandal.

The canons of St Lawrence in Lund decided prior to 1123 not to take vows. In a number of instances, Buus found that the key word *regularis* was omitted in Lund in passages where the Marbach and St Ruf texts have this word. This means that the dividing line between secular canons and regulars in general – which was somewhat blurred by the introduction of regular canons, in contradistinction to monks – was felt in Lund at the same time as it was on the agenda in international church relations during the investiture conflict (cf. Boureau, 1993). The issue has been studied in the Salzburg church province and in the Rhineland in connection with Springiersbach and Klosterrath/Rolduc (*Consuetudines canonicorum*, 1978).

The history of monastic life in Lund must be seen against the background of how the cathedral chapter became organized in the period from the death of Egino in 1072 up to 1123. The few hints we get of Anglo-Saxon mission make it evident that in spite of the Danish–English reign of Cnut the Great with its corresponding Anglo-Saxon influence, impulses from continental Europe took the lead in Scania during the middle decades of the century.

Anglo-Saxon contacts were not forced upon the Scanians by geography. Whereas Jutland is a 'neighbour' to the British Isles, this can certainly not be said about Scania, the eastern extreme of the lands settled by the Danes. The communication system of the Baltic, in which Scania has a central position, included the Swedes, the Finnish and Baltic peoples, and – from this epoch onwards through all the Middle Ages – the Slav republic of Novgorod. Since Norway – 'the Northern Way' – got its name in continuation of the Halland coast beyond the mouth of the Göta Älv to the north, Scanian matters touched directly upon Norwegian issues. Danes and Norwegians met the Swedes a short way up the Göta Älv, the right shore of which belonged to the Norwegians with their stronghold at Konghelle.

The need felt by Svend Estridsen to establish an eastern diocese in Scania for the north-eastern parts of this province, which the king must be supposed to have known well, makes it clear that the idea behind the foundation of Lund in the time of Cnut the Great must have been the concept of a western power trying to get a firm foothold on the western fringe of an eastern country. The experiment of Dalby, on the other hand, was abandoned after no more than a decade.

Two factors seem to have been important here: the Norman conquest of England, and the unchallenged power of Svend Estridsen in the late years of his reign.

The Norman conquest transformed England into a foreign and distant country for those Scandinavian peoples who were not immediately involved in its interests. Western Denmark is in this sense the exception to the general pattern of the rest of Scandinavia. Only to the warrior farmers of Jutland could the dream of reconquering England in 1085 possibly have possessed some realistic prospects. For the rest of Denmark and Scandinavia there is no need to suppose an obstinate desire to restore the old power situation around the North Sea. This means that the death of Bishop Henry of Lund in the late 1060s may very easily have been felt to be the end of an epoch and a signal for a change of politics.

Combining this with the second factor, Svend Estridsen's high reputation and competence, the full command he enjoyed over his realm and his resources after the final battles and his accord with the Norwegians in 1063/64, one should not dismiss the possibility that his friendship with Adam of Bremen, if one might call it that, may have influenced not only Adam but also the king. The collaboration between the two, resulting in one of the most important historical works of the early Middle Ages in Europe, cannot have had its effect upon Adam alone. We can clearly see that Svend Estridsen took Adam into his confidence in allowing him a number of insights into certain intimate spheres of his own family history. In such an atmosphere of confidence, would not, through Adam's influence, the forces represented by the German church and the archbishops of Hamburg-Bremen have gained a higher status and importance in the king's eyes? It must have been obvious to the king that now, after the defeat of Anglo-Saxon England, it would be the right time for the Danes to fall back upon earlier good relations with princes and prelates of continental Europe for the further prosperity of the Danish realm.

On the other hand, as is well known from several studies on Adam's historical work, this priest from upper Germany shows in Book III of his *Gesta Hammaburgensis Ecclesiae Pontificum* that he was perfectly able to take a critical stand against his own superior and employer, Archbishop Adalbert. The portrait Adam gives of Adalbert has justly been viewed as highly remarkable, in all its borrowings from antique biography writing. Adam's honest and tactful description of Adalbert's destiny as a story of increasing decay caused by pride and vanity, as we read it in Book III, may be assumed to have been partly communicated by Adam to the king in private conversation. Svend Estridsen must have been well informed through the private talks between these two.

It would be good to keep this mind when interpreting the king's procedure for procuring a new bishop for Scania after the death of Egino on 19 October 1072. On 16 March of the same year, the great

Archbishop Adalbert had ended his days in personal and political misery, plagued by illness. It must have been the king's explicit choice to select Ricwal, a canon from Paderborn who had been in open conflict with Archbishop Adalbert and excommunicated by him, as the next Bishop of Lund. The new Archbishop of Hamburg-Bremen, Liemar, was nominated in May 1072 by an independent election among the clergy of the Hamburg-Bremen archdiocese and groups around King Henry IV, far away from papal politics dominated by Cardinal Hildebrand, who was elected Pope Gregory VII on 22 April 1073, the very day after Alexander II had died. Ricwal seems to have been used by King Svend as a messenger to Gregory VII to apply to the Pope for the establishment of an archbishopric for Scandinavia, which would make the northern countries independent of Hamburg-Bremen (*SE VI: II*, p. 16; Seegrün, 1967, pp. 74–86). The king could not know, and perhaps never learned before his death in April 1074, that the newly elected pope was on his way to bringing the sword to Europe by provoking a bloody civil war which would rage for the next two decades.[2] It was not least this international conflict that frustrated King Svend's initiative. Scandinavia did not find its way to becoming an independent church province at this time. As this became clear (Seegrün, 1967), however, Ricwal, thanks to King Svend's dispositions, was already in unchallenged possession of the diocese of Lund and went on to carry out this task, first under King Harald Hen (1074/76–80), then under Cnut (1080–86); he died in 1089.

It is very probable that ties were loosened between these two Danish kings and Pope Gregory VII, who was deposed by King Henry IV in 1080 and in 1084 driven out of Rome by the German king, who then had himself crowned emperor by Pope Clement III, his replacement for Hildebrand. An investigation of the sources concerning the St Peter's Pence from Denmark (Nyberg, 1985) shows that Harald Hen may have accepted Clement III and that Cnut, when he succeeded his brother to the throne in 1080, was faced with a *fait accompli* and had no platform from which he might have entered upon a collaboration with Pope Gregory VII.

For the Scanian diocese and its monastic life the general warlike situation in Europe in these years offered good conditions for a collaboration between the two Danish kings, especially Cnut, and Bishop Ricwal of Lund, who apparently was *persona non grata* in Gregorian circles. This must be kept in mind if one wants to understand why the attack which may have been planned against Norman England in 1085 did not materialize, and why instead King Cnut in the same year gave his famous generous donation to the cathedral church of Lund.

Ricwal is held by Cinthio to be the inaugurator of the romanesque cathedral of Lund. More than that: he gives him the honour of having inaugurated All Saints Benedictine abbey (Cinthio, 1989, p. 31) just north of the urban settlement of Lund, which was now in its first period of expansion. All Saints' abbey existed around 1100, and since it does not seem to be a foundation in the spirit of Ricwal's successor Asser, Cinthio's argument is that by a process of elimination we have to assume that it existed before Ricwal's death in 1089. The site was definitely outside the urban settlement of the late eleventh century (Andrén, 1980, maps on pp. 43–4).

Other arguments may be used, however, that speak in favour of Ricwal. Paderborn is an important chain in the discussion of Erich Herzog (1964) regarding the set-up of early episcopal and abbatial towns in a 'Sakrallandschaft' of the tenth and eleventh centuries. Herzog speaks of the 'Ottonian city', a conglomerate of scattered settlements around kernels consisting of ecclesiastical institutions on a distance of 200–500 metres from each other, making it possible to link these institutions liturgically by means of processions and celebrations in sequence from one church to another. In Paderborn we find precisely this type of ecclesiastical institution created at a certain distance from the cathedral, in such a way that they became kernels of settlement separated from each other by open, unsettled areas. West of the cathedral there is the Carolingian Abdinghof, to the east, a little further away, the Busdorf monastery founded by Bishop Meinwerk (1009–36), who rebuilt Abdinghof totally and finally in 1031 had it consecrated, a new and splendid abbey in the style of its time. Its monks came from Lotharingia, but they may have been mingled with a group of Cluniac monks whom Meinwerk invited in 1015 to settle in a special chapel near Abdinghof (Herzog, 1964, 102–15). The idea of elaborating on the original combination of cathedral and monastery by transforming Abdinghof into a full Benedictine abbey and at the same time creating a new monastery at Busdorf, symmetrically on the eastern side of the cathedral, must have influenced Ricwal during his years of formation in Paderborn. One cannot deny that the topography of Lund with the cathedral in the middle, All Saints' abbey to the north and St Peter's nunnery to the west, may also be read in this light, as the idea of a city constituting a liturgical community expressed in a grouping of ecclesiastical institutions capable of sharing a common liturgical event. The topography of Lund can be easily explained if one looks upon it from the point of view of Herzog's 'Ottonian city' – which, on a closer, critical look (Nyberg, 1981a), is in fact something belonging to the eleventh rather than to the tenth century.

In conclusion, Scania stands out as one of the areas of maritime North-Western Europe that was most crucial to the spread of monasticism. Lund became the ecclesiastical metropole of all Scandinavia. By the early implantation of Benedictine monastic life and the early discussions in the metropolitan cathedral chapter on the Rule of St Augustine, Lund took the lead in presenting the most important issues of this sphere of life to all neighbouring regions.

Notes

1. For numismatic evidence of the importance of Ringsted and Slagelse in the eleventh century see Jensen (1995, p. 42).
2. Some scholars, whom Janson (1998) has followed, date Svend Estridsen's death to April 1076.

CHAPTER FIVE

Eleventh-century monasticism: Funen and Jutland

I Funen and the diocese of Odense

The island of Funen must have been of great importance in pre-Carolingian Denmark. In Viking times, an easy approach to Funen was possible from the north. The passage west of the island is favourable, as can be seen from Ohthere's and Wulfstan's descriptions (Jørgensen, 1985; Ottar og Wulfstan, 1983). Adam of Bremen describes a route north of Funen to Zealand taking in the two bays cutting in from the north into the interior of the two islands, the bay of Odense and the Isefjord leading to the bay of Roskilde. The fact that Odense, on the estuary of the island's biggest river, has a name commemorating Odin, claimed as a divine ancestor by the Danish kings, indicates that it was a centre of political power (Hald, 1963). No other place on the island competes in importance with Odense.

Although a bishopric was established here through an agreement between the regency of Otto III under Theophanu and Swein Forkbeard made 29 March 988 in Wildeshausen in Saxony, no bishop seems to have been nominated then. At least no name of a bishop is known until Cnut the Great, according to Adam, appointed an Anglo-Saxon, Reginbert, to Funen about 1020. The further story of the pastoral care of Christian life in this conglomeration of islands is unclear, since Adam's few glimpses into the career of the next bishop of Funen are difficult to interpret. According to Adam, Archbishop Adalbert assigned pastoral work on Funen to a certain Eilbert, *quem tradunt, conversum a piratis, Farriam insulam ... primum reperisse constructoque ibi monasterio fecisse habitabilem* (who, a convert from the Vikings, is said as the first to have discovered the island of *Farria* and, after having built a monastery there, to have made it inhabitable) (*Adam*, IV, ch. 3, with skolion nos 106 and 107). If we disregard Adam's effort to place the island of Farria 'around the mouth of the river Elbe far away out in the ocean' identifying it with Heligoland, we must conclude that Adam had heard that Eilbert was a 'convert from the pirates', in other words a former Viking but in any case not born of Christian parents, a man who for a while had made his living in a pioneer effort to cultivate a certain island where he tried to practise the life of a Christian in a religious community. Whoever told Adam this story, and whatever he might have known or believed about the island indicated by the name Farria, he was evidently fascinated by the strength of the Christian religion and wanted to tell the reader about its power to transform the life of a rough Viking. Since the meaning of the word *monasterium* in Adam's texts is generally not very exact, we may take the *monasterium* founded by Eilbert in Farria to indicate that Adam had heard of a kind of religious community of a group af men there, held together by the force of a common religious discipline.

Adam's reason for reporting this story may partly have been the geographical position of Farria, although from the point of view of literary composition it is irrelevant. The fact that he situates this island in relation to a place well known to the reader – the river Elbe – and yet 'far out in the ocean', identifying it as Heligoland, is in tune with Adam's wish to make his text as exotic as possible.

Scholars have discussed whether Farria stands for Heligoland, the Faeroe Islands or the North Frisian island of Föhr off the west coast of southern Jutland (cf. *SE VI: II*, p. 58, n. 58). Still another solution may be proposed: the small island of Farø in the waters east of Falster, near Vordingborg on Zealand. An argument for placing Farria here could be that Falster was later part of the Odense diocese, but such a theory has not been tested so far.

The geographical position of Farria, however, cannot have been the most important reason why Adam reports the story. In Adam's mind there may have been some connection between the difficult and sometimes rebellious attitude of Bishop Eilbert of Funen on the one hand, and his monastic background on the other, described in such a way that Adam may have looked upon it as 'odd'. Bishop Eilbert refused to participate in provincial synods convoked by Archbishop Adalbert, something Adam knew from documents he found and quoted (*Adam*, III, ch. 75–7; *Diplomatarium Danicum* [*DD*] *1,2*, nos 5 and 6, dated [1061–72]). According to Adam, Eilbert died in the same year as Adalbert, 1072 (*Adam*, IV, ch. 9), and Adam apparently did not learn the name of any successor before his *Gesta* were finished and dedicated to Adalbert's successor (cf. *SE VI: II*, p. 59).

Was it the case that a recently converted Viking spontaneously chose to promote the monastic life? The tension which clearly appears and is documented between Eilbert and his ecclesiastical superior, the Archbishop of Hamburg-Bremen, might indicate a tension between the 'church in the world', the ordinary hierarchy, and the 'church of the elect', the chosen way of life in renouncement of the world and intimacy with God in solitude. The fact that Pope Alexander II had to write to the king himself, Svend Estridsen, whose power he was well aware of, warning the king not to have anything to do with Eilbert until Eilbert's differences with the archbishop were settled, gives us the impression that Eilbert was a man under royal protection, perhaps one of the very few converted Christians of the period whom the king could propose for a bishopric.

We do not know if Eilbert was nominated bishop of Funen upon the death of Reginbert, or only after the diocesan reform had been negotiated by the king and the archbishop c. 1060. Some of the new bishops nominated for Danish episcopal sees *c.* 1060 (*Adam*, III, ch. 77) were evidently the king's candidates, to balance some of the archbishop's nominees. Christian of Aarhus and the Anglo-Saxon Henry of Lund, former bishop of the Orkneys, seem to have been proposed by the king, while Egino of Dalby and the 'monk' Magnus for *Wendila* apparently were the archbishop's men. Upon the sudden death of Magnus on his way to his see (*Adam*, IV, ch. 2), Archbishop Adalbert ordained the former provost of the cathedral chapter in Bremen, Albricus, as his successor (*SE VI: II*, p. 49), perhaps an indication that an agreement had been reached between king and archbishop on the succession in this diocese. Eilbert may have belonged to the king's candidates for bishops in the situation of 1060; in such a case, he may have been the only convert from paganism sufficiently formed in Christian faith and the monastic tradition to become a bishop. A certain reputation must have surrounded him to make him a candidate.

The result is, however, that a man with irrefutably monastic inclinations administered the diocese of Funen and surrounding islands during at least one decade of Svend Estridsen's reign. His ecclesiastical reputation certainly suffered from his conflict with Archbishop Adalbert, and King Svend, who spoke several times to Adam about holy men and martyrs for the Christian faith, must have realized that Eilbert was not made of the material that produces saints. He may, however, have introduced among the members of his flock a consciousness of a difference between a secular and a monastic interpretation of Christian life.

King Svend died in 1074 or 1076 and his son Harald was made king, reigning until his death in 1080 (cf. Hoffmann, 1976). The younger brother, Cnut, carried out military expeditions to England during Harald's reign, bringing relics of St Oswald and St Alban home to Odense. Elected king in 1080 he tried to introduce a strong royal administration based on English and continental models, and to introduce new forms of taxation to replace a royal economy based upon plundering abroad, as practised in the Viking epoch. Cnut married Adela, daughter of

Count Robert I 'the Frisian' of Flanders (Gallén, 1985), whereby he became related to one of the most noble aristocratic families of Europe, tracing its ancestors back to Carolingian times; his mother-in-law, Gertrud, who lived until 1103, was a daughter of Count Bernhard II of Saxony.

King Cnut made a great donation to the cathedral of Lund in 1085, the year when he found it more important to defend the southern border of his reign than to lead his men on a sea expedition against Norman England. When a rebellion broke out in northern Jutland in the early summer of 1086, Cnut fled southwards and went via Slesvig to Funen, where he was killed with his men on 10 July 1086 in St Alban's church in Odense.

The reputation for holiness which Cnut acquired during the following years was due to miracles performed at his tomb and the interpretation of his death as that of a martyr for the Christian faith (Nyberg, 1981b; 1995/96). The reign of his brother Oluf 1086–95 meant nine years of famine, hunger and bad luck, until the next brother and son of Svend Estridsen, Erik the Good, called in monks from Evesham to found a monastery in Odense *c.* 1095. It is in this connection that Hubald, the first Bishop of Odense after Eilbert, is mentioned in the sources.

There is one important point to make here, before we enter into the question of the monastic foundation as such. King Cnut stands in Danish history as the man who gave up the idea of a Danish recuperation of England. He was identified as such already by the armed men of the Viking fleet, who in the summer of 1085 could not enforce their wish to attack Norman England. Ten years later, monks from Evesham arrived in Denmark to found a monastery there and stay. Evesham was one of the abbeys in Mercia which had been able to prosper under Norman rule, thanks to its abbot, Ethelwig, who from the very beginning had declared himself loyal to William the Conqueror and continued to work as his trusted official until his death in 1077. The Anglo-Saxon aristocracy suffered heavy losses during William's reign, those in worldy office as well as the ecclesiastical community. However, the Evesham monks succeeded in resettling some of the old abbeys in Northumbria whose history went back to Bede's times. There was a strong Anglo-Saxon vitality in Evesham, which continued under its next abbot, a monk from Caen, Walter (1077–1104 [Mason, 1990, p. 128]).[1] During his time in office the priory of Odense was founded and settled by Evesham monks, most or all of whom must have been Anglo-Saxons (Mason, 1990, pp. 124–8; Abrams, 1995). A letter confirming the mutual prayer duties, the mutual freedom for monks from both communities to live in each other's monastery, and the prerogative of Evesham at the election of a prior in Odense was set up (*DD 1,2*, no. 24).

King Erik the Good favoured the memory of his brother Cnut and doubtless shared the view of his brother that a Danish–English North Sea condominium would not be restored. The monks from Evesham in Odense must have found their ultimate task as a continuation of Benedictine monastic life on foreign soil, without prospects for a return to England.

If we try to place the Evesham mission in the context of North-Western European monasticism in the eleventh century, it must be clear from what has been said so far, and from the history of early monasticism in Norway, that their arrival in Odense cannot be hailed as Denmark's first monastic foundation. The documentation is certainly more complete for Odense, due to the spectacular beginning of monasticism there in veneration for the holy martyr king, whose canonization was carried out in Odense by Bishop Hubald in a solemn ceremony on 19 April in a year which, on the basis of Aelnoth's *Gesta*, must have been 1100, in which case the day would have been Thursday in the third week after Easter. The only alternative would be 1101, but since the choice of this year would place the elevation on Good Friday, it must be dismissed. According to Aelnoth (quoted in *DD 1,2*, no. 26), the king had sent a delegation to Rome to seek papal authorization of the procedure, which the Pope duly gave. Aelnoth does not say which pope it was who gave his placet, however. Urban II died 29 July 1099, Paschal II was elected 13 August; theoretically, it could have been any of the two (cf. below). The documentation is a direct result of the continued existence and recruitment to this community, which inspired Aelnoth, probably a member of the community, to write *c.* 1122 the principal narrative of Cnut's life and death, his famous *Gesta Swenomagni regis et filiorum eius et passio gloriosissimi Canuti regis et martyris* (*Vitae Sanctorum Danorum* [*VSD*], pp. 77–136).

Regardless of the comparatively solid documentation for the Odense foundation of 1095, the Anglo-Saxon monks must have known that the Bishops of Lund and Roskilde already had Benedictine communities in their dioceses. Moreover, St Michael's outside Slesvig and Our Lady's in Seem outside Ribe must have been in existence by then, although we cannot fix the dates of their foundation. During the reign of Oluf (1086–95), which must have seemed more and more ominous the longer rain and famine continued, negotiations must have begun which ultimately led to the exodus of a number of Evesham monks, thereby repeating age-old patterns in the insular interpretation of missionary Christianity: the fulfilment of the perfect Christian life by voluntary exile.

There is no evidence that there were Anglo-Saxon monks in Denmark prior to 1095. As we have seen, Bishop Svend the Norwegian must have established the Ringsted community prior to 1088, Bishop Ricwal that of Lund prior to 1089. For neither of the two foundations is there any hint of an Anglo-Saxon connection. On the contrary, in the case of Lund all the signs point to a German inspiration, and in Ringsted a connection with the German-inspired foundations outside Slesvig and Ribe seems reasonable. I would therefore think that the existence of presumably three, perhaps four, Benedictine communities in Denmark during the difficult famine years of King Oluf may have incited some of the Evesham monks to risk an exodus from England to seek an unknown destiny in the country which had brought such a confrontation to England for at least two centuries.

Then there is the question of papal schism. A careful analysis of the influence the two conflicting popes exerted upon ecclesiastical institutions all over Europe in the early 1090s shows that Clement III was accepted as pope by a number of princes, secular as well as ecclesiastical, closely linked to Henry IV who had been crowned emperor in 1084 at Clement's hands (Nyberg, 1985; Ziese, 1982). The position of Pope Gregory VII's successor, Victor III, alias Desiderius (1086–87) was very weak, that of Pope Urban II (1088–99) much weaker than many historians of the crusades would have us believe. Urban's travels in France, where he had his main support, and his council in Clermont in 1095 took place under the pressure of doing something spectacular to counteract Pope Clement's and King Henry's various moves. In the end he was successful, but only partly so, and much of his success has been ascribed to him long afterwards.

As for the Scandinavian situation, there is no evidence of a contact between the Danish kingdom and Pope Gregory VII after his deposition in 1080. Among the faithful, lifelong adherents of Henry IV and his pope, Clement III, was the Archbishop of Hamburg-Bremen, Liemar (1072–1101). Unsurprisingly, therefore, there was no contact between Denmark and the papacy in Cnut's reign. To adherents of the Roman pope in the 1090s, when Cnut's reputation for holiness was growing, it would have seemed fatal if the king's career as a saint were not based on the firm ground of rightful obedience to the Pope. With Denmark's schismatic contact to Pope Clement probably continuing through the unhappy reign of Oluf, it would be easy for his competitors in the family, Erik and perhaps Niels, falling back upon the reputation of King Cnut, to chose as an alternative to recognize Urban and thus obtain a 'new deal' by which they could firmly connect their brother's sanctity to Pope Urban's Roman obedience. The Anglo-Saxon monks were not stained by any suspicion of schismatic adherence to the emperor's pope, which may have been the case with the other Benedictines in Denmark in those years.

The main argument in favour of such a construction lies in the analysis of what the emissary of Pope Clement, the Papal Nuntius, Teuzo, did in Denmark during his stay there in King Oluf's reign. Apparently he collected Peter's pence for Pope Clement (Nyberg, 1985), as can be concluded from the formula used later by Pope Paschal II when, on 8 May 1104, he asked the Danish bishops to reassume the payment of Peter's pence, *ne in ipso negotio fraudem Romana ecclesia ulterius patiatur* (so that in this matter the Roman Church shall not suffer further detriment) (*DD 1,2*, no. 30). Thus, the Roman Church had in fact felt cheated of Peter's pence for a while, according to Pope Paschal, who must be the one who, shortly after his election in August 1099, gave his permission to King Erik for the canonization of Cnut. Previous *predecessores* of the addressee – earlier bishops – had paid this tribute to the papacy, says the letter. One must think of the situation under Alexander II (1061–73) and King Svend, and under Gregory VII until his deposition (1073–80) and King Harald, with influential bishops of that epoch like Ricwal of Lund and Svend of Roskilde.

Anglo-Saxon monks from Evesham would, in this situation, be able to promote the sanctity of King Cnut without much ado about the consequences of the papal schism. Once the position of the Roman papacy had improved, especially after Clermont and the Jerusalem expedition, Anglo-Saxon monks familiar with the cult of holy kings (Hoffmann, 1975; Ridyard, 1988; Rollason, 1989) would be most useful to King Erik in order to secure the cult of his brother as a royal saint. Odense even possessed relics of their holy king, St Oswald, brought there by King Cnut himself. By such a connection, a foundation in Odense made by monks from England would be a strong support for a reformed and strengthened Danish kingdom.

Thus, although the Anglo-Saxon Benedictines of Odense did not constitute Denmark's first monastic community, they were probably the first monks to enter into the role of recipients of a special royal favour, of a demonstrative gesture of royal benevolence, accompanied by the necessary holy literature and the corresponding liturgical performances. What King Cnut granted in 1085 to Lund cathedral, Erik and Niels granted in 1095 and 1117 to St Cnut's Benedictine monastery in Odense. This again leads us to a closer examination of the function entrusted to them by their founders during their formative period covering the first two decades of their stay in Denmark, *c.* 1095–1117.

When the monks from England arrived, Odense was not an empty space from a Christian point of view. The church, situated on the ridge mentioned earlier, where King Cnut and his 17 men were killed and buried under the church floor, was still there. Styled by Aelnoth as *basilica preciosi martyris Albani*, it was defined as being *haud longe sitam* (situated not very far away) from the *locus regie sedis* (royal house), where the king first took refuge on the day he was killed (*VSD*, p. 116). St Alban's church was found in an exemplary excavation. Under the foundations of the twelfth-century stone church, the archaeologists (Arentoft, 1985) discovered traces of two earlier wooden churches, the earliest one dating back to the middle of the eleventh century and thus contemporary with the earliest traces of trade and business activities in the area around the fish market just north of the church (*Odense bys historie*, 1982, pp. 160–75). The later state of royal property in Odense leads us to look for the *locus regie sedis* west of St Alban's church (Nyberg, 1995), probably around the place where the construction of a crypt for a stone church was inaugurated, either by Cnut himself, or immediately after his death (Krins, 1968, pp. 38–42; *Danmarks Kirker* [*DK*], IX, 1, 1995, p. 173).

At a short distance to the north of the ridge where St Alban's church and the new crypt stood, placed at a slightly lower level more or less at the same distance from the river bed in the south and the innermost strand of the bay leading in to the inhabited area in the north, we find a church dedicated to St Michael, one of the most popular dedications of churches from the early missionary period. Excavations have not been carried out under the twelfth-century construction hidden in the present-day building, now dedicated to St John the Baptist. It may once have been a village church, or a baptismal chapel from the first 50 years of Christian religion.

The call to settle in Odense meant to the monks that they had to share the place with an episcopal residence. Scattered hints at a lost charter issued by King Niels (1104–34), mentioning a royal grant to *ecclesiae Christi et sanctae Mariae necnon beatorum martyrum Albani atque Canuti, quae est in Othense* (to the church of Christ and of Holy Mary as well as of the blessed martyrs Alban and Cnut, which is in Odense) (*DD 1,2*, no. 34) may be interpreted to mean that the first stone church was meant from the beginning to become a 'Christ Church', a dedication which very seldom survives in this form in Scandinavia (Lidén 1970; also Nyberg, 1986, p. 121, n. 525). If furthermore this church was dedicated to both martyrs, St Alban and St Cnut, the idea may have been to transfer the relics of St Alban to this new stone church. That this was the explanation current in Odense in the thirteenth century is evident from the following passage in a version of St Cnut's *Passio* copied *c.* 1220–50 (*VSD 552*, quoted in *DK*, IX, 1, 1995, p. 173, n. 95):

> *Erat enim monasterium ligneum, in honore sancti Albani consecratum, in quo tunc temporis sedes erat episcopalis, que postea ad monasterium beati Kanuti, cuius hodie festum celebramus, insigni de lateribus edificio constructum translata est.*
> (For there was a wooden monastery, dedicated to St Alban, where at that time the episcopal see had its place; this was later transferred to the monastery of St Cnut, whose feast we celebrate today, built as an excellent building in brick.)

In the summary of another lost charter, the church is said to have been called *ecclesia sancti Canuti quae est Othensi* (Saint Cnut's church which is in Odense) (*DD 1,2*, no. 35).

By the twelfth century, for which fuller documentation survives, St Alban's had become the parish church. The cathedral figures in the first papal letter for the monastery of 13 October 1117 (*DD 1,2*, no. 42). After negotiations and reports – the content of which we do not know – at the court of Pope Paschal II, who knew the Danish situation since the beginning of his pontificate, the Pope issued a mandate to Bishop Hubald in which he refers to a letter from King Niels. Upon the advice and acceptance of Bishop Hubald, the king had 'adorned' *locus sedis vestrae* (the place of your episcopal see) by the presence of *religiosorum monachorum cetus* (a group of monks living according to vows). The clear distinction between the two, the episcopal see and the group of monks, is being transformed into a firm union between the two. The king and the bishop may assign property *ad eiusdem congregationis victum sustentationemque* (to this community's food and living), and the monks' right to own and retain such property is confirmed.

Of all Scandinavian monastic foundations, the Odense case is the only one from the eleventh century that can be elucidated by charters. The case is the first in Scandinavia following a well-known pattern of several English episcopal sees. We are dealing with a monastic community, the establishment of which, during a time span of about 20 years, as the clergy of a cathedral at an episcopal see was negotiated between the bishop and the king, and approved by the Pope. The best parallel example is Durham, which was instituted in a corresponding way, under the direct inspiration by monks from Evesham via its re-establishment of monastic life in Jarrow (Burton, 1994). Had this not been the case, we might have known just as little about Odense as about all the other early Benedictine abbeys of Denmark and Norway.

With this, however, we also admit that the case of Odense, far from taking the lead in the interpretation of what happened on the Benedictine scene in eleventh-century Scandinavia, is entirely untypical of the monastic foundations of the period, and that this untypical character is responsible for the comparatively good foundation evidence preserved up to our time. An exceptional institution needs more explicit documentation for its status, whereas what is normal will be understood to be self-evident and not worth paying too much attention to.

While in the dioceses of Lund, Ribe and Slesvig the monks were on the outskirts of the town which grew up around the episcopal see, and the diocese of Roskilde had its nuns in the same position but its monks in Ringsted, the diocese of Odense had nowhere to place its monks other than in the very centre, next to St Alban's church, which by this arrangement seemingly displayed the typical picture of a parish church beside a monastery. Historically, however, St Alban's was not built as the parish church of a monastery. It was the royal church which probably at an early stage was also the bishop's church. Only thanks to the murder of King Cnut, which led to the dedication of the new stone church to the holy martyr king, did St Alban's achieve the status of a parish church for the civil settlement growing up around the fish market.

To summarize, instead of a 'secular' bishop's church at the centre of liturgy and administration and a 'regular' community at a distance, as in other Danish episcopal sees, what we see in Odense, for the first time in Denmark, is the combination of a 'regular' community at the centre of liturgy and church administration and the 'secular' church at a distance.

The distance between the two grows as the settlement expands. The 'regular' cathedral community tends to dominate the western inhabited part of Odense, whereas the parish of the main 'secular' church, St Alban's, where we find the bishop's residence and civil settlement, expands eastwards, until this expansion leads to the establishment, presumably around 1200, of a new parish in the east, Our Lady's. The expansion to the north of St Alban's parish stops when it reaches the area around St Michael's church, which therefore must have formed an early, autonomous parish.

The inevitable consequence of this development is that in Odense, for the first time in Denmark as far as we know, a monastic community was also responsible for supervising an important saint's cult, so that the monks receiving pilgrims visiting St Cnut's tomb in search of help and divine intercession had to fulfil pastoral duties (also following English examples [Mason, 1990]). Instead of unworldly seclusion, the monks had to display care and pity for the bodily and spiritual needs of people arriving as pilgrims from all parts of the island diocese. The ordinary church administration, then, had to adopt other, more special forms in this diocese, since the bishop could not count on his cathedral clergy for ordinary administrative tasks, but was forced to establish an organization of his own for such purposes.

Map II Monasteries and episcopal sees in North-Western Europe, *c.* 1100. (Drawn by Inger Bjerg Poulsen.)

It is therefore a reasonable assumption (recently stressed again in *DK*, IX, 1, 1995), that there existed some kind of a community life of unmarried clergy in the church of St Alban in Odense before 1086, which deserved to be called a *monasterium* by the author of the younger *Passio*. Whether or not such a college of clerics continued to exist at St Alban's church from *c.* 1100 onwards to carry out administrative tasks of the bishop, as has been proposed by scholars of earlier generations, is very unclear. There were troublesome legal questions to be settled between St Alban's parish and the bishop in the middle of the twelfth century (see, for example, Nyborg, 1979), and the parish church may have had a group of clergy to defend its interests, but such a group of clergy hardly lived a monastic community life any more, since any monastic way of life existing earlier had moved to the stone cathedral. Finally, with the establishment of Our Lady's church and parish in the eastern part of the inhabited area, the local dean came to the fore as the main prelate here, taking upon himself a number of tasks normally assigned to the cathedral clergy, such as the training of future priests and ecclesiastical legal procedure.

It is thus important to remember that Odense does not represent typical Benedictine monasticism in the traditional sense. Such a conclusion would have been tempting if the Benedictine foundation of 1095 in Odense had been the first settlement of Benedictine monks in Denmark. Since this is not the case, and since it is even possible that a certain monastic tradition had been active in Odense before the Anglo-Saxon monks arrived – I refer again to Adam's notes on Bishop Eilbert who died in 1072 – monasticism in Odense in the legal and religious form it acquired between 1095 and 1117 was a very special combination of Benedictine spirituality and pastoral care for pilgrims. There was a forced symbiosis between a monastic community and an episcopal see, which probably drew heavily upon the administrative resources of the bishop. This special combination seems to have had no predecessor in Scandinavia. For the first time in Scandinavia we find here a pilgrim church where monks are wardens of a sanctuary dear to church and kingdom alike. For some decades this close link between a cult of saints and renunciation of the world, introduced from England, was to work as a model in Scandinavian Christianity.

II The three new dioceses of Jutland

At the Diet of Ingelheim in 948 three dioceses apparently were meant to cover all Jutland. Two of them, Slesvig and Ribe, are mentioned in *Vita*

Anskarii as St Ansgar's church foundations, the third, Aarhus, is not recorded before 948. The diocesan reform under the agreement between King Svend Estridsen and Archbishop Adalbert of Hamburg-Bremen *c.* 1060 created a group of three new dioceses: Aarhus, Viberg and Vendel. We do not know if the 948 diocese of Aarhus ever functioned as its founders intended it to. It may have covered the area of all the three dioceses which replaced it *c.* 1060, but even that we do not know. In the middle of the eleventh century, Christian affairs in all the region were supervised by Bishop Wal of Ribe, whose death prompted a reform of diocesan boundaries.

Two of the three new dioceses of *c.* 1060, Aarhus and Viberg, covered the north-eastern part of mainland Jutland. A natural border consisting of rivers and hills running from north-west to south-east across the peninsula constitutes the north-eastern border of the Ribe bishopric. It begins some 50 km inside the western mouth of the Limfjorden, follows the present-day River Karup south-east and meets the eastern coast north of Vejle, not far from Jelling, the sacred centre of royal power in the tenth century.

Of the two, Aarhus contains the River Gudenå basin from its source lakes in the south to its estuary north of Djursland. The diocese mainly coincides with two of the administrative districts, called *sysler*, upon which the land register in the so-called 'Kong Valdemars Jordebog' from 1231 is organized – the Aabosyssel and the Loversyssel (cf. Nyberg, 1982).

The diocese of Viberg may originally have covered the same area which was later defined as the three *sysler* to the north and west of Aabosyssel – Ommersyssel, Himmerland or Himmersyssel and Salling(syssel). In this way the diocese included all the northern coast of mainland Jutland until Limfjorden, but not the island of Mors, although it also was part of Sallingsyssel. In the southern part of the diocese, the eastern section of Ommersyssel as far as the narrow bay separating this land from Himmerland soon came under the administration of the bishops of Aarhus. Viberg itself lies in the western part of Ommersyssel (Dahlerup, 1968, map).

The name 'Viborg' does not contain the element -borg 'borough' or 'castle'. It was originally written Viberg or Vibjerg, composed of vi 'holy grove', 'pre-Christian cultplace' and berg or bjerg 'hill' (cf. *SE VI: II*, p. 117). Viberg was the Thing-place for all Jutland. One can easily understand the reasons why Archbishop Adalbert *c.* 1060 wanted to place a bishop on this spot, considering his perspective over the entire northern mission. Paganism was alive among the Swedes who according to the reconstruction of Henriksson (1995) had celebrated their Uppsala sacrifices in 1052 and now were ready for the next celebration towards the end of February 1060, a year which Bishop Adalvard, then working in Sweden, reported to be one of strong pagan resistance against Christian mission (*Adam*, IV, ch. 23, with skolion no. 136). Adam reports generally that the Norwegians were the most 'superstitious' of the Scandinavian peoples, in other words, still adhering strongly to pagan soothsayers. There was, in 1060, every reason to try to 'Christianize' whatever remnants there were in Denmark of pre-Christian cult. Viberg would be one of those places, and it was chosen to become the new diocesan centre for northern mainland Jutland.

A secondary effect of the creation of the diocese of Viberg was that a new diocese of Aarhus came into being. The Gudenå, Denmark's longest river, with its many lakes and rich fishing waters, was a source of prosperity and, as it turned out, offered ideal surroundings for monastic life. Aarhus had had a longer Christian tradition than Viberg, since it must already have had a Christian community in the tenth century. Aarhus also enjoyed better sea communications, being directly accessible from the entirely Danish waters between Jutland, Zealand and Halland, and, as Adam explains, situated on an equal sailing distance from Odense and Roskilde (Jørgensen and Nyberg, 1992).

In order to gain access to the sea, Viberg, in contrast to Aarhus, had no other choice but to use the harbour of Hjarbæk in the innermost corner of a southern branch of the Limfjorden. On the other hand, the settlement at Viberg grew up on both sides of a lake offering favourable conditions for an urban development. Viberg occupied a central position in inland communications – the main inland route from south to north on the ridge through the peninsula, later called Hærvejen, passed through Viberg if it did not in fact end there.

Beyond the Limfjorden followed a number of bigger and smaller islands set apart to become a diocese of their own, an insular diocese like Funen and Zealand. Adam never mentions the name of an episcopal see in this region but speaks of the diocese by the name of its biggest island – which he calls Wendila – Vendel (cf. Vendsyssel, its present-day name). He also knows the names of two more islands, Thy and Mors. The first occurrence of the title of the see is *c.* 1122 in the *Notitia Galliarum*, a Roman *provinciale* enumerating, in an extension, the dioceses of the Polish and Scandinavian church provinces. The text we have dates from *c.* 1122 but the Scandinavian extension ought to have been created in connection with the erection, in 1104, of a Scandinavian church province with Lund as its *metropolis* (Kumlien, 1962; Nyberg, 1991). Here occurs, as a name for the eighth Danish diocese, Birgila, which has been identified with the royal manor Burhlanis mentioned by

Aelnoth (*VSD*, p. 104). This name later becomes the proper name of the bishopric, *episcopatus Burglanensis*, after the cathedral and the residence of the bishop, Børglum.

We do not know to what extent the new dioceses copied patterns already worked out in other Danish dioceses. The three dioceses that came out of the process differed very much from each other. None of them was headed by an outstanding personality whose name has been recorded for later generations. Beyond the four names of the first bishops ordained by Archbishop Adalbert as mentioned by Adam – Christian for Aarhus, Heribert for Viberg and first Magnus, then Albricus for Wendila – no other early bishop is known but Henry of Børglum, mentioned as a faithful supporter of King Cnut in the 1086 rising (*VSD*, p. 105). One might believe that the three dioceses existed only in theory for the first four decades.

Today we know that this was not so. In the two new mainland dioceses, the first priority was to build a church in stone to correspond to what according to continental European ideas ought to mark an episcopal see. These first remarkable stone churches in Aarhus and Viberg were not begun much later than those of Dalby and Roskilde, and may even have been inaugurated prior to the first Odense *basilica*.

In Aarhus, the crypt under present-day St Nicholas, the first cathedral, built outside the semicircular wall surrounding the civil settlement since the tenth century, has its parallels in a number of churches in the Rhineland, the most recent of which were built in the middle of the eleventh century. Krins (1968, pp. 85–90) dates it to 1070–80 and *DK* (XVI, 3, 1976, pp. 1036–7) accepts these results and assumes a construction period which began 'in the first decades after 1060'. At Viberg, the earliest stone church, completed *c.* 1090 (Krins, 1968, pp. 21–6; Vellev, 1990), was not built on the hill west of the lake which gave Viberg its name, but on low-lying land called Asmild to the east of the lake. Krins found parallels to Asmild in Brabant, Flanders, Hildesheim and Essen. On stylistic criteria, the earliest church of Asmild with its principal nave and square choir with an apse and its two narrow choir wings each ending in an apse is thought to have been finished by 1090 (Vellev, 1990, p. 12). Its heavy western part must have been marked by a tower towards the lake, and here Krins specifically draws a parallel with Abdinghof in Paderborn mentioned above in connection with Bishop Ricwal of Lund. Until the level of the lake was raised in the fourteenth century, communication between Asmild and the hill of Viberg must have been fairly easy, probably by a bridge over the narrow water between them (Vellev, 1990, pp. 17 and 11, map).

For the island diocese of Birgila to the north of Jutland, there is so far no evidence for the construction of a church in stone as early as the eleventh century. Recent excavations in Vrejlev, however, where later we find the monastic church of the Norbertine canonesses from the early thirteenth century, have uncovered older foundations indicating the site of an older church from *c.* 1150, perhaps the very site of the first cathedral of the diocese. On the other hand, there is evidence of the early foundations of a wooden church from the eleventh century in Hjørring, a place with two early churches, one dedicated to St John, the other to St Olav, which developed into an urban settlement but never was the residence of the bishop. Other early churches like Vrensted, dedicated to St Thøger – as the only church in Wendila; Thøger's cult was centred on the island of Thy where he had lived and was buried – or Tise with its old stone sculpture may be drawn into a future discussion.

For the island diocese, we have instead the hagiographical sources about St Thøger or Theodgarus to help elucidate its history in the eleventh century. He was a priest and former chaplain of King Olav of Norway, who after the king's death in 1030, came to the island of Thy and preached the Christian message there. There are records of his reputation as a saint, of miracles and of the elevation of his body dated tentatively to 1067; the records refer to Bishop Alfric's change of mind on the question of his reputation for sanctity (*VSD*, pp. 3–26).

There is no mention of a monastic inspiration in the story of St Thøger, however. In the diocese of Aarhus, the monastic option may have had an early place in the Gudenå basin (Garner, 1993), where all later monasteries of this diocese are found. In Viberg the cathedral clergy, unlike their collegues at Lund, chose to become regular canons following the Rule of St Augustine. We will return later to the question of the earliest evidence for their choice, but the chronology of the construction of the Viberg cathedral west of the lake suggests that the decision may have already been made during their stay in Asmild, after the church there was finished *c.* 1090.

Note

1. Skyum-Nielsen quoted (*DD 1*,2, no. 24), hesitatingly, Monasticon Anglicanum's assertion (II, p. 37) that the Abbot of Evesham 1086–96 should have been Robert of Jumièges.

CHAPTER SIX

Eleventh-century monasticism: Norway and Sweden

I Norway

Christianity was propagated actively as Norway's official religion by King Olav Haraldsson, who was driven out of Norway by adherents of King Cnut the Great and was killed in the battle of Stiklestad in 1030 when he tried to regain his throne. He enjoyed the reputation of a saint and martyr for the faith as early as five years later. Cnut the Great, the aggressor, died in 1035. Olav's kin ensured the succession of his son, Magnus, to the Danish throne in 1042 after the death of Harthacnut, and his short reign (1042–47) brought Norwegian influence and made his father's cult widely known in Denmark. He became known as Magnus the Good after he defeated a Slavic fleet near Slesvig in 1043, pacifying the southern Danish waters for a time (Radtke, 1992). King Harald Hardrada of Norway (1045–66) opposed his successor Svend Estridsen until the middle of the century when, after the battle off the river Nissan in 1062, an agreement between the two in 1064 put an end to rivalries, and Harold fell in England in 1066.

The Christian heritage in Norway in this period was centred around the holy king and martyr St Olav. His tomb in Nidaros/Trondheim was the goal of Christian pilgrims from all northern regions already in Adam's times (*Adam*, II, ch. 61, IV, p. 32). Many bishops, mostly of English origin, were active in Norway during the first half of the eleventh century, but, as Adam stresses, there were no fixed diocesan borders in this initial phase, missionaries being sent out from England ordained as bishops but without a residence (*Adam*, IV, ch. 34), left to find protection with kings or mighty families.

Two areas deserve the title of *civitas* in Adam (IV, ch. 33): Trondheim, *metropolis civitas Nortmannorum est Trondemnis* (the main *civitas* of the Northmen is Trondheim), and 'Viken', the name for the inhabited area around what today is called the Oslo fjord, *ab Alaburg vel Wendila Danorum ... transeatur ad Wig, civitatem Nortmannorum* (from Aalborg or *Wendila* of the Danes ... one crosses over to Viken, *civitas* of the Northmen) (*Adam*, IV, ch. 33; cf. Nyberg, 1984).

However, a third important place in Norway's Christian history attracted Adam's attention in the concluding phase of his work when he added a number of glosses, the *skolia*, to his original text of *c.* 1072. In skolion nos 129 and 145, he tells the story of the *septem dormientium*, the 'Seven Sleepers', who, according to a widespread legend also handed down by, among others, Paul the Deacon, lay sleeping in a cave on the ocean far away in the North, waiting for the end of the world to stand up and preach. 'There Olav even built a church', skolion no. 145 concludes. Apparently Adam had heard of the island of Selja, situated on the most extreme north-western tip of the 'Northern Way' between present-day Bergen and Trondheim, north-west from Nordfjord, the northernmost bay of Sogn on the border with Møre. Sogn is the northernmost district belonging to the Gulatingslag, the West Norwegian law district (cf., for all the following, *Selja*, 1997).

There is general agreement among Norwegian scholars that the reign of King Olav Kyrre, the son of Harold and Tora, who was made king in Norway in 1067 together with his elder brother Magnus, saw the birth and stabilization of a number of Christian institutions according to the pattern prevalent in Western Europe and England at the time. After the death of his brother Magnus in 1069, Olav brought stability to Norway for 24 years until his death in 1093, when he was followed by his natural son, Magnus Barefoot, who continued his father's style of rule for another decade until 1103. In Norway, this was a decisive period for the establishment of Christian institutions such as fixed dioceses and monastic houses.

But who was the Olav who built the church on Selja? The legend of the 'Holy men of Selja' would have it that Irish monks arrived in the reign of King Olav Tryggvesson (995–1000) but suffered persecution and therefore took refuge in a cave, asking for divine protection; a landslide blocked the entrance, they were all trapped inside and died, later to be found intact and venerated as holy men and martyrs. The land inside Selja was a densely populated area in the tenth century, where Hove with its many Iron Age graves must have had an important function (Hommedal, 1993, pp. 97–9). Olav Tryggvesson is said to have met with his men there in 996.

If holy men – perhaps Irish monks – arrived at Selja in the reign of Olav Tryggvesson, then local farmers, adherents of the old gods, may well have been aggressive towards them. The finding of their dead bodies and their veneration as saints might also have taken place in the same period, since Olav Tryggvesson had received baptism in England and was surrounded in legend and literature by the aura of being the first Christian King of Norway. Yet it could just as well be that the Olav who built the church on Selja was Olav Haraldsson, St Olav. In last instance, Adam could also have added his information in skolion no. 145 from recent sources; in that case, it could refer to a church built by Olav Kyrre, thus at the earliest in 1067.

The legend of the 'Holy men of Selja' was apparently widespread in Norway at the latest in the reign of Olav Kyrre, who made the island the residence of a bishop. Here we have the first signs of the monastic option in Norway – no wonder, since the place was sanctified by martyrs who according to the legend were monks. But prior to any evidence for a monastery on the island, we hear *c.* 1070 of Selja as the see of a bishop. Apparently, very early in his reign, Olav Kyrre decided to make this holy place into the residence of a bishop. Such a decision is understandable against the background of pagan practices prevalent everywhere in Norway, according to Adam, in spite of official adherence to the Christian faith. For a Christian king it was necessary to build upon such Christian centres that already existed, before it would be possible to proceed to new organizational forms.

The first bishop of Selja was *Bjarnhardr hinn saxlenzki* (Bernhard 'the Saxon') (Abrams, 1995). Bernhard became bishop of Selja *c.* 1070 after having been active on Iceland and returned home after a visit to Rome *c.* 1068 (Andersen, 1977, pp. 311–12; Johnsen 1968). It is odd, however, that Olav Kyrre began the construction of a Christ Church (Kristkirken) in Bergen at about the same time, *c.* 1070. The Icelandic account of the history of early bishops, Húngrvaka, says that Bishop Bernhard left Selja for Bergen as he felt death approaching. Apparently there was already a scheme to move the episcopal see for the Gulatingslag law district from the distant holy island of Selja to the more central Bergen, to communications along the coast and ultimately to a unified Norwegian kingdom. Not until 1170, however, was the episcopal see formally transferred from Selja to Bergen, together with the relics of the 'Holy men of Selja', now enriched by the relics of St Sunniva, a legendary Irish princess supposed to have arrived with the men and dying the death of a martyr with them.

The diocese of Selja may have comprised all the western coastland from Møre to Agder (Hommedal, 1993, p. 101). Along this outstretched coastal region monastic life began in two different places, both intimately linked to the bishopric: Selja and Bergen.

Selja

The sacred complex in Selja consisted in its later, elaborated form of at least five elements, according to Oddr Snorrason's *Saga Óláfs*

Tryggvasonar of *c.* 1190 (ed. F. Jónsson, 1932, chapter 21 in the second recension). After having mentioned the translation of the relics of St Sunniva in 1170, the text continues in translation:

> And Alban lies in Selja, and there is his main church at the monastery and there is much richness and a very precious and beautiful shrine and in it precious relics ... In Selja there are five churches, namely: the *fylke* church and Christ Church and St Mary's church and Michael's, Alban's church and Sunniva's church, and the great feast is kept by the Northmen on 8 July which is called Seljumannamass.

Something has been interpolated in this enumeration of six church dedications for the announced five churches (Hommedal, 1993; Nielsen 1905). Excavations have uncovered the foundations of St Alban's stone church which has been dated to the last decades of the eleventh century with parallels among other early Norwegian stone churches in Trondheim, Bergen and Oslo. St Alban's seems to have been built first, and accomodation building around a square courtyard, indicating a monastery, seems to have been quickly added. This leads Hommedal to assume that the earliest intention in Selja was to build a cathedral, and that monks arrived when the cathedral was ready to inaugurate a monastic community there (Hommedal, 1993, p. 103). Higher up, near the cave where the dead bodies once were found, St Sunniva's church was built at about the same time (Kvalheim, 1949). The place, then, seems to have been a pilgrim centre administered by Benedictine monks who are believed to have arrived some time between 1080 and 1110.

On the basis of the general cultural situation of Norway and especially the dedication of this early church to St Alban, it is generally believed that the monks came from England. Hommedal points to the recently established Durham Benedictine chapter as a close parallel, perhaps the model for the combination in Selja of episcopal see, Benedictine monks and pilgrimage shrine. In Durham Evesham's inspiration was at work as in the daughter foundation in Odense. Norwegian contacts on the British Isles were normally centred north, with York as an important place of cultural exchange. In this combination of functions and, even more strikingly, in the dedication to St Alban, Selja resembles Odense.

In contrast to what happened in Odense, however, the bishops of Selja were relatively soon drawn away from the island to mainland Bergen further south, so that one rather gets the impression of a predominantly monastic settlement in Selja which the bishops gradually began to regard as a traditional background only. This probably reflects the difference in strength and solid tradition between the ordinary hierarchical structure in Denmark and that in Norway. Here we are dealing with the phenomenon of the lonely bishop, devoted to monastic solitude, but travelling around preaching in different areas where the ordinary hierarchy was not yet established.

The last Danish bishop reminiscent of this type was probably Eilbert of Funen, who died in 1072. He was not highly rated by Adam, who laid much stress on the formal authorization of such a bishop by his superior in the hierarchy, the Archbishop of Hamburg-Bremen. But Adam's devotion to a well-ordered hierarchy was waived in the case of Norway, since he realized that for the mission so far north the situation of wandering bishops preaching without the limitation of diocesan boundaries was inevitable and still a necessity at this stage of mission. Therefore, he is not biased against the famous missionary Bishop Sigfrid, or Sigafrid, for instance, who must have gone from southern Norway (present day Bohuslän, former Ranrike) into western Sweden (the province of Västergötland, already established as diocese of Skara), from there to proceed to Växjö in the south-eastern part of the Swedish highlands, an area soon to be assigned to the diocese of Linköping in the province of Östergötland. There is no evidence that Sigfrid, who died *c.* 1060, had a monastic background. He is mentioned in the same context as Odinkar of Ribe, who died in 1043, and the Norwegian Bishop Rudolf, supposed to be a relative of King Edward, who was active in Norway under King Olaf Haraldsson and then after 1030 went to Iceland, from where he returned to England in 1050 to become Abbot of Abingdon and died there in 1052. The three bishops have in common that they paid a formal visit to the archbishop – not necessarily at the same time, however – *narrantes ei quanta fecerit Dominus in salute gentium quae cotidie convertebantur* (telling him what great deeds the Lord had done for the salvation of the gentiles who daily came and were received in the church) (*Adam*, II, ch. 64). This resulted in the renewal of their authorization to preach – *quos pontifex, ut par fuit, honorifice dimissos ad predicationem denuo misit* (these the archbishop, as was fair enough, dispatched again with honour into the mission) (*Adam*, II, ch. 64).

A monastery such as Selja would be a refuge to which precisely this type of wandering preacher-bishop could withdraw to collect his thoughts, for spiritual nourishment and further study. Nor should one dismiss the importance of such a spiritual centre for the scholarly education of future missionaries, even if they did not take monastic vows themselves. There is scattered evidence of educational activity in Selja in the twelfth century; Kvalheim (1949) believes that several Icelandic bishops received part of their basic theological training here.

This leads us on to the second Benedictine foundation in the west-Norwegian diocese soon to have its centre in Bergen.

Munkeliv

Nicolaysen (1892) compared the three monastic sites of Selja, Munkeliv and Nidarholm, and came to the conclusion that all three were founded at about the same time, *c.* 1110. As we have seen, recent Norwegian scholars do not accept such a late dating for Selja. If we turn to Munkeliv, it is evident from what has been said above that this foundation on Nordnes, the southern side of the bay of Vågen, whose northern shore became the site of Bjørgvin/Bergen, must have been intimately linked to the earliest development of the Bergen settlement. The king's house, later Bergenhus, the bishop's cathedral and residence, and the civil settlement adjoining such grandiose projects would demand at least temporary lodgings for missionaries with a monastic background as were mentioned above. It is by no means certain that the episcopal court would be the obvious refuge, resting place and educational centre for preaching missionaries in the situation of *c.* 1070–1100. Once this pattern was known and had become familiar to the clergy in the diocese of western Norway, the need for a new monastic foundation in Bergen comparable to that in Selja would certainly arise, as soon as it was clear that Bergen was destined to be the new centre of spiritual and ecclesiastical activity in western Norway.

The foundations of Munkeliv, excavated by N. Nicolaysen in 1860 and re-examined several times subsequently, especially by Lidén (1961), do not point to such an early period of origin but are rather to be attributed to the 1130s at the earliest. The papal letter of protection for Munkeliv, of 1146, presupposes a founding period which does not need to have comprised more than one or two decades but which very well may go further back in time. In the following quotation from the *Historia de antiquitate regum Norwagiensium* (1880, ch. 32, p. 64), King Eystein Magnusson, a son of Magnus Barefoot who came to the royal throne in 1103 together with his brother Sigurd 'Jerusalem-farer', is given credit for the construction of Munkeliv – although, according to Lidén, this can only be true for the beginning of building activities:

> Eystein was a man of outstanding honesty, by moderation and prudence keeping command no less over himself than over his subjects, a peace-making king, a circumspect administrator of the state, particularly devout to the Christian religion – this the reason why he also built the monastery in honour of the archangel St Michael near Bergen as it stands today.

If this is to be taken at face value, it reflects a tradition alive towards the end of the twelfth century, namely that Munkeliv, as it stood at that time, owed its origin to King Eystein. The tradition could refer either to the king's earlier period in Norway, 1103–07, for example, or to the years when Sigurd was absent on his pilgrimage to Jerusalem, 1107–10 (Helle, 1995, pp. 137–9).

Whether the foundation is to be dated earlier or later, it is clear that since Munkeliv was the second Benedictine monastery in this diocese, there was time to look around for other models than Selja while construction took place. Thus a number of architectural details have been found which point to Lund and its team of stonemasons in the 1130s (Lidén, 1961). The final shape of Munkeliv, therefore, does not belong to the first period of Benedictine monasticism in Scandinavia, but to the second.

Nidarholm

Munkholmen is a small island situated in the bay directly north of the city of Trondheim. It derives its name from the Benedictine monastery of Nidarholm which occupied it entirely. The monastery was constructed on the island's eastern shore, its church making up the northern wing of a regular monastic complex (McLees, 1988–89, plate 12, reconstruction drawn by Arne Berg). Facing east, the monks could see the mainland.

Excavations have brought to light the foundations of a square eastern choir, to the north of which a slightly recessed apse was discovered, indicating a northern chapel. One has to imagine an original, smaller church with a straight choir to which side chapels were added later, probably as extensions of aisles which had been added on. Such a construction process has been postulated for Christ Church Cathedral, Kristkirke, at Trondheim, and following the chronology of the building process of the cathedral, the earliest Nidarholm church would have been constructed in the latter part of the eleventh century and the addition of the aisles with their chapels could have been finished around 1100.

Trøndelag, the region of fjords, bays, and mountain valleys, the centre of which became Trondheim, was the key to Norway in this early, seafaring period. At the arrival of Christianity around 1000, the region was already divided into a number of *fylken*, natural subregions often following the valleys. Each *fylke* seems to have received a *fylke* church, apparently as a foundation made by the king personally, after his acceptance of the Christian religion on behalf of his realm. What Olav Tryggvesson and Olav Haraldsson inaugurated may even have been reinforced with harsher methods by Cnut the Great, King of England and Denmark 1018–35, who expelled Olav Haraldsson in the 1020s, and may have continued under Magnus 'the Good' (Sandnes, 1993).

But can any of these kings be shown to have introduced monastic life in Norway, as earlier scholars believed? Among historians of the early nineteenth century, Nidarholm, dedicated to St Lawrence, used to be a reasonable candidate for being accounted as the first Benedictine abbey of Norway, founded by Cnut the Great. Against such an idea we have the story told in 'Historia de antiquitate regum Norwagiensium', that a certain Sigurd Ullstreng, one of the great men of King Magnus Barefoot (1093–1103) who was deeply involved in Shetland and Orkney affairs, founded the monastery of Nidarholm. In spite of the theory proposed by Lange, that this monastery followed after an early foundation from the time of Cnut the Great which became extinct with the ending of Danish occupation, the prevalent view today, especially on the basis of the excavations, is that monastic life can hardly have been introduced on the island earlier than towards the end of the eleventh century, or even after 1100. Nothing can be said for certain of the use of the early church, except that it could have been well adapted to the needs of a small colony of monks or hermits arriving from the British Isles. We have the written evidence in *Historia de antiquitate regum Norwagiensium* (1880, ch. 31, p. 62), however, which relates that:

> There were at that time several noble men in King Magnus' [Barefoot's] army, the most excellent of whom, no less by character than by noble birth, was Sigvard Ullstreng, who later built a noble monastery in honour of St Benedict and Christ's most precious and victorious martyr [St] Lawrence in a very small island which is situated close to the archiepiscopal city of Trondheim. After that Magnus left for the Orkneys ...

This information, given 1177–80 by 'Theodoricus monachus' – identical with one Bishop Tore, possibly the Archbishop of Trondheim of that name, who died in 1214? – was taken up and used again by the Benedictine monk Gunnlaugr Leifsson of Þingeyrar, who died 1218/19, in his *Jóns saga ens helga* (*Biskupa sögur*, 1858, I, p. 226), here translated by Peter Foote (forthcoming):

> Notable and truly informed men say that St Jón proposed to him, or rather ordered him as part of his penance, that he should set up a Benedictine monastery on Nidarholm, using his property and giving so much of it that the servants of God might live well and decently from it. It is known to many men that Sigurðr ullstrengr received the island from King Magnús and was the first man to initiate the foundation of the said monastery, donated to it his patrimony, Vigg, and many other large estates.

There is no documentary evidence for the existence of such a community until 1135, when King Magnus the Blind visited the island and donated a farm (McLees, 1988–89, p. 91). However, the written evidence, as well as two more important reasons, tend to support the years around 1100 as date of foundation.

First, Selja and Munkeliv further south, predecessors of the bishopric of Bjørgvin/Bergen, both seem to have been established during these years as centres of Benedictine monastic life. Since the completion of the church on Munkholmen has been dated to *c.* 1100, there is no reason to believe that powerful families of Trøndelag like that of Sigurd Ullstreng should not have been eager to support the monks, once the church on this hermit island stood ready to receive them.

Second, Selja was dedicated to St Alban, the English martyr, just like the first church of Odense on Funen in Denmark. This points to Anglo-Saxon monks. One generation after William had conquered England with his Norman troops there seems to have been a movement among Anglo-Saxon monks in England to follow their Irish forefathers in the highest penitence possible for a monk: to leave one's own *patria* for ever. Such an exodus is easier to imagine one generation after the conquest than two. The most probable hypothesis then, to my mind, is to assume that Anglo-Saxon monks settled in Odense as well as in Selja and Nidarholm at around the same time: during the last decade of the eleventh century. The basis of evidence is, for Odense, Aelnoth's *Gesta* from c. 1122, for Selja and Nidarholm the written sources as well as the excavations of the two church foundations and the evaluation of them.

The Viken area – the diocese of Oslo

No monastery in the diocese of Oslo has been able to trace its history back to the eleventh century. Some scholars have discussed whether there may have been monks on the island of Hovedøya in the Oslo fjord before the Cistercians came there in 1147. Even if such a Benedictine predecessor is possible, it is unlikely that such a community would have existed already by 1100. The oldest churches of the Viken diocese, situated in the area of the later town of Oslo, were under construction towards the end of the eleventh century, but there are no hints of a monastic community at any of them.

One explanation for the absence of monasticism in this area, which had been Christian since the beginning of the century, may be that impulses from many sides, especially from Sweden and Denmark, were here mixed with Norwegian interests in a rich and densely populated area. This may have split up and delayed the development of Christian institutions and created several less powerful centres, each of which was too weak to shelter a monastic community.

An old trade centre, Kaupang, has been excavated south of Tønsberg in Vestfold on the western shore of the bay. Early in the twelfth century Tønsberg was already an important urban centre, which apparently took over some of Kaupang's functions. Borg in Østfold, on the eastern shore of the bay, gave its name to the law code of the region, Borgartingslag, and was apparently an urban settlement already in Olav Haraldsson's days – Cnut the Great was hailed there as king of Norway in 1028, and in Olav Kyrre's reign it was an important commercial centre (Helle and Nedkvitne, 1977) – but had no ecclesiastical function.

In search of a residence for a bishop, Oslo was nearer at hand. It had a Christ Church and a royal house with a St Clement's church as early as 1100. Soon afterwards it got its cathedral, dedicated to St Hallvard, a farmer killed because he protected a pregnant woman against her relatives, mentioned by Adam under the name of Alfwardus (*Adam*, III, ch. 54; Gjerløw, 1961).

In the extreme south of Norwegian territory, on the right bank of the Göta Älv, was the city of Konghelle. Olav Kyrre, Magnus Barefoot and Sigurd the Jerusalem-farer made this city a strong competitor against the Swedes. Their only opening to the west was further upstream on the left bank of the Göta Älv – the city of Lödöse. Magnus is said to have welcomed Erik the Good of Denmark and Inge the elder of Sweden to a meeting in Konghelle in 1100 or 1101, probably to discuss, among other issues, the subordination of Scandinavian bishops under the Archbishop of Hamburg-Bremen, Liemar, who as a follower of the German emperor Henry IV was at that time increasingly isolated in regard to his missionary task in Scandinavia. Within a few years (1104) Pope Paschal II gave his permission for the establishment of a Scandinavian church province; Bishop Asser of Lund became the first archbishop for all Scandinavia. In the corresponding list of dioceses (Nyberg, 1991), Norway was enumerated with three episcopal sees: Nidaros, Bergen and Oslo. This means that the clergy in these three ecclesiastical centres from 1104 onwards brought influences home not only from English centres but also from Lund instead of, as they may have done occasionally before, from Hamburg-Bremen and adjacent German regions.

Under such circumstances, Christian life in the Viken region underwent changes which may have hindered the pattern prevalent in most of the dioceses treated above: the bishop recognized the need to found a monastery in his diocese. It is not always possible to know which bishops mentioned in the Norse literature belonged to which dioceses, so possibly most bishops were still wandering missionaries or royal chaplains or court bishops without leadership in the hierarchy, and no planning on a longer perspective could be expected from them. Instead it would be up to the kings to listen to the signals from abroad and prepare the way for the first monastery in the region. Olav Kyrre concentrated upon Vestlandet, destined to be the centre of royal power. There and in Trøndelag the monastic alternative was realized earlier than in the Oslo diocese.

II Sweden

King Magnus Barefoot of Norway (1093–1103) was married to Margareta Fredkulla, a daughter of the Swedish King Inge and his queen, Helena. Inge was the son of Stenkil, the first Swedish Christian king capable of enforcing effectively the introduction of Christian faith and customs.

In Adam's and Stenkil's time, the different Swedish regions had already begun to develop different characteristic ways of being Christian. The most developed Christian region was Västergötland, the region south of Lake Väner, comprising the lowlands along this huge lake, the two slate hills Kinnekulle and Billingen, and the highlands further south. King Olof Skötkonung had already founded the episcopal see of Skara here.

Lake Vätter on the eastern border of this settlement area led to another fertile agricultural region between Lake Vätter and the Baltic Sea. The first Christian kings reigning over Swedish regions owned their lands west or east of Lake Vätter. On the northern tip of the little island in Lake Vätter, Visingsö, there are remains of a royal stone house, today partly covered by the lake. There is every reason to believe that this island was a favourite residence of the early Christian kings, although, due to the exigencies of early economy, a king could not afford to stay in one place but was constantly on the move between the regions where he had won acceptance.

The inhabitants in these two densely inhabited central districts had accepted Christian faith under the first Christian kings, Olof Skötkonung, Emund and Stenkil. The open lands were rather small, however, compared to the huge forests surrounding them on all sides. Adherents of the existing religion withdrew to the forests and continued practicing their rites and lifestyle there. The contrast between the open land and the forest was given a symbolic connotation in the building of churches with bell towers in the open landscape. In folklore, the sound of the bells is reported to be a horror to all enemies of the Christian faith; the nearer it came to the forest, the heavier was its threat against the old faith. The struggle between the open, cultivated Christian land and the forest with its secrets, where the old gods were still alive, made it evident that principal Christian institutions could only be established on the plains, in the densely inhabited areas where Christianity had been accepted or enforced as the only legal public cult.

In Adam's time, Skara in the middle of the plains south of Lake Väner was the oldest episcopal see among the Swedes. Sigtuna in the rich agricultural region on the northern shore of Lake Mälar came next. A bishop had been consecrated for a see called Birka, which Archbishop Adalbert knew from Rimbert's *Vita Anskarii* and from reports by missionaries. In the *provinciale* mentioned earlier under Denmark and Norway, probably related to the establishment of the Lund church province in 1104, there is a list of seven names of places that clearly can be localized to Swedish regions. The only possible interpretation of the function of these names is that they mark diocesan sees, either already existing or only planned (Nyberg, 1991). Skara and Sigtuna are among them, not Birka, however, for which contradictory information is scattered around in Adam's work. Instead, the list comprises a locality called Liunga, a form related to the present-day place-name Jung as well as to Lin in Linköping, another derivation of Liunga. Shortly after the establishment of the Scandinavian church province in 1104 Linköping emerged as a diocesan see of its own for the region between Lake Vätter and the Baltic Sea (Schück, 1959, pp. 44–6). Weighty arguments can be adduced in favour of the opinion that, in the concept of Archbishop Adalbert and his assistants in Bremen in the 1060s, the diocese of Linköping was the successor of the 'diocese of Birka', the position and borders of which were probably not very clear to the archbishop (Nyberg, 1991).

Adam coins the name Gothi for the inhabitants of the two plains with their adjacent mountain and forest regions between Lake Väner, Lake Vätter and the Baltic Sea. Adam recalled the Goths who plundered Rome in 410 and established an Arian kingdom in Italy under Odoakar (cf. Hyenstrand, 1996, pp. 67–72). His geographical information on the Gothi of Scandinavia is scanty, however. The 'western *Gothia*' he defines as being 'situated closest to the Danes or the Northmen' (*Adam*, II, ch. 58). Then 'there are other [Gothi] who are [called] the eastern ones' or 'there are others east [of them]' (*Adam*, IV, ch. 23). Westragothia he defines as 'neighbouring on Danish Scania' while Ostrogothia 'stretches along that sea which is called the Baltic [Sea] as far as to Birka' (cf. *Adam*, IV, ch. 21 and 29).

The Ostrogothia of Adam, today's Östergötland, was the region where Stenkil and his family were at home. It was natural that the Christian institutions he held to be necessary for the preservation and spread of the Christian faith were to be placed there. The fertile central area of Östergötland is divided by the river Stångan (or Stångån) running northwards from the southern forests and flowing into Lake Roxen, virtually dividing Östergötland into a western and an eastern section. In the land west of Stångan we find the most fertile ground, contrary to the less populated land east of Stångan, more exposed to rough winds from the Baltic. Two east–west waterways cut through the province. At the eastern end of the southern one is the important medieval harbour town of Söderköping and its old stronghold Stegeborg, while the northern waterway ends in Bråviken where later the urban centre of Norrköping grew up.

No place in this province would be better adapted to the needs of an ecclesiastical centre than the area around Lake Roxen. Here, a position on the river Stångan with its royal house called Stång and its important bridge, the Stångebro, would guarantee the necessary good conditions, including communications east and west to the province's two cultural districts (Ahlkvist and Tollin, 1994, pp. 27f).

For the origin of such an ecclesiastical centre the reformulation of the chronology of pagan sacrifices may fittingly be taken into account. According to Henriksson's (1995) reconstruction, the great sacrifices took place every eighth year, always between mid-January and mid-February (cf. *Adam*, skolion no. 141). The main agent in these sacrifices was the king himself; therefore, it was inevitable that a Christian king would get into trouble each time the fixed term for the sacrifice approached, if he was not willing to preside over it. The years 1052 and 1060 would have been years of sacrifice, for which Henriksson finds support in references to growing resistance against the Christians *c.* 1060. Stenkil seized power and was acclaimed king *c.* 1060/61. He died in 1066 and his son, Erik, had to fight one Erik who was an adherent of the sacrifices; both fell in 1067, and another of Stenkil's sons, Hallsten, was hailed as king (*Adam*, III, ch. 53 and skolion no. 84). But Hallsten was a minor and not able to prevent the sacrifice of 1068, says Henriksson, who integrates Adam's note about the election of Anund from Russia into his timetable and proposes that after the 1068 sacrifice Anund was accepted as king by a non-Christian majority, as although he himself was a Christian he had the reputation of being a strong ruler.

As the next year of sacrifice approached, however, Anund is reported by Adam to have refused to preside and therefore to have been deposed (*Adam*, skolion no. 140). According to Henriksson, this would then have been in the sacrificial year of 1076. A certain Håkon, belonging to the non-Christian fraction, governed for a time afterwards, until Hallsten and his brother Inge, the sons of Stenkil, seized the kingdom in 1080. The story repeated itself next time the sacrifice was due, which then would have been in 1084: Inge was driven out and a certain Sven, who carried out the sacrifice, reigned for three years until Inge succeeded in defeating and killing him in battle. After *c.* 1088, Inge and Hallsten, and after Hallsten's death in 1090 Inge alone, would have kept the power firmly in Christian hands and prevented the sacrifice being celebrated in 1092.

This chronology is relevant to monasticism in Sweden, since careful research initiated by Nils Ahnlund (1945) into fragments of chronicles and accounts from the later convent of Cistercian nuns in Vreta led to the conclusion that Vreta must have been Sweden's first monastic foundation, initiated by a King Inge and a Queen Helena. This means that in the synchronism of early Benedictine monastic foundations, it lines up with Lund, Ringsted, Odense, Selja and Nidarholm.

The founder must have been King Inge Stenkilsson, in Swedish history called 'the elder', not to be confused with the younger King Inge, his nephew, a son of his brother Hallsten. The elder King Inge is often said to have died *c.* 1110. Hans Gillingstam's research into the genealogy of the kings has cast doubt over this. Inge is said to have participated in the meeting with Magnus Barefoot, his son-in-law, in Konghelle in 1100 or 1101 but there is no reference to him after this. He may therefore have died rather soon afterwards. His queen, Helena, must have survived him.

The foundation of Vreta was a highly significant act. King Inge and his wife Helena, standing in the middle of a hard struggle against non-Christian sacrifices, must have understood the importance of a monastic foundation. Their daughter Margareta was married in Norway, where her father-in-law, Olav Kyrre, protected Selja and where Nidarholm, according to the *Historia de antiquitate regum Norwagiensium*, was founded by Sigurd Ullstreng before he went with King Magnus to the Orkneys, which was in 1098 (Andersen, 1977, p. 175). King Inge was a son of Christian parents. He could have learned how to carry out a monastic foundation from King Magnus Barefoot, whom he met in Konghelle in 1100 or 1101, if not earlier. Among his own clergy there were some with a monastic education and background who could give him advice (Janson, 1998).

In its context, founding a monastery in one of the Swedish regions where Christianity had been generally accepted at an early stage by a majority of people (thanks *inter alia* to Bishop Thurgot's activities [*Adam*, IV, ch. 56]) would be the first effort of a Swedish king ever to secure for his reign in an institutional way the intercessory prayers of holy men living a life of purity and seclusion. This confidence in the strength and power of monastic prayer was part of the medieval Christian mission. The foundation of a monastery by King Inge and his Queen Helena would be a sign that they shared this faith in a manner which befitted their royal responsibility according to the ideas of a Christian kingdom.

In his analysis of excerpts made by Rasmus Ludvigsson in the seventeenth century (Fh 7, Royal Library, Stockholm) on the property of Vreta, from material now lost, Ahnlund picked out all later donations and reached a kernel of property said to have been donated by King Inge and Queen Helena to Vreta in Vreta village, Bro, Brunneby, Håckla and Mjölorp. In the copy of a register in D 18, Royal Library, Stockholm, Ahnlund quotes the following excerpt from Rasmus Ludvigsson: 'This King Inge with his consort Queen Helena founded the monastery of Vreta and donated to the monastery these lands: 4 ottungar in Little Vreta, 2 ottungar in Bro, 3 ottungar in Brunneby, 4 ottungar in Håckla, 2 ottungar in Mjölorp, 2 ottungar in Broby in Dal hundred'. The two excerpts basically agree, except that the number of *ottungar* in Brunneby is given with three in the one, and nine in the other excerpt. We have to deal with 17 or 21 *ottungar* in all as the presumed foundation estate. Functionally, *ottung* or *attung* has to be treated as a term corresponding to *mansus* in Carolingian and Ottonian sources; with this, however, nothing is said about the size of such a unit. Ahnlund (1945, p. 325) seems to understand an *otting* here to signify a whole village.

In Östergötland, the regional divisions called hundreds (*härad*) extend in rectangular shapes north and south from the middle line marked by the main waterway mentioned earlier. The localities mentioned are situated in Hanekind härad south of Lake Roxen, the region of Linköping, and in Gullbergs härad to the north, where Vreta belongs. Dal is the coastal district far to the west on the shore of Lake Vätter.

An error in the reading of medieval sources led King John III (1569–91) astray, when he tried to re-establish monasteries that had survived so far but were threatened by extinction. In search of the royal tombs in Vreta, he was presented with an old document that was interpreted as saying that the younger King Inge had been poisoned and died in Vreta. Thus, King John built a cenotaph in Vreta to the honour of King Inge 'the younger' and his alleged Queen Helena, and this error remained in Swedish history books for centuries. The younger King Inge may have died *c.* 1120, his first wife was Ragnhild from Söderköping, while his second wife who survived him, Ulvhild, afterwards married King Sverker, who died in 1156.

Was Vreta a monastery for men or for women? Johannes Messenius, the Catholic Swedish historian of the seventeenth century, who had access to many sources that have been lost since, says that Inge and Helena founded Vreta and that Helena entered the monastery after Inge's death. This story has been repeated in many historical works (for example, Parikh, 1991, p. 50). Since we have no knowledge of the way Vreta continued to exist until its transformation into a Cistercian nunnery in the 1160s (cf. Gustavi, 1983), we cannot say for certain whether there were monks or nuns in Vreta. We only know that it did continue to exist, since the excerpts referred to above contain information of further gifts during the reigns of King Sverker (killed in 1156) and the Danish usurper Magnus Henriksson, who killed King Erik Jedvardsson and apparently was hailed as king in both Väster- and Östergötland in 1160–61 (Ahnlund, 1945, p. 327), prior to the transformation of Vreta into a Cistercian nunnery.

Architecture shows, according to Curman and Lundberg (1935), that what remains of the earliest monastic church points to a north French and German background. The similarity in proportions of Vreta and the earliest cathedral of Linköping is striking (cf. Curman and Lundberg 1935, p. 27; Gustavi, 1983, p. 132): the exterior length of the oldest Linköping cathedral was 12.0 m as against the oldest Vreta's length of 11.4 m, whereas the interior length was 10.5 m as against 10.2 m; the interior width in both was 12.0 m. In both churches, the transept had an interior width of 4.7 m, while the transept in Linköping was longer, 17.4 m as against Vreta's 16.8 m. The side aisle was 2.4 m wide in both churches, the main nave of the oldest Linköping cathedral 5.1 m wide as against that of the oldest Vreta church with 5.4 m (Figure 6.1).

Such a striking similarity raises the question of the model for the arrangement we may attribute to the elder King Inge: Linköping a diocesan centre with Vreta in its neighbourhood as a monastic site.

If we compare this with the foundation stories in Denmark and Norway treated so far, the typological similarity with Bergen is most striking. Structurally, the Odense and Selja models with a cathedral simultaneously intended to be a monastic church is not the closest parallel to Linköping and Vreta. In Bergen, on the other hand, the combination of a cathedral on the northern side of Vågen with a monastic church on its southern side is comparable to the construction of a bishop's cathedral on the river Stångan, and a monastic church north of the river Svartån at a distance of about 10 km from the cathedral. Both churches were meant to be monumental and representative, as in Bergen. They display architectural affinities.

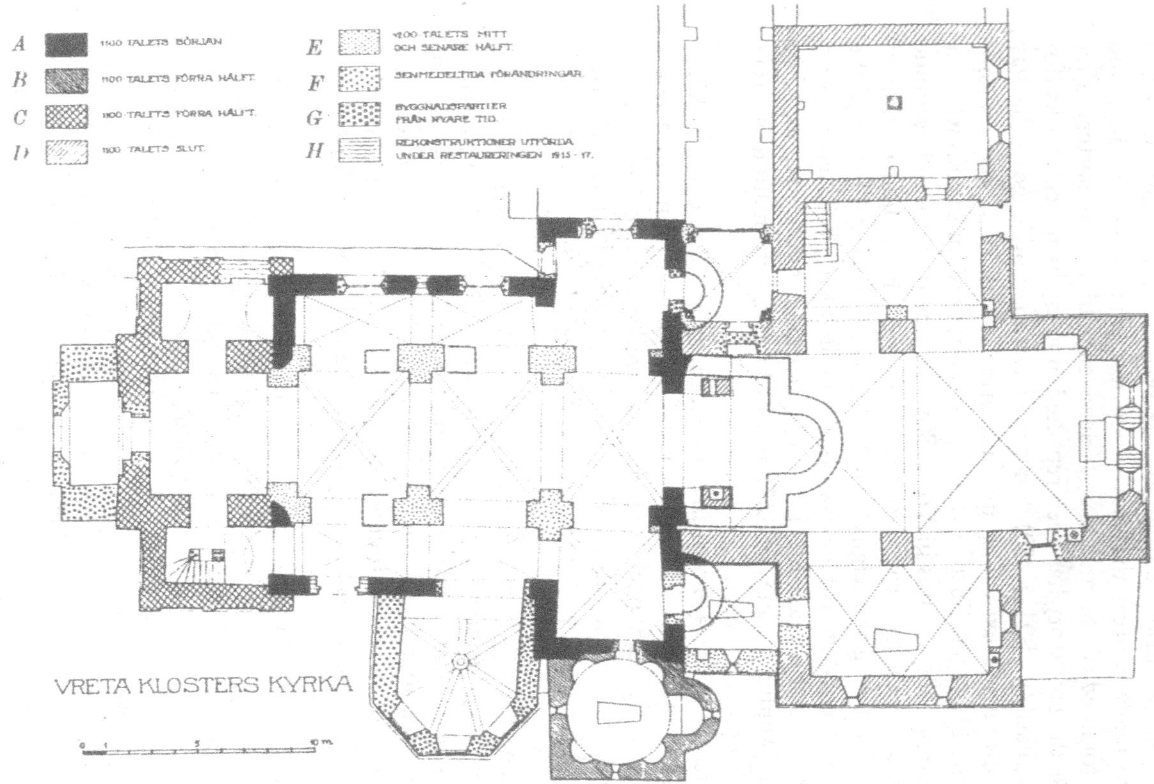

6.1 Vreta abbey church with the foundations of its earliest church, dated to the beginning of the twelfth century, in black ('A'), further extensions to the west and south from the middle of the twelfth century ('B', 'C') and, in Cistercian times, the abolition of the round choir endings and the eastward extension ('D')

Source: Curman and Lundberg (1935).

The early beginnings of monasticism in Norway and Sweden was a pioneer achievement. To continental European and British churchmen it made clear that Scandinavia had a reservoir of potential Christian believers. In the few places, situated far away from each other, where monastic life became established, members of prominent families dominated the scene and took upon themselves the task of transmitting the monastic heritage to second and third generations of Christians soon to follow their example. Royal and episcopal initiative went hand in hand and were not being referred to the Pope or to decisions in Rome – the nearest contacts in the monastic sphere were found in monastic circles of neighbouring countries. They found so faint an echo in the surrounding world that we know practically nothing about the inner life in the communities of Selja, Munkeliv or Vreta, although we have to count them as existing and functioning cradles of monastic life.

CHAPTER SEVEN

Eleventh-century monasticism: Saxony, Slesvig, Ribe

We have seen how bishops arranged with monastic communities to settle in or near their episcopal sees in the dioceses of Roskilde and Lund, and probably Slesvig and Ribe, how the Danish king laid the foundations of monastic life in Odense, the Norwegian king in Selja and Bergen, the Swedish king in Vreta, and how a man in high royal service founded Nidarholm near Trondheim. One could be tempted to ascribe the synchronism of this early monastic movement to special Scandinavian conditions. Strikingly enough, however, this development is synchronic to that of one of the north German dioceses, the very archdiocese of Hamburg-Bremen that even in the 1070s still pretended to control all Christian mission in Scandinavia. In the middle of the eleventh century the rich development of Saxon monasticism reaching as far north as to St Michael's abbey in Lüneburg in the diocese of Verden – thus in the church province of Mainz – still had no counterpart in the Hamburg-Bremen archdiocese. Religious congregations there were, but they were communities of secular canons without vows, like Reepsholt in the north-western part of the old Bremen diocese or, further south, Wildeshausen on the Hunte, a western tributary of the Weser.

The first Benedictine monasteries in the archbishopric of Hamburg-Bremen only came into being in the last decade of the eleventh century. Rastede in the county of Rüstringen had existed before as a foundation of one Count Huno, who, according to the monastic chronicle, in 1059 had asked and received the permission of Archbishop Adalbert to found a 'house of prayer' and a convent of nuns here. The county of Rüstringen in the so-called Ammerland was later absorbed into the county of Oldenburg. It occupied a fertile section of the hilly lowlands west of the Weser estuary. Count Huno had the church he built dedicated to St Ulrich, the holy Bishop of Augsburg who had died in 973 and been canonized in 993, the first canonization ever to be carried out by a pope – until far into the twelfth century the declaration of a person's holiness was normally given by the diocesan bishop. After Count Huno's death, his widow, Willa, entered the convent, for which the count apparently also had secured support from King Henry IV.

In addition to the church of St Ulrich, Huno, Willa and their son Frederick also founded a college of secular canons at an Our Lady's church, for the pastoral and liturgical service of the parish. Since Frederick was the sole heir and unmarried, after the death of his parents he decided to have this foundation transformed into a Benedictine abbey. Hermann Lübbing counts the time in office of the first abbot, Thetmar, from the year 1091; he died in 1123 (*Die Rasteder Chronik*, 1976, p. 20 cf. *MGH SS, xxv*, p. 500).

It is perhaps no mere chance that Rastede became important to the Scandinavian mission by the stay there of a former Bishop of Uppsala, Siward, who became the fourth abbot in 1142 and died whilst abbot in 1157. Compared to neighbouring German dioceses, the archdiocese was indeed late in giving shelter to its first Benedictine abbey, which was finally realized as the foundation of a count, to which the archbishop gave his placet. Thereby Rastede acquired a position in its surroundings comparable to that of the simultaneous Scandinavian monasteries treated above, founded towards the end of the eleventh century in their respective ecclesiastical milieux.

The second Benedictine foundation of the archdiocese came just around the turn of the century, in Harsefeld west of Hamburg, in an area surrounded on nearly all sides by lands subject to the bishops of Verden. Here again, a foundation for secular canons at Our Lady's and St Bartholomew's church made by Count Henry of Stade, who died in 1016, was transformed into a Benedictine abbey towards the end of the century by accepting the full regular life with vows under the leadership of monks from Ilsenburg (Streich, 1986, p. 69). In 1102, Pope Paschal II made Harseburg exempt from archepiscopal authority and directly subordinated it to St Peter's chair – no wonder, since these were just the decisive years of the investiture conflict and Archbishop Liemar still stood firm on the emperor's side. This was only two years before the Scandinavian church province with its centre in Lund was established by the same pope, who in the first year of his pontificate may have given his permission to the canonization of St Cnut, Martyr King of Denmark. Harsefeld in the Duchy of Stade became the northernmost representative of Saxony's monastic reform movement in these years.

Thus the archdiocese of Hamburg-Bremen was far from taking the lead and serving as a model for monasticism in its missionary dioceses in the north. The missionary area where the monastic alternative still had to be discovered includes even the mother of Scandinavian mission, the German archdiocese itself. In the 32 years from the death of Archbishop Adalbert in 1072 to the approval of Lund as the head of a church province in 1104, the synchronism of monasticism in Scandinavia with that in the German lands subject to the Hamburg-Bremen archbishop is openly demonstrated. Perhaps the papal schism, as in the cases of Rastede and Harsefeld, was a decisive factor in finally making room for the monastic alternative, which then advanced in close collaboration with the papal party (cf. Janson, 1998).

This leads us back to the two northern neighbours of the archdiocese, the dioceses of Slesvig and Ribe, with their two monastic institutions St Michael's and Seem, for which the year 1026 was given as *terminus post quem*. But how do we approach the *terminus ante quem* for St Michael's in Slesvig and Our Lady's in Seem?

Vilhelm Lorenzen thought (1933, p. 147), that the Benedictine monastery of St Michael in Slesvig came into being 'in the second third of the eleventh century' but placed the construction of the circular church to *c.* 1140–50. He discussed whether a circular church would have been practical for the use of a monastic community and came to the conclusion that it very well could have been, since St Michael's is said to have been a double monastery and the nuns could have had their place in the gallery of the two sides of the circular church. Since then, however, excavations, including those of 1971–72, have shown no traces of monastic buildings directly built together with the church, neither north nor south of it. The most recent publication concludes that the monastic buildings must have stood at a distance from the church. A foundation *c.* 1100 is suggested (Lafrenz, 1985, p. 298).

Faced with such uncertainty, it is worth reflecting once more upon the bishops of Slesvig in the search for a possible benefactor and inspirator to St Michael's. Ekkihard, educated in Hildesheim, who died in 1026 on his way to regain his diocese after the years it had laid waste, has already been mentioned, although only his successor Rodulf (1026–47), who came from Cologne, had a realistic chance of taking an initiative which included settling a monastic community on the spot. In the environment Rodulf came from, the monastic movement was highly esteemed and Rodulf seems to have been in touch with important men in this movement, such as Bishop Godehard of Hildesheim and Abbot Poppo of Stablo (Radtke, 1984, p. 146).

It is clear that Rodulf's successor Ratolf, who came from Bremen, must be regarded as a much less probable candidate for having carried out a monastic foundation in his diocese, although the destruction that ravaged Slesvig *c.* 1050 and in 1066 during his time in office (Radtke, 1984, p. 147) must be taken into consideration in any discussion of when St Michael's came into being. A certain Siward, only known from the donation charter of King Cnut for the cathedral of Lund in 1085, is commonly held to have been the next Bishop of Slesvig after Ratolf's death in 1072/75. Gunner, mentioned next, can probably not have become bishop earlier than 1104. He died on 23 April between 1121 and 1125. Could Siward or Gunner – their names suggest that they were Scandinavians – have founded St Michael's abbey? With these two bishops we approach the latest possible decades when the circular church is thought to have been constructed, which makes it less probable that the foundation of the monastery took place that late. To assume the time in office of their successor Bishop Adalbero (1121/25–35) for the foundation of St Michael's is definitely too late. It is easier to conceive of a foundation taking place under Bishop Rodulf (1026–47), who knew from his Rhineland background the Cluniac inspiration and the function of such a monastery near the episcopal see.

As for Our Lady's in Seem, Bishop Odinkar, who must have become bishop at the latest in 1005 and who died in 1043 (*SE VI: II*, p. 68), could very well have been its founder. Also Wal and Oddo, both according to Adam ordained by Archbishop Adalbert, are possible candidates for this honour. In some publications, Seem is still seriously seen as a foundation made by Bishop Odinkar, favoured by the cultural exchange in Cnut the Great's North Sea empire (*Germania Benedictina VI*, 1979, p. 459). In the CER (1933–35, 27), however, there is no allusion to a monastic foundation of Odinkar. Instead, Odinkar's ambitions to secure his family's influence in the diocese for the future is mentioned in a somewhat ironic wording: *procuravit a papa, ut sua semper posteritas Ripensi ecclesiae praesideret. Quod non diu duravit* (he procured from the Pope that his descendants should always govern the diocese of Ribe. This did not last long). Some effect it must have had, however, since the chronicle mentions as the third Bishop of Ribe a certain Christian, allegedly Odinkar's son and in his turn allegedly father of Wal.[1] Conversely, Oddo, whom Adam mentions, is not found in the bishops' chronicle, which makes Christian or Wal the third, Jareld/Gerald the fourth Bishop of Ribe and raises the question, whether Oddo, ordained by Archbishop Adalbert, was perhaps not really accepted by the family clan of Odinkar in Ribe.

The CER says about Bishop Gerald, a German and former chaplain of King Cnut, who participated in a synod in Worms in 1113, that he was an *extraneus*, which probably means someone coming from outside, not belonging to the inner circle previously dominating the affairs of the diocese. If it is true that Wal was the son of Christian who also acted as a bishop, and that Christian in turn was the son of Odinkar, then this family must truly have governed the diocese for quite a while, something higher authorities would not be willing to tolerate in the long run. We will therefore have to see in Gerald/Jareld a man with another attitude towards his episcopal office than the family of Odinkar and Wal, and also a man nominated to the episcopal office out of motives and intentions different from, and perhaps directly opposed to, the Odinkar family's dominance.

Aelnoth expressedly states (*VSD*, p. 95) that King Cnut took advice from two of his chaplains, *Geroldo scilicet et Arnoldo*, both of whom were at that time (1080–86) *regalis curiae capellanis* (chaplains at the royal court), but 'now' – at the time Aelnoth wrote, *c.* 1122 – *pontificibus venerandis* (venerable bishops). For the time in office of Gerald, then, at least the two years 1113 and *c.* 1122 are certain. Arnold is known to have died as Bishop of Roskilde on 24 May 1124 or 1125.

We are thus faced with two alternatives. Either Odinkar or one of the members of his family are to be given the credit for having called in Benedictines to settle in Seem (which would have been before *c.* 1060, as Wal died), or Seem was founded by Oddo, who is omitted in the CER but may have been in office some years from 1060 onwards, or even by Gerald who – from the point of view of local Ribe interests – may have been regarded as an outsider, since apart from what has been said above on the family dynasty of Odinkar, Gerald may have been of German origin. The fact that he had served as a chaplain under King Cnut may also have aroused the scepticism of the previous group interests in Ribe.

The choice stands between an earlier phase, prior to *c.* 1060, when an Our Lady's abbey in Seem could have been founded as an episcopal *Eigenkloster* (propriety monastery) – to speculate about a royal foundation by Svend Estridsen is not realistic – and a later phase, after *c.* 1095, when, under the auspices of the cult of St Cnut, such a double monastery could have been favoured by King Erik the Good (1095–1103) and/or his successor King Niels, and by Bishop Gerald.

There is a strange passage in the CER which may hint at Bishop Gerald in this connection. The author of the chronicle writes, in Ellen Jørgensen's edition (CER, 1933–35): *qui propter regios sumptus possessiones ecclesiae alienavit et collecta pecunia clam discessit* (who because of royal expenses lay hands upon church property and left secretly with the collected money). It is a strange accusation raised here against Gerald, who just one line earlier is said to have been elected by *maiori et saniori parte populi* (the greater and better half of the people), this well-known formula which often covers over a political faction that got its own way. However, two of the three copies upon which the edition rests produce another reading: instead of *regios sumptus* they read *religiosos sumptus* which, if this were the expression intended by the author, would indicate not expenses made by the king or for the king, but 'religious expenses' – *religiosos* in the sense of 'religious', 'monastic'

– which would have misled the bishop, according to the author, (unjustly) to lay hands on ecclesiastical property.

In another curious coincidence, the chronicle of the Counts of Stade (*MGH SS*, XVI, p. 320), enumerating the evil deeds of two brothers, both Counts of Stade, brings a strange story of the passage of three Danish bishops through their lands in 1112, who,

> preparing to pass through this land [the county of Stade] brought much money with them, and after they had been drowned [*submersis*] in the Elbe with all their company by the aforesaid brothers, the money was robbed, and although they [the two brothers] had deserved God's wrath for this, nevertheless they prospered very much in transitory things.

Although *submersis* literally means that the three bishops and all their men were 'drowned', and one would presume that it led to their death, it could easily be that the author here refers to something he had heard but deliberately made it worse in order to underline the evilness of the two counts. Allowing for such an interpretation, one of the bishops could very well have been Bishop Gerald who, according to the CER, left the diocese with a sum of money that belonged to the church.

It also fits in with his documented presence in Worms on 6 April 1113. On this day, Emperor Henry V, upon the request of the Abbot of St Maximin in Trier, confirmed property which the abbey had received earlier but which was now contested. This the emperor does, it says, on the advice of the Archbishop of Trier and the bishops of Würzburg, Basle, Strasbourg, Speyer, Münster, Constance and Novara, ending with *Geraldi Rifensis* – the Bishop of Ribe in the last place. The abbots of Metz, Reichenau and Marbach were also present. This was certainly a very special company in which Bishop Gerald was allowed to mingle. Moving in such circles, he would without doubt be capable of finding people who wanted to establish a Benedictine monastery in Denmark.

The *religiosos sumptus* as well as the story of the money which brought him a bad reputation in the local Ribe tradition may well have to do with certain interests of Bishop Gerald that were not identical with those of his clergy. Yet a few years later Aelnoth calls him a 'venerable bishop'. If the two pieces of information from Ribe and Stade deal with the same bishop and the same event, it throws some light upon the person, a bishop who apparently was not afraid of conflicts but followed his own intentions at the price of his good reputation among his clergy. Such a man may easily have been able to support or even inaugurate a Benedictine monastery for monks and nuns, perhaps against the wishes of his clergy.

It is clearly stated in the sources telling about the take-over of Seem by the Cistercians, that Seem was founded as a double monastery. Its site has not been excavated; local tradition places the monastic buildings on the lake 2 km south-east of the present parish church of Seem, on the land of *Munkegård*, probably the main manor of the monastery. But in the later twelfth century double monasteries increasingly became targets of criticism by monastic purists (Bolton, 1973). A double monastery in Seem can hardly have been founded later than in the early part of the twelfth century. The end of the eleventh century would be just as probable, if we may ascribe such an undertaking to Oddo or to Gerald in his earlier years of office. In 1131, when Bishop Godehard of Hildesheim was canonized and part of his relics were acquired for the parish church in Seem, the double monastery must have been flourishing, looking back over several decades of study and liturgical prayer.

There is a huge time span between the ordination of Oddo at the hands of Archbishop Adalbert *c.* 1060, and the death of his successor *c.* 1125. If there was no bishop between them, Oddo must have lived until the 1090s and the former chaplain of King Cnut must have been ordained under Erik the Good or in the first years of the reign of King Niels. To explain such long periods in office of two bishops of whom so little is known, a reminder of the papal schism could be useful. If Ribe had a bishop siding with Archbishop Liemar and Emperor Henry IV in the 1080s and 1090s, and this bishop was not Oddo, then the name of such a bishop could easily be erased from records and given over to oblivion. This is, of course, speculation, but it helps us understand the role of Bishop Gerard and the negative attitude some of his clergy may have had towards him, since he certainly represented the new kingship, which from 1095 onwards tried to carry out the basic ideas of the holy king, St Cnut.

In conclusion, it is hardly possible to imagine that Our Lady's Benedictine double monastery in Seem was founded later than under Bishop Gerald in the first quarter of the twelfth century. Since we know neither when Gerald became Bishop of Ribe, nor how long Bishop Oddo, who was ordained by Archbishop Adalbert, remained in office, if he was accepted in Ribe at all, the main alternative remains as stated above: either Seem was a foundation of the Odinkar family and in that case it belongs to the period before *c.* 1060, or Seem was founded by one of the German bishops, Oddo or Gerald, some time between *c.* 1060 and 1120. If we prefer the later alternative, Seem was probably controversial to some circles within the Ribe clergy. As we will see in the process of its transition to the Cistercians, there must have been a faction in the cathedral chapter which, for whatever reasons, was anything but friendly towards this Benedictine institution.

Monasticism, then, made just as slow progress in the neighbouring German and mixed German–Danish regions of South Jutland as further north in Scandinavia.

Note

1. Christian is omitted in *SE VI: II*.

CHAPTER EIGHT

The great period: civil war 1

I The spirit of the epoch: revenge and penitence

The context

Around the year 1100, North European history was given a new turn by changes which decisively influenced all forms of life in society for the centuries that followed.

It is not so much the acts of one or a few single personalities which brought these changes about. Singular acts like the penitence of King Henry IV in Canossa in 1076 or the killing of King Cnut of Denmark in 1086 only paved the way; changes came in the next generation as conclusions were drawn. Aelnoth wrote the history of King Cnut one generation after his lifetime; but we can be fairly sure that much of what he ascribed to King Cnut in reality was just the policy the younger brother King Niels was about to carry out – or he held a mirror up to the king to show him how to deal with the problems of society and his own power, a *speculum regale* (mirror of princes). In Sweden, the elder King Inge was followed by the younger King Inge, succeeded in turn by King Sverker, who owned his family lands in Östergötland. In Norway, the period from the return of King Sigurd from Jerusalem in 1112 until his death in 1130 meant a slow penetration of new values deeper into society. Not least, the independence in religious matters under the archbishops of Lund from 1104 onwards was highly esteemed and highly relevant in all branches of the church in Scandinavia, including Iceland. It was also not without importance in Saxony, since now other forces came to the fore and the archbishops of Hamburg-Bremen for a while were reduced to a provincial role only, while the eastward colonization movement of Westphalian and Dutch farmers run in ever broader streams.

The clash of values brought conflict to the following generation. Norway for a short while entered a state of internecine war, violently ended by a new form of collaboration (from 1153) between a Norwegian archbishop and a political group formed around a boy crowned king by this archbishop in 1163 or 1164. In Sweden, a competitor to the Sverker family arose in Västergötland with the family of Erik Jedvardsson, and the war between them affected the power in the Lake Mälar region. Denmark's civil war began with the murder of Cnut

Lavard in 1131, which finally carried his son Valdemar to a unique authoritarian power position over the entire country in 1157. Iceland defended its independent republic but also had to accept growing contrasts between the wealthy and the poor.

There is every reason to see the end of a period in the 1170s. The final outcome of new values, conflict and war stabilized into forms of society which remained stable until the middle of the thirteenth century. The period covering roughly the years 1100–80 coincides almost completely with the time of foundation of most of the monasteries which put their mark on society and daily life in North-Western Europe for the next 300 years. Without discussing here the changing role and function of monasteries in a changing society when we move into the fourteenth and fifteenth century, it is clear that the institutions founded in this way created patterns of behaviour that tended to multiply and reproduce themselves for generations as long as the institutions existed. Strong, more or less usurper dynasties governed in Norway and Sweden – they even entered into marriage coalitions – and tried from their power platform to realize the same integration of monasticism into their power structure as that which came to dominate in Denmark. In Saxony, imperial authority gave in to ducal power and only with great difficulty succeeded for a while in halting the centrifugal forces of the German realm. Towards the end of the period, even Denmark participated in the colonization movement into neighbouring Slav territory, which thereby lost much of its identity and its language, as far east as to the principalities that were united in their Christian cult and their faith in a united Polish kingdom.

Uncontroversial foundations

Until the war in Denmark began after the murder of Cnut Lavard in 1131, monasteries were not of particular interest to those in power.

We can follow this in the peaceful transformation of the central clerical community in the diocese of Viberg, the cathedral chapter, into a monastery of Austin canons (Figure 8.1). We do not know every particular stage in this development, but it is a fair conjecture that the former canon of Lund, Bishop Eskil, who held office in Viberg, perhaps as early as in 1115 and at all events in 1122 (*SE VI: II*, p. 119), inspired the canons to choose St Augustine's rule instead of the secular way of canons which his brethren in Lund preferred. He was loyal to King Niels, and therefore he was killed before the altar in the church of Asmild on 20 October 1132 or 1133. In his cathedral chapter of regular canons a saintly man lived his life, Ketillus or Kjeld, whom Bishop Eskil

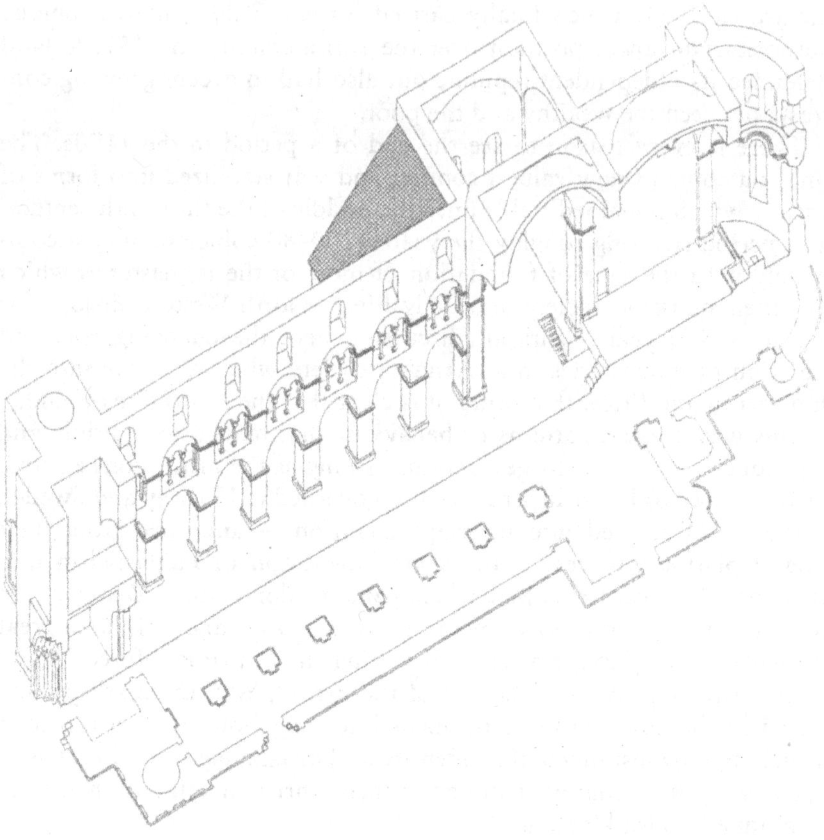

8.1 The Romanesque cathedral of Viberg (Viborg) as it may have looked prior to its late Romanesque completion. The roof of the chapel of St Kjeld (Ketillus) is seen west of the northern side chapel.

Source: Vellev (1991).

had ordained to the priesthood (*VSD*, p. 263) and whom the community elected to its prelate perhaps in the 1130s. He died, as related in his *Vita*, on 27 September 1150 and was canonized in 1188 (*VSD*, pp. 251–83). The canons of Lund entered into mutual prayer union with those in Viberg in the 1130s, and in the necrology from Lund the names of three canons from Viberg have been entered by the earliest hand as identified by Weibull: Thorkillus *presbiter et kanonicus sancte Marie Wiberge*, Geruasius *diaconus canonicus sancte Marie Wiberge* and Blithmannus *presbiter Wibergensis canonicus* (*NL*, p. LXIV), thus one 'priest and canon of Our Lady's in Viberg', one 'deacon and canon of

Our Lady's in Viberg', and one 'priest and canon of Viberg'. Besides Eskil's successor Bishop Svend, who was elected from among the canons and died 1153 or 1154, and besides *bone memorie sanctus Ketillus prelatus sancte Marie Wibergensis ecclesie* (Saint Ketil [Kjeld], of blessed memory, prelate [prior] of Our Lady's church in Viberg) and Willo, Ketil's predecessor as prior (*VSD*, p. 264), we find three priests styled *sacerdos et canonicus*, six priests styled *presbiter et canonicus*, one deacon, one subdeacon, one *laicus et canonicus*, and finally three *conversi*, in all 18 names of deceased members of this community styled *sancte Marie Wibergis* 'Our Lady's at Viberg' from its establishment in the 1130s to *c*. 1170. Another eight canons and a *soror* Thorgart are found in *Liber daticus Lundensis* until the entries from Viberg come to an end *c*. 1200. The introduction of vows according to the Rule of St Augustine, whereby the canons became regular, took place at an unknown point in time, either as the new cathedral on the hill was taken for use in regular service, or earlier, in Asmild.

We can also follow the foundation of another Augustinian community, at St Saviour's church in Lund, on a very central place west of the main square, where excavations have uncovered the foundations of a large Romanesque church from the middle of the twelfth century, with traces of a wooden church below. It was probably the first religious community in Scandinavia to follow the statutes of Prémontré, the monastic home of Norbert of Xanten in the early 1120s until, in 1126, he was nominated Archbishop of Magdeburg (Nyberg, 1975–76). St Saviour's in the centre of Lund must have been formally established and organized before *c*. 1150, since the Rule of St Augustine with the Premonstratensian statutes was then activated for the second time in Scania by the foundation of a second Premonstratensian abbey at St Peter's church in Tommarp far out in the south-eastern corner of the province. The Lund abbey had entered into a prayer union with the canons of the cathedral, and among the earliest entries in the *NL* we find what we may take to be the two very first obituary notices for the community's first abbot and one pioneer canon: *Huclek primus abbas eterni Salvatoris in Lundis* (Huglek, the first Abbot of the Eternal Saviour['s] in Lund) and *Osmundus canonicus et sacerdos ecclesiae sancti Salvatoris Lundis* (Osmund, canon and priest at the Holy Saviour's church in Lund), to be dated before *c*. 1170. *Liber daticus Lundensis* brings a third deceased canon styled in the same way: *frater Hector diaconus et canonicus sancti Salvatoris* (brother Hector, deacon and canon of the Holy Saviour['s]). However, church and abbey soon took on the name of the Holy Trinity: Abbot John, known from charters 1173 and 1180, was entered as *abbas sancte Trinitatis Lundis*, and we meet *canonicus et sacerdos* Thort (Tord) *sancte Trinitatis Lundis* and three lay brothers as *conversus sancte Trinitatis Lundis*, thus one abbot, one canon priest, and three lay brothers of the Holy Trinity['s] in Lund.

A third rather uncontroversial introduction of monastic life took place in the Norwegian dioceses from *c.* 1130 onwards with the growing independence of the Norwegian church from the archbishops of Lund. Nicolas Brakespear, the English papal legate, who in 1154 became Pope Hadrian IV, had been in Norway the year before and laid the foundations of a Norwegian church province; the Bishop of Trondheim became its archbishop. To prepare for this event in a country which until recently had had only three dioceses, the southern part of Vestlandet had been taken out of the district of the Bergen bishops by 1125 and made a diocese of its own with its see in Stavanger, to which also Valdres and Hallingdal, two inland valleys opening westwards, were added. Shortly before 1153, the diocese of Hamar was established, covering the upper, inner parts of the Viken area previously belonging to the Oslo diocese. With five mainland and two island dioceses, comprising the Orkneys and the Isle of Man with adjacent islands, Norway was ready for church independence from Lund, although within a short time (Nyberg, 1986, pp. 58–72) it was clear that the Faeroe Islands, Iceland with its two dioceses, and Greenland with a bishop of its own for the Norse settlers there, would also have resort to the Archbishop of Trondheim.

The five mainland dioceses were each in the process of establishing one cathedral chapter. Apparently, however, the secular chapters were only slowly getting organized. Perhaps it was easier to raise small communities of regular canons to assist in urgent pastoral duties or, as in the case of Stavanger, a community like St Olav's Austin monastery may have been inaugurated by Bishop Reinald (executed by the king in 1135) as a provisory solution before the cathedral could be used for the daily hours of prayers by a chapter of secular canons. Stylistic criteria class Stavanger cathedral together with St Swithun's in Winchester, from where relics of St Swithun and probably also clergy came to Stavanger (Hohler, 1963–64; 1964). Helle (1975) believes that St Olav's in Stavanger may have been the first house of Austin regular canons in Norway, and that the example from there spread to Bergen, where Jonskloster was their site, and to Trondheim with (H)Elgeseter. At the beginning of the Norwegian development, the regular canons were integrated into the tasks of the diocese by being located very close to the cathedral (cf. Herzog, 1964).

Also without much controversy, the monastic life was introduced to Iceland when in 1133 Þingeyrar was founded after a long period of planning, in which allegedly the saintly Bishop Jón Ögundarsson, who died in 1121, is also said to have been involved. With Þingeyrar, the Icelanders obtained their first Benedictine abbey, probably a foundation of very moderate size, but tremendously important for the development of literary life and culture in Iceland. New categories of saints' lives and other religous literature found their way to Iceland and to the desks of monastic translators and interpreters. Vilmundr Thórólfsson und Hreinn Styrmisson are two of the early abbots of Þingeyrar, which was situated in the diocese of Hólar established in 1106 for Iceland's northern quarter as a first step towards improvement after the supremacy of Lund in Scandinavian church matters had become a reality in 1104. The pattern prevalent in other dioceses of two complementary institutions, the episcopal see with its cathedral, chapter and school, and the monastery with its liturgical devotion, prayers and literary and cultural work, reproduced itself in this new diocese, while the three remaining quarters of the island making up the diocese of Skálholt had as yet no monastic foundation.

The fighters

The decisive year of change for monasticism was 1135. This is the year when in Denmark Cnut Lavard's brother, the usurper Erik Emune, who had defeated and killed his uncle, King Niels, in revenge for the murder of his brother by the hands of King Niels's son, Magnus, in thanksgiving for his victory and/or penitence for his crimes made a considerable donation to the already existing Benedictine abbey of Ringsted in Zealand, where Cnut Lavard had been buried. This was the first comeback of the family of Erik the Good after the frightful blow it had suffered by the death of Cnut Lavard.

Late in the same year, one of the great magnates of Southern Zealand, Peder Bodilsen, together with his brothers, Hemming and Jørgen, and their mother, Bodil, made a very generous donation for the establishment of a Benedictine abbey in Næstved near the southern shore of Zealand.

The two monastic enterprises of 1135 have not always been seen in their mutual dependency and in their context with the civil war that raged in these years, which in the first instance led to the violent death of King Erik Emune in 1137.

We know next to nothing of what happened to the monastery of Ringsted after Bishop Svend the Norwegian's foundation in the 1080s. Our Lady's church in Ringsted is dated *c.* 1080 and its architectural models have been found in the Rhineland, for instance in

Mönchengladbach and St Lucius in Essen (Krins, 1968, p. 44). The heavy stone construction is archaic with a number of parallels in Roskilde cathedral and Our Lady's in Roskilde. One cannot explain such investments in stone church constructions, had not each of these three churches been built for an ecclesiastical corporation and community constituting its living heart: the Benedictine monks in Ringsted, the Benedictine nuns in Our Lady's in Roskilde, and the cathedral chapter, as it later turns out.

The church in Ringsted is situated west of an open place which constitutes the north–south passage through the island. The land slopes towards the south with the open place and its church at a middle distance between the high and low levels. Earlier town historians made much out of the supposed pre-Christian cult practised in Ringsted in connection with Thing meetings and tried to see a link from there to the foundation of a monastery (Hassø, 1932, pp. 24–34). From a topographical point of view, the regular orientation of the church with its choir facing the open place and its entrance at the rear as it were, suggests that earlier other buildings may have determined the layout of this open place on the slope, perhaps a temple of some sort facing east, and thereby, as in many non-Christian religions and even in early Roman Christianity, with the entrance doors facing the rising morning sun.

In the 1080s, during King Cnut's reign, the royal mint for a while was active in Ringsted. Jørgen Steen Jensen writes (*Tusindtallets*, 1995, p. 42): 'No coins are known to have been struck at Ringsted under Cnut's [the Great] immediate successors, but during the reigns of Cnut the Holy [1080–86], Oluf Hunger [1086–95] and Erik Ejegod [1095–1103] coins were again produced with the name of Ringsted, struck by the moneyer Alfvord or Alfvart.'

That minting in Ringsted came to an end with the reign of King Niels is an indication of his contentration upon Roskilde. Among the clergy in Roskilde, if we conclude from 'Chronicon Roskildense' (CR) (*SM*, I, p. 25), there was some resentment against Erik as well as against Niels at the time the chronicle was written: *multas iniquas et iniustas leges adinvenit* (he introduced many evil and unjust laws' during his eight years) reign, it says about King Erik the Good, who after his death in Cyprus in 1103 paved the way for King Niels, *virum mansuetum et simplicem, minime rectorem* (a gentle man and plain, [but] no leader).

Although we do not know what the presence of Benedictine monks in Ringsted meant to the decision of King Niels to withdraw from there previous activities like the royal mint, it is clear from the sources that the king lavished his gifts in quite another direction: it was to the

Benedictines of Odense that he made a considerable donation (*DD 1,2*, no. 32) and for whom he procured the papal bull of October 1117 (*DD 1,2*, no. 42), by which the monks were formally confirmed in their task of being a regular cathedral chapter.

To understand King Niels's attitude towards monks and monastic observance, one passage in CR (*SM*, I, p. 26) is relevant. In 1124 or 1125, the king had made a certain Peter, the chaplain of his son Magnus, Bishop of Roskilde after the death of Bishop Arnold, who was in office as Aelnoth dedicated his *Gesta* to King Niels. Arnold had had a conflict with Peder Bodilsen, who had urged him to enforce celibacy among the clergy, something Arnold apparently was too weak or too old to do. His successor, Peter, changed the nature of the question – he must have taken the letter of Pope Paschal II to King Niels of April 1117 (*DD 1,2*, no. 41) as a model – by forbidding complaints about the clergy in secular public Thing meetings, reserving such discussions for an ecclesiastical synod. Bishop Peter was praised in the chronicle for being *vir eruditus et litteratus* (an educated and learned man) and the most steadfast of Danish bishops at the time. He could well distinguish between 'what belonged to God and what belonged to Caesar', it says, but used to say that he was ready to 'claim also what belonged to God in order to secure peace and traquillity'. 'To fulfil the [good] work he planned in his mind and in his words, he added some houses to the church of St Clement in order that a congregation of monks should settle there', the chronicle continues, 'but he sowed such discord among the Danes that there never arose a greater tribulation over clergy and laity since Christianity came to Denmark'. What the chronicle refers to, is of course the murder of Cnut Lavard in 1131, carried out by the very prince whose chaplain Peter had been, or still was. The bishop later fell together with the king's son in the battle of 1134 against Erik Emune.

Sometime between 1125 and 1131, then, Bishop Peter of Roskilde, the king's chaplain and presumably confident of his son, made preparations for the settlement of monks at St Clement's downhill north of the cathedral area in Roskilde, today St Jørgensbjerg church, built in the last decades of the eleventh century (Krins, 1968, pp. 59–62). Peder Bodilsen had made objections against the married state of the clergy, and now Bishop Peter wanted to establish a house for monks living in celibacy and obedience. Did he try to temper Peder Bodilsen's criticism by reinforcing monastic life – not unlike the honour the king had bestowed upon the monks in Odense?

Whatever the background, it all came to nothing as a consequence of the murder of 1131 and the ensuing civil war, which brought death and catastrophe to the whole royal family. But the situation considered here as a possibility may explain something of the tension between Peder Bodilsen and King Niels, which paved the way for a collaboration between Peder Bodilsen and King Erik at least for a while around 1135.

A tendency to politicize the presence of monks is visible here in two variations. First the Odense case. It is by no means certain that Erik the Good called the monks from Evesham to settle in Odense with the explicit purpose of having them fulfil the function of a cathedral chapter – our knowledge of the situation in Odense around 1100 is, in spite of what we find in the literature about St Cnut, still insufficient for a final conclusion on that point. But clearly enough, King Niels picked up the thread of his brother's Evesham initiative and had the monks accept – if they themselves were not the ones to propose it – a role as a Benedictine regular cathedral chapter, as we know from the papal mandate to Bishop Hubald of 1117. An initial foundation charter for the Odense monastery has not been handed down to us and we do not know if it ever existed (Andresen, 1990). We have the royal charter which styles itself an *edictum* (*DD 1,2*, no. 32) – not dated but it must have been issued before 1117 and have been part of the documentation presented to the Pope before 23 April 1117 – in which King Niels, as the editor, Skyum-Nielsen, points out, makes known that he has refrained from his claim to certain royal rights and revenues due from such land as the church of Odense and the monks already own or dispose of:

> I have openly made known the following law of freedom to the church of St Cnut in Odense and to the brethren who live there: for all future times I have donated to their own use whatever income under whatever name belongs to us according to the king's legal rights for all fields, villages and lands that are theirs already now or will be theirs later. I have excepted from this rule only ...

Then follow the royal reservations, among others the right to wrecks and to the income derived from the *leding* duties – the tax paid in place of participating in seaborne war expeditions. We have two fragments of the king's donation letters, one to the church of Odense concerning fishing rights (*DD 1,2*, no. 34), and one to the church and the monks in Odense on a revenue due from Jutland (*DD 1,2*, no. 35). But the final legal construction by which the community of monks was made a regular cathedral chapter we only know from the mandate of Pope Paschal II, dated 23 April 1117, to the Bishop of Odense.

It is important to remember that the whole process was carried out in collaboration with one and the same pope, he who had given his approval to the canonization of King Cnut, Paschal II (1099–1119). Continuity in office was essential to the realization over a period of time of such a complicated church project. The Pope wrote to the bishop: 'We have received the letter of Niels, the illustrious king of the Danes, by which he tells us that upon your advice and with your consent he has caused a community of religious – of monks – to be brought together at your [episcopal] see'. The king must have sent sufficient documentation by the clergymen who went to Anagni for him, proving that he already had given all legal securities necessary for the union of the community of monks with the 'church of Odense', the episcopal see.

In the same period, as we have seen, the king reduced the importance of Ringsted in his administrative system by withdrawing the royal mint from there. After 1117 he accepted or stimulated the Bishop of Roskilde's efforts to settle monks in St Clement's church in Roskilde, presumably by removing some from Ringsted. If not, recruitment to the Odense community – of which we know nothing – could produce a surplus of monks that would help fill up a daughter foundation in Roskilde. In any case, the initiative concerning St Clement's in Roskilde may be interpreted as an attempt to include the Zealand Benedictines in his administrative system as well, since Ringsted apparently was no longer a place of special interest to him.

Then everything was turned upside down by the crime his son committed, bringing blood and revenge on his head. The brother of the murdered Cnut Lavard stood victorious after a period of unequalled bloodshed, comprising not only the death of the king's son and many bishops and magnates, but also of the king himself, who was murdered in Slesvig a few weeks after the battle of 4 June 1134, while he was trying to hide and save his life after the defeat.

This led indirectly to further politicizing of monasticism. First, Ringsted again became the focus of attention. In 1131, Cnut Lavard had been buried before the high altar of the monastic church there, allegedly because King Niels had refused to have him properly buried in Roskilde. Some time in 1135, probably early in the year, his brother Erik Emune, now king, came to the church of Ringsted and declared, in a solemn act in front of the high altar, that he now had assembled around his brother's tomb, 'namely in the church of Ringsted', 'the congregation of brothers living a regular life' and that he now, 'with God's help, wanted to serve them in food and living overflowingly, as is fitting, by a benevolent royal gift'. Then comes the notification of what he just has given to the brothers and the promise that more will follow (*DD 1,2*, no. 65). In its form, the document is partly similar to the charter issued by King Niels for the monks in Odense (*DD 1,2*, no. 32), in that Erik assigned to the church and monks ten marks *ex eiusdem villae censu qui dicitur mit sommers gield* (out of that payment of the town [of Ringsted] which is called Midsummer tax). But later in the letter, King Erik also makes a donation in *mansus* (farms or *bol*).

Against the background of what has been related above on the role of Ringsted and on the plan to settle monks in Roskilde, King Erik Emune's act is without doubt the most contrary act he was able to perform against the plans of the defeated and deceased King Niels. From now on, and continuously throughout the Danish history of the following centuries, the two holy Cnuts of Denmark symbolized a constant tension, representing different value systems and calling different groups of society to be their followers. Two Benedictine abbeys, in Odense and Ringsted, had received the support of two consecutive kings, the one the victim of the other, in order to each preserve the memory of one powerful and sacred magnate, the already canonized St Cnut in Odense, and the other Cnut whose canonization was soon fervently hoped for. Two Benedictine communities were being dragged into a political role which must have been felt to be adverse to some of those who for other reasons had chosen the monastic option.

The act in Our Lady's church in Ringsted must have taken place at the latest in October or November 1135, since *Rykone capellano*, one of the witnesses, must be identical with the next bishop of Slesvig, nominated at the earliest one and a half years after the battle of Fotevig which took place on 4 June 1134. According to CR (*SM*, I, p. 29), Bishop Adalbero ('Adelbyorn') of Slesvig was wounded in the battle and lived *vix annum et dimidium* (hardly one year and a half) after the battle. Apparently, King Erik celebrated Christmas 1134 and the following *Yule* season in Scania where he founded a prebend in the cathedral of Lund (*DD 1,2*, no. 63, 6 January 1135). Later in that year, his wrath was directed against his own half-brother, Harald Kesje, who had betrayed him and joined with King Niels; King Eric hunted him down and killed him.

The first witness to the king's donation to Ringsted mentioned in the undated charter of 1135 (*DD 1,2*, no. 65) is Peder Bodilsen. He is the main agent in the second politicizing act which affected Danish monasticism in 1135: the foundation of St Peter's abbey in Næstved on 29 November, a date most probably following that of the king's donation.

II The alternative: disinterested prayer

St Peter's in Næstved

Ringsted is situated half-way between Roskilde in the north, to which there is access from the sea through Roskilde Bay, and Næstved near the mouth of the river Susåen in the south, one of Zealand's main water courses.

Not far from Susåen's estuary we find Store (Greater) Næstved on the river's left bank (east), and Lille (Lesser) Næstved on its right (west) bank, separated from each other by the *herred* boundary: *Nestuet ex utraque parte amnis* (Næstved on both sides of the river) (*DD 1,4*, no. 49 [dated 1202–05]) (cf. Helms, 1940, pp. 498f.). Both Næstveds seem to have been mainly part of the Bodilsen family's property. According to Aage Andersen (1987), Store Næstved got the monastery and the adjacent town because it was situated higher, about 12 metres above sea level, and because Lille Næstved, being closer to the coast, was more exposed to attacks from the Vends. 'The urban community probably arose against a background of agrarian changes in the late Viking Age or beginning of the Middle Ages', writes Andersen (1987, pp. 95f.) in his summary about Medieval Næstved, who stresses that the economic life of the town depended on a restricted local market. The Viking village on the plateau of the left bank of Susåen, which here flows south-east, must have existed at the time when Christianity arrived. The church immediately to the east of the area where archaeological work uncovered this village is thought to be identical with that *ecclesia in Næstweth* which was part of the foundation of the monastery in 1135 (*DD 1,2*, no. 64) and which in 1140 is said to have been dedicated to St Peter (*DD 1,2*, nos 75 and 78). It may have been the cult of St Peter which gave rise to the dedication of a guild to his brother St Andrew in neighbouring Ladby. The church of Vejlø further south, although younger, was probably dedicated to St Andrew.

There has been some discussion about where the first abbey was situated, since no traces attributable to an early abbey have been identified around the present St Peter's, a construction of the late thirteenth century on the site of an earlier church. Excavations have brought to light the foundations of that earlier, small Romanesque village church with an apsidal choir. At some point, however, the abbey moved out of town and a new St Peter's abbey church was built in the forest north-west of the town, in the parish of Ladby, which later together with Vridsløse was called Herlufsholm parish. Practically all of Ladby parish, including a locality called Bukkerup, was part of the monastery's original endowment (Helms, 1940, pp. 450, 503f.).

The main donation of Peder Bodilsen in 1135 (*DD 1,2*, no. 64) was his *curia*, described in the confirmation charter of Bishop Eskil: *in Lathbu et Bukkæthorp curiam suam ... et sextam partem silve que Foxingiworæ dicitur, in Møn in villa Kælbu quinque mansos et dimidum* ... (his farm in Ladby and Bukkerup ... and the sixth part of the forest called Faksinge and five and a half lands in Keldby on [the island of] Møn). There follow the gifts of Hemming and Jørgen, partly on the island of Falster, and of their mother Bodil, all confirmed by the bishop. The monastery also received St Peter's in Næstved, as well as Tjæreby and Haarlev churches, from Bishop Eskil, who gave them extended tithe privileges and asked for intercessory prayer.

It is characteristic that an urban settlement came into being on the border of two *herred* in the farmers' open village landscape with its meeting places for the Thing. To Viking farmers, an estuary just meant a place from which to embark on war expeditions, whereas merchants profited from navigable rivers for quite other purposes. This favoured the town of Næstved in its early growth. But it favoured the monastery as well, since previously peripheral property near the *herred* and *syssel* boundary now could be kept together by a new gravitation centre undisturbed by distant Thing meetings of the land-owning farmers. As in the course of the twelfth century royal power and influence upon the Thing communities grew, a monastery, well endowed and equipped with royal confirmation, would enjoy excellent conditions in such a border area between administrative districts, close to an estuary comfortably accessible for ships of the type used then.

All this makes evident that what Peder Bodilsen did in November 1135 was something new in Scandinavian monastic history. After a thorough consideration of the chances for a future monastery in Næstved and the resources of his own family to sustain it, he – or his mother, Bodil – decided to emulate the king and instigate a monastic foundation by his own family. To be able to do that, he must have made an agreement with a group of monks who were able to settle in Næstved. Where did he get them from? There is no evidence of any contacts abroad on the establishment of the first monastery in Næstved. The monks must have come from Denmark. Nearest at hand were the monks in Ringsted and in Odense. What could have persuaded monks from Odense or Ringsted to go to Næstved? There is no other explanation for such a decision but the gift of King Erik Emune to Ringsted abbey, which transformed that place into a memorial to his brother.

The situation of the parties is clear from the fact that the charter for Næstved stating the gift of Peder Bodilsen (*DD 1,2*, no. 64) was issued by the new Bishop of Roskilde, Eskil, who in 1137 rose to the archbishopric of Lund and became a potent opponent to the family clan stemming from Erik the Good, including his sons Cnut Lavard, Erik Emune and Harald Kesje, and his daughter Ragnhild, the mother of Erik 'the Sheep' or Agnus, King of Denmark 1137–46, who ended his life as a monk in Odense.

The Danish civil wars that began in 1131 and ended in 1157 were fought between Erik the Good's descendants on the one side, ultimately rendering victory to Cnut Lavard's and Ingeborg's son Valdemar, and King Niels and his branch of the family on the other side, systematically defeated and ostracized right down to the persecution of its last descendant, Bishop Valdemar of Slesvig who died, deposed and exiled, in 1236.

The foundation of Næstved may have been an effort to counteract the tendency of politicizing monasticism by its contra-position to the political role the Benedictine monks had been given in Odense by King Niels and now in Ringsted by King Erik Emune. Ringsted was initially not a royal abbey, but a foundation of Bishop Svend 'the Norwegian' of Roskilde. In 1135, the king 'usurped' it for his political purposes, as his uncle and predecessor had done in a slightly different way with the Odense community. There must have been a number of monks in Ringsted and perhaps also in Odense who were not happy with the political bias their abbeys had been forced into by the two kings. In that situation, Peder Bodilsen, supported by Bishop Eskil, may have tried to open a monastic alternative without looking askance at pilgrimages to a royal tomb and the pastoral care of pilgrims.

Already here we witness one of the factors that were so decisive in the development of monastic life in Denmark during the following decades: the love of Bishop Eskil for a monastic observance outside the reach of the king or worldly magnates. One may interpret the foundation of Næstved abbey as a demonstration that power politics among rulers of this world, be it the dead King Niels or the reigning King Erik, would have to step back when faced with the monastic alternative as such, by which man in the monastic interpretation of Christianity finds his true self beyond all the sophistry of the world.

When the term 'political purposes' is used in connection with the three Benedictine monasteries of Ringsted, Odense and Næstved, this is of course still to be understood in the medieval not in the nineteenth-century context of this notion. A Danish king four to five generations after the baptism of Harald Blueteeth would be just as convinced as Harthacnut or Gorm before that first baptism that it is absolutely necessary for a king to be in close and intimate commune and friendship with gods and divine powers, expressed by a decent treatment of their representations in society. For a king to reach this status, which to the whole realm was looked upon as essential to the royal office, thanksgiving and penitence in humility were necessary parts of a process by which the king became a kind of mediator between God and men – the essence of presiding over a sacrifice. The two royal acts favouring the Benedictines in Odense and Ringsted were instrumental to this purpose, in that they enabled a community of men who preferred the monastic alternative to devote themselves to prayer, study and meditation, to the benefit of the same realm which the king was to administer. Their thanksgiving would have to direct itself also to the king for the gifts which God through the king had bestowed upon them. Thereby the king and his family would be included in the power of this prayer in life as well as after life.

The ideal monastic alternative, on the other hand, is to disregard political interests and cultivate that indifference of mind according to which it does not matter who is striving to exert power in secular matters. In this sense, prayer is not just a radiation of power which has to be forced to flow in the 'right' direction, but an attitude to life basically uninterested in the division and separation of power between decision-makers or lobby groups. The Benedictine *pax*, fundamental to monasticism and not exposed to fluctuations of fashion or style, turned out to be precious to Archbishop Eskil throughout the rest of his life.

Seen in this perspective, one might ask if Bishop Eskil, by accepting the Bodilsen's gift (*DD 1,2*, no. 64), had not 'run away with the blessing' under the very nose of the king in office. The Bodilsens' gifts were given *pro remedio animarum suarum suorumque, pro salute videlicet viventium, pro refrigerio decedentium* (for the remedy of their souls and [the souls] of their [kin], for the spiritual health of the living and for the refreshment of the dying). The monks, being *servi Dei* (God's slaves or servants), should enjoy these gifts in freedom. Eskil liberates them from all dues which normally ought to be paid to the bishop and orders that from now on 'they shall not be subdued to secular or ecclesiastical persons in anything, except that they shall exhibit due subordination to the bishop of their diocese and an obedience which is befitting for those who are holy' (*que sanctos decet obedientiam exhibeant*). The bishop is to exert the role of an arbiter in case of conflicts that the *prelatus*, their abbot or prior, cannot solve, and the tithe he awards to the monks should be used for their participation in synods if they are called thereto by the bishop.

Denmark had several Benedictine abbeys founded by bishops, and it is possible that the form given here by Bishop Eskil in November 1135 has utilized some earlier, now lost, document as a model. It is an interesting point that the bishop stated his supremacy over the future monastery and declared himself to be an arbiter in case of conflicts which the monks could not solve by themselves. Could this have been copied from a lost charter given by Bishop Svend the Norwegian to Ringsted Abbey prior to 1088? Such a charter would have been available for a bishop of Roskilde at that time. It looks as if the subordination of monks under the bishop of the diocese was still taken to be the normal arrangement for a Benedictine abbey, so that further exemption from episcopal authority would require documents from higher authorities.

It is a reasonable conjecture that the foundation of Næstved enabled Zealand monks to continue living the way of life they had been living in Ringsted from the 1080s up to 1135. St Peter's abbey in Næstved presumably did not inaugurate a new monastic observance and we would not have to ask from where it got its pioneers and its customs. They would be a continuation of monastic traditions that had been practised under episcopal supervision in the Zealand diocese since the 1080s. St Peter's in Næstved may, under such circumstances, be our source of knowledge for how Benedictine life was practised at the same time in All Saints' abbey outside Lund, in Seem, in St Michael's outside Slesvig, in the first Benedictine abbey in the diocese of Aarhus, in Nidarholm, Selja and Munkeliv, in Þingeyrar – all those places where the monastic alternative had been established in collaboration with the bishop of the diocese and was not burdened by royal duties limiting the scope of the monks' task or stained by involvement in civil war.

The diocese of Aarhus

The earliest beginnings of monasticism in the diocese of Aarhus are difficult to find in the sources. Two early monasteries doubtlessly belong to the foundation period we have treated so far, Veng and Randers.

According to the Cistercian chronicle of Øm, there was in the 1160s a Benedictine abbey in Veng in the middle part of the river Gudenå basin which is described in such a way that it must have existed there for at least one generation.

The church of Veng or Venge has been the object of much research. A number of reminiscences of Anglo-Norman architecture have been evaluated and have led to different conclusions as to the time and context of its construction. The church has generally been taken to be the monastic church of the Benedictine community mentioned in the 1160s. Krins (1968, pp. 73–84) refers, however, to a number of details in Veng that are also frequently found in the Rhineland and other German regions, for example the west portal may be compared to that of St Lucius in Essen, a church which was consecrated in 1063, or to the decorations in the blindings on the inside of the choir, which resemble those of St Michael's in Lüneburg, consecrated in 1033 (Figure 8.2). Although Krins may not be right when he, following earlier Danish scholars, finds

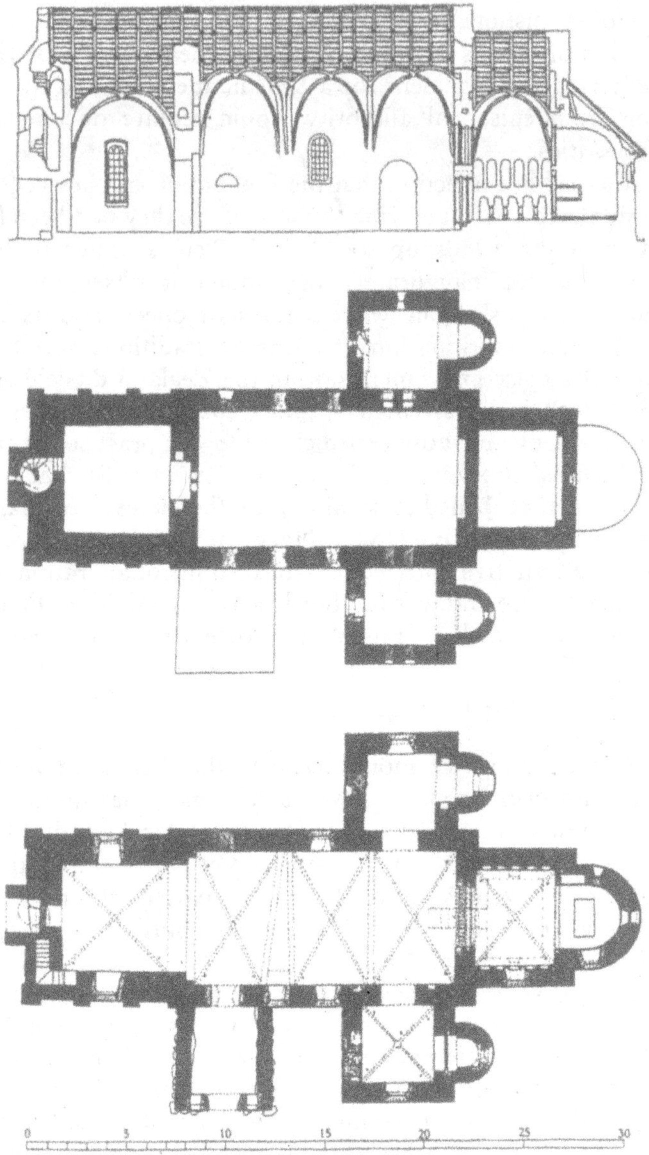

8.2 Ground plan and longitudinal section of the abbey church of Veng, Jutland

Source: *Danmarks Kirker* (1988–89, 16:6, p. 3197).

parallels to English churches like Deerhurst not far from Evesham and Repton, his reference to the stone constructions in Roskilde and Ringsted from the same period leads him to characterize the construction of Veng as 'archaic', placing it in the time around 1100, as against other later dates, for example, *c.* 1125.

The Anglo-Norman characteristics of the church in Veng have led scholars to postulate a connection to the Anglo-Saxon Benedictines in Odense. As has been pointed out earlier in this book, the evidence is much better for Odense than for any other Benedictine abbey in Denmark from the end of the eleventh century. But, as also has been pointed out, Odense is much more exceptional than most scholars have thought, by the very fact that in Odense, for the first time in Denmark, a Benedictine community was honoured but also burdened with the extra tasks of caring for pilgrims gathering around the tomb of a royal saint and of carrying out the duties of a cathedral chapter. There is no doubt that such a function in the structure of the state–church relations of the twelfth century was seen as a public office in the service of the king and the whole realm. In other words, the monks in Odense were being used for purposes which – although there were models for it in many places in Europe including England – must have been understood to be more princely than religious.

Against such a background, it is conceivable that a move of Anglo-Saxon monks to Denmark in the years around 1100 may have split them, so that some sought to escape from the exposed role in Danish society they would have to play in Odense according to the plans of King Niels. At the latest *c.* 1115, the Odense monks must have negotiated their future status with the king and with Bishop Hubald, a status which was then confirmed by Pope Paschal II in 1117. Basically there must have been different ideas among Anglo-Saxon monks in general on how to carry out monastic life in recently Christianized Denmark, considering the many variations of Benedictine lifestyle that England could offer.

We do not know very much about the situation at the see of Aarhus in these years. There is no name of a bishop between Christian, who was ordained by Adalbert *c.* 1060 as the first bishop after Aarhus had been reorganized, and Ulkil, who seems to have been one of King Niels's men, since he is said to have been deposed by Erik Emune after King Niels had been murdered in June, 1134 (*SE VI: II*, p. 42). Perhaps we have to introduce here again the strange story from the chronicle of the Counts of Stade, about three Danish bishops who were 'drowned' on their passage through Stade in 1112. One of them could have been a Bishop of Aarhus unknown to us, perhaps a man nominated under King

Oluf (1086–95) and therefore later identified as schismatic. Whether or not he died in 1112, his name could in that case have been intentionally suppressed. This speculation shows that there is no help to be obtained from information about bishops of Aarhus when considering the circumstances under which monasticism materialized in Veng. The diocese was not led by any of those outstanding personalities known from chronicles and Saxo's *Gesta*, whom we could credit with taking a stand for or against the arrival of monks. Rather, Anglo-Saxon monks in 1100 would have to rely upon royal support and privileges, be it under Erik the Good or under King Niels, if they thought to move to a second Danish diocese for the foundation of a 'normal' monastery, free from the burden of administering a cathedral. The choice of Veng as a monastic site may be explained in such a way.

The only existing evidence states the basic fact that Veng was a royal foundation. In the 1160s, Veng was abolished and its property incorporated with the new abbey of Øm. Papal letters were needed for the suppression of the abbey, and in one of them, issued by Pope Alexander III, the style of the papal court required that the founder of Veng be mentioned. Therefore the papal letter to King Valdemar *c.* 1165 (*DD* 1,2, no. 167) speaks about Veng *quod antecessores tui pro anime sue remedio fundarunt et largis et magnis possessionibus ampliarunt* (which your predecessors founded for the remedy of their souls and dotated with lavish and great property). The passage in the papal document confirms that a Danish king founded Veng abbey with generous endowments. Theoretically any of the Danish kings between Svend Estridsen and Erik Agnus could have been the founder. A later foundation puts us in some difficulty, however; for how then to explain that we hear nothing of such a foundation during the civil wars, when so many other things are being recorded? If the foundation of Veng does not go back to Erik the Good, King Valdemar's grandfather, we are left with the long reign of King Niels as the best choice.

The most careful, recent statement (*DK* XVI, 8, 1988–89, pp. 3213, 3250f. n. 41) sets 1080 as *terminus post* – thus including even the possibility of King Cnut as founder – and 1134 as *terminus ante*, but the years around 1100 as the most probable ones for the construction, carried out by one very gifted man who must have been well versed in all the architectural possibilities for a Benedictine monastic church including side altars on two levels. No exact parallel has yet been found to the combination of architectural elements in Veng so far, although St Peter's in Sigtuna has been mentioned for numerous similar elements. Veng church is supposed to have been built in one single construction phase. The royal endowment apparently put resources to build this church at the disposal of a group of monks, some of whom may be assumed to have been Anglo-Saxons.

The royal abbey of Veng was destined to be the cradle of Benedictine life in mid-Jutland. The church was grandiose in its proportions, in its decorations and liturgical equipment in the form of side chapels and altars; the somewhat reduced church that is left today is enough to imagine its past glory. During its existence for two or three generations, Veng represented the monastic alternative for men in a rich and fertile part of Denmark, where the new Christian religion had begun to penetrate at least into the layers of land-owning nobility and better-off farmers. The monasteries may have had a certain appeal in families of such status, perhaps in the beginning for child oblates, or for younger sons too numerous to prosper through war or in colonizing new land.

A second Benedictine foundation in the region may have been inspired or led by monks from Veng: Our Lady's monastery in Randers, the growing urban settlement on the left shore of the Gudenå estuary. It is not clear to which diocese Randers may have pertained from the beginning. If the original plan had been to make the Viberg diocese comprise all hundreds that in the land register of King Valdemar II 1231 are entered under Ommersyssel, then the River Gudenå in its lower, north-eastern to eastern course would have been the southern border of the diocese of Viberg, making Randers part of that diocese. As far back as the sources go, however, church life in the four eastern hundreds of Ommersyssel were administered by the bishops of Aarhus.

Randers is situated on the slope down to the river on the northern shore of the Gudenå river. The church, belonging to a settlement from the eleventh century next to the water, was dedicated to St Clement. Excavated foundations have been dated to *c.* 1160 (Vellev, 1977). Further up the slope, east of the main northwards road, were a church and convent of Our Lady and a church dedicated to St Peter. West of the main road, a parish church dedicated to St Morten (Martin), known from written evidence of the fourteenth century, corresponds to the medieval expansion of settlement in this north-western direction; the present construction is from *c.* 1500.

Randers belongs to the places in Jutland which were favoured by King Cnut (1080–86). It was apparently a royal mint for a short time:

> Cnut the Holy's three mints in Jutland – Viborg, Ålborg and Randers – are only known from coins of the last years of his reign. All coins are struck with the same types ... The obverse type is new. It shows an enthroned king wearing a crown in Byzantine style. The right hand is holding a sword and the left hand is supporting a shield.

> The design is related to effigies on certain German coins and on medieval seals but no direct prototype has been found ...

Minting in Randers continued under Erik the Good (*Tusindtallets*, 1995, pp. 120, 126). The coins correspond to the results of excavations in the area around St Clement's. According to Cinthio (1968), St Clement was a favourite for the dedication of churches or chapels belonging to a royal manor in the formative period up to *c.* 1150. There is no doubt that Randers was important to the king on a spot well adapted to cross the Gudenå river.

As we have seen, there was no strong leadership in the diocese of Aarhus in the decades around 1100. A monastery or convent higher up on the slope above the water level of the river Gudenå can hardly have been inaugurated by anyone else than one of the kings. We are back with the same situation as in Veng. Commonly, Our Lady's monastic complex is thought to have been built *c.* 1130–50 (*Randers købstads historie*, 1952, p. 46). Recent excavations of Our Lady's monastic complex support this (Schelde-Jensen and Juhl, 1991).

It has generally been assumed that the Benedictine monks who later lived in Essenbæk resided in Randers first. However, in the late twelfth century, Our Lady's in Randers was a convent of Benedictine nuns. A grandson of the Zealand magnate Skjalm Hvide, who died *c.* 1113, Stig Hvide or Tokesen, is the only person mentioned as founder of the Benedictine monastery of Essenbæk east of Randers but south of the river. There is only one single piece of evidence for Stig's role as a monastery founder, an entry in the so-called *Annales Essenbecenses* (*Danmarks middelalderlige annaler* [DMA], 1980, pp. 274–83) under 1151: *Stig Huithæ, fundator claustri Eskinbeck, interfectus est* (Stig Hvide, the founder of the monastery of Essenbæk, was killed). Very few descendants of the Zealand magnate Skjalm Hvide actually used the Hvide name for themselves, although the famous 'Hvides' are found in many scholars' minds as a conglomeration of a number of family branches stemming from Skjalm (Hill, 1992, p. 207). Stig belongs to these few. He was married to Margarete, the eldest daughter of Cnut Lavard (and eldest sister of Valdemar I) and was killed in the battle of Viborg 1151, when Svend Grathe and Valdemar defeated Knud Magnussen. Clearly enough, the founder of Essenbæk was a man on a par with Peder Bodilsen, at least as far as family connections go.

We cannot doubt, then, that what remained in Randers was the royal foundation of Our Lady's convent for Benedictine nuns, St Peter's church apparently being part of that complex. What we have in Essenbæk, is the foundation by a member of an influential noble family, if we believe the annals' entry of 1151. How this separation between nuns in a royal abbey situated in an increasingly urbanized settlement, and monks in an abbey in the countryside founded by a local magnate, was carried out in practice we cannot say for sure. But the so-called Essenbæk annals contain besides the entry under 1151 only one more entry dealing with the monastery of Essenbæk. Under 1179 it says: *Mutatio claustri Eskinbeck*. Earlier scholars tentatively interpreted the *mutatio* of this entry as a 'move' of the male community from Randers to Essenbæk. This is admittedly not the literal translation, which is 'change' in the sense of 'revolution', normally used for a change of leadership or presidency. But the *mutatio* of Essenbæk in 1179 might refer to just such a change of legal status achieved by the final cutting of legal bonds between the royal abbey in town and the nobelman's foundation on the countryside. In that case it appears as the final 'move' of the monks to Essenbæk, although physically that move could have taken place earlier. Possibly one will have to calculate with a construction period for an abbey church and a monastery *c.* 1150–75. One single entry in the Lund necrology proves the existence of Our Lady's nuns' convent in Randers at the latest *c.* 1170. After an *Anniversarius Gunnolfi laici* on the 20 September, another hand has added the obituary entry of 'Thrugund, nun of Our Lady's in Randers': *et Thrugundis sanctimonialis sancte Marie de Randrusia* (*NL*, p. 95), which suggests another anniversary foundation at the cathedral chapter in Lund just for the soul of this sister Thrugund, who may have had relatives in Lund to make the foundation for her.

CHAPTER NINE

The great period: civil war 2

I Monasticism in times of threat

The losses

Violence left its mark upon the first years when Eskil, educated in Hildesheim, was Bishop of Roskilde. He was nominated in 1134 by the victor, Cnut Lavard's brother, Erik Emune, to replace Bishop Peter who had fallen in the battle of 4 June that year on the side of King Niels. Not only the murder of Cnut Lavard, but now the fall of the king's son Magnus in the same battle, the murder of his father King Niels in Slesvig shortly afterwards, the bloody execution of Erik Emune, the new king, and not least the extinction of his own brother Harald Kesje and his family, created an apocalyptic mood which first inspired Bishop Eskil to support Peder Bodilsen's monastic foundation in Næstved and then brought him into opposition with the king himself. *Hec vita Herici, hec incessio, talis introitus; sed nunc, quis sit exitus, videamus* (This was the life of Erik, this was how he developed, such was the way he came [to power]; but now, let us see how he left), says CR (*SM*, I, p. 31), which was written shortly afterwards and in the same mood. King Erik was slain in a way which in his time was regarded as unworthy: *surrexit quidam nomine Plouh, quod latine aratrum sonat, et regem incautum mortali vulnere prostravit, vir deformis, brevis stature, per se nichil faciens ...* (a certain man by the name of Plouh which in Latin means 'plough' stood up and felled the king, who did not observe him, with a deadly wound – an ugly creature, of small stature, of no doings on his own account ...) but merely representing God's wrath over such an unworthy reign.

Among the minor sons of the fallen combatants none could be put forward as the successor to King Erik, so another Erik, the son of the dead king's sister, Ragnhild, in her marriage with Håkon Jyde or Håkon the Norwegian – his mother Sunniva came from Norway – was accepted as king (1137–46). The decision for Erik called Agnus 'the Lamb' (Erik Lam, also Erik III), fell in the months after the death of Scandinavia's first Archbishop Asser on 5 May 1137. Thanks to Peder Bodilsen, the competition between Eskil of Roskilde and Rico of Slesvig on the succession to the metropolitan chair of Lund was solved in favour of Eskil, while Rico instead became Eskil's successor in Roskilde, where he died in October 1139. The collaboration from Næstved in November 1135 between Eskil and Peder Bodilsen thereby bore fruit in a most spectacular way, which must have given both the feeling that their efforts in favour of the true monastic option was providential and blessed.

In the mean time Hartwig, Archbishop of Hamburg-Bremen, had tried to make good the schismatic politics of his predecessor, Liemar, which in 1104 had cost his see the supervision of the Scandinavian mission. Now he claimed the mission back for his see. Hartwig's collaboration with Pope Innocent II (1130–43) was useful, and in 1133 it secured him papal charters which would have brought the whole of the Scandinavian mission once more under the supervision of German authorities, had they ever been legally accomplished. To counteract this, Eskil dispatched his recent chaplain, Hermann from Klosterrath, to Rome, the 1133 charters were anulled and both succeeded in 1139 in getting the papal legate, Theodewin, to Denmark where he presided at a provincial council in Lund. The charters, by the way, had never reached Scandinavia, but were in Bremen where they have remained in the archives to the present time.

It must have been during these years that Archbishop Eskil bought from King Erik Agnus the territory of Esrum. This is testified in a letter given by King Svend (1151–57). The king states that Esrum, which *iuri pertinebat regio* (belonged to the king) but now was set aside for sacred use, had been bought by Archbishop Eskil from 'my predecessor King Erik' and given to the *usui immo necessitati fratrum ibidem Deo servientium* (use and subsistence of the brothers who serve God there). Different interpretations of the details regarding the earliest property of Esrom abbey have been brought forward by Niels Skyum-Nielsen (*DD 1,2*, no. 107), McGuire (1982, p. 50) and Jack Overgaard Jørgensen (1989, p. 11). The formulas in the different charters belonging to the story are blurred because of the political tensions which gave rise to different claims and pretensions in the description of what really happened. Basically, however, there is agreement that Bishop Eskil by some kind of a bargain, which was differently interpreted, acquired Esrum from King Erik Agnus, i.e. prior to 1146, and that property in Nybo, Nødebo, Nørre Herlev, perhaps Jonstrup, and Villingerød, all situated in northern Zealand, were at an early stage Eskil's property and reserved for the foundation of a monastery, which then may have come into being during the 1140s. One of the problems with this early property is the transfer of Eskil from the see of Roskilde to Lund 1137/38, whereby he could no longer exert jurisdictional rights in the diocese of Roskilde. The diocese was governed by Rico until October 1139, then by the Austin canon, Asser, from the community of Eskilsø in the Roskilde bay until 1158. Eskil of course had enough strength to exert his will anyhow, but possibly the legal transactions necessary in order to define the foundation lands for Esrum as Eskil's private property were open to doubt.

There is no doubt, however, that during these years the decision must have ripened in the mind of Bishop, later Archbishop, Eskil to carry out a monastic foundation of his own in thanksgiving for everything which seemed to be going well for him and the legitimate interests of the church towards the end of the 1130s. That he planned to do so in Zealand indicates that the idea was mature before he moved to Lund. The transfer made the matter somewhat more complicated, but since he apparently managed to make a bargain with King Erik Agnus regarding the lands of Esrum on the northern tip of north-eastern Zealand's great lake, not far from the North Sea (Kattegat), and since he held more property ready for the purpose, the foundation must have come into being some time in the 1140s. Possibly, also, monks arrived to initiate the foundation – they may have come from Næstved or from All Saints in Lund.

In founding the Benedictine abbey of Esrum, Archbishop Eskil was in line with other measures whereby monasteries tried to protect their office of prayer and detachment in these years. In his own church province, the Benedictines of Norwegian Munkeliv near Bergen in 1145 sent a delegation to Rome to provide a papal letter of protection for their abbey, which was given on 7 January 1146 by Pope Eugene III, a former monk who had been elected pope on 15 February 1145.

According to Arne Odd Johnsen's (1965) careful analysis, the struggle for royal power and authority in Norway after the death of Sigurd the Jerusalem-farer in 1130 was no less dramatic and cruel than the civil war in Denmark, characterized by unhindered crime and oppression against ecclesiastical institutions. To Munkeliv, this meant a new cultural orientation which carried the monks abroad, to Lund, the ecclesiastical metropole of Norway since 1104. As has been brought out by art historians (Lidén, 1961), a number of details in the fragments of the abbey church of Munkeliv excavated in the nineteenth century point to Lund cathedral, which was under construction between its inauguration in 1123 and the consecration of the crypt in 1145. For construction works in Munkeliv, workers must have been taken from Lund, as continental artistic tendencies show, which can only be explained by assuming Lund as an intermediate stage. The request for a papal letter of protection may well have to do with a concluding stage in construction works at Munkeliv in the beginning of the 1140s.

Moreover, new contacts and impulses, not least from Eskil himself, had focused attention upon the new type of reformed Benedictine monasticism, represented by Bernard of Clairvaux and originating in the Cîteaux filiation of reformed monasticism, which made great strides by the nomination of the new Pope in 1145, Eugene III, one of Bernard's followers and monks. Even this new movement and the growing sympathies for it in competition with traditional Benedictine customs may have contributed to the costly expedition to Rome which the Munkeliv monks set in motion in order to save their monastery's status within the framework of the monastic alternative.

For his own archdiocese, Eskil had in fact already addressed himself to the representatives of the reformed Benedictine monasticism of Bernard of Clairvaux. Much has been written about the relations of Archbishop Eskil to Bernard of Clairvaux and his love for the monastic alternative, which ultimately moved him to resign his office in 1177 and withdraw to Clairvaux, where he died as a monk in 1181.

It is important here to state from the beginning that the reform movement emanating from Cîteaux and Clairvaux was a movement with the aim of reforming Benedictine monasticism. Every abbey that followed the statutes of Cîteaux and sent its abbot there for the annual meeting at the general chapter was a Benedictine abbey, following first and foremost the Rule of St Benedict as a guide for its material and spiritual life. In the first instance, therefore, there was no insoluble conflict between either type of Benedictine monasticism. To the degree that such a conflict was construed out of variations in clothes, daily habits and liturgical practice, it did not touch on the central purpose of monasticism as such, which at any epoch will remain the same: a way to achieve the detachment of mind by which prayer, meditation and other religious acts provide their value for the monks themselves and for their surroundings.

Today, after the thorough analysis by McGuire (1982), we cannot cast any doubt upon Eskil's merits in the foundation of Herrisvad abbey in the north-western corner of Scania in his own archdiocese. In the tradition of the Cistercians, Eskil has always been regarded as the founder of Herrisvad, which came into being and was taken into use by monks from Cîteaux in 1144. The year before, the Swedish King Sverker had received monks from Clairvaux for two foundations, Alvastra and Lurö. Eskil, the metropolitan for all Swedish dioceses including Linköping, covering Östergötland and Småland, plays a decisive role in these two monastic foundations as well.

II The Danish model in Sweden

Religious ambush in the forest

To understand the first monastic foundations in Sweden properly, it is necessary to dwell upon the background situation during the first decades of the twelfth century. Religious tensions between Christians and non-Christians in this period have normally been minimized by scholars treating Sweden already as a properly Christian country in the twelfth century. But there was still much tension between the Christians and those who adhered to the ancient sacrificial rites in Sweden. The people were split. To take the Folkland region north of Lake Mälar as an example – today the province of Uppland – the inhabitants in the south, in Attundaland, closest to the lake, were well-to-do Christian farmers who expressed their fortune in the famous memorial slabs with runic inscriptions, most of them adorned with Christian symbols. In the north, in Tiundaland, people seem to have been more resistant against the Christians, there are no runic stones, and the building of churches and the organization of a parish system came considerably later.

Henriksson's (1995) research on the sacrificial cycle has demonstrated the longevity of the astronomical calculations behind the dating of the sacrifices to January/February every eighth year. According to his table the non-Christians ought to have calculated the performance of their main sacrifice in 1092, 1100, 1108, 1116, 1124, 1132 and 1140. In the 1120s we hear about a certain Erik Årsäll performing non-Christian sacrificial rites. The 'Vita Sancti Botvidi' about the fisherman Botvid, who is said to have died for his Christian faith in 1120, tells us about the elevation of his bones nine years later – 1128 or 1129 – which would correspond to the mid-term between 1124 and 1132, the two closest years of sacrifice. The same source informs us that when, in 1129, the wooden church of St Botvid was ready, 'they' (the people) 'called upon two bishops, men of good remembrance, namely Henrik of Uppsala and Gerder of Strängnäs, and they consecrated the church to the honour of God and St Botvid'.

The fate of Bishop Henrik is significant for the situation. The stone church of St Botvid was consecrated in 1176, says the *Vita*, seeing the events in a rather long time perspective. But Henrik was called *Vpsalensem* which does not fit to that year, since Henrik fell in the battle of 4 June 1134 at Danish Fotevig in Scania when Erik Emune defeated King Niels and Magnus Nielsen and a number of bishops were killed. The title, therefore, probably refers not to 1176 but to the elevation in 1128 or 1129. Henrik is the last after the Danish bishops to be mentioned in this series of bishops who fell in the battle. In CR (*SM*, I, p. 29) he is called *Henricus expulsus de Swethia* (driven out of Sweden), in *NL Henricus Sictunensis* (Bishop of Sigtuna). Both sources are more weighty than the 'Vita Sancti Botvidi' which dates from a period when Sigtuna's role was finished.

Thus, Bishop Henrik was in Denmark in the summer of 1134, fighting on the side of King Niels – why? Synchronizing this with Henrikssons's table, we can see that 1132 would have been a year of sacrifice, when the non-Christians in the Swedish forests may easily have recalled their old religion. Every such year would mean new dangers and threats for the Christians, including their bishops. It is reasonable to see Bishop Henrik's stay in Denmark as a flight from the threatening situation in the mission field after the sacrificial winter of 1132.

A decade earlier, around 1122, according to Norse literature, King Niels had made an agreement with King Sigurd of Norway to carry out a war expedition to the highlands of Småland, the southern part of the diocese of Linköping, the region immediately bordering Danish Scania. Although one of its central regions, Värend, with the church of Växjö, is said to have been Sigfrid's field of mission in the eleventh century, many non-Christians were said to live in the forests here, so the expedition could be styled a 'crusade'. It was carried out in 1123, 'in the summer before the eclipse of the sun', which fell on 11 August 1124. In the end, however, the Danish king did not come, allegedly because he did not want to wait longer for the Norwegians, who were late. Thus, they alone carried out this *Kalmare ledung* (sea borne expedition to Kalmar), as it is called (Blomkvist, 1978).

It might seem strange that the King of Denmark should feel entitled to pacify non-Christians in the highland forest areas between Danish Scania and the agricultural central part of Swedish Östergötland. According to Henriksson's table, however, the sacrifice next in time to the 'crusade' would be calculated to occur in January–February, 1124. If the Kings Niels and Sigurd knew that – and they must be assumed to have known such a thing, considering its touchy character in the missionary process – an expedition to such areas where there were many non-Christians in the year 1123, the summer preceding the sacrifice, may have seemed an appropriate measure in favour of the Christian faith, in order to deter non-Christians from organizing a sacrifice which from any point of view would be illegal.

King Niels's role as a promoter of Christianity may well have induced him later to support a Bishop of Sigtuna, the Christian centre nearest to Uppsala, if the bishop had been forced to leave Sweden in the face of non-Christian resistance.

Why did such a bishop enter the battle of 4 June 1134 on the king's side – a battle which after all was part of a Danish civil war and not a matter of Swedish politics? An answer to this may be found in the person of the queen, Margareta Fredkulla, whom we met earlier in dealing with the foundation of Vreta abbey. After the death of Magnus Barefoot in 1103, Margareta, by marrying King Niels, became Queen of Denmark. In this capacity she exerted considerable influence. She is one of the witnesses to the charter mentioned earlier by which King Niels gave fishing rights to the Benedictines in Odense (*DD 1,2*, no. 34). One of the annals notes 1117 as the year of her death, but scholars take this to be an error and suppose that she lived much longer (Aksel E. Christensen in *Dansk Biografisk Lexicon* [*DBL*]). The fact that we find a Swedish Bishop Henrik dying in battle for King Niels in 1134 may indicate, therefore, that beyond the bonds of interest between King Niels and the Christian hierarchy in the Småland and Lake Mälar regions, the queen may have been instrumental in giving refuge to clergy and other Christians exposed to resistance from the side of the non-Christians in the missionary field. For a bishop in remote Swedish regions, confronted with the cycle of sacrifice which may have caused upheavals at regular intervals (such as 1124 and 1132), it may have been a better alternative to associate with King Niels and his queen, than to rely upon Archbishop Asser of Lund, since Denmark's queen came from Sweden and ultimately represented the tradition from the Christian kingdom of her father, the founder of Vreta, King Inge 'the elder'.

Then there is the case of Bishop Siward consecrated to a see in the Lake Mälar region. Tönnes Kleberg (1968) has made the most recent analysis of his career. Siward is an interesting man in monastic context since after having left the Swedish mission he entered Rastede abbey west of Bremen and became its abbot.[1] In the chronicle of Rastede ('Historia Monasterii Rastedensis', 1880, p. 502; *Die Rasteder Chronik*, 1976, p. 24) he is said to have arrived there during the time of its third abbot, Simon, who was elected *c.* 1130:

> In the time of the said Abbot Simon a Bishop of Uppsala by the name of Siward, who had been driven out [from there] by the audacity of the pagans (*propter insolentiam paganorum*) and now came from Ireland, which is one of the English islands, found joy in staying here because of the beauty of the place.

Kleberg especially focuses upon the enumeration of books which according to the chronicle Siward brought with him to the monastery. He was called on to serve Archbishop Adalbero (1123–48) and in this vein he consecrated a chapel in Elmendorf; the chronicle dates this act to 1134. The chronicle of Disibodenberg (*MGH SS*, XVII, p. 25) then informs us that one altar on the northern side of the new monastery had been consecrated 'by the Lord Siward Bishop of [Upp]sala ... This venerable bishop, who unjustly had been driven away from his church, came to the bishopric of Mainz ... '. The event is dated to 1138, which makes it probable that Siward here met Hildegard of Bingen, who lived in Disibodenberg during these years (Kleberg, 1968, pp. 17–22). We find his name written as the first one among the witnesses in two charters issued by Archbishop Hartwig of Hamburg-Bremen in 1141 and 1142: *Siwardus Obsalensis episcopus*. In 1441 he was elected Abbot of Rastede and according to the chronology of the chronicle he must have died in 1157. Arne Odd Johnsen found the date of his death in an obituary from Canterbury: on 30 October *Obiit Siwardus episcopus Ubsallensis* (Johnsen, 1970).

Moreover, Kleberg believes that the notice of Arnold from Lübeck (*MGH SS*, VI, p. 60) about a cleric from the company of Archbishop Adalbero in Rome, 1123, whom the Pope *Suethis episcopum ordinavit* (ordained bishop to the Swedes), concerns Siward. Had he gone to Sweden already in the following year to find his diocese, then he would have arrived just after sacrifices pertaining to the winter of 1124 may have been celebrated secretly among non-Christians. If he succeeded in staying and working some years for his diocese, in the spirit of Adam of Bremen trying to fight the non-Christians, he must have been in a risky situation at the latest in 1132, the presumed next year of sacrifice. He may have been driven out of Sweden at any time between 1124 and 1132 and could yet have gone to Ireland and back to Bremen and Rastede and been accepted there, before he performed his episcopal service of consecrating the altar in Bremen in 1134. After that time he certainly never returned to Sweden.

Earlier scholars saw Bishop Siward primarily as a representative of the Hamburg-Bremen desire for total supervision of the Scandinavian mission and for the abolition of the independent Scandinavian church province and suppression of the metropolitan rights of Lund. This framework of interpretation was launched by the Swedish church historian, Knut B. Westman, in his important analysis of the tendencies and conflicts of this epoch (Westman, 1915). It was used for Bishop Henrik as well: both bishops were supposed to have run into problems because of internal conflicts between Lund and Hamburg-Bremen interests on the mission field. That they were seriously threatened by non-Christians was dismissed out of the preconceived conviction of scholars at the time that Sweden was Christianized and, therefore, the reference to the violence of non-Christian resistance was nothing but a pretence to cover up other differences.

Without preconceived concepts, however, one cannot easily dismiss the references in the sources to a non-Christian resistance which must have been more than symbolic. As can be seen from the timing of the evidence for bishops Henrik and Siward, they may have been present in Sweden simultaneously for a few years, Siward as Bishop of Uppsala and Henrik as Bishop of Sigtuna. That Bishop Henrik is being called 'of Uppsala' as he consecrated the church of Botkyrka south of Stockholm in 1129 – in a region which must have belonged to the original Sigtuna diocese and later was part of the diocese of Strängnäs – must be ascribed to the hagiographic author's adjustment to the diocesan boundaries valid at the time when 'Vita sancti Botvidi' was composed.

Bishop Henrik had been working in the missionary field and had gone to Denmark, where he died in battle in 1134. Bishop Siward may have been working in the field in the 1120s, to be back in Germany at the latest in 1132/33, never to return to Sweden. Nothing is known about Bishop Gerder's function and the actual state of a possible episcopal see in Strängnäs. All three were working in the mission. Henrik and Siward seem to have met a non-Christian resistance strong enough to drive them out of the country. This shows that the Christian Church was weak in several parts of Sweden still in the 1120s and 1130s, perhaps especially vulnerable in the years of secret 'illegal' sacrifice: 1124, 1132 and 1140, if we prolong Henriksson's reconstructed list of the sacrificial cycle that far.

In Hamburg-Bremen, the tradition from Adam of Bremen was strong. His description of the sacrifices in Uppsala had spread in all circles of literary men of the period. It must have seemed most appropriate for an Archbishop of Hamburg-Bremen, once he was reinstalled in his authority over the Scandinavian mission, to try to sequester the famous Uppsala name and transform it into a Christian symbol, expressing the victory over false gods and sacrifices to them. It was clearly within his competence to establish new dioceses. If in 1123 he decided to consecrate a cleric to an episcopal see named after the famous Uppsala, he would without doubt find himself surrounded by understanding and support. Henrik, on the other side, built upon the existing Christian centre and episcopal see of Sigtuna, where the heavy stone constructions from the period, today impressive ruins of considerable size, give witness to the empirical foundations of his office. Sigtuna was based upon reality, whereas Uppsala may have been part of a programme for the future as set down by Archbishop Adalbero of Hamburg-Bremen in the 1120s.

The see of Uppsala took the lead, Sigtuna fell into ruins. The idea behind Uppsala was probably just to prove the victory of Christianity over non-Christian gentile religion with all its allegedly atrocious practices. This would explain how finally Pope Alexander III in 1164 made Uppsala the metropolitan see of a new Swedish church province.

The analysis of the situation surrounding two of the three bishops in the Lake Mälar region has made evident, that there was no strong authority in that region, neither secular nor ecclesiastic, that could protect missionaries exposed to confrontation with non-Christian practices and beliefs. The *Kalmare ledung* styled as a 'crusade' shows non-Christian resistence leading to a proper war expedition against them. The Christians in central Östergötland around the episcopal see of Linköping, as well as those in the correspondingly Christianized region in central Västergötland around Skara, may have felt as though they were living on islands amidst non-Christians who threatened them from north and south.

This makes it understandable that the realization of monasticism among the Swedes would probably be out of the question in any region other than the central areas of Östergötland and Västergötland around the episcopal sees of Skara and Linköping. The existence of a strong royal power would be a necessary prerequisite. This was the background for the foundation of Vreta around the year 1100. That two bishops were driven out of the Lake Mälar region in the 1120s and/or 1130s is a strong indication that the situation there cannot have improved very much in the 1140s at the time of the foundation of Alvastra, Lurö and Nydala. The monastic alternative had to be implanted among the Swedes with much greater circumspection than was necessary at that time, and perhaps at any time, in Denmark and Norway.

Alvastra and Nydala – royal Östergötland under Sverker

Swedish monasticism began with two women, two Swedish queens: Margareta Fredkulla and Ulvhild.

Margareta was the daughter of the elder King Inge, the founder of Vreta; her role in connection with that monastic foundation c. 1100 has been mentioned earlier. She was first given in marriage to King Magnus Barefoot of Norway (died 1103), then to King Niels of Denmark, whereby she became the mother of Magnus Nielsen. The younger King Inge, her nephew, must have died in the beginning of the 1120s, the non-Christian King Erik Årsäll may have been king in 1124, if this was a year of sacrifice. Margareta's son, Magnus, would have had a claim to the Swedish succession, and according to Saxo he also raised this claim. But since sources from Västergötland mention the name of a certain Ragnvald, who for a short while was accepted as king there but met an evil end, Magnus Nielsen's Swedish supporters may have been found solely in Östergötland (Tunberg, 1926, p. 39). His crime of 1131, as he killed Cnut Lavard, must have interrupted his possible interference in Swedish affairs, and his death on 4 June 1134 put an end to it. In one of these years, Sverker, probably of a local Östergötland family, was accepted as king by the Swedes.

The battle of 4 June 1134 also brought the death of Bishop Peter of Roskilde, which paved the way for Eskil's appointment to that see. As was pointed out earlier, connections to Sweden had to concentrate upon the regions that were thoroughly Christian. Sverker made contact with the Danish royal family. According to Saxo (*Saxon's Gesta Danorum*, 1931, Lib. 13, X, p. 362), King Niels after Margareta Fredkulla's death married the Norwegian Ulvhild, who in Norwegian tradition is said to have been married before to the younger King Inge. Ulvhild became Sverker's first wife. Her marriage to Sverker must have lasted far into the 1140s. The couple were credited with two monastic foundations: Alvastra in Östergötland and Lurö in Västergötland ('Narratiuncula', in *SM*, II, p. 138). Ulvhild is the *religiosa femina regina Suecie* (the devout lady, the Queen of Sweden) mentioned in the *Exordium magnum Cisterciensis ordinis* as the one who asked Bernard of Clairvaux to send monks to the northern peoples (quoted in the Old Zealand Chronicle, in *SM*, II, p. 35). Monastic tradition insists on the year 1143 for the foundation of Alvastra, and Lurö must have followed suit.

The circumstances and problems connected with the earliest evidence for these monastic foundations have been described recently by France (1992, pp. 27–30). The sources group in two different ways the three monasteries that came into being in the Christianized parts of Sweden in the 1140s. The 'Narratiuncula' (see below) couples Alvastra with Lurö in Västergötland, the nucleus of Varnhem, stating that these two abbeys were initiated by the royal couple, Sverker and Ulvhild, at the time Bernard was still alive. One of the annals, however, links Alvastra to Nydala on the basis that these two abbeys were founded in the same year: *1143 conventus missus est in Alvastrum et in Novam Vallem* ('Annales Colbazenses', in *DMA*, p. 10), rewritten by France (1992, pp. 27–30) as: 'The party of monks which set out from Clairvaux to Sweden in 1143 consisted of the two groups which, when they neared their destination, split up to form the twin abbeys of Alvastra and Nydala'. This way of looking at the situation of 1143 is, however, not the best if one is searching for the forces and personalities behind the three foundations Alvastra, Lurö and Nydala.

If Saxo's story of the marriage of Sverker to Ulvhild, King Niels's second wife, has any historical credence, then at least it shows that one string of Danish historical tales towards the end of the twelfth century wanted to denigrate King Niels as well as King Sverker. For, as the story goes (*Saxonis Gesta Danorum*, 1931, Lib. 13, X, p. 362), Sverker was already courting Ulvhild before the death of King Niels and even seduced her, taking her away from her husband. Whatever truth there might be in that story, power and marriage politics among rulers were not always up to the moral standards of bishops and prelates. There is every reason to believe that the new Bishop of Roskilde, Eskil, saw the moral shortcomings of King Niels and King Sverker just as well as those of Erik Emune. Above we followed the collaboration of Eskil and Peder Bodilsen in the foundation of Næstved abbey in 1135. In 1138 Eskil was already Archbishop of Lund. From 1139 onwards, when the Hamburg-Bremen archbishop's claim for supremacy over the Scandinavian mission had finally been silenced, Eskil could take full responsibility for his Norwegian and Swedish suffragan dioceses.

The problems for Christianity in Sweden must have seemed urgent to him. Eskil cannot have had any illusions about the weak position of Christianity in the Lake Mälar region and generally in the forest districts. His mind must have turned to the same remedy, the same medicine as in Denmark: Sweden needed the strength of prayer and the example of monks living a perfect life according to monastic traditions, so that not only the Danes but the Swedes as well could be aware of the strength of monasticism, which they had not learned so far. But like in Denmark under Erik Emune, the founding of a monastery for the king's own glory or, for that matter, as a public act of penitence for crimes and transgressions the king might have been guilty of during his struggle to reach power, might just have been in King Sverker's mind as well. The result would follow the Erik Emune model of making use of the prayers of monks for dynastic purposes, such as had been developing in Ringsted, though for the time being it had been stopped due to King Erik Agnus. In the world horizon of the archbishop, the same could easily happen in Sweden, if attention was not paid to the process of foundation and the legal basis for the future of the monks.

Seen with the eyes of Archbishop Eskil, it is not enough merely to recount that Nydala was the foundation of Bishop Gisle of Linköping or that the monks loyally accepted the need to have their monastery confirmed by the bishop of the diocese. Rather, the bishop's role is one of the most crucial ones in the whole story, politically as well as from the point of view of the mission. How can one explain that three abbeys in the same region were founded in one and the same year? How was it possible to convince Bernard to enter into such a project, so heavily tapping his convent in Clairvaux for men that he refused to stand by Eskil's own foundation in Herrisvad in Scania the following year? There must have been strong reasons for this investment in material resources and manpower. It is striking that one single source, the Ryd annals (*DMA*, p. 165) does not link Nydala to Alvastra and the year 1143, but with Herrisvad and the year 1144: *Conventus missus est in Heriuadum et in Nidal* (a community of monks was sent to Herrisvad and to Nydala). Under 1142, the Ryd annals had entered: *Atque conventus missus est in Aluastrum* (and a community of monks was sent to Alvastra). Evidently, to some people, even inside the monastic tradition, the foundation of Nydala was not associated with that of Alvastra but is recorded as having taken place later.

The intrinsic relation between the Alvastra and the Nydala foundations is rather to be sought in the events of 1135. Erik Emune's great donation to Ringsted in the first part of that year, motivated by his veneration for his murdered brother, had alarmed Eskil to such a degree that later in the same year he entered into collaboration with Peder Bodilsen on the great project of Næstved. Here, a true cradle of monastic life, undisturbed by royal prerogatives, was to constitute the counterweight to Ringsted, now usurped by political interests.

This event must have created a basic pattern of interpreting the value of religious life in Eskil's mind. Prayer as a magic stream of energy, forced to flow where its founder wanted and exploited by him, must have appeared to Eskil to be diametrically opposed to disinterested prayer subordinated to God alone in the detachment of true monastic observance. I would propose to interpret the Alvastra and Nydala foundations in the light of such basic categories in Eskil's mind. In the eyes of Eskil even Sverker and Ulvhild were secular rulers, incalculable and elusive as far as religious matters went, no less than Erik Emune had been. Eskil would simply not allow a royal monastic foundation to stand alone in Sweden in the situation of the 1140s. One would be inclined to assume that to influence the situation he had to negotiate directly with Bernard, the most prominent and prophetic religious leader of the time. But there is no evidence that he visited France in these years (McGuire, 1982, p. 46). Had he done so, it would certainly not have been omitted in the Clairvaux or Cîteaux sources dealing with him. Only the queen is mentioned in the *Exordium* as the one who handed in the petition for monks. Queen Ulvhild's (and the king's?) letters, as well as letters from Eskil which we no longer possess, may have worked together to convince Bernard of the urgency of the matter (cf. McGuire, 1985) – if we do not prefer another explanation, namely that Nydala was offered to the French monks upon their arrival in Sweden by the local bishop, backed up by Eskil.

For the procedure of foundation, Eskil had to resort to the bishop of the region where the first monastery might be established. Bishop Gisle of Linköping happened to be a strong and impressive personality who could be brought into close collaboration with Eskil. He participated in the synod in Lund of 1139 (*DD 1*,2, no. 77) and both Gisle 'of Östergötland' (Østgocie) and Ödgrim 'of Västergötland' (Westgocie) stood loyally on the side of Eskil in September 1145 at the dedication of the Lund Cathedral (*NL*, pp. 50–52). In 1143, when the first landed property was put at the disposal of the monks who were in the process of founding Alvastra and Nydala, Bishop Gisle, backed up by Eskil, must have been alert to a number of aspects of the local situation. The proposal to split up the group of monks that were arriving and settle some in the bishop's own foundation in Nydala may even have been a surprise. The *Exordium magnum* does not mention Nydala at all. It is as if it was not scheduled.

This discussion also has a bearing upon the sites of the two abbeys, and has been interpreted differently by different scholars.

One may find it ironic (France, 1992, p. 29) that Alvastra is situated in the middle of the best cultivated land near the eastern shore of Lake Vättern, in the hundred of Aska, where most of the land belonged to the abbey (Holmström and Tollin, 1990). That the intention of choosing the site of Alvastra was not to achieve monastic seclusion in a remote colonizing area underlines the fact that this was a royal foundation, called into existence on the conditions of the royal couple and not primarily on those of the monks. To place the first monastery on a site in the midst of a fully Christianized population in a fully cultivated part of the country was evidently born of the need of the royal couple to manifest their Christian conviction in a most visible way, so that no one would be in doubt as to where the resources of the realm were to be found. The estate at the foot of the Omberg hill is said to have been 'Queen Ulfhild's *morgongåva* or morning-gift, that is the husband's gift to his bride following the wedding night', to use James France's (1992, p. 29) formulation. The site is uniquely central in all possible respects.

For Nydala (Figure 9.1), on the other side, its comparatively remote position has been stressed: 'Built on a very secluded and remote site on the shores of Lake Rusken in the province of Småland, Nydala was much closer to the Cistercian ideal than was Alvastra' (France, 1992, p. 31). Rusken is one of the lakes of considerable size of which there are great numbers in Småland. It is situated midway between Växjö, where Sigfrid is said to have preached prior to *c*. 1060, and the southern tip of Lake Vättern. One main south–north route passed by Vrigstad and Lake Rusken, and Nydala got its property and was built in the old

9.1 The choir of Nydala abbey church. (Photograph: Tore Nyberg.)

settlement just north of the lake (Swartling, 1967; for its early documents see Gejrot, 1994; cf. Tollin, 1998). The area later called Småland, 'the small lands', consisted of three greater lands in the south: from west to east Njudung, Värend with Växjö, and the coastland Möre, the goal of the 1123 war expedition of King Sigurd of Norway, where later Kalmar became the great urban centre. North of these, a number of smaller 'lands' – furthest east Tjust – filled up the number of units in the conglomeration called Småland.

Nydala was not more remote from the central regions of Östergötland in this land of great distances than Næstved in relation to Ringsted within the proportions of Zealand. In its position it would be more confronted with problems of mission among the non-Christians in southern Småland than the Alvastra monks could ever be. In the area of Rusken, the bishop certainly had more opportunities to play a decisive role than in the royal domains of Alvastra. It really looks as if Eskil had communicated his experiences from Zealand in 1135 to Gisle, in order to make clear to him that a royal abbey alone would not impart the full blessings of monasticism to a country which, so far, was not familiar with monks.

The arrival of monks in Sweden – and monks from France, moreover – made an indelible impact upon the process of mission. It eased something of the fear the Christians had had of the easily inflammable anti-Christian feelings – between two presumed years of sacrifice according to the old calculation, 1140 and 1148. In the 20 years from 1143 to 1164, the situation developed according to the given premises, especially in regard to the royal house of Sverker. The king, after Ulvhild, married the Polish princess Rikissa and was himself killed by a thrall while celebrating *jul* or 'Yule' in 1156. Alvastra took the lead in the growth of monasticism in Sweden, but the power of the Sverker family was under severe pressure.

Lurö/Varnhem – monasticism in Västergötland

The genre of monastic foundation history furnishes us with further sources for the earliest history of the Cistercian way of monastic life in Scandinavia. The well-known foundation story of Vitskøl abbey in northern Jutland, the so-called 'Narratiuncula de fundatione monasterii Vitaescholae in Cimbria' (*SM*, II, pp. 138–42) proves that the 1140s were a highly intensive time for Christianity in Sweden with decisive events for the future position of monasticism. The existing copy of the 'Narratiuncula' from 1608 is thought to be based upon a manuscript from 1409, but the author was probably a monk from Varnhem in the twelfth century (Edenheim and Rosell, 1982). *Swercho, rex Swecie, et Wluildis regina, duos conuentus monachorum temporibus beati Bernhardi ex Claraualle, eiusdem patris monasterio, assumentes, duas ex eis abbatias in regno Swecie et patrimonio fundauerunt, Aluastrum scilicet et Lwdrhe* (Sverker, King of Sweden, and Queen Ulvhild, in bringing, at the time of St Bernard, two convents of monks from Clairvaux, the monastery of that Father, founded two abbeys in the Kingdom of Sweden with these [monks] and from his [their?] patrimony, Alvastra and Lurö) is the formula used by the Varnhem brothers in recounting the first item of their story. It makes a clear distinction between the 'bringing of two convents' from Clairvaux, referring to the monks involved, and the foundation proper, made in the form of an assignment of property from the patrimony.

Although the formula used by the monk at first sight suggests a similar or comparable development of the two abbeys from this starting-point – the two 'convents' of monks from Clairvaux were Alvastra and Lurö, Nydala is not mentioned – the formula is a rhetorical trick, of course, since the Varnhem monk knew very well how differently the two foundations developed within but a few years. Out of their patrimony, King Sverker and Queen Ulvhild founded two Cistercian abbeys – one in the central agrarian areas of Sverker's own province Östergötland, one on a little island in Lake Väner belonging to the province of Västergötland – and they settled monks from Clairvaux in both. This is the content of the first statement.

The little island of Lurö in Lake Väner is situated between two peninsulas stretching out into the huge lake from the south and from the north towards each other, thereby separating the lake into a western and an eastern half. The southern peninsula, Kålland, is one of the central and most ancient settled areas of Västergötland. In this period it constituted a hundred of its own. The northern peninsula, today Värmlandsnäs, stretches out from the province of Värmland as part of an old transit road from Norway where the distance over to Kålland could be easily traversed by boat. This was where one of the well-known pilgrim routes to St Olav in Trondheim crossed the lake (Widéen, 1949).

However, the very next paragraph tells us how the monks soon moved to Lugnås – inside the southern shore of the lake 'in the forest' – but later 'with the help of a noble woman' were 'transferred to a rich ground called Varnhem', (*de hac sylua per quandam nobilem feminam ad diuitem fundum, qui Warnhem dicitur, translatus est*), nearer to the central parts of Västergötland. Excavations on Lurö have shown that the monks must have been living long enough on this tiny island to build a proper church, the foundations of which are well preserved (Sigsjö, 1990). But Lugnås in the area east of Kålland, the Kinne hundred, is also a rather humble place, still today situated in a huge forest beyond the eastern border of the densely cultivated and inhabited part of Kinne hundred on the lake and around the hill, Kinnekulle. The seat of the monks is indicated by the place-name, Klosterängen, a small hill near the parish church of Lugnås.

Neither of the two places was well adapted for convent life: Lurö was too small, Lugnås too much out of the way. *Propter nimiam suam paupertatem* (because of utmost poverty) the monks are said to have moved from Lurö to Lugnås. If we recall that there is no record that the Alvastra monks were ever burdened by 'utmost poverty', the difference between the two royal foundations is evident. One has the impression that King Sverker did not have much ground in Västergötland to offer the monks and that he could not dispose of royal domains there. Did Sverker and Ulvhild possess real royal power only in their own province of Östergötland?

The final location for the Lurö-Lugnås abbey was given to the monks not by Sverker and Ulvhild but by a noble woman, Sigrid, who was a relative of the next queen, Christina, married to Erik Jedvardsson, in the 'Narratiuncula' styled *Christina regina vxor Erici regis Swecie consanguinea Sigridis* (one relative of Sigrid's, Queen Christina, wife of Erik the King of Sweden) (*SM*, II, p. 138).

The explanation must be found in the power of the Erik family in Västergötland. The formula used for Erik and his consort seems to indicate that the chronicle was composed after Erik had been generally accepted as king of all Sweden, which he hardly can have been – especially not by the author of the 'Narratiuncula' – before Sverker's death in 1156. According to the later legend St Erik governed Sweden for ten years, which normally has been understood to cover the 1150s.

Sigrid, the relative of his consort, first transferred Abbot Henry and his convent to Varnhem on the fruitful plains of Västergötland, then, *consilio cuiusdam potentis viri deprauata* (misled by the advice of a powerful man), forced them to move out, but hit by sudden blindness and leprosy she called them back again, whereupon she died. After her death there were a number of aggressive actions against the monks, carried out especially by local women, who gained access to the monastery, improperly dressed and badly behaved, some of whom allegedly had been sent there on Palm Sunday by a priest in the neighbourhood. These actions appeared to the chronicler as a well thought out intrigue against the monks: *Christina regina ... abbatem et eius conventum molestabat, quatinus eis expulsis locum illum possideret* (Queen Christina pressed the abbot and his monks in order to take over the place when they were driven out). Finally, when Queen Christina tried to convince Abbot Henry that he had to tear down the house where he lived 'and was used to copy his books' and have another house built nearby instead, he gave up and went abroad to plead for help and assistance (Damsholt, 1985, pp. 97–9; Edenheim and Rosell, 1982; Johansson, 1964). This in turn, so the story runs, led to the foundation of Vitskøl, for which the 'Narratiuncula' gives the date 1 April 1158.

The move from Lugnås in the north-eastern corner of Kinne hundred to Varnhem (Figure 9.2) was a move directly southwards, into the smaller, well-hidden and well-protected area of Valle hundred, cut through by a number of rivers and small lakes, which made it in a way a natural resort of exceptional character between the open plains of Skara and Skövde and – south of Valle – the hundred of Gudhem with its early nuns' convent. The migration of the Lurö monks from the island in the lake to a forest on the outskirts of neighbouring Kinne hundred, and then to a central site in Valle hundred, is a move in three stages from the periphery of the province of Västergötland into a protected site between its central agricultural districts.

For determining the chronology of the move there are several options. The chronicle states that convents of monks arrived at Alvastra as well as at Lurö in Bernard's lifetime, i.e. before 1153. It also states, that when Abbot Henry arrived in Denmark on his way to the Cistercian General Chapter and to the Pope, Erik Emune's son, Svend Grathe, and Magnus Nielsen's son, Knud Magnussen, were still alive and in power there following an agreement with Valdemar, the son of Cnut Lavard. The decisive battle, where Valdemar defeated and killed Svend, took place on 23 October 1157, so Abbot Henry must have arrived in Denmark with his monks before that date.

Sverker was dead since 'Christmas' 1156. The date for Sigrid's death is not given, but the chronicle's royal title for Erik Jedvardsson and his wife Christina indicates 1156/57 as the time when the queen forced Abbot Henry to move his house to another place. This gives us a minimum period of at least four years for the settlement of the monks on Lurö, their move to Lugnås, their transfer to Varnhem, and the conflict around them after the death of Sverker.

Evidently the span of time for the same sequence of events including Sigrid's donation of land at Varnhem, her change of attitude towards them and, finally, her illness, 'conversion' and death, may have been much longer. If we could assume that the settlement on the island of Lurö followed in the same year as Alvastra 1143 or shortly afterwards, the period may have been as long as 14 years.

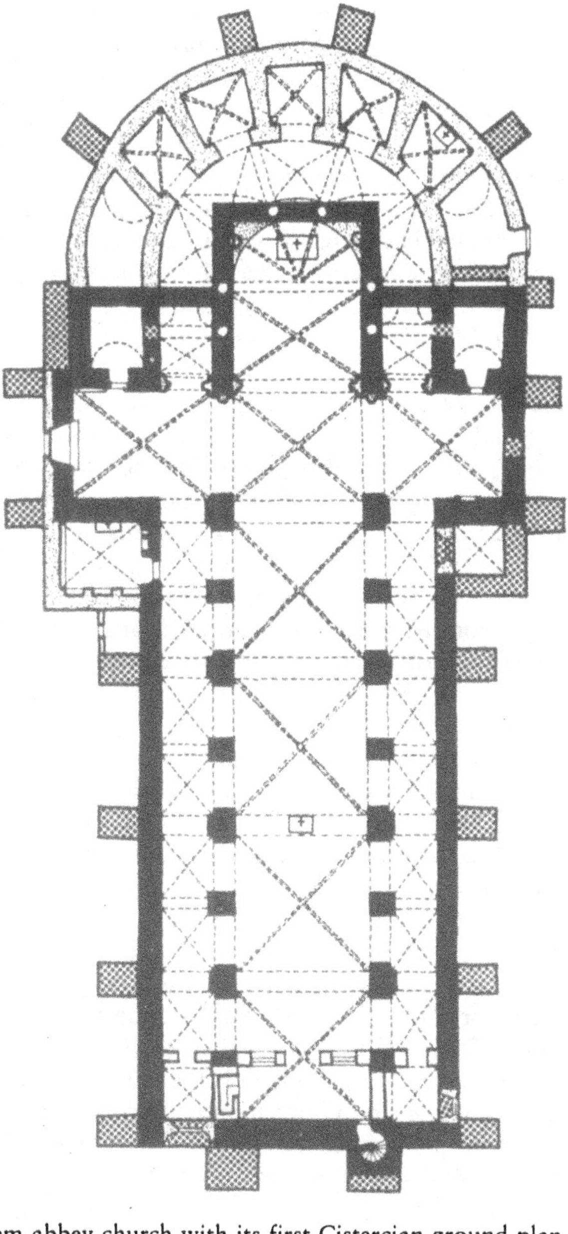

9.2 Varnhem abbey church with its first Cistercian ground plan and its later choir extension

Source: Karlsson and Sigsjö (1987, p. 33).

The information given in some of the annals, which state that the monks arrived in Varnhem in 1150, have been used to support a third option. The monks in Ryd Abbey recorded the year 1150 with the formula *Conuentus mittitur in Warnhem* (*DMA*, p. 165; cf. pp. 196 and 227). They even gave a date: *Kal.Maii.*, but the notice is blurred by the addition: *qui profectus est postea in Esrom*, which is difficult to interpret, if one does not take it literally to mean that Esrum 1153 got its monks from Varnhem. The Danish–Swedish annals 826–1415 originating in Östergötland say explicitly under 1150: *Conventus fratrum venit in Warnhem* (*DMA*, p. 301; Paulsson, 1974, 32, 375), and the annals 266–1430 state under 1150: *Conuentus missus est in Wærnem* (Paulsson, 1974, p. 276).

James France (1992, pp. 37–9) has opposed this interpretation of the entries in the annals, using entries for Øm and Løgum as an argument: these two abbeys are said to have been founded in 1165 and 1172 respectively, whereas in reality the two years refer to the very first beginning of the community, and not yet at the final spot, to which they did not arrive until 1172 and 1175. Correspondingly, he argues, the year 1150 might well refer to the first settlement of the Clairvaux monks – coming from Alvastra then – on the island of Lurö. We would then have a time span of seven years from the coming of the monks to Lurö 1150 to the clash between Queen Christina and Abbot Henry in 1156/57.

There is one remarkable detail around the death of King Sverker, however. Continuing Henriksson's series of sacrificial years beyond 1084 when non-Christian sacrifices are said officially to have come to an end, we have seen above that the years 1124 (Erik Årsäll) and 1132 (the two Bishops of Uppsala and Sigtuna forced to leave) may have been relevant for strong non-Christian reactions against Christian mission. Now, the series continues with the years 1140, 1148 and 1156. Would it be possible to set the death of Sverker at 'Christmas' of 1156 in relation to the recurring year of sacrifical offering among adherents of the old religion? To say that Sverker died at 'Christmas' must be a Christian rendering of *jul* 'Yule', which is the name for a whole season of pre-Christian origin, covering one month after the winter solstice, to be determined by the position of the moon. If we combine this information with the possibility that some Christian missionaries used the nativity style of counting the beginning of the year, i.e., making 25 December the first day of a new year, then 'Christmas 1156' might very well denote the period from 25 December 1155 to the beginning of February 1156. Since the Julian calendar was in force, 25 December would anyhow correspond to the position of the sun on 4 January according to a Gregorian time-reckoning. It is quite possible, then, that Sverker was killed in the beginning of the year 1156, and not in the last week of that year, as we would be inclined to deduce from the expression 'Christmas 1156'. In that case we would have to date the death of Sverker to the calculated sacrificial time according to the old time-reckoning, January–February 1156. His death could have had something to do with the imminent act of non-Christian sacrifice, the performance of which was once more impeded by a Christian king. This would mean that Erik Jedvardsson, perhaps already made king in Västergötland, could have already begun his establishment as king of all Sweden in the spring of 1156.

The chronicler points out that Varnhem was 'always' subordinated to Alvastra. This may indicate, not only that the repopulation was carried out with monks from Alvastra, but also that the original group of settlers did not go directly from abroad to Västergötland but gathered at the outset in Alvastra, from where some went to Lurö some time after their arrival in Sweden (Edenheim and Rosell, 1982, p. 52; Johansson, 1964, p. 68). This is at least the impression the chronicler wants to create. It is highly possible, as France also assumes, that Erik Jedvardsson was that very powerful man in Västergötland who even before the death of Sverker tried to make Sigrid give up her support of the Cistercian monks. However, there is no reason, as Knut B. Westman did (1915; 1954), to bring up a whole system of church ideologies in order to interpret the resistance of Erik Jedvardsson and Christina to the monks from Alvastra. The two may simply have felt it to be an insult and a threat that Erik's rival, King Sverker, had been trying for several years to establish a monastery in Västergötland, Erik's sphere of interest. We have to take his resistance as evidence of the limits of Sverker's power. It would be perfectly understandable, if Erik, after the death of Sverker, busy trying to succeed him and be recognized by all the Swedes, left his Queen Christina behind to attend to the further destiny of the monastic foundation in Varnhem. The sudden shift in Swedish politics towards Norway brought about by King Erik is evidence of his quick action following the death of Sverker: Erik apparently gave his support to the Norwegian Sigurd in the latter's fight against King Harald Gille, and left Sigurd's party to get organized in Västergötland during the winter of 1157–58 (Westman, 1954, p. 62).

Abbot Henry, then, must have arrived in Denmark, made his complaints and established his contacts with Valdemar before 23 October 1157. Then came Valdemar's victory. The foundation of another abbey, Vitskøl, seemed to offer a solution to the difficulties of the implantation of monasticism in Västergötland. At the same time it gave Valdemar the

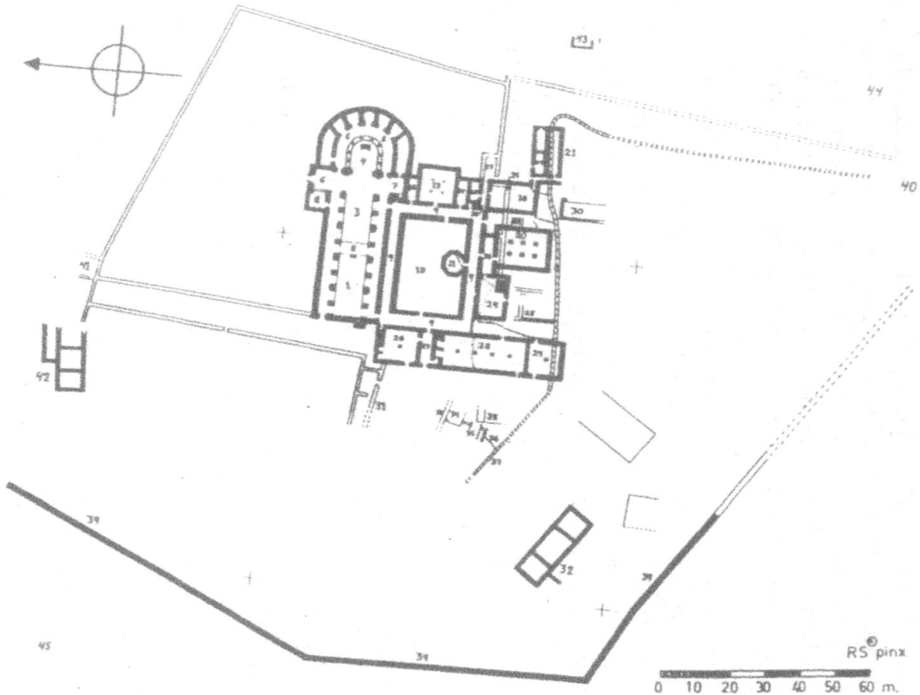

9.3 Ground plan of the church and foundations of monastic buildings of Varnhem abbey in the Middle Ages. The medieval sacristy (12), the chapter hall (13) and the parlour (14) fill the eastern wing, with the adjacent auditorium and the abbot's house (21). In the south wing there is a common entrance room (23) to the refectory (20) and the kitchen (24). The west wing is assumed to be the area of the lay brothers according to the regular plan. There is running water under the abbot's house and outside the kitchen area (37, cf. 33–6). It has not been possible to assign any specific function to a number of rooms and buildings (29–32, 38, 41–3). The foundations of the wall around the precinct have been found (39).

Source: Sigsjö (1979–80, p. 15).

chance of demonstrating his gratitude to God for his victory. The foundation charter for Vitskøl abbey was given before 18 April 1158 – as has been mentioned, the chronicle gives the date 1 April (*DD 1,2*, nos 120 and 121).

This does not mean, however, that Varnhem (Figure 9.3) ceased to exist. King Erik and Queen Christina soon 'changed their mind', as the chronicler puts it. Varnhem, he states, after having been abandoned for a time, was repopulated with monks from Alvastra and given a new abbot, Laurentius. Since Erik only lived until May 1160, he cannot have waited long to make good what the monks in the spring of 1157 apparently understood to be an evil intrigue against them. As the chronicle puts it: *Post hec cum Ericus rex supradictus et Christina regina Swecie pro discessione monachorum de Varnhem circum locum mitiores essent* ... (After this, while the above mentioned King Erik and Queen Christina had become milder concerning the discord with the monks about the place ...) (*SM*, II p. 141). Edenheim and Rosell (1982, p. 52) think that the re-establishment of Varnhem took place '*c.* 1160'; there is probably no other support for that assumption than the traditional date of King Erik's death, 18 May 1160, which is then taken to be the *terminus ante*.

Conclusion

Christianity, severely under pressure from civil wars in Denmark and Norway, and by non-Christian resistance in Sweden, found new leadership under Archbishop Eskil. From his episcopal see, first that of Roskilde, then Lund, Eskil finally won full papal approbation of Scandinavian independence from the Hamburg-Bremen archbishop in matters of religion in 1139. But after settling such questions of obedience and subordination, Eskil must have had the monastic option in mind as early as the 1130s as one of the main remedies to the threat against Christian values which he witnessed all around in different forms. Since one must accept the clear evidence of a non-Christian persecution of two bishops in the Lake Mälar region in the 1130s, the prospects for the introduction of monasticism in Sweden are clearly defined: only densely populated and thoroughly Christian agricultural regions like the central districts of Östergötland and Västergötland could be seriously considered as sites for monastic life. In the interpretation of the events that led to Alvastra, Lurö/Varnhem and Nydala, however, Eskil's personal intervention is not to be followed primarily in the choice of Clairvaux to find the monks for Sweden. More important is probably Eskil's experiences from 1135. King Erik Emune's donation to Ringsted and the foundation of St Peter's in Næstved by Peder Bodilsen and Eskil established a model and created categories of thought in Eskil which may be adduced to interpret the new Swedish beginnings of monasticism. Ringsted corresponds neatly to Sverker's and Ulvhild's foundation of Alvastra and Lurö, based on a rich royal patrimony, while Nydala, founded by Bishop Gisle, functionally plays the same role of a counterbalance to Alvastra as Næstved came to play in relation to royal Ringsted (cf. Swartling, 1967). Lurö, transferred to Lugnås and from there to Varnhem, was absolutely unsuccessful in its role as a royal foundation and was saved thanks mainly to a noblewoman who was related to the wife of Västergötland's grand magnate Erik, made king in that province probably by *c.* 1150 and accepted as king of all Swedes after Sverker had been murdered in the *jul* of 1156.

III The Danish model in Norway?

Can we find the pattern postulated above, as manifest in the Ringsted and Næstved story of 1135, in the Norwegian monastic foundations of the 1140s?

As mentioned earlier, the papal letter for Munkeliv of 7 January 1146, according to Arne Odd Johnsen's careful analysis, could partly owe its timing to the plans to introduce the Cistercian interpretation of the Benedictine rule in the diocese of Bergen. In fact, the new monks came from England. In the course of 1146, they were given the manor of Lyse at the bottom of the Lyse Fjord south-west of Bergen, part of the bishop's patrimony, and kept that name as Lyse abbey, playing with the meaning of the Scandinavian word *lys* or *lius* meaning 'light' or 'candle', from the same root as Latin *lux*.

Bishop Sigurd or Siward of Bergen (1135/39–56) was a native of his diocese. Narrative sources mention him as priest in Bergen in 1128. His predecessor, Ottar, who is known to have been in Lund on the occasion of King Erik Emune's donation to Lund cathedral on 6 January 1135 (*DD 1,2*, no. 63), must have died during the following years of violent civil war between Harald Gille and Sigurd Slembe, for at Archbishop Eskil's synod in Lund 1139, where Gisle of Linköping was also present, Sigurd took part as the new Bishop of Bergen.

Sigurd may have belonged to one of the powerful Norwegian noble families, *nobili prosapia oriundus*, as the fragmentary foundation story of Lyse tells us ('Historia Fundationis Monasterii Lysensis', 1776). The story makes him explicitly the *fundator* of Lyse (France, 1992, pp. 78–85), describing him pondering, *calore superno respersus* (as heavenly heat was heaped upon him), the fact that the *Cisterciensis consonantiae* (Cistercian concord) and the Rule of St Benedict were to be preferred to other orders because of their purity, *caeteris pro suae puritatis merito praeferendum ordinibus*. By his foundation, so the story relates, Sigurd showed the same mercy towards the poor as that which Jesus defined for those who would take their place on the judge's right hand at the day of judgement. Formally the text appears as an exhortation to intercessory prayer for the deceased founder.

At first sight, a Norwegian Cistercian abbey settled with monks from England could be thought of as being further from the original Cistercian inspiration than the Swedish abbeys to which monks had come directly from Clairvaux. A closer look at the English background makes it evident, however, that by bringing monks to Lyse abbey from Fountains abbey, the Norwegians shared the heartbeat of Cistercian inspiration and spirituality. The *Narratio de fundatione Fontanis monasterii in comitatu Eboracensi* (Walbran, 1862) tells the story of how a number of monks from Our Lady's Benedictine abbey in York in 1132 began to fear in their conscience, in words put into the mouth of a certain Richard, later first Abbot of Fountains, addressing his abbot: 'when they recalled what they had promised before God and his saints according to the Rule of the holy Abbot St Benedict at the beginning of their conversion, about staying for ever in their monastery, changing their daily habits and living in obedience'. The speech ends with Richard's conclusion: 'No one is in doubt that in the last analysis all monks make their profession, not according to the Cluniac daily customs, but according to the Rule of St Benedict'. That *adinventiones* (inventions) which are against the holy rule ought not to be defended, forms one of the arguments. Finally, in 1132, with the archbishop's help, a number of monks left the Our Lady's community in York. The following year the community entered into closer connection with Bernard and Clairvaux. Fountains abbey soon settled monks in Newminster, Kirkstead and Haverholme. The Norwegian foundation took place under the third Abbot Henry Murdak (1143–46, Archbishop of York 1146–53). One of the eight pioneer monks, Rannulph, became Lyse's first abbot.

Lyse, then, was not only a monastery in the prophetic stream of Bernhardine inspiration. It was also the foundation of Sigurd, an inspired bishop on the see of Bergen. Not only did he found the monastery, pay the expenses and bring the monks what they needed, he also held them in the greatest respect and veneration, says the author of the memorial speech about him, describing himself and his fellow monks as:

> we who have carried the burden and the heat of the day, we who have left everything and followed Christ, who have sold everything that we had, given it to the poor and followed Jesus, we who have left the borders of our homeland, resigned the heritage of our parents, given up our beautiful fields, we who have not given in to flesh and blood but have forgotten what is behind, attending the world to come, holding everything as dung for the sake of Christ, for ours is to live for Christ, death is our profit. If we have food and clothes, we are content, for we brought nothing into this world, and no one is in doubt: we will not be able to take anything away from this world. ('Historia Fundationis Monasterii Lysensis', 1776, p. 408.)

This is the monastic option in its short form, giving evidence of the very regular foundation process we have in Lyse. It was based on fundamental values of monasticism in a way that could be true for any monastery, including neighbouring Munkeliv.

What, then, was the difference between the two recently founded and neighbouring abbeys of the diocese, Munkeliv and Lyse? The question might seem ridiculous and superfluous to those historians and scholars who see the answer in a simple reference to the religious 'orders' the two abbeys belonged to: would not the contrast between black Benedictines and Cistercians offer explanation enough?

In the 1140s, however, it is very much the question whether such a difference was a decisive distingishing mark in the ecclesiastical milieu within which Lyse became a monastic site. The two abbeys differed in observance but were basically organized on the basis of the same monastic values. Instead of searching for the difference between them in an abstract entity, the adherence to two different 'orders', we ought to ask what contemporaries may have seen as the main difference between them.

First and foremost, they must have seen Munkeliv as a royal foundation and Lyse as an episcopal one. In the beginning of the twelfth century one could have confidence in Christian kingship to the degree of seeing the conviction of a king and his religious decisions as inspired in him from above, the king as an instrument of God's power surrounded by holy awe. After the murder of Cnut Lavard in 1131 and the violent revenge of Erik Emune 1134–37 – with parallel phenomena in Norway – such an outlook was shaken. The CR (*SM*, I, pp. 27–33) is our best evidence for this change of mind. It was in Denmark with Archbishop Eskil that a decisive mental change took place in these years. In the 1140s the faith in the king as mediator of holy decisions was gone. In just this situation, a bishop adhering to the principles of the Gregorian reform would seem to be nearer to an understanding of what was required for the purity of a monastic life.

Seen in this light, Lyse cannot primarily have been understood only as an abbey following the Cistercian interpretation of the Rule of St Benedict. It must have been viewed principally as an episcopal foundation, the act of its foundation thereby 'illuminated' by the Holy Spirit in quite another way than might be possible with a royal monastic foundation, depicted as tainted by the danger of greed and political purposes. Instead of referring to the Cistercians as a 'reform movement', one ought rather to point to the authority that helped implement the purity of monastic life in the situation of the 1140s. The monks themselves were not carriers of the eternal call for *conversio morum*; in the missionary period, it was the king first of all who brought into reality the institutions where monks could fulfil this call, then the bishop.

The model is that of the Ringsted–Næstved twins in the Roskilde diocese and the Alvastra and Nydala couple in the Linköping diocese. As opposed to the first, royal founder, being the first strongly to support the monastic option in the three dioceses of Roskilde, Linköping and Bergen – and here, Selja is included together with Munkeliv – we find three bishops as second founders: Eskil, Gisle and Sigurd, all three collaborating in the synod of Lund in 1139.

Moreover, as pointed out earlier, it was not Erik Emune who inaugurated monastic life in Zealand, as some scholars have believed until now. He rather usurped it for his purposes, appropriating the monastery of Ringsted, which was originally an episcopal foundation of the 1080s, and making it a royal abbey, thereby probably forcing some monks to leave for the foundation of Næstved.

So instead of understanding monastic history in twelfth-century Scandinavia as a sequence of religious orders competing on the issue of monastic virtues, it is preferable to put a pragmatic interpretation on these events and interpret the sequence of singular monastic foundations in the light of twelfth-century tensions between 'the two swords', wielded respectively within the secular and ecclesiastical spheres. The praise of the Lyse monk for his great founder is less an expression of 'Cistercian spirituality', than an example of the new confidence monks of this epoch had developed towards strong prelates, who shared their conviction of the importance of monastic purity.

The traces of these illuminated prelates – of popes, archbishops and bishops – we find in all corners of Europe in the twelfth century. The distinctive mark of Næstved, Nydala and Lyse was not the 'order' they belonged to, but the conviction of their founders and monks alike that they were members and representatives of the 'new community' of Christ in their respective dioceses, ready to take over from the old 'evil' forces dominant until these decades (cf. Newman, 1995).

Contemporaries may have observed the difference in religious habits and other observances between the monks in Munkeliv and those in Lyse, perhaps also in their attitude to the surrounding world and the way monks mixed or did not mix with people living near the abbey. What they could not know in the 1140s, however, was the long-term effects of the yearly meetings of abbots in Cîteaux upon religious observance. In this respect, there was from the beginning the institutionally installed controlling instance of the general chapter to check deviations and any slip in monastic behaviour. The two abbeys of Munkeliv and Lyse developed along different tracks in a way which must have been clearly visible to everybody after some decades. Abbots of Lyse went regularly to France, whereas abbots of Munkeliv went nowhere and were not institutionally bound to check by personal experience their stand on religious observance with that achieved in other monasteries. Not until 1206 did the logical conclusion of this set of experiences come to light by the introduction of general chapters for all Danish Benedictine abbeys under the supervision of All Saints' in Lund (*DD 1,4*, no. 111).

One year after Lyse came into being, monks from Kirkstead, a daughter abbey of Fountains, settled on the island of Hovedøya in the Oslo Fjord near an existing church dedicated to the English martyr king St Edmund (France, 1992, pp. 85–9; Johnsen, 1974). If we apply the above considerations to Hovedøya, it seems advisable not to focus too much upon the Cistercian side of this foundation. Earlier we saw that there was no male monastery in this diocese when the monks arrived in 1147. Hovedøya was the first site where the monastic life could be lived by men in this diocese – there probably were nunneries, but the problem is the dating of their foundation.

Scholars agree that our knowledge of the Bishop of Oslo during these decades, William, is very sparse. He must have been elected in the 1130s; he died in 1157 according to Icelandic annals. But scholars also agree that royal gifts played a role in the establishment of the Hovedøya property. These gifts may have been originally made by previous kings to the church of St Edmund. Whatever the procedure, the kings later stressed the royal donations to Hovedøya. In the 1140s, the Oslo region was mainly governed by the men around the young King Inge Haraldsson Krokrygg, a son of Harald Gille who had been murdered in 1136. Inge's men and their party were influential in the Oslo region and in Vestlandet and fought against influential groups in Trøndelag. In such a situation it would be strange had the people around King Inge not wanted to stress royal influence over monasticism in Hovedøya. They had the example of Lyse before them and they had the chance of being the first in the

Oslo diocese to express royal Christian intentions by founding a monastery for monks representing the essence of monastic purity.

In the following period, the new united Norwegian kingdom established in collaboration with the first Archbishop of Trondheim, Eystein, from 1153 onwards would have no problems in continuing the claims of being successors to the donations of King Inge and earlier kings.

France (1992, p. 88) has found the name of the first Abbot of Hovedøya: a certain William who appears with the title of *abbate de Hovedeie* in two charters of Rievaulx abbey prior to 1150. Abbot Philip, who previously was held to be the first Abbot of Hovedøya, later Abbot of Meaux 1160–82, is said in the chronicles of that abbey to have governed Hovedøya for seven years, which must have been in the middle of the 1150s, but *propter aeris intemperiem ad monasterium suum de Kyrkstede reversus et ibidem prior effectus in nostrum abbatem de Melsa electus fuit* (because of the rough climate he returned to his abbey of Kirkstead and became prior there. Then he was chosen abbot of our abbey of Meaux).

Returning finally to Denmark, Esrum may be mentioned in support of the view presented here. How is it that Archbishop Eskil himself all through the 1140s, as these great events happened, of which he must have been a strong promoter, was still working on the idea of collecting Benedictine monks for Esrum, part of his own property but situated in Zealand, where he was no longer bishop, when at the same time he achieved the miracle of getting monks from Cîteaux to settle in Herrisvad in his own archdiocese in 1144? Esrum must have been impracticable, and it was in any case not a success, until *c.* 1151 when Clairvaux was able to send out again a handful monks for a mission to the north, making Esrum the mother abbey for most later Danish abbeys of the Clairvaux filiation. If we believe that the role of the monastic founder was regarded as more decisive than the choice of religious order and observance, Eskil may have felt that it was more important that a bishop promoted monasticism, than that for lack of monasteries in a region a secular ruler would pick up the idea and use or misuse it for his own purpose by becoming a *fundator.* From that point of view, there would be no difference between Eskil's efforts for Herrisvad in Scania and for Esrum in Zealand in the 1140s. Esrum may have been a preventive action in the situation of a civil war in Zealand, in which one could fear that the royal usurpation of Ringsted might be cemented.

No new and previously unknown source material can be adduced in support of this view. But it may explain better the fact that in the 1140s Eskil still tried to assign to the Benedictine monks in Esrum the same role of renewal as he must had felt with regard to Næstved in 1135 and

Herrisvad in 1144. As an archbishop, he was a neighbour to the Benedictines of Lund and must have seen the possibilities linked to their observance. However, All Saints' in Lund was probably the foundation of Bishop Ricwal from before 1089. Seen in this light, there is no contradiction in Eskil's attitude concerning Esrum. An episcopal foundation would be just as good, whatever observance the monks would follow.

Finally, however, Eskil got his monks from Clairvaux. I will return to the relevance of this fact in a following chapter.

Conclusion

Monastic life in the three Scandinavian kingdoms must be said to have gone through a decisive phase in the 1140s. In the foundation process of three monasteries for men in Sweden and two in Norway, a pattern of competition between secular and ecclesiastical power has been detected, with regard to which of the two powers was best fitted to understand the monks in their struggle for the purity of the monastic alternative. King Erik Emune appropriated Ringsted for his own purposes in 1135, King Sverker founded Alvastra in 1143, Munkeliv became part of royal and episcopal Bergen by virtue of its great construction works, crowned by the papal letter of 1146, and royal intervention may have played a role as Hovedøya church dedicated to an English martyr king became the site of English monks in 1147. In spite of all that, bishops were still felt to be more apt to understand the essence of monastic life. Thus we find Bishop Eskil giving his support to Næstved in 1135, Bishop Gisle his to Nydala in 1143, Bishop Sigurd his to Lyse in 1146, and, parallel to these events, Archbishop Eskil founding Herrisvad in Scania in 1144 while working on the establishment of his own abbey of Esrum in Zealand. As McGuire (1982, p. 39) and France (1992, p. 44) unanimously have stressed against some scholars who have belittled Eskil's monastic efforts, the evidence of the *Exordium magnum* and the Øm chronicle cannot be dismissed: by being the proper founder of Herrisvad and Esrum, Eskil made it possible for men in two Danish dioceses, Lund and Roskilde, to live monastic Christianity according to the new interpretation of the Rule of St Benedict. But we may go further than that and conclude that the same urge for the monastic alternative made him effectuate the same opening for two more Scandinavian dioceses: Linköping and Bergen. Eskil's crucial role is not only Danish but Scandinavian.

Note

1. For the possibility that he founded a nunnery in the Lake Mälar area see Chapter 10 in this volume.

CHAPTER TEN

The great period: civil war 3

The king

Civil war and the overall tension between the two branches of the royal house continued until 1157, personified in the reigns of Erik Emune's (killed 1137) son Svend, made king by the Scanians and the Zealanders, against Magnus Nielsen's (killed 1134) son Knud, made king by the Jutlanders. Yet, during the minority of these boys, there was another intermediate period of peace 1137–46, when Denmark was united under one king, Erik III Agnus, a nephew of Erik Emune from his sister Ragnhild and thus a cousin of Svend.

Much of the monastic history accounted for above took place under King Erik III: the synod of Lund in 1139, the foundation of Alvastra and Nydala 1143, Herrisvad 1144, Lyse 1146, Hovedøya 1147 and the preparations for Esrum, but these were small and inconspicuous events, easily hidden from the greedy eyes of politicians.

Much more striking was the king's support for the Benedictines in Odense, which because of its public character (*DD 1,2*, no. 71, introduction, p. 138) could not be hidden. Although it is difficult to state in detail the juridical extent of the Act whereby the king settled a controversy between St Cnut's monastery and the local (or regional) dean at St Alban's church, Livo (cf. Nyberg 1986, p. 118f.; Nyborg 1979), it basically dealt with the construction of St Alban's church and was to the advantage of the monks, protecting them from claims brought forward by the dean on behalf of a group of *parochiani* (members of the parish?). St Alban's church is taken out of the *dominium* of the monks, who are not to bear the expenses of its construction. Royal gifts to the monks are recorded under 1141 and 1142 (*DD 1,2*, nos 81, 84 and 85) and *c.* 1145 an exchange of lands donated to the monks was approved at a synod in Odense (*DD 1,2*, no. 86).

More important are the entries in a number of Danish annals about how and when King Erik III died. The year must have been 1147, but only some of the annals mention that the king joined the Benedictines of Odense and died as a monk. It is easy to see that some annalists were not interested in recording such a circumstance surrounding his death. We find it in ecclesiastical milieux, as in the Lund annals, *monachus factus est, obiit Othænsø* (he became a monk and died in Odense), in the old Sorø annals, *monachus obiit Othense* (he died as a monk in Odense) and in the Ryd annals, *Ericus Lam obiit, factus monachus in Odenseh* (Erik the Lamb died after he had become a monk in Odense), from where it entered the Ribe, the Essenbæk, the Visby and other annals (*DMA*, pp. 57, 90, 146, 165, 257, 276, 301, 307). Erik III is the only Danish king who died as a monk, so these entries and the fact that all other annals only record the king's death make visible the split between major factions of society. To some, it mattered more that a double royal election followed upon his death, than that he died as a monk.

Crucial for the future was also King Erik III's privilege for Næstved of 21 March 1140 (*DD 1,2*, no. 78). For the first time, a Danish king gave to an abbey *forum ville*, the market-place in the merchant settlement surrounding the abbey, together with *omnia fori iura cum omni iustitia ac Danorum consuetudine* (the public rights connected with the market-place with all penalties [according to written law] and all revenues customary in Denmark). The special rent *quod Danico vocabulo dicitur mithsumeres chield* (which in Danish is called Midsummer tax) is also to be paid to the monks from now on instead of to the king. The money the tenants on the abbey's lands used to pay to the king for not participating in the *leding*, the Viking war expeditions, was from now on to be paid to the abbey instead (Lund, 1996, pp. 168f.), in exchange, however, for the duty of transporting the king and his men for one day once a year, if asked to do so, from Zealand to Falster, Lolland or other islands, *ut me vel meos ad Falstriam vel Lalandiam vel ad alias insulas circumiacentes deducendo semel in anno si necesse fuerit per unum diem deserviant.* There is no doubt that King Erik III, counselled by Archbishop Eskil, decided to make good the exclusive support his predecessor had given to Ringsted by favouring Næstved here in a very special and new way, which became the model for King Valdemar's similar engagement in supporting Veng and Tommarp abbeys 20 years later (Lund, 1996, pp. 170–75).

It is also interesting to put the question: why in the winter of 1138/39 the Prior of Ringsted asked the Pope for a letter of his and St Peter's protection, which was given on 1 March 1139 (*DD 1,2*, no. 76)? Did the monks feel disturbed because Erik III did not offer them the same royal protection as Erik Emune had done? Or was it important to Eskil to have the episcopal authority over the monastery, now exerted by Rico, in the form *salva nimirum iustitia canonica atque reverentia diocesani episcopi* (without offending canon law and due observation of the rights of the diocesan bishop) explicitly stated in a papal letter? Eskil did not favour the idea of making Cnut Lavard a saint and

Ringsted a shrine. Quite the other way round: on 8 August 1139, Eskil, supported by the papal legate, Cardinal Theodevin, confirmed the status of the Odense monks in their service of the diocese as a Benedictine regular cathedral chapter, a community independent of royal obligations. The Ringsted monks could not claim such a public function.

The nuns

Another aspect of monasticism relevant to the decades before 1157 may be touched upon here: the nunneries. Cinthio (1989, p. 37) believes that 'some time soon after 1145' (the consecration of Lund Cathedral), Eskil may have inaugurated Our Lady's and St Peter's convent for nuns in Lund. There are indications of royal participation in the foundation. King Erik (until 1147) or King Svend may have been instrumental in this, in collaboration with Archbishop Eskil. Numerous early entries regarding deceased nuns in the Lund necrologies show that the communion of prayer between the cathedral chapter and the nuns was at work from the very beginning. The earliest layer of entries, dated *c.* 1145–60, contains 12 names of deceased nuns. Thrugunnu/Trugundis and Gunloch may have died before the first prioress Cristina, followed by Topa and Gunnildis – if their title *monacha* is archaic. *Sanctimonialis* is used for Ida, Thora, Gudne, Wifridis, Reinburgis, Brigida, Alwigis. One Anna is *puella conversa*, but then there are four male members of the convent in the same layer: Goszuinus and Helgi are styled *conuersus et monacus sancte Marie et sancti Petri Lundis*, Galt just *monacus*, and Bertoldus *conuersus* correspondingly.

In the diocese of Oslo, the foundation of two Benedictine nunneries demands attention as early examples of the realization of the monastic option. As already mentioned, we know very little about the bishop in office, William, who died in 1157, so his share in the two foundations is unknown.

The first nunnery is Our Lady's or Nonneseter in the area of present-day Oslo, mentioned for the first time in 1161. It was generously donated and must have been founded earlier than 1161, perhaps even before the death of King Sigurd in 1130. It was located and excavated in the 1880s and its ground plan, a single nave church with square choir and a western tower as the south wing of the monastic precinct, has been reconstructed on the basis of a number of finds by Gerhard Fischer and Alf Tore Hommedal (Lunde, 1987, p. 90). In the shires of Oslo, Akershus and Hedmark, the convent owned no less than 126 *bol* and disposed of extended revenues from fishing – eels and salmon – as well as from the administration of water-mills and forests (Eriksson, 1994).

The second is Gimsøy abbey. The site lies in an area inhabited today, so its physical foundations have never been identified. Its foundation is linked to a son of Dag Eilivsson and his wife Ragnhild, residents of Bratsberg Manor near Tønsberg. Gregorius Dagsson had immersed himself in regional politics in favour of the King of the Viken area, Inge Haraldsson (Krokrygg, 1137–61) whom he had followed even during the civil wars from 1155 onwards; he fell in defence of Inge in January 1161. Regional political groups from Vestlandet and Trøndelag had slowly driven the Gregorius–Inge coalition back, but after Inge's death, one of their kind, Erling Skakke, succeeded in having his 5-year-old son Magnus accepted as king of all Norway, an event which inaugurated the Magnus Erlingsson era, beginning with the coronation of the boy king in 1163. Dag had once participated in Sigurd's expedition to Jerusalem (1108–11) and Einar Østvedt (1971) believes that the foundation of the nuns' convent at Gimsøy goes back to a promise given in return for a splint of the Holy Cross which Dag brought back from the Holy Land. Dag may have completed the foundation of Gimsøy at the latest in the 1140s (Lunde, 1987, p. 99); his daughter, Baugeid, Gregorius's sister, entered as the first abbess. Situated on the river leading up to the later town of Skien, backed up by Upper Telemark as its hinterland, the convent apparently profited from its access to water, both as a source of power for water-mills, maybe also for textile production and its processes, and for fishing rights (Eriksson, 1994). From the thirteenth century there is evidence that the convent administered lands distant from its site: in Gjerpen and Mælum parishes in Telemark, the convent owned 15 *bol*, in Tanum in Vestfold 6 *bol*, in the parishes of Skee and Bro in today's Bohuslän it owned altogether 27 *bol*.

Gimsøy was a foundation of a magnate but certainly its success rested partly upon the political influence exerted by Gregorius Dagsson.

Contrary to the two nunneries in the Oslo diocese, the convent of Our Lady or Nonneseter in Bergen possibly took shape on the initiative of its bishop, Sigurd, the founder of Lyse. At a very much later stage (fifteenth century), the nuns followed the customs of Cîteaux, but their original observance is unknown. After all, Munkeliv was the most influential monastic community in the diocese in the 1140s. Helle (1995, pp. 140–41) assumes, on the basis of its property, which among other lands also comprised the royal manor Alrekstad, that the king may have carried out the foundation of Nonnester already in the 1140s.

The site, today part of downtown Bergen, has been excavated, but it was known earlier because the southern choir chapel is still standing and in use. Its dating to *c.* 1150 rests upon its architectural relation to the constructions going on in Bergen under the influence of the Lombard building constructors from Lund who were active in Bergen in the period *c.* 1130–60, as carefully analysed by Lidén (1961), who used Cinthio's research in the construction history of Lund cathedral as a background. The foundations of a heavy west tower indicate an early date of construction within that period, which does not, of course, prove the existence of a convent at that stage. The single nave church probably had a northern side chapel in symmetry with the southern one which is still standing. The shape of the choir is not known; fragments of convent building foundations have been found south of the church (Lunde, 1987, pp. 104, measurements from 1872, 1891).

As far as Bergen, the contact system of Archbishop Eskil to ecclesiastical centres in Norway was fully at work. Probably they did not to the same degree reach the diocese of Trondheim, which now got its nuns' convent (Lunde, 1977, p. 142; 1987, p. 115). It is mentioned in scaldic verses dated *c.* 1150 at the latest, as well as in Sverre's saga, referring to events of 1183, as *Nonneseter på Bakka*. It is assumed that the nuns followed St Benedict's rule and that the convent already existed when Trondheim obtained its archbishop in 1153. Only the monks of Nidarholm represented the monastic option in the diocese, and they did in a nearly eremitical fashion, so that their share in the foundation of Nonneseter may have been greatly reduced. There is no hint as to which Bishop of Trondheim was instrumental in the process: Simon who was still in office in 1139, the Icelander Ivar Kalfsson in the 1140s, or possibly Reidar, who died in 1151.

Following the communications across the sea, northern Jutland was always closely linked to Norway. The growing harbour town of Aalborg (Knudsen and Kock, 1992, pp. 112–18), well known already by Adam of Bremen, was given its Our Lady's convent for nuns at the latest *c.* 1150. There were early contacts with Norway, and the church served as burial place to two Norwegians involved in civil wars: the royal impostor Sigurd Slembe in 1139 and a saintly man, Olaf, in 1169.

Aalborg grew up on both sides of a river running northwards and is situated just before it flows into Limfjorden, where the passage over to the island of Vendel is especially narrow. West of the river a wooden church has been dug out under present-day St Budolfi's church, which became the centrally placed middle parish between St Peter's to the west and Our Lady's church and convent to the east. Anglo-Norman decorative details characterize Our Lady's church, dated to the first half of the twelfth century. It has generally been assumed that the church was built for the convent. Apparently it was already in use as a convent church in 1139 and known as such in Norway.

Aalborg lay in the diocese of Viberg. It is a reasonable guess that Bishop Svend (1133/34–1153/54), former prior of Our Lady's regular chapter in Viberg, during his 20 years as bishop, with the many possibilities he had to create favourable conditions for monasticism, also founded Our Lady's in Aalborg for nuns. For some time *c.* 1147–50 during his conflict with his community, Prior Kjeld of Viberg had *accepta licentia in ecclesiam Aleburgensis oppiduli declinavit* (with permission withdrawn to the Christian community of the town of Aalborg) (*VSD*, 268). Every nunnery needed a priest, often called prior, for daily mass, confession and spiritual guidance, and Kjeld no doubt also fulfilled this service to the nuns during his time in Aalborg in 1147/48.

Our Lady's in Aalborg must have been one of the early projects for female monasticism in the diocese of Viberg, the two other convents of the diocese being younger: Our Lady's and St Budolfi's convent in Viberg, and St Margaret's convent in Asmild. All the nuns of the diocese of Viberg may have followed the Rule of St Augustine, like the cathedral chapter, but this is not known for certain.

Earlier it has been pointed out that we do not know if Vreta, neighbour to Linköping, in its early period *c.* 1100–60 was a monastery for men or for women. Most probably, it was a community of Benedictine monks. We would expect that after the monastic option for men had been realized among the Swedes, at some time it would also be opened for women. An early beginning of monastic life for women in Sweden has been proposed by Gunnar Annell (1983). The starting-point for Annell's conclusions is the land register of the convent of Vårfruberga on the southern shore of Lake Mälar, which had been edited by F. Ossiannilsson in 1945 and analysed by Ivar Ståhle in 1948. It was known that the nuns of Vårfruberga had moved there from Fogdö in the same area. In the land register, a kernel of lands around Fogdö is said to have been donated by a certain earl (*jarl*) Siward. Since we know all Swedish earls since 1160, says Annell, it must be an earl who lived prior to 1160. He finds Bishop Siward of Uppsala, Archbishop Adalbero's man, probably the one who was ordained in Rome in 1123 for the Scandinavian mission and was driven out *c.* 1132/34, the later abbot of Rastede abbey. Other instances of bishops who had the title of *jarl* are known, says Annell. Fogdö, then, would have been founded during Siward's time in office in the Lake Mälar region prior to 1134.

To explain how Bishop Siward as earl could dispose of lands for a monastic foundation, one would either have to assume that he was a native Swede and used family property for the purpose, or that he, in the course of missionary work in the 1120s, obtained lands which may have been used for non-Christian cult purposes or in other ways donated to him by Christian families.

Although Annell's theory seems hazardous, one must admit – considering the great number of stones with Christian runic inscriptions of the eleventh and twelfth centuries from both shores of Lake Mälar – that there is nothing in it which directly contradicts what we know of the general Christian situation in the region by 1130. An audacious explanation in accordance with the sequence of non-Christian sacrificial years could even be that a sequestration of lands destined for a non-Christian cult by Siward, for the foundation of a convent, would have been felt to be especially offensive in the sacrificial year 1132, and might in that case have given non-Christians good reasons for expelling him, as discussed in Chapter 9 of this volume.

Although Siward could be called *jarl* in Scandinavian sources, efforts from his side to found a convent for women would be in complete harmony with his general duties as a bishop for his diocese. Whatever the link between Fogdö and Bishop Siward of Uppsala, the Lake Mälar region must have had its earliest convent for nuns prior to the 1170s, because of a passage in a papal letter to King Knut Eriksson (1167–93) concerning the stay in a nunnery of his wife, the queen, prior to their marriage. There is no other candidate for such a nunnery than Fogdö, which then leads Annell to his explanation.

Augustinian monasticism

Augustinian monasticism has been mentioned earlier in connection with Dalby in Scania, the cathedral chapter of Asmild-Viberg and the early beginnings of Stavanger. For the decades around 1150 there is no doubt that Augustinian monasticism was an increasingly important religious phenomenon within the Scandinavian Christian tradition. Recruitment to this form of community life may be studied in the case of Dalby, the Augustinian community which grew up in place of the abolished episcopal see, 10 km from Lund.

Listing communities with which they had a communion of prayer for the deceased, the Lund cathedral canons mention Dalby first, followed by the cathedral chapters of Roskilde, Odense, Viberg, Slesvig and Vestervig in that order (*NL*, p. 127). In the necrology, until *c.* 1170, we find the names of the canons from Dalby for whom one ought to pray. They are indicated as *presbyter Dalbyensis canonicus*, *presbyter et canonicus Dalbyensis ecclesie*, *presbyter sancte Crucis*, *presbyter et regularis* or *regularis canonicus* and other combinations. We find one *Lothen Dalbyensis canonicus et decanus*, a dean or prior. The priestly title *presbiter* is used for Ascerus, Gerungus, Magnus, Richardus *qui et Pa dictus* (who is also called Pa), Franco, Arnoldus, Alwinus, Gerbernus, Effrem *dictus Suno*, Brother, Faderus and, further, one deacon, Gudmundus, and one subdeacon, Windane. Most extraordinary is this entry: *Anniversarius Simeonis pueri sancte Crucis canonici paralitici vij annorum* (the anniversary of Simeon, a *puer* of the Holy Cross and a canon, paralysed, seven years). Is *puer* to be taken here as 'boy' – a boy 7 years old – or as 'servant'? After all he is indicated as *canonicus*, canon. Could he have been one of the pupils at school?

We do not know how far back these entries reach, or if they cover all dead from the beginning of Augustinian regular canonical life in Dalby. Even had we known that, the year community life began is not recorded. It is therefore difficult to draw any conclusions about the size of the community from this list of deceased canons until *c.* 1170. In any case the list tells us that until *c.* 1170 the cathedral canons of Lund were informed of 15 canons who had died in the monastery of the Holy Cross in Dalby, and for whose souls they had the religious obligation to pray. Among them were 12 priests, one deacon, one subdeacon and one a 'boy' or 'servant'. One cannot disregard the religious importance of the pastoral work and the monastic observance of such a community for the archdiocese as well as for Augustinian monasticism generally in Denmark. The most famous evidence for the existence of a monastic scriptorium in Denmark is the 'Dalby Book', an illuminated Gospel manuscript written in Dalby before 1100 and the oldest extant manuscript produced in Denmark (Royal Library, Copenhagen, GKS 1325, 4°).

There are several aspects in the spread of Augustinian monasticism. The historical background for the *vita communis* of the clergy, the object of many scholarly efforts, must be found in the revitalization in the eleventh century of clerical and canonical communities that in the course of 'privatization' had given up their *mensa communis* and common property, and lifted the strict rules of celibacy. But to explain the spread of Augustinian monasticism in the twelfth century, this historical background is not enough. The 'rediscovery' of the Rule of St Augustine and its successive acceptance in a number of clerical communities opened them to influences from Benedictine monasticism in its new and actual forms, especially as personified by Bernard of Clairvaux. It is enough here to recall the mutual sympathy and friendship between Bernard and Norbert of Xanten, who in the 1120s founded Prémontré in northern France, where his successor Hugo worked out the rules for a monastic life of regular canons, after Norbert had accepted the office of Archbishop of Magdeburg (1126–34) (*Norbert von Xanten*, 1984).

In many variations, other communities of canons adopted St Augustine's monastic rule and composed statutes for its implementation. As we have seen in the case of Lund, communities might well vote against the adoption of this rule and thereby remain 'secular', as the term was coined, contrary to 'regular'. The oscillation between these two forms can be studied in several instances in Scandinavia in the twelfth century.

In spite of its different historical background, then, basically the same monastic inspiration was at work among the regular canons as among the monks. Their respective ways of life had come to resemble each other in many respects. Both were governed by the clerical members for whom the daily sung office hours and the celebration of one sung high mass and further private masses was an essential part of their daily duties. Both in principle 'withdrew' from the 'world' in a spiritual as well as – mostly – a material sense, in that the idea of an urban abbey was not the most important model; urbanization generally grew outside the reach of monasticism. Both depended upon landowning and – in spite of all ideal claims – rents paid from land cultivated by tenants. Both enjoyed comparable freedom from royal and episcopal exactions and fees. Both had lay brothers in their service for more or less extended duties inside and outside the abbey precinct. Research during the last decades has even made it evident that the role played by monks and canons in pastoral work, for example, in fulfilling the office of a *rector* (a parish priest), was totally comparable: both categories were cautious about adopting such tasks, both understood the incorporation of parish churches mainly as an addition to the monastic revenues.

As mentioned in Chapter 8, the Viberg canons must have adopted the Rule of St Augustine some time in the first quarter of the twelfth century. St Ketillus or Kjeld, who died in 1150, is the most outstanding and well-known figure of this community. The *Vita sancti Ketilli* (*VSD*, pp. 251–79), apparently written in preparation for his canonization in 1188 (*DD 1,3*, no. 150), gives some insights into the spirituality of the Austin canons' community in Viberg. Kjeld's birth is placed in 'King Niels' time' (*DD 1,3*, no. 279), which – considering his career – must have been in the early years of Niels's reign. As a young man, *vivens adhuc inter peccatores* (still living among sinners), he *transferri ad meliorem vitam desideravit* (wanted to be transferred to a better life), so he *non tantum sua sed et se ipsum disposuit pro Domino reliquere nudusque crucem post Christum baiulare* (prepared himself to deliver not only his things but also his own self for the Lord and naked carry the cross in following Christ). Through the intervention of Bishop Eskil he entered among the 'brethren in the main church who in great charity lived together there following the Rule of St Augustine'. This cannot have been much later than *c.* 1125, for after a time as *magister puerorum* when he was 'not lazy in teaching and writing', as the *Vita* says, he received 'the yoke of the priestly office'. He was ordained by Bishop Eskil, who 'after some years' was killed before the altar in the church of Asmild, an event which took place in October 1132 or 1133. The *prepositus*, Svend, whom Willo succeeded, became bishop; after Willo had died, Kjeld was elected *prepositus*.

Bishop Svend participated in the synod in Lund in 1139 together with the papal legate, Theodevin, at which a number of important issues were treated. Formed in the discipline of a regular Augustinian community he must have been a vigorous proponent of monastic life when such issues were being discussed at Lund with Archbishop Eskil, other Danish bishops, Sigurd the Norwegian and Gisle the Swede.

During the civil war, Kjeld travelled to Lund but was taken prisoner by Slav pirates and liberated, then 'friendlily received by king and archbishop' in a situation when there existed in Denmark 'another king'. Thus the king must have been Svend Grathe, and Kjeld's visit in Lund must have taken place after the double royal election of 1147. Having out of pity shared the royal gifts, which he had brought with him from Svend for 'the other king', with the poor instead, he ran into trouble with his community and spent some time in Aalborg, then went to Rome to try to obtain Pope Eugenius III's permission to preach among the Slavs. What he actually obtained was a letter reinstating him in his office in Viberg. He died on 27 September 1150. In one of the antiphons for the vespers of his feast (*VSD*), p. 280), he is being hailed as:

> *Clarus honestate, rutilans mira bonitate,*
> *Mitis, mansuetus, humilis, pius atque modestus,*
> *Induit algentes, satiavit et esurientes.*
> (Outstanding in honesty, shining in admirable goodness,
> mild, kind, modest, devout and considerate,
> he clothed those who were shivering from the cold and fed those who were starving.)

Kjeld is held up as the model for a religious. The works of mercy according to Matthew 25 are the ones held in high esteem since the days of the Roman deacon and martyr, St Lawrence and the Frankish soldier and Bishop, St Martin of Tours. The regular canons of St Augustine in Viberg have imparted the basic doctrines of monasticism. Their decision to adopt the Rule of St Augustine must have been made at the same time as the decision of the Lund canons not to do so. Instead, for Lund the same solution was found as in the Norwegian diocesan centres: a community of regular canons representing the monastic alternative arose as a neighbour to and parallel with the secular cathedral chapter.

As described earlier, the regular canons who followed the statutes of Prémontré took over St Saviour's church near the market-place (Wallin, 1989). This church was built in stone between 1123 and *c.* 1150, on a site where traces of three early wooden churches have been identified (Nilsson, 1989). It may have been used by the secular cathedral chapter between 1123, when the crypt of the St Lawrence cathedral was consecrated, and 1145 when the new cathedral could be used for daily service. Some time between those years, then, a community of regular canons took over St Saviour's church. Perhaps some of them were former cathedral canons who had not followed the decision of the majority to be 'secular canons' and therefore were on the lookout for statutes that could be used in connection with the Rule of St Augustine. During such a process the statutes of Prémontré must have become known to them very early; the Prémontré statutes began their spread throughout Europe in the 1130s.

But the spirit of the Augustinan monastic rule was not only prevalent in Viberg, Lund and Dalby. Another bishop who took part in the synod of Lund in 1139 was Sylvester of Børglum, nominated after the death of Bishop Ketil, who fell in the battle of 4 June 1134. Archbishop Eskil must have negotiated with Sylvester on a par with Svend of Viberg, Sigurd and Gisle on the future of monasticism in the Scandinavian church province. Did it have an effect?

According to earlier historians, the cathedral canons of Børglum followed the Rule of St Augustine and the statutes of Prémontré from about 1180. This dating was based on Abbot William of Æbelholt's correspondence with a great number of recipients all over Denmark and Europe mostly relating to real events in the period *c.* 1170–95. Some of these letters deal with the canonical communities in the diocese of Børglum, from where the previous dating of the origin of these communities was taken.

Yet, Abbot William speaks about them in a way which indicates that they must have existed for at least some decades when he wrote. If we consider what little evidence there is for the earliest period of a number of monasteries that are known to have existed, these letters – which are undated – cannot have any bearing upon our idea of when these communities arose. Such considerations, together with an analysis of lists of Premonstratensian abbeys which rank Børglum after Lund, but before Tommarp (Nyberg, 1975–76, 1978), and a study of the situation in the abbey of Steinfeld in the Rhineland, given as mother abbey of Børglum in some of these lists (Nyberg, 1986), lead to the conclusion that an inspiration from Steinfeld for the monastic option in the diocese of Børglum seems ever less probable the further one proceeds forwards from 1139.

First, in the early 1140s, the canons of Steinfeld had not yet adopted the statutes of Prémontré but were active in founding daughter abbeys according to papal permission given in 1136. To someone familiar with the monastic option as it had developed in northern Jutland, for instance in Viberg, Steinfeld in the 1140s must have looked just like a fervent community of Augustinian regular canons. It kept in close touch with its mother community of Springiersbach and the neighbouring Klosterrath or Rolduc, from where Archbishop Eskil's chaplain, Hermann, had arrived in Denmark.

Second, under their *prepositus* Count Evervin von Helfenstein, the Steinfeld canons responded to a call to settle in Strahow in Prague in 1142/43 – Zeliv in Bohemia followed in 1149. It was a heavy task which they took upon themselves. Evervin joined Bernard of Clairvaux in 1147 in preaching the crusade in German lands. Evervin's successor, Ulrich (1152–70), presided, when in 1163 the abbey of Mariëngaarde in West Frisia made Steinfeld its mother abbey.

During the Danish negotiations with the Rhineland monastery, Hermann must have been a key figure. Eskil had made him Bishop of Slesvig and in that capacity he participated in the 1139 synod in Lund. The period of King Erik III (1137–46) had made possible the synod and brought support to the Benedictines in Næstved in 1140 and to the Benedictines of Odense by donations in the following years. Whoever was searching for contacts within the circles of regular canons in these years would have been made aware of the Steinfeld canons, among others.

In 1139, in Lund, Sylvester had met Hermann from Klosterrath, the archbishop's confidant. Sylvester must have been well acquainted with Bishop Svend of Viberg, his neighbouring colleague, himself a regular canon and a man capable of establishing further contacts abroad. The favourable situation under King Erik III with the Næstved charter of 1140 and royal gifts to the Odense Benedictines on the one hand, and on the other the foundation of Nydala in 1143 and of Herrisvad in 1144, makes it most probable that contacts relating to a future presence of regular canonical life in the diocese of Børglum were made in these same years, as a result of a collaboration between Bishop Sylvester and Hermann from Klosterrath, inspired by Eskil. Since the lists of Premonstratensian abbeys insist on Steinfeld as the mother abbey of Børglum, the most natural interpretation is that contacts were established by Silvester and Hermann for Evervin in Steinfeld soon after 1139, before the Strahow foundation was initiated.

That this was a favourable time to create such a link can also be derived from Hermann's fate in Slesvig. Hermann was not accepted there but was seen as an intruder by the ecclesiastical community of Slesvig, which in 1137 had elected another bishop, Occo, and supported him, refusing to accept Lund and Eskil as their proper metropolitan authority (*SE VI: II*, pp. 109–11). While trying to be accepted as Bishop of Slesvig, Hermann had plenty of time to cultivate his old relations with the regular canons in the Rhineland where he came from. In fact he never got access to Slesvig. He and Eskil had to resign from their claims (1145); he died 1151 in Lund.

The most favourable constellation for contacts between a Jutland diocese and the group of regular canons in the Rhineland would seem to have been irreversibly lost, once Hermann and Eskil had had to give up their claims to Slesvig, and Sylvester had died shortly before King Erik in 1145/46. Yet, Hermann lived until 1151 and Bishop Svend may be seen to have participated at a synod in Trier in January 1148 presided over by Pope Eugenius III, so these years would still have been reasonably well suited to such contacts, provided the new Bishop of Børglum favoured them.

This, however, was hardly the case. Sylvester's successor Tuco, or Tyge, was still a royal chaplain in 1145 but is said by Saxo (Lib. 14, LIV, 29, p. 510) to have been nominated the new Bishop of Børglum by King Erik III, thus before August 1146. Then came the double royal election and Knud Magnussen was the separate King of Jutland for ten years, 1147–57. No special occasions comparable to the synod of 1139, where we would find Bishop Tyge in close touch with Archbishop Eskil, are recorded in the following years. No bishop from Jutland participated in the consecration of Lund cathedral in 1145 – the war must have made it impossible. As Tyge witnessed King Svend Grathe's gift to Ringsted abbey dated 1148 in Zealand (*DD 1,2*, no. 101), it was an expression of loyalty to Svend rather than to the archbishop, whose sanctions were quoted in the king's letter. There is nothing which allows us to assume special contacts between Bishop Tyge and his neighbour Bishop Svend, who died on a pilgrimage to Jerusalem in 1153 or 1154. After Steinfeld's provost, Evervin, had died in 1152, Tyge would have had to take up contact with his successor Ulrich, had he been the one to inaugurate the presence of Steinfeld in the North Jutland diocese. But there are no traces of such contacts in the many letters of Ulrich's that have been handed down to us.

The conclusion (Nyberg, 1986, pp. 99–102) is, that a mother–daughter relationship between Steinfeld and a regular canonical community in the diocese of Børglum was most likely established under Bishop Sylvester, still in the reign of King Erik III – that is, prior to 1146 – with the help of bishops Hermann of Slesvig and Svend of Viberg, as a direct follow-up of decisions made at the synod of Lund in 1139.

Two lists of Premonstratensian abbeys, Ninivensis II and the list from 1320, rank the monasteries of the Scandinavian circary of the order in the sequence: Lund – Børglum – Tommarp, implying that Børglum was founded prior to the abbey of Tommarp. Can the date of Tommarp's foundation help us fix Børglum's date of origin?

The south-eastern corner of Scania, where Tommarp is situated, had been a densely populated area since Viking times at least. *Terminus ante* for the foundation of an abbey of regular canons there following the statutes of Prémontré is the papal charter for Tommarp of 22 November 1155 (*DD 1,2*, no. 116). Other contemporary written testimony of the founding and construction process is lacking. But on the basis of what the charter says of Archbishop Eskil, *terminus post* is the accession of Eskil to Lund 1138, or rather the synod of 1139 as the starting-point for a planning process comprising both Herrisvad in north-western Scania (cf. France, 1992, pp. 45f.), and Tommarp in south-eastern Scania.

In his charter, Pope Hadrian IV, who had just created the church province of Trondheim, took the abbey of Tommarp under St Peter's protection, as Innocent II had done for Ringsted in 1139 (*DD 1,2*, no. 76) and Eugenius III for Munkeliv in 1146 (Johnsen, 1965). All three charters are adressed to the prior or abbot – in Tommarp his name was Patricius. All three confirm the abbey's right to the undisturbed ownership of property. The first item is always the papal guarantee that monastic order is to be preserved in the recipient's monastery for all times. The three charters display the same formula in three different variations:

> *Statuentes, ut* (we ordinate that)
>
> [Ringsted] *ordo monasticus qui secundum sanctorum patrum regulam ibidem noscitur institutus* (the monastic order which is known to have been instituted there according to the rule of the holy fathers)
>
> [Munkeliv] *ordo monasticus secundum beati Benedicti regulam* (the monastic order according to St Benedict's rule)
>
> [Tommarp] *ordo canonicus qui secundum Deum et beati Augustini regulam ... in eodem loco noscitur institutus* (the canonical order which is known to have been instituted there according to God and the Rule of St Augustine)
>
> *perpetuis ibi(dem) temporibus* or *futuris perpetuis temporibus inviolabiliter conservetur* (shall be kept unviolable there for all times to come).

The Tommarp charter mentions Eskil no less than twice – compared to no mention at all of a founder or benefactor in the Ringsted and Munkeliv charters. First, the *ordo canonicus* is said to have been introduced in Tommarp *per studium et providentiam venerabilis fratris nostri Eschilli* (by the energy and foresight of our venerable brother Eskil). Second, Eskil *concessit* (gave) the two churches of Tommarp to *ecclesie tibi commisse* (to the church which is confided to you [= Abbot Patrick]) – 'church' is here used in the more spiritual sense of 'holy community'.

Curt Wallin (1955–91, I, p. 150; 1961; 1989) has tried to work out the precise role Eskil played in regard to the foundation of Tommarp. The papal charter of 1155 does not disclose whether Eskil was a founder in the technical sense or not and, if not, who else may have been the founder of Tommarp. But we get a hint in a charter of Archbishop Esger Juul from 1322 (*DD* 2,8, no. 451) who states that Eskil *locum, monasterium et ecclesiam beati Petri in Tummathorp et conventum ibidem Premonstratensis ordinis de bonis suis fundavit et dotavit* (out of his own property founded and donated the place, the monastery and St Peter's church in Tommarp as well as the convent of the order of Prémontré there). The text proceeds to enumerate the parish churches Eskil had incorporated with the abbey: Our Lady's in Tommarp as well as Järrestad, Gladsax, Simrishamn and Vallby. Curt Wallin has demonstrated that the church dedicated to St Peter was the abbey church, the foundations of which were uncovered in 1955. The church, which is still extant in Tommarp, is Our Lady's parochial church for what soon became the town of Tommarp.

The formula from 1322 *de bonis suis* (out of his own property), however, does not correspond to reality, says Wallin. Eskil did not own anything that he could give away in south-eastern Scania, except what he as archbishop disposed of from parish churches in his diocese. Tommarp, including its water-mills, which have been excavated, belonged to the king.

This very fact provides the key to understanding how the charter of 1155 for Tommarp, although it explicitly mentions Eskil twice, nevertheless continues the line from Ringsted with its recent royal support, and Munkeliv: Tommarp was a royal abbey and as such raised to a level which entitled it to the special protection of St Peter. Could the founder have been King Erik III? We may seriously doubt that Erik, after all he had done for several monastic institutions focusing upon Odense, still possessed power and interest enough to found a monastery in south-eastern Scania, the archbishop's land. So the more, then, could his successor in Scania and Zealand, King Svend Grathe, come under consideration as the founder of Tommarp. Svend would have every reason to do much for Eskil, whose support he urgently needed. A monastic foundation according to the archbishop's wishes would be of great value to him. If so, Valdemar the Great, after his victory, would have no reason to stress the role of his predecessor, as will be seen below in analysing his 1161 charter for Tommarp.

It seems, therefore, reasonable to accept the sequence presented in the two abbey lists, and date the Lund foundation at St Saviour's church to the 1130s or possibly the years just after the synod of 1139, the foundation of a house of regular canons in the diocese of Børglum to the remaining years of Erik III's reign, 1139–46, and the foundation of Tommarp to Svend Grathe's reign in Scania and Zealand after 1147. This sequence would be reasonable from a chronological point of view and could be supported by political arguments. Construction works to secure sufficient dwellings for some canons at St Peter's church in Tommarp – which was already in existence – would not need more than the seven years 1147–54, so that a delegation bearing the supplication for a papal letter of protection could be dispatched to Italy in the summer of 1155, to be signed by the Pope and cardinals in Benevent on 22 November.

Although the Lund Premonstratensian community was not regarded as a mother abbey for Børglum, its existence in 1139 in Lund, where the synod took place, must have given it a key role for Bishops Svend of Viberg, Sylvester of Børglum and Hermann of Slesvig in their discussions with the archbishop on the future of the monastic option in Denmark. In the situation of 1139, the prospects for a foundation drawing upon the regular canons in the Springiersbach–Klosterrath–Steinfeld group must have seemed very promising, considering Hermann's background. The plans for an abbey in Scania may have seemed more distant and may even have become more concrete only after the political situation had changed with the election of King Svend in 1147.

Where did the first regular canons settle in the diocese of Børglum? As a forthcoming publication will show, the construction dates of Børglum cathedral and monastic buildings point to the beginning of the thirteenth century, which is not compatible with the above considerations. But if we give up the dogma that the canons from the Rhineland or the Danish adepts taught by them necessarily came to Børglum, another possibility opens up. The question has long been raised as to why Vrejlev, the monastic church of a convent of canonesses from the thirteenth century south-east of Børglum, displays such archaic foundations and details pointing to the late twelfth century as the time of construction. The answer is probably that Vrejlev was the place where regular canons following the Steinfeld tradition first settled when they arrived in Denmark. This first community must have gone through the same *rapprochement* towards Prémontré as the Steinfeld community did in the years after their arrival in Denmark.

Vrejlev church burned down in the early thirteenth century. In the reconstruction period which followed, old materials were reused for the windows in the northern wall that must have their original function in a church of the last third of the twelfth century. From the point of view of timing, this would fit well with the organization of a community of regular canons, which may have had its beginnings in the 1140s and acquired resources in the course of the following decades to build the first church in stone.

In the second half of the twelfth century, a community of regular canons committed to the Rule of St Augustine also arose in Vestervig in Thy, in the western half of the diocese of Børglum, the place where St Thøger had lived in the eleventh century. The relics of St Thøger had been venerated in the parish church of Vestervig since 1117 at the latest, but in the second half of the twelfth century, a huge monastic church was built nearby for a community of these Augustinian regular canons who did not adopt the statutes of Prémontré. There is no evidence as to where these canons came from. One of the bishops of Børglum, Ketillus, who fell in the battle of 1134, was apparently a native of Vestervig: *Ketillus Westervicensis* (Nyberg, 1986, pp. 84–6), but a community can hardly have existed there that early. Former scholars, who assumed that Vestervig was the episcopal see of Ketillus, consequently dated the monastic church earlier than justified by the architectural features it displays. The history of the community of regular canons in Vestervig on the island of Thy cannot go much further back than the community of those who followed the statutes of Prémontré and whom we tentatively placed in Vrejlev on the island of Vendel. Perhaps the simple answer to the existence of the two communities in the diocese of Børglum is that Vestervig was inhabited by canons who followed the original inspiration from Steinfeld, before this abbey had taken over the statutes of Prémontré, while the other community, which ultimately settled in Børglum, opted in favour of these statutes. The question will be taken up in connection with William of Æbelholt (see Chapter 13 in this volume).

Finally, from the career of one of the bishops of Roskilde, but only from that source, we learn about the early existence of yet another convent of Augustinian regular canons: on the little island of Eskilsø in the Roskilde Bay. On 18 October 1139, Bishop Rico of Roskilde had been killed in one of the many encounters in the civil war. His successor was one Asser, or Asker, who participated in the consecration of the cathedral of Lund on 1 September 1145 and in the foundation of Vitskøl abbey in 1157. After his death in April 1158, this unique entry in the Lund necrology records his *memoria*: *Ascerus episcopus*

Roscheldensis professus sancti Thome Eskils ø (Asker, Bishop of Roskilde, professed at St Thomas in Eskilsø) (*NL*, p. 67; cf. Skyum-Nielsen, 1971, p. 95). From the sources concerning Abbot William, who founded the house of Augustinian regular canons in Æbelholt, we know that Eskilsø was the first place he came to when arriving from France in 1165 or 1166. The foundations of the church in Eskilsø have been excavated; it is a small, one-nave church with apse from the early twelfth century, about 18 m long if the tower, which was added in the second half of the century, is not counted (*DK*, II, 4, 1975, pp. 2635–9).

But when did Asker make his profession in Eskilsø, and when did he actually succeed to the episcopal see? His unique necrology entry with its singular mention of St Thomas in Eskilsø must have been meant as a positive connotation in the eyes of the Lund cathedral scribe. We do not know what Asker did between his nomination in 1139/40 until 1 September 1145, when he as *Aszerus Selandie episcopus* was mentioned before Gisle, Ödgrim and Hermann in the notification of the consecration of Lund cathedral (*DD 1,2*, no. 88). The community of St Thomas would seem to have existed in Eskilsø in 1139, or at least in the early 1140s. There is, however, another possibility: that Asker made his profession late in life, perhaps on his deathbed, or that he resigned or was forced to retire from the chair of Roskilde to a monastic site in connection with the nomination of Absalon as Bishop of Roskilde in 1157/58. In that case, the obituary notice would not prove the existence of St Thomas's Augustinian monastery in Eskilsø in 1139, but *c.* 1158.

Whatever alternative is most probable, we are faced with the quest for the intentions and motives which could have led to the establishment of this little monastic community. We have the choice between the mid-1130s with Eskil as Bishop of Roskilde, an initiative taken under the warrior Bishop Rico, who fell in 1139, and a foundation dating from Bishop Asker's own time in office 1139/40–1158. If Asker's own profession as a regular canon occurred only after the victory of King Valdemar in 1157, then the community had been in existence only a few years when Abbot William arrived.

Abbot William reacted negatively when King Valdemar sent himself and three more canons from Paris via Ringsted to Eskilsø in August of 1165 or 1166 to try to clear up the situation there. Although the description of the state of Eskilsø upon the arrival of Abbot William belongs to his *Vita* and carries the mark of an element in his life story (*VSD*, pp. 320ff.), it is nevertheless striking that there is no mention of a founder or of the origin of the property which the few canons had at their disposal, though in great poverty. The whole account has been styled to extol the humility and endurance of Abbot William. Eskilsø itself seems to have been born out of nothing, and it was also, logically, given up in favour of Æbelholt. An explanation of this silence could be that Bishop or Archbishop Eskil was in fact the man who inspired the foundation and that his role was suppressed, because at the time the *Vita* was composed – Abbot William died in 1203 and was canonized in 1224 – Eskil was *persona non grata* in Danish history writing. Eskilsø may well have been a monastic foundation initiated by Eskil and carried on for a while by Asser of Roskilde without this being said explicitly, except for the entry on Asser's death in the Lund necrology.

Summing up, monasticism was a dynamic movement everywhere around the middle of the twelfth century. But no single institution was the pioneer. Monasticism was favoured and patronized for pastoral reasons by upright bishops and prelates, who sometimes were able to convince those in power of the necessity or the religious merit of making donations to monastic institutions. In this epoch, the monastic alternative could be realized only if revenues from landed property could be diverted to the use of the 'poor of Christ'. They were *pauperes Christi* because they had promised to refrain from exerting their natural right of disposing of individual property.

How old were those who took their monastic vows we seldom know. If the general trend of the epoch holds true for North-Western Europe as well, younger sons and daughters, often brought up in close contact with religious and/or monastic institutions, made up the bulk of monks and nuns. They must have come from all those better-off families to whom the new Christian religion opened up new perspectives upon crucial issues of society.

Since the beginning of civil war in Denmark and Norway *c.* 1130 and the demonstration of still serious resistance against the Christian mission in Sweden at the same time, monasteries must also have been felt to offer protection against violence of all kinds. The implantation of the Christian message against the background of a monastic community kept together by a strong group consciousness could be understood as a primary pastoral task, as we may suppose, for example, was the case at the foundation of Tommarp. The special use which the highest political authority made of monasteries in some cases, in the service of their forefathers and their own *memoria* for all eternity, may in other, more religious, circles have been understood as a deviation. Whatever intentions were behind each particular monastic foundation, they all take shape within a general pattern which remains more or less the same for all monastic institutions, without decisive distinguishing marks, until well into the twelfth century.

CHAPTER ELEVEN

The Valdemarian age 1: 1157 and the coming of competition

In the preceding chapters on early monasticism in Scandinavia the civil wars of Denmark and Norway have been assigned the significance of putting their stamp upon an entire epoch. The final victory of Valdemar the Great over his competitors in 1157 has given to Danish historiography the symbol of transition from the period of the civil wars to that of the new dynasty of the 'Valdemarians' governing Denmark until 1241 under Valdemar the Great (1157–82) and his two sons Cnut VI (1182–1202) and Valdemar II (1202–41). Denmark's weight in the Scandinavian approach to Christian European culture was considerable, which makes Valdemar's victory in 1157 equally important to the two neighbouring kingdoms of Norway and Sweden. As already demonstrated, the Danish period of civil wars corresponded in Norway to a similar period of bloody interior clashes, whereas the Swedish situation in the same decades is better characterized as a period of religious war. The scholarly treatment of monasticism in Scandinavia in the decades following Valdemar's victory in 1157 must take into account the overwhelming importance of this Danish dynasty for the two neighbouring kingdoms and for the whole North Sea and Baltic region. Although the three Valdemarian kings never 'reigned' in Norway and Sweden, the Danish influence was so strong that all important events in Danish politics and public life had their repercussions in the region.

I Summing up: kings in the secular church and the monasteries

Interaction where religious orders and institutions are involved can mean many things. One may think of interaction as a form of confrontation and competition. There are several examples of competition and tensions between monastic orders and houses in Scandinavia even prior to the 1220s, when the Mendicants arrived. Tension arose where new monks arrived from abroad, when the existence of smaller communities was threatened by bigger ones that had better means to propagate their religious values. Tensions arose about goods and property, and about individual monks who were at odds with their superiors. Tensions between regular and secular clergy are more or less built into the whole system of a hierarchical, as opposed to a monastic, church, both with their supreme head in the Pope, the successor of St Peter and the vicar of Christ.

But one may also think of interaction in the sense of collaboration, when one community learns from another how to tackle common problems of monastic life, or when two superiors of religious houses are closely linked to each other by bonds of friendship, sharing religious ideals and aims. Correspondingly, the relationship between a bishop and/or his cathedral chapter, and a religious house mostly implies a learning process which affects both parties and contributes to a change and adjustment of their views.

Evidently, monasticism is unthinkable without monks and nuns entering into collaboration with the secular power, either with the supreme authority of one country, the king, or with mighty families and dynasties invested with regional or local power. But in order to grasp the idea of monastic life as such, northerners had first to go through the experience of conversion. This process was intimately connected with the emergence of a Christian kingship, by force of which not only tribes and regions, but whole conglomerates of such local units were brought together into more comprehensive structures, following patterns prevalent in continental and insular Europe.

After the first Christian kings had enforced baptism upon their men – Harald Blueteeth in Denmark in the 960s, Olav Tryggvesson in Norway in the 990s, Olof Skötkonung in Sweden in the first decade of the eleventh century – the story of Christian kingship began in Scandinavia.

Kingship was still inspired by the memory of the origin of royal good fortune in divine forefathers, but it received new strength from the sacred character which the hierarchy of the church bestowed upon kings. Last but not least, kingship was reinforced by the ideology of the holy kings, kings venerated as saints and protecting their people from beneath the throne of God. The first holy king of Scandinavia, Olav Haraldsson of Norway, who fell in the battle of Stiklestad in 1030, gave rise to the first centre of pilgrimage in Scandinavia, his tomb in Trondheim, which had an immense importance for the further development of this idea. Of the following holy kings of Scandinavia, St Cnut (Knud) of Denmark, killed in 1086, was venerated in Odense, St Erik of Sweden, killed in 1160, in Uppsala.

One may say that Christian kingship was the first institution outside the ecclesiastical sphere with which monasticism was confronted when it entered Scandinavia some time in the eleventh century.

The first monasteries in Scandinavia were not created by the power and grace of strong kings. Scandinavian kings of the first Christian generations saw themselves confronted, not with hermits and religious idealists gathering in the forest, but with a common European culture, in which monasteries made up a formidable pressure group, evoking fascination and attraction as well as awe and fear among recently Christianized magnates of a peripheral culture. At first, the royal contribution to the establishment of monasteries consisted of fulfilling a duty towards the new religion, to which monasteries were as essential as bishoprics in order to make it function.

Yet, as has been demonstrated in one of the preceding chapters, even in the first half of the eleventh century there is still no trace of monasticism in Scandinavia, except that some of the Anglo-Saxon missionaries working in Sweden – St David of Munktorp, and 'Unaman, Vinaman, and Sunaman', the nephews of St Sigfrid in Växjö – are said in their legendary *Vitae* to have had a Cluniac background. No evidence is found to substantiate the idea that Cnut the Great, King of England and Denmark 1016–35, introduced Benedictine monasticism in Denmark. The few hints that Celtic monasticism may already have spread from Scotland and Ireland to Iceland in the eighth and ninth centuries cannot build a bridge over the century of Norse non-Christian religion in Iceland. Besides scattered references in the Icelandic sagas, one piece of evidence for Celtic influence in Norway would be the legend of the Holy Men of Selja. But even this has been deeply dipped into the bath of legend and must remain part of a general aspect of cultural exchange.

No charter is preserved which could testify to the participation of Scandinavian Christian kings in a monastic foundation in the eleventh century. Among numerous references given by Adam of Bremen on the efforts of King Svend Estridsen (1047–74) to organize Christian life in Denmark, there is none concerning the foundation of a monastery. The rich treasure of Old Norse literature has more to say about monasticism in Norway, but the information is casual and seldom praises a king because of his participation in a monastic foundation. The closest we get is King Olav Kyrre (1066–93) and his successor Magnus Barefoot (1093–1103). For Denmark, the literature around the canonization of King Cnut (1080–86) gives several hints to the monastic role of King Erik the Good (1095–1103). But since it was not a typical pattern of a Scandinavian king of the eleventh century to contribute to monastic foundations, one has to refer to indirect arguments on royal participation in such foundations, as has been done in some cases earlier in this book.

In the early period of interaction between kingdom and church, the latter was represented by its bishops. The sagas mention a number of bishops in the courts of the Norwegian kings of the eleventh century, many of them without an indication of the particular diocese to which they were assigned. Preaching, administering of baptism and counselling the kings were typical occupations of these first missionary bishops, if it was not the question of a sensational miracle as, for example, that of the ordeal of Bishop Poppo in the presence of the Danish king. Regular liturgical service and a cathedral school were among the first prerequisites for an ecclesiastical centre, as soon as a see was fixed to which individual bishops may be assigned.

In some cases a regular religious life in community came into being rather early among the clergy of the episcopal cities. In the second half of the eleventh century, however, when we hear of the earliest monastic foundations in Denmark and Norway, we can also take into account the part of bishops in these foundations. The geographical distribution of early foundations suggests that there was not yet any effort from any single community to 'cover' a specific area by trying to recruit new members from that very area. The few indications we have suggest that foreigners were the first members of monastic communities in Scandinavia. During the early formative period of Scandinavian monasticism – roughly covering the period *c.* 1050–1140 – existing monastic communities, scattered far from each other, seem to have made themselves known in the same limited circles of possible adepts to monastic life: the nobility and the warrior class with property. For the second and third generations of Danish, Norwegian and Icelandic male Christians – people born between say 1020 and 1100 – the options, if one wanted to give service to the church, were limited to either one of the recently established episcopal sees, or one of the very few monasteries, both normally to be found in the same area. The monastic option was doubtless more strict and severe than the path to ordinary priesthood or lower range of ecclesiastical service at the cathedral, especially since celibacy could not yet be enforced upon the secular clergy.

II Bishops and monasteries

From the preceding chapters we have seen that every diocese had its own monastery. There was virtually no monasticism outside densely settled and already intensively Christian areas. There is no trace of a monasticism of remote wilderness in the forests or mountains of which Scandinavia had such plenty. In the Swedish forests paganism still reigned, it could be dangerous to be a Christian out there until far into the twelfth century. Monasticism rather seems to have been understood as an alternative way of serving God in a region filled with fervent Christians and equipped with a secured number of ecclesiastical institutions.

Under such conditions, the institutions of secular and regular ways of Christian life were left to their own mutual understanding and collaboration in a constant process of interaction and exchange. The hierarchical church might have felt the need to adopt monastic characteristics and a regulated life in common with the clerics, thus paving the way for the introduction of communities of regular canons. Monasteries, on their side, had to establish potent links to all parts of society in order to survive: the royal house, great landowning families, and bishops would be their support. Liturgy and literacy would be a common heritage of both main branches of church life, and neither the clergy around the bishop, nor monks and canons, could afford to withdraw from pastoral concerns.

During the reorganization of the Norwegian church under King Olav Kyrre (1066–93) the first bishop explicitly nominated to the see of Nidaros was Adalbert or *Aðalbriktr*, mentioned by Adam of Bremen as Bishop of the Orkneys. The Benedictine settlement on the island of Nidarholm outside Nidaros is believed to have come into being *c.* 1100, which probably means during the time in office of this bishop.

Selja with St Alban's abbey arose under the first Bishop of Vestlandet, the German Bernhard *hinn saxlenzki*, who after years in Rome and on Iceland took up residence on Selja from *c.* 1070. This abbey cannot possibly have been founded without the bishop's active assistance, which might have been motivated by his wish to leave an institution behind on the pilgrimage island while moving the bishopric to the growing urban settlement of Bergen, where he died.

That the diocese of Skara, covering the regions of Västergötland and Värmland, does not prove any Benedictine presence must be explained by the early and rather special process of Christianization of this province. Paganism was still strong in the 1060s after Skara had been the episcopal see already for some time, as testified by Adam (IV, ch. 9). He combines the destruction of idols with Bishop Egino of Dalby's travels in the diocese of Skara in support of the Christians there: *Ibi etiam opinatissimum Fricconis simulacrum in frusta concidit* (here he even cut to pieces a widely renowned idol of Frey). The diocese was presided over by two strong German bishops, the older Adalvard (1060–64) and the younger Adalvard (*c.* 1066–72?) (Johansson, 1985, pp. 411–15). Their successors Rodulvard, Rikulf and Hervard were of French or English origin with only short periods in office (Hellström, 1979). Probably during their time, the eastern part of the diocese constituted itself as a separate unit within the framework of the original single diocese of the Göta provinces, covering Västergötland and Östergötland and Småland. In this eastern part we find Vreta founded by King Inge *c.* 1100, as has been discussed earlier. It has even been discussed, whether Vreta just in these years possibly may have been planned as a future episcopal see.

Still the Swedish-born Bishop Styrbjörn, who died *c.* 1130, may have presided over the undivided West and East Göta diocese. He must have had his hands full in organizing the hierarchical church in the central agricultural areas of Västergötland with an extremely high number of parish churches, many of them being propriety churches (*Eigenkirchen*) built by well-to-do landowners (Claesson, 1989). To the east of Lake Vätter, in the central parts of the later Linköping diocese, Benedictine monasticism was present and must have contributed to the variety of church life in this highly agricultural area in the first decades of the twelfth century.

III The new interpretation: peace and tension

In Scandinavia, the fundamentally reciprocal relationship between bishops and monasteries in the earliest Christian epoch changed with the civil wars and the arrival of the Cistercians. The monks of St Bernard were filled with that spirit of crusade which looked upon the world in black and white (cf. Newman, 1995). The Cistercians introduced what in other parts of Europe may have been called the spirit of monastic reform into Scandinavia, which here is better described as a spirit of monastic competition. Monasticism of the ancient world often bore the stamp of heroic and athletic sanctity, and the Cistercians arriving in Scandinavia reproduced this new aspect of monasticism which, I believe, had only occasionally been looked upon so far as a specific characteristic of monasticism by Scandinavians.

It was easy for the Cistercians to misrepresent previous Scandinavian monasticism as decadent and in need of reform. Their vocabulary was well adapted to such language since the excessive rhetoric of St Bernard had echoed throughout Europe. They threw Germany into the second crusade in the late 1140s following the foundation of the first Cistercian abbeys in Scandinavia. The spirit of crusade associated with the Cistercians was much stronger since it was now that German mission in the Slav countries east of Brandenburg began to be called a crusade. The shock caused to Scandinavians by confrontational monasticism must have been immense, even if it did not make itself felt until after some decades of Cistercian presence.

Previous monastic centres in Scandinavia seem to have loosened their ties with any foreign mother abbey soon after their establishment. Benedictine abbots were sovereign lords and independent fathers of their abbeys. There was no oath of obedience by Scandinavian religious superiors to any mother abbey or foreign religious institution like a general chapter previous to the Cistercians. A fraternity link of common prayer was the main element in the community with foreign abbeys of, for example, All Saints' in Lund (*NL*) and St Cnut's in Odense (*DD 1,2*, nos 24, 66, 67). Although a number of Benedictine abbeys of Scandinavia sometimes are being styled Cluniac, there is no proof that any Scandinavian abbey was ever bound by the proper oath of obedience to the Abbot of Cluny as might be understood in a strict interpretation of the term.

Contrary to this, the Frankish orientation webbed into Cistercian origins was continually reinforced by the regular visits of the order's abbots to the general chapter of Cîteaux. The Cistercian allegiance towards the general chapter of Cîteaux, and thereby towards the Pope as the supreme authority behind the institution of the general chapter among the Cistercians, was a new experience to Scandinavia. It meant a first direct confrontation between the loyalty due to the ordinary bishops of the country and the internal loyalty of monks among themselves.

Before his death in 1153, Bernard managed to put his very personal stamp upon Scandinavian Cistercian tradition, not least by force of his conviction that it was a very special vocation of the order to enter into the recently Christianized Scandinavian kingdoms (McGuire, 1985). In Archbishop Eskil the new Scandinavian church province had the greatest promoter of Cistercian spirituality, a true local counterpart of St Bernard. The first wave of Cistercian foundations in the 1140s took place while Scandinavia was still the one united church province of Lund with Eskil as its mighty head, as not until 1153 was Norway loosened from it and got its own archbishop, followed by Sweden in 1164.

There is some similarity between the reform drive of the Cistercians and that of the Austin canons of Æbelholt led by the French Abbot William from Sainte-Geneviève in Paris. But the Order of Prémontré, the Norbertines, who founded the community in Lund in the 1140s and soon established three abbeys on the Scanian countryside, as well as the regular cathedral chapter of Børglum in northern Jutland, have not left any traces of a critical or condemning attitude towards existing canonical communities. The Premonstratensians also called on their abbots to travel to the general chapter of Prémontré. But probably because of the strong authority of their abbot-general, the *Dominus Præmonstratensis*, in the early period, they did not have an institution which could foster a crusading spirit comparable to that emanating from Cîteaux. The difference is so considerable that the 'reform movement' clause does not seem to be useful as a common denominator for all the participants in the new wave of monastic foundations beginning with the period of civil wars in Denmark and Norway in the 1130s and that of the Sverker dynasty in Östergötland in the 1140s. Methods and attitudes varied considerably. Scandinavians had to learn a new lesson in regard to monasticism.

The purpose of general chapter decisions was to enforce common observance of rule and statutes in those abbeys who had bound themselves to such a common observance. But one must also keep in mind that the procedure used to enforce such common observance was a distinguishing mark compared to what had been usual until then. Deviations were reported at the general chapter and one, two or three abbots in the region of the offender were ordered to investigate the matter reported, correct and report back at the general chapter on the next occasion. Any abbot could be in the position of correcting another abbot or his monks on behalf of the general chapter. The Cistercian abbot was no more an independent and sovereign lord and father in his monastery. The traditional Benedictine autonomy of the abbey as an independent family, the *ecclesia* in miniature, was slowly replaced by a feeling of universality in the striving for one and the same uniform observance and purity.

Those who favoured and gave their support to the monks of the Cîteaux interpretation of the Rule of St Benedict in Scandinavia in the 1140s cannot have been aware of the full long-term effects of what they were doing. Neither Archbishop Eskil and Bishops Gisle and Sigurd, nor King Sverker or – as we soon shall see – King Valdemar were prophetic enough to envisage the spirit of competition and a certain arrogance which would soon come out of this exclusive cultivation of religious perfection (cf. Newman, 1995, pp. 123–40). After 20 years of new monasticism, however, some results were clearly visible.

There was a growing conviction among the monks of the new observance that monastic purity and strictness does not exclude personal affection among the brethren in that monastic friendship which Brian Patrick McGuire (1988) has described with such eloquency. The first abbey in Denmark to cherish the new type of fraternal community was Herrisvad in north-western Scania. Reference has been made to its foundation most probably being a result of negotiations on the synod of Lund in 1139 (France, 1992, p. 45). Since monks from Clairvaux had long been going out to all corners of central and insular Europe to settle in new abbeys and ultimately also came to distant Alvastra, Lurö and

Nydala in 1143/44, Bernard did not wish any more of his monks to leave. Good connections must have been necessary for Eskil to secure that the mother abbey, Cîteaux, which so far had not patronized any foundation abroad, would offer its monks to Eskil. After all, not often in the 1140s did an archbishop personally found a monastery from his own property, as we must assume Eskil did, although we do not know the details (France, 1992, p. 46).

Being the first Benedictine abbey in Denmark to follow the new interpretation of the Rule of St Benedict, Herrisvad doubtless was spared and left in peace for perhaps a decade after its inauguration in 1144. It is situated on the northern shore of the River Rönneå which receives its water from the greatest lake in the middle of Scania, Lake Ringsjön, and leads it in a straight north-west direction to its estuary in the deep bay of Skälderviken. Excavations have uncovered an early three-aisle church with transept and square choir endings (Olsson, 1947). The community stood in prayer union with the Lund cathedral chapter. *Necrologium Lundense* mentions seven monks styled *sancte Marie de Herivado* who died before *c.* 1170: Stephen *presbiter et monachus*, Hugo, Henricus and Walterus called *monacus*, and Haste, Henricus and Tuki (Tyge) styled *conversus*. The *Liber daticus Lundensis* brings more names of deceased for whom the canons in Lund had promised to pray. On palaeographical criteria, an Abbot Hugo, the monks Constantius and Cristianus, a *laicus monacus* Toko (Tyge), a *conversus et monachus* Ascerus, and no less than six *conversi*: Ascerus, Azerus, Bertolfus, Glip, Ricardus and Tuky, must have died before *c.* 1200. Names of Herrisvad monks deceased *c.* 1200–1220 are a Prior Esbernus, Ako and Lucas styled *monacus et sacerdos*, and one Nicolaus *monachus*. These obituary entries do not correspond to the real number of first generation monks in Herrisvad, however, since in the 1170s the abbey inaugurated the daughter foundations for which its monks went out to settle and die in the abbeys they had migrated to.

There was never a competition between Herrisvad and any Benedictine abbey of another observance. The prayer union in the archdiocese went on undisturbed by conflicts in other Danish lands. We hear nothing of verbal attacks from the Herrisvad side against, for example, Benedictine life in All Saints' in Lund, nor in their politics of populating their first daughter abbeys, as will be seen below. Eskil governed the archdiocese long enough (until 1177) to be able to keep effective control over these monks while they began building their abbey church and monastery, and sent their brethren westwards for new foundations.

The first sign of competition between monks of the new observance and the traditional Benedictines came in Esrum, founded by the

Benedictines in the 1140s, in 1151 taken over by monks from Clairvaux who then for the first time were able to settle in Denmark. We have no sources to throw light upon the transition from one type of monk to another. It did not change anything regarding the founder family which remained the same, as we have seen above on the foundation property. There had not been enough time for a Benedictine community in Esrum to stabilize and create conditions for conflict. The number of monks may have been reduced, Eskil's authority in any case was too renowned to permit real competition between the two types of monks in Esrum.

Narrative sources, such as the Cistercian foundation stories, give us more insight into the spirit of competition between different types of monks. They were written down by the newcomers as a documentation of their vocation and their divinely committed mission. The earliest specimen of this type is, however, the introduction to the collection of deeds made by the Cistercians from Esrum, concerning their take-over in 1161 of Sorø abbey, the Benedictine foundation of the influencial family of the Hvide, the 'Whites', on Zealand west of Ringsted, and so it is hard to imagine this polemic as belonging to a later period. 'The memory of the Benedictine foundation was quite fresh when our Cistercian chronicler wrote so arrogantly about it,' wrote Brian Patrick McGuire (1974, p. 8). 'According to the author of the account, the Benedictine house founded at Sorø, probably in the 1140s was a den of sin ... the Sorø Cistercians were so totally convinced of their moral superiority to their predecessors.'

The theme of the 'blacks', the *nigri*, the old, non-reformed Benedictines, against the 'white', the *grisei*, the new, reformed orders with their monastic habit made by naturally coloured wool, was a popular literary pattern of the twelfth century to express changes and conflicts of regular life at the time. It has its prototype in the competition between Cîteaux and Cluny on the most correct interpretation of the Rule of St Benedict, the controversy between Bernard and Peter the Venerable. The Cistercians in Denmark followed this well-known pattern of sacred competition between the *nigri* and the *grisei*.

IV Danish kingship and the new interpretation

In order to find the right perspective for interpreting a few more of these narration stories, it is necessary to pause for a while at the foundation of Vitskøl abbey which predates the take-over in Sorø by four years. Vitskøl's ruins can still be seen on an eastern shore of the bay of Limfjorden leading in to the area around Viberg. Vitskøl, *Vitae schola* as its original Danish name was re-Latinized, was the first and only royal monastic foundation of Valdemar I 'the Great'. It came immediately after his victory in October 1157 over his competitor, King Svend Grathe. The king's intention to make the foundation of Vitskøl the expression of his gratefulness to God for his victory is quite explicit: *Porro miseratio divina non defuit quae me nullo opem ferente protexit et de mediis armatorum cuneis potenter eripuit* (Divine misery was not lacking; it protected me without any other help and mightily liberated me from the midst of the attacks of armed men) (*DD 1,2*, no. 120). Therefore he gave, in accordance with the vow he had solemnly made, out of his patrimony, as explicitly stated, *villam ... quae Withscuele vocatur*, to Abbot Henry and his brothers who were living *secundum Cisterciensem ordinem*, (according to the manner of Cîteaux). It is inevitable that we use this translation of the Latin expression, since at this early stage in the development of monasticism in Denmark, there is no evidence for a consciousness of a 'Cistercian Order' in the way we use this expression today, among scholars as well as in ordinary usage. The brothers were monks like monks always were, following the Rule of St Benedict. The distinguishing factor was that they followed this rule in the same way as in Cîteaux and other abbeys of the same observance.

The significance of the consent of Archbishop Eskil, who was present with the king in Roskilde in October 1157, is underlined by the king's use of the archbishop's new title and office: *apostolicae sedis legato*. The title of an apostolic legate must have been given to Eskil shortly before and this is the first time it appears. Eskil used it until the end; it was renewed for his successors Absalon and Anders Sunesen (resigned 1223) but thereafter no longer bestowed upon the Lund archbishops (Skyum-Nielsen, 1969). But I would not agree with France's way of describing this situation (1992, p. 63): 'Eskil's part in bringing the first two colonies of monks to Denmark, one from Cîteaux to Herrevad and the other from Clairvaux to Esrum, has already been mentioned. He was equally responsible for the third foundation, at Vitskøl in 1158, this time acting in close collaboration with King Valdemar'. Vitskøl is not the foundation of Eskil, but a public royal act of penitence and a demonstration of power and wealth. The monks came as a gift from heaven, exiled from Sweden, and the king seized the opportunity to combine these monks with the fulfilment of his vow. Eskil played his best card: his new papal title, which the king would have to use, in case he wanted the archbishop's acceptance. And that he surely needed.

Eskil was in no way responsible for the situation. He had no hand in the exile of the monks from Varnhem and their sudden and probably unexpected arrival in Denmark after Valdemar's victory. Against the background of previous royal monastic foundations, we can clearly identify Eskil's problems. Ringsted was one of the early cases which had alarmed him and which caused him to assist so actively in the foundation of Næstved abbey. Alvastra and Varnhem were royal Swedish foundations, not the archbishop's. Theories about some influence of Eskil upon King Sverker and Queen Ulvhild are deductions from the general situation and not supported by evidence, whereas Bishop Gisle's episcopal foundation of Nydala can be linked to Lund, 1139, and Herrisvad, 1144. Eskil's most urgent move in this situation of 1157/58 was to ensure that he was not kept outside the king's foundation. For that reason, he was able to pluck his new apostolic title out of the hat.

The source we have to deal with here is the famous 'Narratiuncula de fundatione monasterii Vitaescholae in Cimbria' (*SM*, II, pp. 138–42). McGuire (1982, p. 58) dates it to Varnhem in the early thirteenth century, whereas Johansson (1964, pp. 49f.) supported by Toni Schmid (1934, pp. 100, 204) places it in the late twelfth century and leaves open whether it was written in Varnhem or in Vitskøl. The text runs:

> *Factum est abbate Henrico de Swecia decedente et per regnum Danorum transeunte, ut in Selandie ciuitate Roschildensi synodus magna ageretur, in qua rex Waldemarus et archiepiscopus Eschillus presidebant.*
> (It so happened, while Abbot Henry was leaving Sweden and was travelling around in Denmark, that a great synod was held in Roskilde in Zealand, where King Valdemar and Archbishop Eskil [both] presided.) (*SM*, II, p. 139)

After some words about the civil war and the vow which the king had made in case the victory fell to him, the text goes on to say that Eskil found Abbot Henry to be *literatum et honestum virum* (an erudite and honest man), which is why he convinced the king that the monks roaming around would be well fitted for the monastic foundation the king had promised to establish, 'advising the king that he should put such a man in charge of the abbey which he had promised to establish'. As the abbot easily accepted and asked for a place to live,

> the king some days later sent his men to Jutland and ordered them to show the abbot the best parts of his patrimony, so that he could choose the one which fitted best the requirements of *Cisterciensi ordini*. After negotiations with the archbishop and other prudent men, the abbot made the decision for Vitskøl and immediately sent messengers and letters to Varnhem and invited all his convent to the new place which the king of Denmark had given to them. (*SM*, II, p. 140.)

Some important details can be drawn from this description. The king owned estates in Jutland which he thought might aptly be used for the foundation of a monastery. These were estates belonging to his own family property, his *patrimonium*. The king's men took Henry with them to show him some of the chosen sites. Returning with this information, the abbot turned to consult the archbishop and others. This description seems to imply that the abbot possibly did not have too much of a choice. He may have been allowed to see only a few places, some that Valdemar thought he could go without.

As for the monks of the new settlement, Abbot Henry is said to have invited all monks in Varnhem, *omnem conventum suum*, to Denmark. From that point of view the following paragraph, which tells the story of how Gerard, the Abbot of Alvastra, on his visit in Varnhem, gave the Varnhem monks the freedom of choice to go or to stay, is of interest for our understanding of the so-called persecution the monks are supposed to have been exposed to in Varnhem by King Erik's queen, Christina. It cannot have been as bad as scholars who take the Cistercian story at face value sometimes depict it. To the father abbot in Alvastra, it may have seemed too risky to let all the monks leave Varnhem – the place could have been lost althogether as a monastic site if they all left. When it says, then, that 22 monks and a number of *conversi* left for Denmark, we have to assume that the total number of monks in Varnhem was higher, and that the father abbot succeeded in keeping convent life in Varnhem going. Anyhow, as the author states, 'most of them returned to Varnhem, where they had come from': *e quibus plures et meliores ad locum Varnhem redierunt, unde exierant*. This, in turn, implies, however, that convent life cannot have been extinct in Varnhem, in spite of local problems and the Danish exodus, since we cannot assume that the view of the father abbot was ignored.

The story ends with the foundation's canonical date: *kalendas aprilis* of the year 1158. In the foundation charter from the letter-book of Vitskøl abbey (*DD 1,2*, no. 120) the king states that at a synod in Roskilde, *in Roschildensi synodo*, he had solemnly, fulfilling all legal formalities, given by holy donation, *contuli*, a village from his patrimony called Withscuele to Abbot Henry for the construction of an abbey.

The charter must have been issued between 23 October, 1157, the day of the battle of Grate hede, and 18 April 1158, when one of the witnesses, Bishop Asser of Roskilde, died. It carries no date, but the list of witnesses presenting the names of seven of Denmark's eight bishops seems to confirm that it was issued at a synod in Roskilde, which might be identical with the synod mentioned in the foundation story; we have no other source to tell us when such a synod following the victory of 1157 was held. Since, however, Abbot Henry is said to have journeyed to Jutland to inspect some possible sites after the negotiations at the synod, the charter may be a post-issue from the royal chancery, fixing in writing a gift made orally at the meeting in Roskilde.

It cannot have been often that seven bishops were gathered around the king. Their names do not, as might be expected, follow in the order of years of office, according to which, for example, Tyge of Børglum ought to be listed before Eskil of Aarhus and Niels of Viberg. The text expressly states that the charter was issued with the king's seal only *cum testium annotatione*, which supports the understanding of the charter as a post-issue confirming the narrative's report of Abbot Henry's journey to Jutland following the synod. Within the order, the 1 April 1158 was handed down as the day of foundation of Vitskøl abbey.

There is no doubt that in the situation after Valdemar's victory, Vitskøl became the most prominent royal abbey in Denmark. Within the group of royal Danish abbeys comprising Odense, Veng, Tommarp and recently Ringsted, usurped by Erik Emune from an original episcopal foundation, Vitskøl took the lead and claimed the highest rank.

Concomitantly, however, the king was not forgetful of his royal duties towards other 'poor of Christ' living their lives in renunciation for the good of the realm, in monasteries founded by his predecessors, and what could be gained by a serious effort to secure their existence. As has been pointed out before, and has again recently been stressed by Niels Lund (1996), King Valdemar gave important privileges to Veng and Tommarp abbeys 'not too long after his victory', as Skyum-Nielsen puts it in relation to Veng, whose charter has been handed down undated (*DD 1*,2, no. 123). The Tommarp privilege is dated 27 March 1161 (*DD 1*,2, no. 143). The Veng privilege (*DD 1*,2, no. 123) is a patent charter with an *arenga*[1] expressing a motivation for royal support to monasteries in general:

> *Quoniam Deo disponente, quamvis meritis nostris minime exigentibus, totius regni monarchiam suscepimus, ob id scilicet universis et divinis et humanis quantum Domino opitulante nostra sufficit valitudo prodesse curabimus. Credentes igitur resurrectionem et post huius vite mortem cum illis qui domum Dei decoraverunt nos in eternis tabernaculis portionem habituros, notificamus nos monasterio apud Weng fratribusque eiusdem cenobii ibidem sub regula beati Benedicti famulantibus colonos suos cum omni iure nostro regali, quod solvere prius consueverant exactoribus nostris propter expeditionem que Danice leyding nuncupatur, contulisse ...*
> (Since we, according to the foresight of God, although our merits in no way deserve it, have been endowed with royal power over all

> the realm, we want to make this advantageous to everyone and everything, be it in divine or in human matters, as far as it stands in our might, God willing. Since now, believing in the resurrection, we believe that we are going to have a share in the eternal mansions and after this life a death together with those who adorn the house of God, we now make known that we have afforded to the monastery of Veng and its brethren, who live there according to the Rule of St Benedict, their tenants, together with all our royal revenue which these [tenants] used to pay to our public officers for [being liberated from] the military service which in Danish is called leding ...)

Such a motivation probably belongs to the beginning of Valdemar's reign. It would be reasonable to assume that Valdemar gave this charter to the monks in Veng on his first passage to Jutland after his victory in 1157. The model for this he found in King Erik III's privilege for Næstved in 1140 (Lund, 1996).

In the royal privilege for Tommarp an *arenga* was apparently seen to be superfluous. The king gave to the abbey the (royal revenue from the) two parish churches of Tommarp together with St Nicholas in Simrishamn, besides five water-mills mentioned by name. The right to donate up to half of one's property to the abbey 'in exchange for a more permanent happiness' is explicitly stated. In the future the abbey is entitled to collect from all the abbey's servants and tenants the fee these people hitherto had paid to the king for their exemption from military service, *eorum fratres seculares, qui se suaque subiectioni eorum dederunt, eorumque colonos omnes ab omni expedicione regio iuri pertinente liberos esse demandamus*. Tommarp was hereby treated on a par with Næstved and Veng. Only one bishop testified: the archbishop himself, together with the two sons of Henrik Skadelår, Cnut and Buris, the *cancellarius* Radulf and the *capellanus regis* Henry.

V Swedish kingship and monasticism

Vitskøl, Veng and Tommarp were the three examples of King Valdemar's benevolence towards monasteries in the first years of his reign.

In Sweden there is an immediate echo of these ambitions from the holders of royal power. Most visible is the extensive new donation of Vreta by King Karl Sverkersson in 1162. Most sources agree that Vreta from then on was a nuns' convent following St Benedict's rule and Cistercian constitutions. A new construction phase set in, and the previous, impressive three-nave church with *Westwerk* was extended eastwards by a square choir with two side chapels. There is no trace of a conflict or contest with any Benedictine monks, however. Was Vreta already at that time, perhaps long since, a convent of Benedictine nuns? We cannot exclude the possibility that Vreta had been in continuous existence on the basis of the early endowment made by the elder King Inge. The impressive church, which existed before 1162, testifies to wealth.

Less studied and recognized by scholars, but opening up broad perspectives, is the creation of a monastic cathedral chapter in Uppsala, which must have happened precisely in these years. We are dealing here with the place today called Gamla Uppsala (cf. Rahmquist, 1986). An undated charter issued by Archbishop Peter of Uppsala (*c.* 1188–97) (*Diplomatarium Suecanum* [*DS*], I, no. 98) mentions it in the *arenga*:

> Be it known to all of you that out of our wish to imitate the form of the ancients, and with the aim of strengthening the state of the Christian religion and the monastic way of life at our archiepiscopal cathedral, for the salvation of ourselves and of the flock which has been confided to us, for the souls of the bishops who preceded us and for the well-being of those who are going to follow after us, we have for all future time given to the canons who dwell before God in the church of Uppsala as alms and maintenance all the tithes which pertain to the right of the bishop in ... To the same brethren we have transferred all our revenue in ...

According to Jarl Gallén (1976), the term *ordo monasticus* is a sure sign of Benedictine presence. He expressly refutes his own earlier opinion that it could denote an Augustinian community of regular canons. Gallén pointed out that the reign of King Erik Jedvardsson would be the closest bet, if we want to situate in time the installation of Benedictine monks in the cathedral of Uppsala. He uses several arguments in favour of his view, such as the Abbot Robert 'from Sweden' mentioned in the foundation story of Sorø. Where was the monastery for which he was the abbot, Gallén asks, and his answer is: it must have been the cathedral chapter of Uppsala, which, then, must have existed in the mid-1150s. Gallén believes to a certain degree that the legend's praise of King Erik's piety and church building ('Erik den heliges legend', 1954, pp. xi–xiii) is based upon reality and takes it as an argument in favour of Erik as a founder and organizer of monastic divine service:

> *Nam Upsalensem ecclesiam ab antiquis regibus suis scilicet progenitoribus fundatam et aliquantulum edificatam primo et pre ceteris aggrediens ac ministros divini cultus inibi ponens opere pregrandi et laborioso sollicite studuit consumare.*
> (For first and before other things he took charge of the church at Uppsala, which was founded by earlier kings, his forefathers, and

> begun to be built. And while installing servants of divine worship therein he strove attentively to bring the church to its final perfection by grandiose and costly constructions.)

Although neither the expressions in the Latin text, nor the existence of Abbot Robert 'from Sweden' in the 1150s can be interpreted as clearly as Gallén wanted it, Uppsala was a contested place, and a symbol for any Christian kingdom among the Swedes because of its significance as evidence of the victory over pre-Christian religion. It was important for a king to get hold of Uppsala and the Lake Mälar region as one of the areas from which traditional royal power among the Swedes had received support since pre-Christian times. Uppsala was of special interest to the family of King Erik as the place of the dynast's violent death, soon transformed into the place of his martyrdom for faith. If it is true that Stephen, the first archbishop (died 1185), was a monk from Alvastra, as later sources claim and most historians have accepted, it would certainly be against his observance to help in establishing such an archaic institution as a monastic chapter in his cathedral. If, on the other hand, he found upon arrival in Uppsala in the 1160s – he was Bishop of Uppsala before its elevation into an archiepiscopal see in 1164 – such a community already in existence, he would certainly not try to dissolve it, provided the monks held to fundamental Christian norms and fulfilled some of the pastoral duties incumbent upon them – the more so, if the monks had left Vreta to make possible the introduction of a stricter observance there. Stephen's action in regard to a regular cathedral chapter in Ribe (see Chapter 13 in this volume) shows clearly that he was not indifferent to that issue.

Gallén may be right in that the introduction of *ordo monasticus* among the cathedral clergy in Uppsala most reasonably can be linked with the cathedral chapter of Benedictine observance with its English roots in Odense. It is not surprising that due to the scarcity of evidence we hear nothing of a connection between Odense and Uppsala on this level. But we cannot exclude the idea that King Erik, if the initiative came from him, may have been influenced by the Odense model and perhaps obtained Danish or English monks from there for his chapter. If there were Benedictine monks in Vreta, Abbot Robert may have been one of them. Members of a community of Benedictine monks in Vreta in the 1150s would hardly have accepted the wish of King Erik to move to Uppsala, had they not been guaranteed the necessary space for continuing their monastic life. The monastic cathedral chapter in Uppsala, then, might just have been a continuation of male Benedictine community life in Vreta, so that it was an easy thing for Karl Sverkersson in 1162, after his victory over the slayer of Erik, King Magnus Henriksen, to oust the last monks and transform Vreta into a nuns' convent following the new signals of the Cistercians.

The most reasonable conclusion, coinciding in the main with Gallén's, is that Erik Jedvardsson in his short years as undisputed King of Sweden tried to secure service and pastoral care at Uppsala by accomodating monks there, making them fulfil cathedral clergy tasks. Such a monastic institution survived or was revitalized during the reign of his son, Knut, after 1167 and remained in existence for the following decades.

Parts of the cathedral church taken care of in this way by King Erik are still standing today, making up the parish church of Gamla Uppsala, 5 km from present-day Uppsala. This very extensive parish displays a distribution of property which is exceptional, and according to Rahmqvist (1986) best explained by the special role and endowment the monastic cathedral chapter enjoyed in the second half of the twelfth century.

Light is thrown upon King Erik's attitude to monasticism from another angle: the story of the foundation of Gudhem (Figure 11.1), the first convent for nuns in the diocese of Skara. Some time under Bishop Ödgrim (died *c.* 1150) and Bishop Benedikt or Bengt (died *c.* 1190 [Johansson, 1985, pp. 418f.]) the royal manor of Gudhem on the fertile Västergötland plain between Falköping and Skara was transformed into a convent. Its very name has been interpreted as denoting its early pertinence to the gods (Roth, 1973). The papal letter of protection given by Pope Alexander III in Anagni on one 19 January (1175? [*DS*, I, no. 72]) is addressed to *dilectis in Christo filiabus monialibus in Gudhem* without the name of a prioress. It confirms the nuns' right to retain what they have received *ex dono regis Canuti vel fratris eius seu aliorum predecessorum suorum* (donated by king Knut, or by his brother, or by others, his predecessors). It is generally assumed that Erik, besides two daughters, had only two sons, Knut and his younger brother, Filip, who may have been the grandfather of Knut Holmgersson called Långe, Swedish king 1229–34, later executed (Erikska ätten, *Svenskt biografiskt lexikon* [*SBL*], XIV). Since Filip had not been king before Knut, Knut's 'predecessors' must point to at least two preceding kings. The nearest one is Karl Sverkersson; correspondingly, earlier scholars thought that it was Karl who gave Gudhem to the nuns in 1161, the year when he became king (Roth, 1973). But Karl's predecessor was Magnus, who in turn had killed his predecessor Erik in Uppsala in 1160. Gudhem was always cherished by the Erik family. In assuming that Karl Sverkersson transformed a royal manor in the province, where his property was so limited, into a nuns' convent, we imply that he grasped the chance given to him by his victory in 1161 to dispose of property which belonged to the royal office. A motive for acting in this way would doubtless have

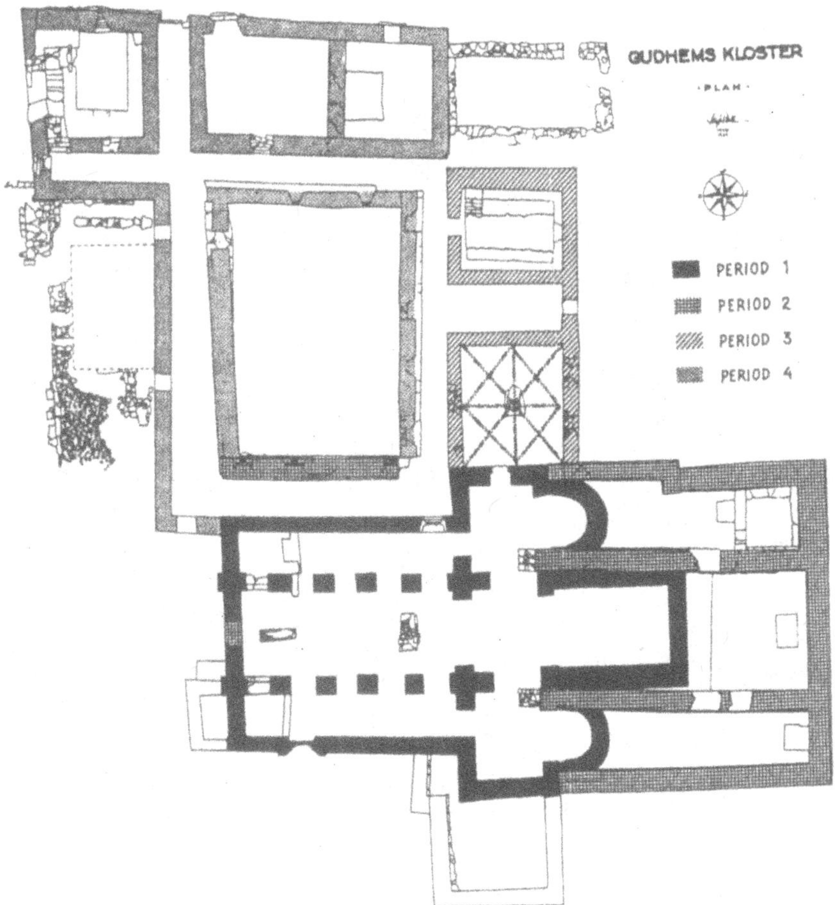

11.1 Gudhem abbey with the foundations of its earliest church in black ('Period 1'), and its Cistercian choir extension in squares ('Period 2')

Source: Roth (1973).

been to try to win support in the province of his competitors. But is this likely to be the royal foundation of a nunnery? The stone church of Gudhem with its nave and aisles is thought originally to have been built to serve the royal manor. It is not known which norm the nuns followed for the observance of the Rule of St Benedict until much later, when they were Cistercians (Roth, 1973). France (1992, p. 172), following Ortved, calls them Benedictines. Whatever hypothesis is brought forth as to when and by whose intervention the royal manor of Gudhem was transformed into a convent, it seems natural to assume that a Benedictine

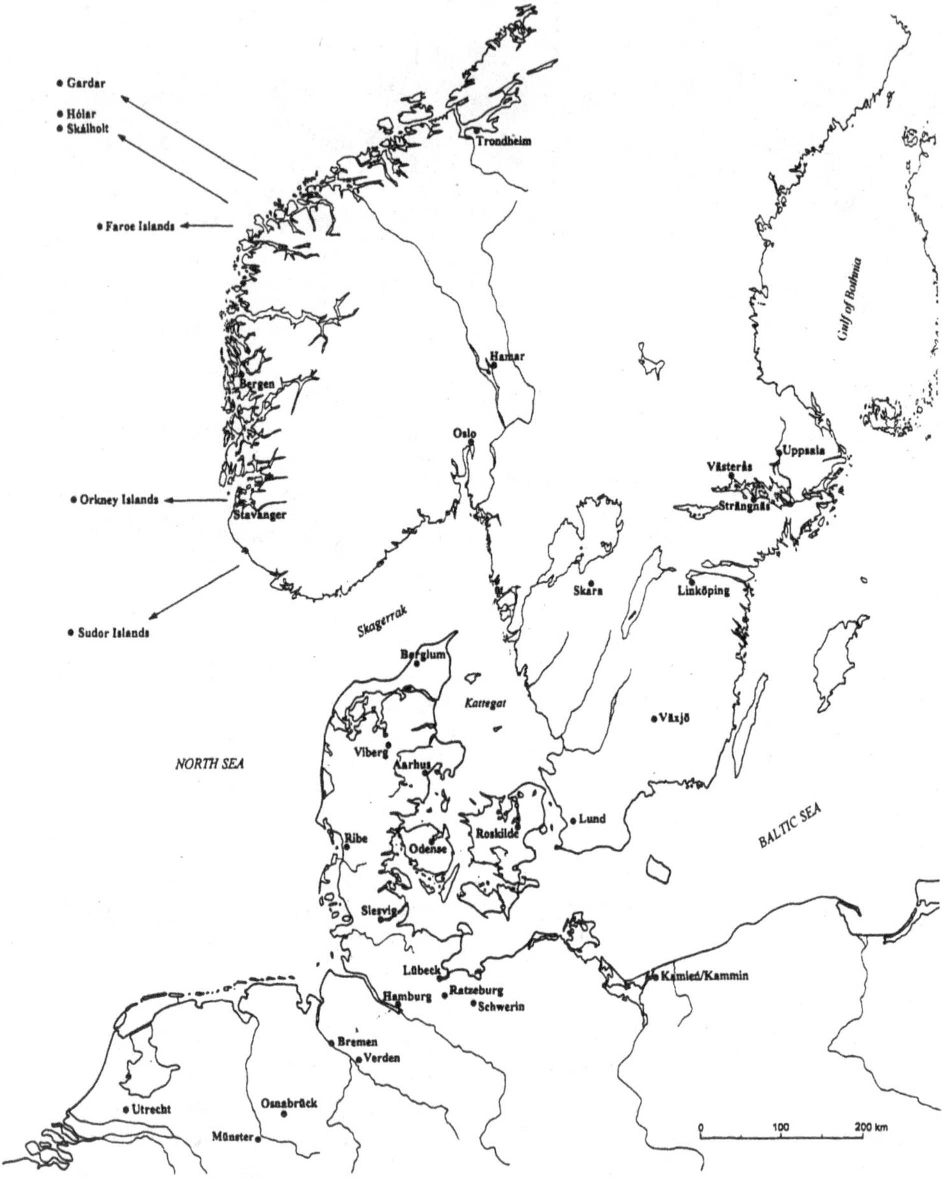

Map III Episcopal sees in North-Western Europe, *c.* 1170. (Drawn by Inger Bjerg Poulsen.)

female community already existed in Västergötland in the diocese of Skara before the death of Erik Jedvardsson in 1160. In that case, he is himself the most probable founder – not necessarily as king, since that would undoubtedly have been seen in some of the sources, but still as a powerful magnate of his province.

The background given in this chapter has generally not formed part of scholarly work on the spread of the Cistercians in Denmark or Scandinavia. The following chapter will make evident that this background is necessary if one wants to describe adequately what happened within monastic circles, especially in Jutland, in the great period of early Valdemarian power.

Note

1. The short rhetoric passage at the beginning of a medieval charter.

CHAPTER TWELVE

The Valdemarian age 2: movements among monks

I The history of 'The Precious Island'

There is no indication of the part the new diocesan bishop for Vitskøl, Niels of Viberg, nominated in 1154, played in the foundation of Vitskøl. Niels later sided with the king whenever this was necessary, also against Archbishop Eskil and Pope Alexander III (*SE VI: II*, p. 121).

We also do not know how and when his southern neighbour Bishop Eskil of Aarhus was nominated, since the charter for Vitskøl is the earliest written evidence of him. The reason for our ignorance lies in his two predecessors and their unknown fate. Ulkil of Aarhus is mentioned as the one in whose place one Illugo or Illuch was installed by King Erik Emune shortly after King Niels had been murdered (25 June 1134). He is known from the undated renewal of prayer communion between the Odense Benedictines and their mother abbey Evesham, handed down in English sources and probably to be dated 1135–39 (*DD 1,2*, no. 66). No bishop of Aarhus participated in the Lund synod of 1139 and we have no evidence for the presence of a Bishop of Aarhus in later situations when several bishops were gathered. If Ulkil was deposed, he may have claimed his rights later against Illugo or Eskil. It seems impossible to clarify whether under King Knud Magnussen, 1147–57, the Aarhus diocese was administered by Ulkil, Illugo, Svend or someone else. Within a few years, however, Eskil of Aarhus played an important role in the history of monasticism in general, and Vitskøl in particular, by opening his diocese to a daughter foundation.

A proper understanding of the history of 'The Precious Island' will include some aspects of the schism between the king and Archbishop Eskil which broke out in these years (Nyberg, 1986, pp. 140–51). It was reinforced by the schism in the universal church between Pope Alexander III and the German king and emperor, Frederik Barbarossa, who had appointed Cardinal Octavian to be his own Pope Victor IV. Archbishop Eskil's castle, Søborg in Zealand, was attacked and plundered by the king in 1161. The archbishop left the country in voluntary exile, which implied, among other stops, several periods in northern France, where Pope Alexander III resided, and a visit to Jerusalem. He returned to Denmark in 1168. The king participated in a synod held by Pope Victor IV in France in 1161. Studies by Michael Gelting on the attitude of the Danish bishops during the conflict have made it evident that all of them except Bishop Simon of Odense stuck to the king as long as Victor IV remained pope (*SE VI: II*, pp. 51, 71–4, 121). After Victor's death on 20 April 1164 there was a gradual return of European powers, including King Valdemar, to the obedience of Pope Alexander.

The schism was an important element in an earlier interpretation of the religious history of Denmark in the early 1160s (Green-Pedersen, 1981). The king's support for Cistercian abbeys in the late 1160s was taken to be significant for his return to the obedience of Pope Alexander III, since the Cistercians had not been inclined to follow the emperor and Victor IV.

In the following text no new hypothesis on the relation between schism and monastic development will be formulated. Only two aspects seem highly relevant for the interpretation of the foundation story of 'The Precious Island'. First, Archbishop Eskil was abroad and could not exert his authority through the channels of ordinary jurisdiction. The bishops who stayed to administer their dioceses had to stick to the prevalent royal policy and make up their own mind in questions of conflict between secular and religious values. Second, royal prerogatives over particular monasteries, based upon foundation rights, patronage or custom, were important issues for any monastery, regardless of a schismatic situation in the arena of power politics which did not always bother lay people and monks in daily life.

Let us now turn to the best known of Danish monastic foundation histories, the chonicle of the Abbey of Øm or *Cara Insula* (The Precious Island), where we find the first serious instance of competition between the 'white' and the 'black' monks (*SM*, II, pp. 154–264).

The chronicle sets out by giving a date of birth for the new community: on the 16 February 1165, a group of monks in the abbey of Vitskøl were sent out by Abbot Henry to a place called Sminge in the diocese of Aarhus on the fertile eastern side of the Jutish peninsula, in order to found a new abbey there. There were no Benedictines in Sminge, and Bishop Eskil of Aarhus had been instrumental in finding the place, so this first move did not yet involve conflicts with any other religious groups.

It is difficult to derive from the chronicle how things turned out next. It states that later in the same year, 1165, Bishop Eskil fell in battle against Slav tribes on the side of the king, and that his successor, Bishop Svend, together with the Abbot of Vitskøl, the mother abbey, went to the king and proposed *quod fratres in ecclesia de Weng collocarent* (that the Sminge monks take up their residence at the church of Veng). The chronicle brings only one argument in support of the proposal: that this church *conculcabatur negligentia nigrorum monachorum* (was then humiliated by the negligence of the black monks). Further on, however, it is stated that Veng had been founded by the king's predecessors. At least two factors must have worked together here: King Valdemar was the patron of Veng, and bishop-elect and abbot could convince him that the actual Benedictine monastic discipline in Veng was unworthy of a holy place and of a royal monastic foundation.

Beyond such arguments, however, one more story is being told here. Abbot John of Veng made repentance, it says; he moved to Vitskøl, wept bitterly over his sins, and converted – which actually means he converted to the way of life of Cîteaux as observed in Vitskøl – later returned to Veng, now taken over by the Sminge monks, and died there in peace. Since the next move of the community came in 1168, his death must have happened during the three years the Cistercians were in Veng. This raises the question: what function does the story of Abbot John of Veng have in the foundation recital? The monks retold it at the papal court and had it included in the papal document approving the take-over of Veng. Pope Alexander III addressed the king as follows: 'You, advised by the council of bishops, and intending its reformation, gave it for the sake of restoring observance to the brethren of the Cistercian customs', *abbate cui fuerat prius concessum de magistro disciplulo facto* 'after the abbot, to whom it was previously bestowed, had changed from being a master to a disciple'. The term *concessum* suggests an abbey *ad commendam*, as if Abbot John had been appointed by the king and not elected by his convent. Regardless of what authority had secured Abbot John his office, the supplicants at the papal court made it look as if his was an office resting upon appointment of the king, although the matter nevertheless seemed important enough to be mentioned.

On the face of it, then, the story deals with the religious impact of the Cistercian lifestyle, leading to the repentance and conversion of a sinful Benedictine abbot. But in a monastery where a royal prerogative, contained in the lost foundation charter, must have been matched by a certain legal independence of the monastery and its abbot, it seems improbable that the king could legally have acted alone in handing it over to another group of monks, as long as it was a Benedictine abbey still inhabited by lawfully professed monks of the observance which had been instituted there from the very beginning. The consent of the abbot must have been required if someone wanted the observance to be changed. The story of the conversion of Abbot John may therefore have fulfilled the purpose of proving that the transfer of Veng to the Cistercians was carried out with the acceptance of the lawful Benedictine community at the place. Abbot John may have wept not only because of his sins, but also because of the pressure put upon him by the king, a bishop-elect and a highly reputed Cistercian father-abbot to consent to the new and stricter interpretation of the Rule of St Benedict introduced by the newcomers.

There were others who did not yield to such pressure, however. One Lady Margaret is said to have carried out a property transaction with the king, intending to establish a nunnery in Veng instead. This deprived the new monks of access to parts of Veng abbey's previous estates, although her deceased brother, Count Eric, had supported the transfer of Veng to the newcomers. The success of Lady Margaret proves that the take-over of Veng by the Cistercians cannot have been legally undisputed.

What were, in the last instance, the objections of Lady Margaret that made the new monks give up Veng? The answer to this question may depend on how we characterize the new monks' attitude to the prerogatives of the king. Were they royal monks, these newcomers from Vitskøl, happy at the prospect of finding a new residence in another royal abbey? It is difficult to explain their behaviour if we interpret their attitude as being loyal in this manner to the king's patronage. I would rather propose the explanation that the royal prerogatives in Veng ultimately made Veng unsuitable in the eyes of the 'white' monks as a place for monastic life according to the Cistercian interpretation of the Rule of St Benedict.

In the case of Bishop Svend of Aarhus we may assume a wish to introduce a better monastic life into his diocese. He may have come to the same conclusion as the monks: that Veng would not offer them more monastic freedom than the royal abbey of Vitskøl, where they came from. Bringing with them the corpses of their deceased founding bishop and Count Eric, the Sminge monks left Veng on paths trodden by their Benedictine predecessors, leading them to a freshwater lake island called Kalvø where a Benedictine community existed as a *cella* under Veng abbey; these gave up immediately on the arrival of the newcomers, says the chronicle, later stressing, however, that the place was humid and lacked communications, thereby furnishing the argument for the monks' final move to Øm (Figures 12.1 and 12.2), the *Cara Insula*.

With the exception of the transition from one observance to another in Esrum and Sorø, where special circumstances made the change less

12.1 Øm abbey in the upper part of the Gudenå valley. The monks dug out three only partly-excavated channels crossing the narrow piece of land where the abbey was built, bringing water from the greater Lake Mossø in the south to Lake Gudensø in the north (both lakes can be seen in the photograph, cf. Ingvordsen, 1990). The river Gudenå running northwards links both lakes and makes a wide turn west of the abbey (not seen in the photograph). The road cutting through the area is of recent date. (With the kind permission of Øm Kloster Museum, DK–8060. Photograph: Erik W. Olsson.)

visible, Veng is the first example of a real Cistercian take-over of a Benedictine monastery in newly Christianized Denmark. That it was controversial must have been clearly understood by contemporaries as well as it is by us. The final result was a loss: neither Veng nor Kalvø became cradles of monastic life after they had been deserted by the Cistercians. But its controversial character can also easily be attributed to another factor: the suppression of Veng meant not only the suppression

12.2 Foundations of Øm abbey. Choir, four chapels and transept of the church, east and south wings of the convent buildings, and the inner and the outer cloisters can be clearly recognized. Excavated abbots' burials in the choir have been made visible *in situ* to the public, with the help of windows. The nave of the church was never completed. (With the kind permission of Øm Kloster Museum, DK–8060. Photograph: Erik W. Olsson.)

of traditional Benedictine observance of the monastic rules in that place, but also the suppression of a royal abbey and, thereby, an expression of episcopal power against royal prerogatives.

Moreover, it has seldom been recognized that Benedictine monastic life in its previous observance continued in the same area of the river Gudenå basin soon after the establishment of the *Cara insula*. It is difficult to conceive that such a continuation would not also have implied continuity on the level of personel. It has been argued (Ingvordsen, 1991, pp. 43–5) that the agreement of Lady Margaret with the king ultimately led to the establishment of the Benedictine nuns' convent at Ring not far from Veng, the origins of which can be traced to the same decades. It seems almost as if the royal side was in retreat and Lady Margaret here intervened to save the king's honour. Furthermore, the earliest mention, in 1183, of an Abbot of *Horø* 'Voer', with its Latin name *Oratorium* (*DD 1,3*, no. 111), gives a hint that Benedictine monasticism, drawing upon the tradition of Veng, probably survived in the same natural basin formed by the Gudenå river and its many lakes, continuing their traditional way of interpreting St Benedict's rule. The place might just as well have been in existence already as what the name expresses: a prayer *cella*, perhaps of the monks of Veng. We may be justified in looking at the monks of Voer abbey as the heirs of Veng, their observance as a continuation of the Benedictine heritage planted in Denmark in the pioneer period *c.* 1100.

II Repeated patterns?

Sorø

In Zealand, traditional Benedictine observance had been practised at Esrum until 1151 and at Sorø until 1161. Predating the wanderings of the pioneer convent of Sminge in Jutland from 1165 onwards is the well-documented transition of the Benedictine Sorø abbey in Zealand to the observance of Clairvaux in 1161. Did the Sorø affair offer a model for the events in Jutland?

We have the extraordinary 20 years in office of Bishop Absalon of Roskilde, 1158–77, the sworn adherent of the king, against the independent Archbishop Eskil in Scania who spent seven of these years in exile. Eskil was more or less forced to resign in 1177, to be succeeded by the same Absalon who refused to give up Roskilde, which gave rise to the 15-year personal union of the two dioceses and regions on the ecclesiastical level between 1177 and 1192, until Roskilde finally got a bishop of its own again, Peder Sunesen, the son of Absalon's cousin.

Being situated in the middle of Zealand, between the old ecclesiastical centres of Ringsted and Slagelse, Sorø was a Benedictine foundation inaugurated by the sons of Skjalm Hvide (died *c.* 1113) in the last years of the 1140s (France, 1992, p. 54; Hill, 1992, pp. 206–87; McGuire, 1974; 1982, p. 74). Toke (died *c.* 1145), Ebbe (died 1151) and Asker were the most prominent of his sons. Absalon and King Valdemar's confidant, Esbern Snare, were brothers, sons of Asker. The family in all its branches was immensely influential in Zealand.

Scholars seem to agree, and Hill has especially stressed, that Sorø's transition in 1161 from the previous observance to that followed in Cîteaux and Clairvaux, did not fundamentally change its role as *Hauskloster* of the Hvide family. It was a place for the burial and the living *memoria* of the family's deceased members and remained so for at least the first hundred years.

What purpose, then, did the family and its most prominent ecclesiastical member, Absalon, pursue by this transition to the observance of Clairvaux as practised in Esrum? After all, Esrum was an episcopal foundation, backed up solely by Eskil, who was the direct opposite to Absalon in the Danish church. In Esrum, an initial Benedictine site had been resettled by monks from Clairvaux. The corresponding transition of Sorø could easily be interpreted as an expression of the same 'reform' movement as was seen by scholars to be at work in Esrum.

But another interpretation is possible: that Absalon saw the success of Esrum and, witnessing the growing cult of St Bernard and the glory of sanctity surrounding the monks of the new observance, realized that his family foundation would not be well off if it could not compete with the reputation of Esrum. He might have been urged on by the need to get rid of those denigrating rumours, now increasingly spreading around Danish society, which were making life difficult for the *nigri*, the 'blacks'. In order to be on a par with Eskil, Absalon would have to make his family foundation a model of at least the same reputation for sanctity and holiness as Esrum. In this interpretation, Absalon's 'friendship' towards the monks of the new observance is seen as based upon care for his own family more than upon a real interest in monasticism. The international communication system of the monks of the new observance would mostly have been attractive to Absalon as it guaranteed a good reputation for his monks.

The main reason for preferring this latter interpretation of Absalon's support for the new observance is the strong contrast between Eskil's personal relationship to, and the inspiration he received, from Bernard and Absalon's many gifts to monasteries during his long time in office in Roskilde and Lund. There is no reason to see in Absalon's many gifts of land an expression of genuine love on his side for the type of monastic observance prevalent among his monks, as long as they fulfilled their duties of intercessory prayer for the realm and for the members of his family. Gifts and donations contribute to stabilizing the institutional character of monasteries, which is not the same as the expression of a genuine love for 'the poor of Christ'. Stability and affluence favour good vocations from well settled families, which ultimately must have been a good purpose worth considerable efforts by a bishop in charge of the pastoral care of his diocese.

Against this background, I strongly doubt that Sorø's transition from the *nigri* to the *grisei* in 1161 would play the role of a model for the handing-over of Veng to the Sminge monks in Jutland in 1165. After all, Denmark was not a unified realm under one central administration, but consisted of at least three regions with each single Thing community capable of accepting or rejecting a candidate for kingship. What happened on the island of Zealand would not necessarily be of importance in Jutland and Scania, if the king did not personally adapt experiences from one region to solve the problems of another.

The first move of a handful of monks from Vitskøl to Sminge could be understood as the act of one bishop, Eskil, loyal to the king, who wished to have a good community of monks from this royal abbey for his diocese. The second move, that from Sminge to Veng, was inspired by another bishop, Svend, apparently with another aim: hypothetically an effort to counterbalance royal influence on the abbey of Veng which had resulted in moral indifference. The motive for the third move, that from Veng to Kalvø and Øm, initiated and motivated by the monks themselves, may have been to get rid of an overwhelming royal influence which may have appeared to be an obstacle to their monastic observance (cf. Appendix). Internal forces inherent in the Vitskøl foundation from the beginning, through its primary experiences in Sweden and the preponderance of the royal foundation act for Vitskøl of 1157/58, must be credited with this migration history. I see an immense symbolic and psychological importance in the new name: the final refuge of these monks on 'The Precious Island'. It was there they finally settled and took root among ordinary people in the region.

Tvis

In the years between the loss of Sorø 1161 and of Veng in 1165 to monks of the new observance, others of the latter were on the move to a third site, this time one without any predecessor. Tvis was the first daughter of Herrisvad in Scania of the Cîteaux line, after nearly 20 years of the abbey's existence. The founder, Buris Henriksen, was greatgrandson of King Svend Estridsen.[1] Thus, he and his brothers were potential claimants to royal dignity in Denmark as well as in Sweden. Buris's brothers had suffered violent death, Magnus as king of a part of Sweden in 1161, and finally Cnut, possibly as late as in the beginning of 1163, so that Buris took over the title of *jarl* 'earl' from him and the earldom linked to this title. Apparently he exercised the corresponding administrative power in the region of Ringkøbing in Western Jutland.

After his victory in 1157, Valdemar had kept Buris close to him to avoid fear of intrigue. The endowment Buris made of his manor Tvis for the foundation of a Cistercian abbey may have been forced upon him by the king, but at all events it directly followed the violent death of his brothers. Whatever background may be assumed, Buris's intention seems to have been to establish a monastery linked to his family and its ambitions. Hill (1992, pp. 160–63) treats Tvis as a 'family monastery', a *Hauskloster*.

The charter of 24 March 1163 is known only in a translation into Middle Danish (*DD 1,2*, no. 152). In this charter, Buris Henriksen addresses himself to an Abbot Peter and his brethren at Tvis, but no such abbot appears among the signatories, the list comprising the king, the Bishops of Børglum and Odense, the abbots of Herrisvad, Esrum and Vitskøl, and noblemen. Besides Tvis manor itself, four districts are contained in the endowment: Skjern, Felding, Hjerm and Kvistrup. The parent abbey, with responsibility for the construction works, is explicitly addressed: Herrisvad. In conclusion, Buris evokes the protection of the king and his fellow peers who by their presence are the guarantors of the realization of his donation.

In 1165, Buris changed the status of his earldom into a hereditary fief, which brought him a violent end: in 1167, Valdemar accused him of rebellion (*1167. Hoc anno Burius captus est* [*DMA*, p. 58]; *1167. Burisius captus est* [ibid., p. 76]), and, according to Saxo, blinded him. The later *Annales Visbyenses* and the *Annales Ryenses* summarize several traditions (*DMA*, pp. 147, 166): *1167. Burisius captus est et oculis effossis castratus* (cf. Annales 980–1286 [ibid., p. 270]). There is no information about his death on this occasion, and it is certainly not necessary to assume that he died, since after such a treatment he could pose no further threat to Valdemar. Instead, there is the popular tradition, found in a number of ballads, that he was buried much later together with Kirsten, possibly a girl of royal Norwegian descent, in a tomb at the cemetery of Vestervig abbey in Northern Jutland. Davidsen and Møller-Christensen (1971, p. 53) have pointed to a manuscript by Hans Svaning (1503–84) which purports to tell the story of how Buris stayed on at his manor, Tvis, long after 1167, living the life of a blinded penitent, while the abbey was built and made ready for convent life.

In the situation of 1163, it must have been important for the king, after his short-lived contact in 1162 with Pope Victor, Frederik Barbarossa's candidate to replace Pope Alexander III, to demonstrate that he was back on the right side in the schism. He was now surrounded by the abbots of three out of four Cistercian abbeys in existence in Denmark, and by Bishop Simon of Odense, whom he had forced to leave his residence in favour of the previous dean, Livo, made schismatic bishop with the help of Pope Victor. But it is significant that the bishop of the diocese, Radulf of Ribe, was not among the signatories. He had been ordained bishop by the schismatic Pope Victor and did not yet belong to the respectable company gathered in Tvis on that day.

Buris himself was less important to the king in this situation. He had treated Buris in the same way since 1157, keeping him in the vicinity of power while being attentive to possible ambitions from his side. But it would be no little advantage to King Valdemar to see Buris bereft of his manor, investing his property in a family monastery, like the king himself had just done in Vitskøl.

Not least significant is the fact that Tvis received monks from the older branch of Cistercians in Denmark, from Herrisvad of the Cîteaux filiation. One might perhaps look upon the Herrisvad monks' decision to take up the settlement in Tvis as a readiness to participate in the act of due penitence expressed in Buris's foundation. It could also be evaluated as an obliging gesture towards Archbishop Eskil, whose castle of Søborg the king had attacked in 1161 with the effect that the archbishop had gone into exile (Riis, 1975). After all, Eskil had personally called in the Cîteaux monks in a situation when he could not get monks from Clairvaux. Whoever made the Herrisvad monks settle in Tvis, the choice may have given a hint that Buris belonged to a group that was more distant from the king's power than other groups in Danish society. Such a symbolic statement could only confirm the king in the attitude he already had towards Buris.

France (1992, p. 63) concludes in a conciliatory way:

> Admittedly, the foundation of both Sorø in 1161 and Tvis in 1163 has been invested with political motivation, the one as a consequence of Bishop Absalon's desire to mediate between the king and his exiled archbishop, and the other as a means of bolstering the power of the founder, Duke Buris Henriksen, a possible claimant to the Danish throne. This interpretation cannot be upheld: in bringing the Cistercians to Sorø Absalon chose the most effective way of continuing the patronage of his family monastery; there is no need to look for any motivation of a wider political nature. As regards Tvis, a more likely interpretation is that the foundation was a conscious political act of *rapprochement* by the king, for in witnessing the foundation charter he found himself in the company not only of the three Cistercian abbots of Herrevad, Esrum, and Vitskøl, but also of the legitimate bishop of Odense, Simon, who had been replaced by the schismatic, Livo.

Tvis never shook off its close involvement in Buris's fate, so that from 1167 onwards, it could no more become a model for monastic life according to the new observance. It was an abbey of penitence, the Cîteaux-Herrisvad monks' first experience of the involuntary involvement of monks in complicated political business.

Seem-Løgum and Holme

In those years another Danish bishop, Radulf of Ribe, carried out an operation similar to that of Veng with another Benedictine abbey. A new group of Herrisvad monks were called upon to leave their Scanian abbey between 1165 and 1171, this time to introduce the new, strict interpretation of the Rule of St Benedict in Seem outside Ribe. An official document 20 years later states that it was a double monastery (*DD 1,3*, no. 163): *Nam et ibidem aliquantis temporibus tam nigrorum monachorum quam sanctimonialium cenobium fuerat institutum* (for once upon a time a monastery with both black monks and nuns had been instituted there). What happened to the existing monks is not known. The nuns of this double monastery may have moved to St Nicholas's church in Ribe, where nuns are found later.

Crucial to the understanding of this transition is the fact that Radulf's successor in 1171 on the chair of Ribe, Bishop Stephen, had previously been a canon of Ribe, had entered Herrisvad and had been elected abbot there some time after 24 March 1163, when his predecessor witnessed the foundation of Tvis abbey (*DD 1,2*, no. 152). Without doubt such a man used his authority and the resources of the bishopric to help accommodate the newcomers. The process ended with a move of site: around 1175 the monks gave up Seem and moved south to Løgum (Figure 12.3) which they Latinized *Locus Dei* (God's Dwelling), leaving Seem bereft of monastic life as their brethren had done in Veng. The above mentioned episcopal confirmation charter opens up with an *arenga* which suggests that quarrels, hatred and rumours were something that was being overcome by the arrival of the Cistercians.

In dealing with the Herrisvad daughter abbeys, the discussion after Tvis and Løgum often turns to Holme abbey on the island of Funen, present-day Brahetrolleborg. No foundation narrative and no foundation charter for Holme abbey are extant. The foundation years of Holme and Løgum in the Cistercian filiation lists have been differently combined by scholars. McGuire (1982, p. 67) picks up the years 1170 or 1171 for Løgum and 1172 for Holme abbey and reflects:

> it would not be surprising if their foundations were due at least in part to Eskil's efforts. Eskil was involved during this period in the

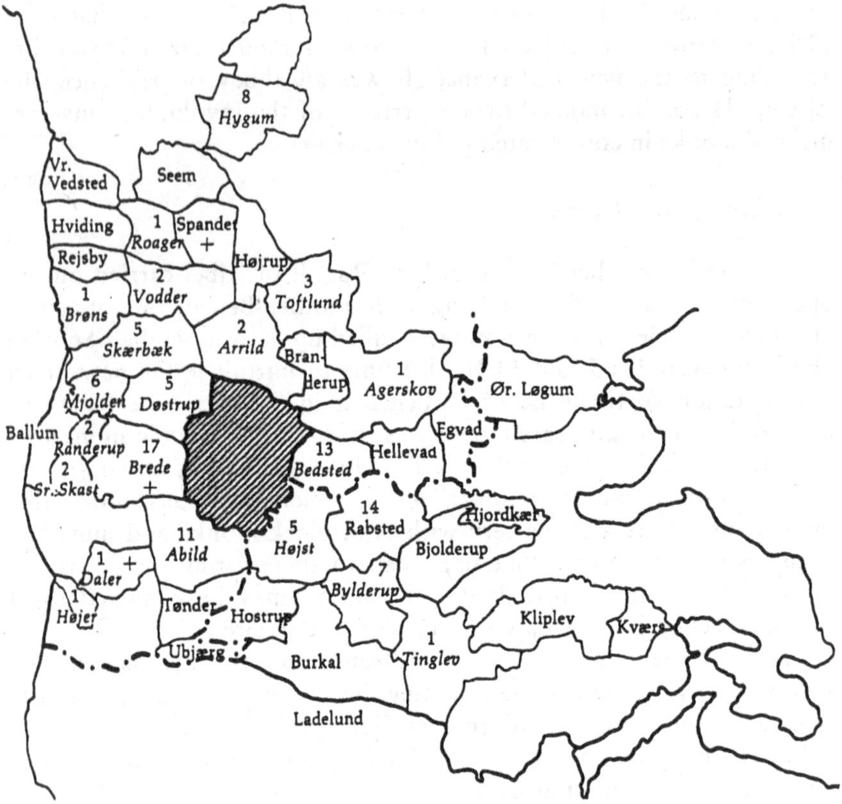

12.3 Map of property belonging to Løgum abbey, the successor of Seem abbey. The indicated area in the centre is the parish of Løgum where the abbey owned all 88 farms. The numbers in parishes with name printed in italics indicate the number of farms belonging to the abbey in that parish at the end of the Middle Ages. In the remaining parishes the abbey owned property at some point in time, which later went out of its hands.

Note: + indicates incorporated parish church; the broken line indicates the boundary between the dioceses of Ribe (west) and Slesvig (east).

Source: Bartholdy (1973).

foundation of the Premonstratensian abbey Væ in Skåne. Even if his support consisted entirely of privileges and not of property gifts, he was still an essential participant in the new religious foundation. In Løgum's case we know that its early privileges were issued by Eskil. These were lost in a fire before the end of the century. In Holme's case, Bishop Simon of Odense legally had to be involved. But here we may have a link with Eskil. Bishop Simon had given Eskil's foundation at Væ the church of St Mary and so can be looked upon as Eskil's ally in starting the new house. Eskil may have reciprocated by helping Bishop Simon found a Cistercian house on Fyn.

Doubts are cast upon these considerations after one scholar has revised the foundation story of Vä abbey. As will be shown (Chapter 13 in this volume), Vä abbey was founded *c.* 1160 rather than in 1170, as previously assumed. But Simon was one of Archbishop Eskil's allies in the papal schism. He must have given his approval to Holme abbey towards the end of the 1160s after the schism was overcome and he had returned to his see of Odense following exile. This does not explain, however, why a Cistercian abbey should come into being here in the southern part of Funen. After all, the Odense Benedictines with their English roots were the cathedral chapter of Odense, taking care of pilgrimages to St Cnut. They must have been capable of depriving the newcomers of their site, had they wanted to do so.

The explanation is probably that there is another type of connection between Løgum and Holme abbeys than hitherto assumed. First, the Cistercian abbey of Løgum did not begin its existence in 1170 or 1171, as McGuire believes, nor in 1172–3, as James France proposes. The new abbey began in Seem, and the process of the reform of Seem with the assistance of monks from Herrisvad had already begun in the late 1160s. Two entries in the Løgum Necrology ('Necrologium Monasterii Loci Dei', 1776, IV, from AM 868 4°) can be referred with certainty to the early period:

1. Under 22 December we find: *Obiit Hellavus, in Seem sepultus et inde translatus Løgum.* Hellavus died while the convent was situated in Seem, and the monks brought his dead body to Løgum in 1175 to be buried there. Most probably such a man would have been a monk or at least a lay brother.
2. Under 22 July we find: *Obiit Torstanus donatus.* Since there is no conjunctive *et* after *Torstanus*, *donatus* cannot be a name here, but apparently denotes a monk who was given to the monastery as a child. Since Cistercians did not receive oblates, Torsten probably was a Benedictine monk of Seem, given to the monastery as a child, who joined the new-comers and died a Cistercian.

Second, Løgum has very much to do with the person of the Bishop of Ribe, who was instrumental in the take-over. The English-born Bishop Radulf, who succeeded the Flemish Bishop Elias on the chair of Ribe under the obedience of Barbarossa's Pope Victor some time between March and September 1162, was consecrated bishop for the second time in France in 1166 by Archbishop Eskil during his exile there (*SE VI: II*, p. 73). The CER (1933–35, p. 28) states: *Tandem data quadam mansione monachis apud Løghum quarto anno electionis consecratur* (Finally, after having given a mansion to the monks at Løgum, he was consecrated in the fourth year of his election). The mentioning of Løgum already in connection with the year 1166 could refer to the 'monks who later lived in Løgum', or that the gift consisted of lands in Løgum. But if Herrisvad monks had not already arrived in Ribe by 1166, the *monachis* could also refer to a gift to monks of traditional Benedictine observance in Seem. In any case, the CER (1933–35, p. 28) asserts that Radulf as a condition for his consecration in 1166 had to show his penitence for *crimina homicidii et apostatiae sibi imputata* (the crimes of manslaughter and apostasy which he was accused of) in the form of a gift to monks, and that this gift (or these monks) had something to do with Løgum. Even if the cause and condition clause is a later construction of the chronicler, we may assume that the Herrisvad monks were active in the Ribe diocese as early as the last years of the 1160s. Abbot Stephen, the former Ribe canon, was an outstanding contact person between the bishopric and Herrisvad. Upon the death of Radulf on 14 February 1171, the canons got the king's permission to elect one of the three Cistercian abbots of Vitskøl, Tvis and Herrisvad Bishop of Ribe. In agreement with the king they chose Stephen (CER). This must have happened during the first half of 1171. Thereby they were able to harvest the result of negotiations which must have been going on for some time. From this time on at the latest, the reform of the abbey of Seem must have been systematically carried out as a question of high priority among the monks of Herrisvad.

The move to Jutland meant that the Herrisvad monks set out on one or more journeys through Danish lands. They may have left by ship from Helsingborg, crossing the Sound to Elsinore, passing Zealand overland, crossing the Bælt, then Funen from east to south-west, debarking either from Assens for Jutland in the direction of Ribe or from Medelfar to Kolding and then overland to Ribe. Setting out from Helsingborg, they could also have sailed north around Zealand and Funen to reach one of the harbours on the eastern coast of Jutland, for example Vejle or Horsens, from where they could procede overland either towards the present-day Ringkøbing region, if Tvis was the goal of the journey, or by means of the narrow passage by Medelfar (today's Lillebelt) to Kolding as above.

Considering the chronology, the situation in Herrisvad in the late 1160s when Bishop Radulf – perhaps without real conviction – deliberated with Abbot Stephen and the monks about the reform of Seem must have been one of waiting and insecurity for the monks. If there were so many monks in Herrisvad that a new foundation would not be problematic from the point of view of personel, it must have been frustrating not to know the outcome of the reform initiative in the diocese of Ribe. One road from Herrisvad to Ribe crossed the island of Funen. With the contact established along this route between travelling Herrisvad monks and Bishop Simon and clergy and other groups on Funen, the idea of establishing a station on the route to Jutland may soon have arisen. Holme is situated on the direct route between Nyborg on the eastern coast of Funen, and Assens, a road which does not pass by Odense. The situation of Holme might be understood as a station on the route of Herrisvad monks travelling to Ribe.

For the development of Herrisvad as mother abbey of Tvis, Seem and Holme one must assume that a positive wave of recruitment characterized the years 1144–63 in Scanian Herrisvad. This must have led first to the decision to accept, in 1162/63, the task of constructing an abbey in Tvis on the manor of Buris Henriksen. Then the reform of Seem, called for by Bishop Radulf, must have been seriously considered during several years in the 1160s without clear prospects of realization. After things had dragged on for some years, the idea of a foundation on Funen, exactly on the land route to Ribe, may have looked ever more realistic, so that preparations may even have been made, seeking out the spot on southern Funen, surrounded by watery areas, which aptly could be called a *holm* (island), and asking Bishop Simon of Odense for his permission which he undoubtedly gave willingly. After Stephen's election to Ribe it was clear that one of these foundations would have very good chances of materializing. We may assume that it was easier to establish a new abbey on virgin soil than to settle all the complicated legal questions connected with taking over and reforming the old abbey of Seem. It is a fair assumption that both options were carried out concomitantly, with the result that Holme happened to count its foundation from the year 1172, whereas Seem, taken into use earlier, never appears as a Cistercian abbey proper.

The lists waver regarding the foundation year of Løgum. Not until the new site called *Locus Dei* was settled, can one say that the foundation of Løgum was a reality. Archbishop Eskil gave his confirmation, followed after 1190 by that of Bishop Omer and Archbishop Absalon as a prerequisite for the protection charter of Pope Celestin III (1191–98) (*DD 1,3*, nos 163, 164, 167).

Essenbæk and Glenstrup

In the same years two more abbeys of Benedictine observance were founded in the neighbourhood of Randers.

The foundation of Essenbæk to the east of Randers in 1151 has already been mentioned. The little evidence we have points at Our Lady's and St Peter's in Randers for its origin. Since 1179 at the latest, the year the Essenbæk annals speak about the *mutatio claustri Eskinbeck*, it must have existed in regular forms as a centre of monastic life.

Glenstrup north-west of Randers, on Lake Glenstrup in the area of the Viking fortress of Fyrkat, present-day Hobro, is known from Pope Alexander III's short confirmation to its Abbot Cato of the abbey's property in Handest, 'Homtofh', Als, Skortorp, (Sønder) Onsild, Karleby, 'Hubæk', Skjellerup, Rold, 'Fælmyng', Katbjerg in Fjelsted, and the episcopal tithe from half of the Hindsted hundred (*DD 1,3*, no. 17), given in Tusculum on a 2 December which could be 1170/72, 1178 or 1180. The letter may have been procured by the monk Ogyrius of Gledingstorp who was received, apparently upon recommendation of Archbishop Eskil and in his company (*presente archiepiscopo Dacie*), into prayer union with St Remi in Reims by its abbot, Peter (*DD 1,2*, no. 150). He was a close collaborator of Archbishop Eskil on his important stay in France in the 1160s and as late as their last meeting in 1176 (*DD 1,2*, no. 149).

This growth of traditional Benedictine monastic life corresponds to what happened on Zealand two decades earlier. Without active support from the diocesan authority they could not have flourished. Svend of Aarhus had engaged himself in the progress of the Sminge monks. He and Archbishop Eskil must have approved of both Essenbæk and Glenstrup, although there is no record that an initiative from their side lay behind them. The two monasteries bear witness to the fact that monasticism had taken deep roots in the area so that the monastic trend of these decades revitalized even traditional Benedictine observance.

III New moves in Sweden

Two Swedish foundations are intertwined with the Danish sequence Sorø–Tvis–Sminge/Veng: the sequence denoted by the names Saba and Gutnalia and the years 1160 and 1164. The *Annales Colbazenses* – originating in Lund and brought after 1177 to Belbuk by its Premonstratensian pioneer canons, from where they later came to Kołbacz/Kolbatz (Kristensen, 1969, pp. 37–61) – as well as the Ryd annals display the sequence Saba–Sorø–Tvis–Gutnalia–Øm with some variations regarding the years of foundation (*DMA*, pp. 10 and 166).

Saba or Sabba is the Latin transcription of a Swedish Säby, a place situated south of Lake Mälar in the diocese of Strängnäs and later called Julita. But this cannot have been the place where the new monks, coming from Alvastra, had been living the first years after 1160. The diocese of Strängnäs was hardly organized, as it was enumerated among the suffragans of the new archbishop of Uppsala in August 1164 (*DD 1,2*, no. 153). After the late mention of a Bishop Gerder of Strängnäs in 1129 (see Chapter 9 in this volume) it is not until 1171 that we know from a papal letter of protection that it was administered by a bishop of its own, William (*DS*, no. 58). It is in Attundaland, on the northern shore of Lake Mälar, that we first meet these monks, in the impressive agglomeration of churches and Christian settlements of early converted farmers around the former episcopal see of Sigtuna, which had existed for decades, but which apparently had been left vacant as the diocese was given the Uppsala name. It is known from an undated charter of Archbishop Stephen, issued under Karl Sverkersson (= 1164/67), that a *Deo dicata femina* (a woman dedicated to God), by the name of Doter, had given her property in Viby near Sigtuna to a community of monks (*DS* no. 51). There were unsettled questions of property rights between her and her son which made the archbishop an arbiter in the question. The king put his seal on the charter for its authorization together with the archbishop and several other nobles and clergymen. In the region around Sigtuna, farmers were very early converted to Christianity – the numerous stone slabs with runic inscriptions and Christian symbols they left behind have already been mentioned. We learn about the monks' move from Viby to Säby/Julita (*DS*, nos 64, 65) between 1174 and 1185 under other auspices (France, 1992, p. 40) through a charter issued, still under Archbishop Stephen, by the then king, Knut (1167–96), the son of Erik Jedvardsson, who in a long *arenga* expresses his (or Archbishop Stephen's?) view of the role of monastic life in the church:

> Christ I adore, praise and honour, the king of the angels, who governs and leads all kingdoms ... To him can nothing more enjoyable or acceptable be offered by mortal man than gifts imparted to those who, giving up themselves and all they have, live a life of poverty in a monastery.

It is an open question, under which political and ecclesiastical constellation Saba was established. The year 1160 is strange. Later Swedish historiography put the entry of Saba before that of the martyr death of King Erik Jedvardsson in Uppsala on 18 May 1160 (*DMA*, p. 301), thereby insinuating that Doter's great donation of her family property took place in the reign of King Erik. But Doter's donation may also have taken place in the reign of the man who killed King Erik, Magnus Henriksen, brother of Buris mentioned above, who was king and exerted power for a while, at least in Västergötland, before he was killed by Karl Sverkersson in 1161. But the year 1160 for the arrival of the convent to Viby excludes the possibility that Doter made her donation after Karl Sverkersson had become king. The most probable solution is that the donation of Doter had nothing to do with the political situation at the top of society. Her decision must have ripened and led to action during the reign of King Erik in the Christian milieu of rich farmers she seems to have belonged to in the fertile area around Sigtuna. Ongoing research and excavations in Viby have brought to light the foundations of a Romanesque church with an apse of considerable size but without any traces of Cistercian construction works (Karlsson, 1999)

The second instance, Gutnalia or Gutualia, also called Roma after the parish of Ruma, and sometimes styled 'Gudvalla', was founded in 1164 in Gotland, an early Christianized and densely populated island in the Baltic, situated at an equal distance from Sweden and Livonia. There are enough hints – the second Abbot Peter is said in the *Exordium magnum* to have been one of the pioneer monks of Clairvaux that came to Nydala – to indicate that the monks came to Gotland from Nydala. Although nothing is known of foundation or founding community (France, 1992, p. 41), there seems to be good reasons to assume that Bishop Gisle of Linköping was still alive and that he negotiated the establishment of this abbey with the Thing community of Gotland, said to have used Gutnalia as its meeting place (Pernler, 1977, pp. 60–65). No royal participation can be expected on this nearly independent island, which functioned as a republic of farmers in the style of Iceland, and where royal Swedish power was not an issue until the thirteenth century. Although the foundation took place during the reign of Karl Sverkersson (1161–67), Gutnalia does not seem to have had anything but an episcopal authorization. In the architecture of the church with its square choir and four adjacent side chapels with slightly rounded apses, parallels have been traced to Clairvaux III (1154/74) (Swartling, 1959). That a pastoral and missionary purpose was infused into this foundation from the start is clearly seen from the fact that the new abbey quite soon acquired lands in Estonia and apparently became involved in mission there as early as the following decades (Johansen, 1951).

IV Women and the monastic option

In the early years of the Valdemarian age, the move towards opening the monastic option for women was a constant process. Again, bishops were instrumental, corresponding to age-old traditions from antiquity. On account of the lack of evidence, it is nearly impossible to state the dates of these monastic foundations for women. One of the most impressive was Bosjö, on an island between the two lakes in the middle of Scania, named under the single heading Lake Ringsjön. This is the lake from which the river Rönneå, passing Herrisvad, takes its source. Since the earliest documentary evidence is the papal letter of 1182, whereby Pope Lucius III takes the convent under his and St Peter's protection (*DD 1,3*, no. 101), we have to assume a history of at least a generation until such a letter could be asked for and issued. The addressees are the Prioress Juliana and her *sororibus tam presentibus quam futuris regularem vitam professis* (now living and future sisters bound by vow to a monastic way of life). The formulas are the same as in protection charters for monks and the Rule of St Benedict is expressedly mentioned as well as the name of the founder, a certain Thordus (Tord), together with names of lands and villages constituting the convent's first property: Fogdarp, Kulleberga, the mills in Sätofta, Gårdstånga, Skarhult and Osby, an unidentifiable piece of forest in the neighbourhood, and half of the fishing rights to the lake; we are told that Tord, the founder, a well-off nobleman of the area, reserved the other half for himself as long as he lived (Cinthio, 1989, p. 41). 'It shall also be permitted to you to receive for monastic education, free and absolved, such persons who want to flee the world and to keep them among you without any objection (from any other party)' was added as a clause probably necessary in order to divert efforts from the side of influential families or knights to make the convent release a nun who is already professed. We may guess that Bosjö was founded already during Eskil's time in office (prior to 1177).

No sisters from Bosjö are found in the Lund necrology, which went out of use *c.* 1170. A great number of them appear, however, in the *Liber daticus Lundensis*, showing that convent life began in the 1160s at the earliest. On palaeographical criteria, Weeke (1884/89) assigns the obituary entries of the prioress Juliana, five sisters, one prior and one *conversus* to the period 1160–1200. This *conversus* is being styled *Sveno filius Thorh conversus*, possibly the son of the founder. The prior is expressedly said to be *sacerdos et monachus ecclesie Omnium Sanctorum Lundis, prior de Bosø* (priest and monk at All Saints' in Lund and prior at Bosjökloster). At least one priest serving the nuns was or had been a secular priest, which must be the meaning of the combination *Sveno sacerdos et conversus sancte Marie et sancti Nicolai de Bose* (Svend priest and lay brother at Our Lady's and St Nicholas of Bosjökloster) in his obituary notice.

The archaeological findings indicate that the Romanesque abbey church was built during the last third of the twelfth century – the apse of the present church remains from this construction period. The nuns did not use the eastern choir of the church, however, but followed the custom of using a gallery in the western part as their choir. The entrance of the nuns from the upper floor of the west wing of the monastic buildings into their gallery can still be traced about 3m above ground level in the southern wall of the church. A further indication of the situation and function of the nuns' gallery are the acoustic tubes walled into the church walls, which in Bosjö are not to be found around the eastern choir, as in many other churches, but in the upper parts of the walls at the church's western end, apparently to make the singing of the nuns from their gallery sound more powerful. The eastern choir seems not to have been built together with the eastern wing of the monastery – a very natural solution, since all that was needed here was room for the priest and his servant. The monastery had cloisters around the inner yard, as indicated by traces in the walls.

Shortly before St Nicholas became the favoured patron saint of a great number of churches in recently founded towns along the northern and southern Baltic coasts, we have him here chosen as the patron of a Benedictine nunnery, which from the beginning took deep roots in the land-owning class of Scanian nobility. The cult of St Nicholas spread after the transfer of the relics of this Bishop of Myra to Bari in Italy in 1087. One of the earliest royal monastic foundations on Zealand, Slangerup nunnery, said to have been founded by King Erik the Good (1095–1103), was dedicated to St Nicholas. A precious memory of the veneration of this bishop is a famous gospel book from the late twelfth century, the so-called Horne book, now in the Royal Library, Copenhagen, where the title-page shows St Nicholas and two donors kneeling. The first owner who wrote his name in this book is Oluf Rosensparre, the son of Sten, who in 1562 was enfeoffed with Bosjö. There is, then, some probability that Sten Rosensparre kept this book from the library of the nuns when he took over, after the last surviving nun had been moved in 1560 to her last asylum with the Benedictine nuns at St Peter's in Lund.

According to the prevalent opinion (Smith, 1973, pp. 5–7), Zealand was given two convents of nuns in the 1160s, both presumably following the Cistercian observance just introduced in Sorø.

At Our Lady's in Roskilde, where the constructions from the eleventh century – assigned by Saxo to Bishop Svend the Norwegian (see Chapter 4 in this volume) – suggest the early existence of a nuns' convent, a *prepositus* Isak, who is known from written evidence *c.* 1160, made a new foundation from his family property (*DD 1,2*, no. 163). Absalon states in his charter, which may have been fabricated afterwards, that he has made a donation to the *claustrum sancte Marie in civitate Roschildense* (the convent of Our Lady in the city of Roskilde) which was *novella fundatione irrigatum et pio iuvantium labore constructum* (irrigated by a new foundation and constructed by the pious efforts of benefactors). There is nothing to indicate that a convent did not already exist as this new foundation was made (cf. France, 1992, p. 174). The signatures of Abbot Simon of Sorø, Isak and some Hospitallers of St John (who had recently arrived in Denmark) follow. What happened seems comparable to Vreta's new foundation of 1162 and could easily have been born out of a similar attitude to the way by which one hoped to gain merit by securing better conditions for the 'poor of Christ' who chose the monastic alternative. Hill (1992, pp. 277–86) enters into a careful analysis of the role of this convent as a centre for the veneration of St Margaret, a relative of the archbishop, and the efforts to initiate her canonization. He treats Our Lady's in Roskilde as a 'family monastery', a *Hauskloster* of Absalon's family (cf. *DD 1,3*, no. 100).

In Slangerup, St Nicholas, a stone construction from *c.* 1100 patronized by King Erik the Good (Krins, 1968, 63–7), was amplified by convent buildings that cannot be older than *c.* 1160. Esrum abbey seems to have assumed responsibility. As in the case of Our Lady's in Roskilde, France (1992, pp. 168, 180) assumes an existing convent of nuns which was aggregated to Esrum at the earliest in the 1160s, thus born out of the same mind.

Nuns' convents could exist for long periods without too much attention paid to what observance they followed. Both nuns' convents in Zealand followed the Rule of St Benedict. Both went through a phase of renewal in the 1160s by which they opened themselves more effectively to women of the land-owning class in Zealand who chose the monastic option. Both profited from the arrival of new monks in Sorø and Esrum, in spite of all fluctuations in the attitude of the Cistercian general chapter to the *cura animarum* of monks towards nuns. Thereby they bear witness to a new movement in monasticism characteristic of the peace which Valdemar the Great had now imposed upon Denmark and which spread to all Scandinavia.

Protected by this imposed peace, the Bishop of Børglum, Tyge (1145/46–76/77), gave his family property to the foundation of Ø Kloster

(*DD 1,3*, no. 7) on an island in the Limfjorden, which constitutes the southern border of his diocese. The nuns followed the Rule of St Benedict, contrary to other religious communities of the diocese – the Augustinian inspiration from Steinfeld has been mentioned earlier. Tyge had signed the donation chart for Vitskøl in 1157 and had followed the king in schism.

Bishop Simon (1157–86) must have been active in the foundation of a Benedictine convent for nuns in the Viking fortress of Odense, called Burg, later Nonnebakken (cf. *DD 1,2*, no. 124), but we have extracts of a charter of King Cnut VI from 1193, which mentions royal privileges given to the nuns by King Valdemar (*DD 1,3*, no. 189; *Odense bys historie*, pp. 208f.). We may be reasonably sure that Nonnebakken, from where, apparently *c.* 1200, the nuns moved to Dalum 5 km upstream on the river Odense Å, came into being out of the same motives and tendencies as those behind the renewal of Roskilde and Slangerup and the foundation of Ø Kloster.

Finally, the bishops of Ribe took care that the monastic option for women, which had had its centre in Seem, got a new refuge after the move of the monks to Løgum: St Nicholas in Ribe. The ancient settlement north of the Ribe river (*Ribe excavations 1970–76*; Nielsen, 1985, pp. 31–9) had lost much of its old urban function after the area south of the river had properly become the cathedral city. St Nicholas is one of the churches to the north of the river now receiving a new profile.

Since the 1160s, each Danish diocese had at least one nunnery, and their number grew during the following century. After Ribe housed the nuns from Seem, Lund those of St Peter, and Aalborg and Randers were ready to receive women from the Viberg and Aarhus dioceses, Børglum got Ø Kloster, Odense Nonnebakken, and Roskilde the renewed Roskilde and Slangerup convents. Only St John's convent in Slesvig came later.

The corresponding pattern was repeated in Swedish dioceses. In the central districts of the diocese of Linköping to the south of Linköping-Vreta, a nunnery existed in Askaby which may have got a letter of protection by Pope Lucius III (1181–85) (France, 1992, p. 172). The evidence is somewhat dubious: the Pope declared St Olav's church in Norrköping to be incorporated to the convent, but there is no other evidence for the existence of that church in the twelfth century. There is, however, some probability that an original genuine papal letter of protection was given to the nuns by Pope Lucius.

In the southern, Småland region of the same diocese, Byarum northwest of Nydala was established where a road from the west, from Halland, met the main transit road leading from the southern tip of

Lake Vätter over Nydala to Växjö, which was a diocesan centre in its own right since at least the 1170s (Persson, 1999).

Finally, in the diocese of Strängnäs, nuns settled in Riseberga where they received gifts from the 'smiling' Earl Birger (presumably the meaning of his nickname, Brosa), still during the reign of Knut Eriksson (*DS*, I, pp. 823–4). Riseberga is situated in Närke, the western part of the diocese, and the property and the fishing rights the nuns received lay further west, in Värmland, a part of the diocese of Skara. The foundation emanated from the highest circles in the Swedish nobility. In the *Liber daticus Lundensis*, we find the convent of Riseberga mentioned only once: in the obituary entry for Birger Brosas's wife, Brigida, daughter of King Harald Gille of Norway. (There was apparently no prayer union between the Lund cathedral chapter and Riseberga.) She must have been born *c.* 1130 and (after Birger's death in 1202 [Beckman in *SBL*, IV, p. 415]) she entered as a 'nun in Riseberga. She was the wife of Duke Birger': *Et Brigida, sanctimonialis de Risibarge. Hec fuit uxor ducis Byrgeri.* It is illuminating to follow her personal history: she was first married to the Earl of Västergötland, Karl Suneson or Karl of Edsvära, mentioned in the list of law-keepers in Västergötland (Sawyer, 1991, p. 39), then to Magnus Henriksen, the Danish usurper, who killed Erik Jedvardsson and was accepted in Västergötland as Swedish king in 1160–61. The monastic foundation of her third husband must have taken place with the goodwill of King Knut Eriksson, whom Birger Brosa served. It is not known according to which observance the nuns of Riseberga followed the Rule of St Benedict.

Summarizing this investigation into the foundation of Øm, Sorø, the Herrisvad, Alvastra and Nydala daughter convents, and the nunneries in Denmark and Sweden, we find that a king only in some cases appears in what might have been a decisive role in the foundation process. It is the age of active bishops, who, with assistance from their equals in the nobility, pursued a distinct policy of founding Benedictine monasteries, regardless of the observance they followed, just like the two Aarhus bishops had done in Sminge and Veng. But whereas Veng was clearly a royal abbey, there is in the case of Seem no mention of the king or his predecessors, but the introduction of a new observance there was a process which only involved the bishop, the cathedral canons and the Herrisvad monks. For Sweden, it is reasonable to assume a connection between Viby abbey and the former Alvastra monk, Bishop Stephen of Uppsala, and that possibly the Bishop of Linköping rather than King Karl Sverkersson (1161–67) made an active effort in the foundation of Gutnalia/Roma in Gotland. But an ostensive royal foundation after the model of Vitskøl, 1157/58 – very much in line with the monastic cathedral chapter of Uppsala from the same years – is nowhere to be found in the 1160s, whereas several monastic foundations of this decade can be linked to bishops and noble families.

Note

1. Whose sons, apart from Svend (died 1104), were Harald, Knud, Oluf, Erik and Niels. Svend's son Henrik, called Skadelår, was married to Ingerid, a niece of King Niels's consort Margareta Fredkulla, daughter of King Inge of Sweden.

CHAPTER THIRTEEN

The Valdemarian age 3: sons and daughters of St Augustine

One might call the followers of the Rule of St Benedict a family, and treat the followers of the Rule of St Augustine correspondingly as another family. In reality, both offered an invitation to a perfect life as pronounced in the Christian gospel. The distinction between the two has no historical bearing until their representatives begin drawing upon the difference, making it an important feature in their attitude towards the world. Scholars have been inclined to predate the process of a gradually growing consciousness about this difference. The monastic world strives to reduce the differences between monastic 'families' by declaring such families to be 'worldly' things, which they also probably were, in the sense that they had more meaning for those outside monastic life intending to embrace it, than for those who already participated in it.

The clergy of collegiate churches were the first to use the Rule of St Augustine as a norm for their community life. This type of religious community life dominated in Scania and northern Jutland, alternated with Benedictine monasticism throughout Norway, but never entered Sweden. Aspects of this peculiar geographical distribution have been hinted at in previous chapters. The following summarizing discussion will focus upon the Augustinian option as it developed under the impression of the extraordinary impact of St Bernard. There is nothing specifically Scandinavian in the growth of Augustinian community life. The particular feature here is its dominance in two Danish regions and its strong position in Norway and in Old Norse culture. From a few early sites where the Rule of St Augustine was cherished as an instrument to attain the perfect life in a community among clerics, it spread to whole areas where Benedictine communities of one or the other observance did not enter.

Scania

The excavation of St Saviour's or Holy Trinity church in Lund makes evident what the *NL* entries show, that here was a fully developed abbey of clerics who followed the Rule of St Augustine by the mid-twelfth century. The background for the foundation of its daughter abbey in Tommarp shortly after 1147, crowned by the papal letter of protection of 1155, has been lined up earlier.

A second foundation of the 'white' canons of Prémontré is found in northern Scania: Öved or Övedskloster. Obituary entries in the *Liber daticus Lundensis* show that the dedication of this abbey to the Holy Trinity could be a derivation of the St Saviour's dedication title of the Lund abbey, so that we have every reason to assume that in functional terms Öved was a follower of the Lund community, though out in the country. All the lists of Premonstratensian abbeys mention Öved before Vä. As we will see below, the beginnings of Vä can now be placed in the period around 1160. The planning of Öved, then, and the first settlement of canons on this *insula sancte Trinitatis* ought to have taken place in the 1150s, be it before or after the victory of King Valdemar in October 1157. The lists refer to it as a daughter of Prémontré (Nyberg, in Wallin, 1955–91, II), and Wallin (1989, pp. 72–4) points at a fragment of a missal from Öved displaying strong French influence. Wallin refutes the interpretation that the *insula* should be taken literally to mean a physical island in Lake Vombsjön, and refers to the oldest known form of the place-name, Ewith with the meaning 'forest near water'.

The obituary entries for canons 'of St Saviour' or 'of the Holy Trinity' in the *Liber daticus Lundensis* may be distributed in four groups (Nyberg, in Wallin, 1955–91, II, pp. 17–19). The first, those indicating 'St Saviour in Lund', and the second, those rendered as belonging to 'Holy Trinity (Church) in Lund', have been treated in Chapter 8 of this volume. A third group consists of canons of the 'Holy Trinity (Church)' without indication of a place. These are, from the last third of the twelfth century, the two canons Manni, priest, and Florentius, deacon, and not less than seven *conversi*: Alle, Amilius, Bo, Hugo, Hugo, Lambertus and Ricardus. From the first third of the thirteenth century date the entries of five deceased canons: Augustinus and Paulus priests, Michael and Olavus acolytes, Asel without an ordination grade, and Aloldus, Bo, Fastolf, Kæto and Thorstanus named *conversus*. The indifference of the scribe, a canon of the cathedral chapter, may indicate that most of these belonged to the Lund abbey, but a relation to Öved is possible. But then we have in a fourth group a number of entries mentioning Öved. Three of them, dated *c.* 1170–1220, give the abbey name in Danish: Johannes and Simon priests and canons *ecclesie sancte Trinitatis de Øwith* and another Johannes correspondingly *in Øwith*, the others by the Latin formula *de insula sancte Trinitatis*. One retired Abbot Sveno of Öved has been entered in the first third of the thirteenth century, other deceased canons carry names like Berthram, Fregerus and Karolus; *conversi* entries from the same years mention Hildolfus, Kato, Therbernus and Thidricus. There are even two sisters assigned to Öved, Margareta and Tova. The southern names, apparently foreign to Danish usage of baptismal names in this epoch, support the impression that the mother abbey function of Prémontré derived from the lists may have been quite real in Öved. According to later lists, the Lund community had lost its dignity of an abbey and was a priory under Öved.

Recent research has completely changed our understanding of how the fourth abbey of this Augustinian branch, Væ or Vä abbey, came into being. The learned diplomatic analysis of Niels Skyum-Nielsen on the foundation documents of Vä, the texts of which he himself had found among seventeenth-century copies (*DD 1,3*, nos 12, 13, 96, 102), had led him to the conclusion that Vä abbey was founded in June 1170 when many prelates were gathered in Ringsted to celebrate the canonization of Cnut Lavard, the king's father. One archaic detail in the charter, however, disturbed this dating but was discharged as unimportant. The invocation formula *In nomine sancte et individue Trinitatis*, which introduces the undated Odense foundation charters of Bishop Simon and Archbishop Eskil (*DD 1,3*, nos 12 and 13), was used in the royal chancery only in the first years of King Valdemar's reign, for example in his charters for Vitskøl, Veng and Tommarp, but had disappeared from usage there in 1164. As art historians entered into a discussion of the age of the Romanesque mural paintings extant in the abbey church, it was important critically to test the arguments that had placed this charter in the year 1170. In her thesis, Inger Ahlstedt Yrlid (1976) refuted the late dating with reference to the usage of the invocation formula in the royal chancery. She also found an argument in the emendation made by Skyum-Nielsen in the title of the second of three prelates witnessing with the formula *subscribo*: after Archbishop Eskil and before Abbot Hugo of Tommarp stands 'Stephen Bishop of Uppsala', *Stephanus Upsalensis episcopus*, changed by Skyum-Nielsen in *<archi>episcopus*. Instead of this emendation, Yrlid claimed that the charter must have been given prior to Stephen's nomination as archbishop in 1164. This means, if the charter was issued in Denmark, that it must have been given between 1158, when Bishop Simon came to office in Odense, and 1161, when Eskil left the country.

The important consequence of this change is, then, that when Simon (*DD 1,3*, no. 12) refers to the church of Our Lady in Vä as something 'I have received as a gift from My Lord the King and the Queen as well as from the Lord the Archbishop of Lund' and that the same donors now wanted to 'complete what I have been striving for for long time', *et inclinavit domini regis et reginae simulque praefati archiepiscopi voluntatem ad perficiendum quod diutius optaveram*, we are dealing with a foundation made *c.* 1158/60 by Bishop Simon of Odense in one of his first years of office and in Valdemar's first period of power, *locum illum ... sicut libere susceptum possederam, ita quoque libere Praemonstratensi ordini perpetuo possidendum contuli* ([that I] have transferred this place to the Premonstratensian order to be its free property for ever just as I owned it freely after having received it). That Stephen was bishop-elect before he became Archbishop of Uppsala is seen in the expression used by Pope Alexander III in his letter of 5 August 1164 to the Swedish bishops (*DD 1,2*, no. 154): *Venerabilem fratrem nostrum Stephanum olim Vpsalensis ecclesie electum nunc vero archiepiscopum vestrum ad sedem apostolicam venientem debita benignitate suscepimus* (we have gently received our venerable brother Stephen, previously bishop elect of the church of Uppsala, now your archbishop, when he came to the apostolic see). With Stephen moving in the company of Eskil, his first election to the see of Uppsala cannot be dated, but there is no weighty argument against assuming that he was chosen for the diocese of Uppsala at a very early stage and therefore could use this title in his signature as early as 1158/60.

The new chronology allows for an earlier dating of the Romanesque mural paintings of Vä and ultimately for the acceptance of the year 1121 for the consecration of the main altar, a date found written on a slip of parchment placed in a reliquary in the main altar, but so far refuted as erroneous. This possibility is also left open by Thun and Anglert (1984, pp. 40–44). The main conclusion is that the church of Our Lady in Vä may have been consecrated in 1121 under the royal patronage of King Niels. Since his own son, Magnus, had died before him, Yrlid argues that after his death in 1134 his daughter-in-law, Rikissa, must have cared for Vä on behalf of her son with Magnus, Knud Magnussen. But soon afterwards Rikissa married prince Volodar of Minsk (Yrlid still adheres to the older but erroneous opinion that her husband was Vladimir of Novgorod [cf. Gallén, 1985]) and by him gave birth to Sofia, who became the consort of Valdemar the Great. Then followed Rikissa's third marriage, to King Sverker (1142/43). During this period Rikissa had an interest in Vä because her son Knud was still a minor, Yrlid argues. Such historical combinations explain, according to her, some of the mural paintings which would be difficult to interpret by a later dating of the monastic foundation. I quote from Yrlid's (1976, p. 116) summary: 'The paintings in the chancel are here dated to the 1130s and associated with the generation before Valdemar I and Sofia. The donors are identified as being Rikissa, Sofia's mother, and, most probably, Magnus Nielsen, Rikissa's first husband.' After

Valdemar's victory in 1157, Vä was of no interest to him, and he and Sofia therefore let Bishop Simon take over and gave their consent to the founding of a regular canonry on the site.

The process must have taken some years, since Archbishop Eskil's letter, still using the invocation formula *In nomine sanctae et individuae Trinitatis*, is addressed to a certain Brother Gilbert and his brethren in Vä and was signed by another series of witnesses: King Valdemar, Stephen now as archbishop, Bishop Stenar of Linköping, Abbot Valbert of Esrum, Deacon Peter of Lund and *prepositus* Palni. This document is the ordinary bishop's final legal *executio* of the transformation of Our Lady's church in Vä into a Premonstratensian abbey, *exequentes ... ecclesiam ... ad faciendam abbatiam Praemonstratensi ordini perpetuo liberam concedimus*, and is therefore necessarily given at the end of the process. *Terminus post* is Eskil's return to Denmark in 1167, *terminus ante* is the summer of 1172, the latest date when Bishop Stenar of Linköping can have tendered his resignation (it could just as well have been in the summer of 1171) (*DD 1,3*, no. 24). The deacon, Peter of Lund, witnessed another charter issued by Eskil in 1171 (*DD 1,3*, no. 19). Thus, the community of these regular canons must have been organized in Vä between 1158/61 and 1167/72.

Northern Jutland: dioceses of Viberg and Aarhus

The Augustinian cathedral chapter of Viberg was the home of Kjeld, who died 'in the odour of sanctity' in 1150. On 9 June 1188, Pope Clement III allowed his life and merits to be scrutinized by Archbishop Absalon with a formal elevation of the relics in mind (*DD 1,3*, no. 150), still the only valid form of canonization. This followed on 11 July 1189. As Archbishop Eskil defended the canons' right to visit the sick and dispense all the sacraments (1164/77) (*DD 1,2*, no. 161), he recalled that this had been practised by them for more than 50 years. Bishop Niels transformed the parish church of St Michael in Viberg, which belonged to the chapter, into a hospital (*DD 1,2*, nos 136, 169). In 1167 Pope Alexander III took St Margaret's in Asmild under St Peter's protection (*DD 1,2*, no. 175), and on 21 February 1170 the same grace was bestowed upon the cathedral chapter (*DD 1,3*, no. 11), expressly stating the incorporation of St Margaret's in Asmild and St Martin's in the island of Fur in Limfjorden; later the chapter also got St Vincent's in Lime (*DD 1,3*, no. 54). The right of the canons to vote at the election of a bishop was confirmed. It was all repeated in Clement III's nearly identical charter of 8 June 1188 (*DD 1,3*, no. 149).

In a remarkable document from 1176, Bishop Niels confirmed, on his own authority and with the consent of the *parrochiani* of the church of St Peter's in Grinderslev, a *societatis et fraternitatis confoederationem* (a confederation of community and brotherhood) between that church, where *fratres* also lived, led by a prior, and the cathedral chapter (*DD 1,3*, no. 56). This way of founding a 'daughter abbey' differs from that practised among monks. On the highest plateau in the centre of the Salling peninsula which stretches out northwards into Limfjorden, there is a site called Oddense, apparently a former cult-place of Odin. The Salling peninsula was divided into two hundreds. Grinderslev north-east of Oddense is centrally placed in the northern hundred, on an important road leading from the island of Mors eastwards over the peninsula to the crossing passage over Valpsund to the Limfjorden coast of Himmerland where, further north, Vitskøl is situated. From Viberg's vantage point, the position of Grinderslev must have seemed profitable for the establishment of a pastoral and spiritual centre.

Tapping their spiritual energy from roots other than the monkish tradition, the Viberg canons of the twelfth century constitute one of the most remarkable regular communities in Scandinavia. Its counterpart and twin was not any of the agrarian monasteries on the Danish countryside, but the St Lawrence metropolitan chapter in Lund. The synthesis of Viberg's ecclesiastical history achieved by Severinsen (1932) is still the most relevant contribution to an understanding of the monastic alternative as it was offered to dozens of men and women by the Augustinan canonical tradition in the diocese of Viberg.

Augustinian community life also sought the renowned Gudenå river basin. Benedictine inspiration from the original Veng abbey had attracted the Sminge monks from Vitskøl. We have seen how, in the process of their taking over Veng and Kalvø before their final move to Øm, these monks had indirectly made room for the male Benedictine abbey of Voer and the Benedictine nuns in Ring. Further downstream the Gudenå river, after the lakes where Øm, Voer and Ring were already established, at the height of Sminge, which is situated on an tributary from the east, Augustinian canons became established at Vejerslev on a western tributary of the river. It is not known when this happened, but in 1203, an Abbot Ingemar presided over the abbey. He and the prior of Ring were the only witnesses to a donation of Bishop Peter Vognsen to the cathedral (*DD 1,4*, no. 82), perhaps a hint that the bishop had stimulated the Augustinian canons to settle in his diocese as a counterweight to the two types of Benedictine monks he already had. That Vejerslev was the original site of an Augustinian house, which moved to Alling in the 1240s, was argued by Rasmussen (1956) in his analysis of the property of Alling abbey, since at the Reformation it owned all 26 manors in the district of Vejerslev.

One striking piece of evidence for the spread of Augustinian canonical life in Denmark is seen in the discussions in the cathedral chapter of Ribe about whether to adopt Augustinian regular life there or not, *ut vel formam Vibergensis ecclesiae sub regulari conversatione vel saecularium canonicorum Hildensemensium concorditer sectarentur* (that they in unity either follow the form of the church of Viberg under regular observance, or that of the secular canons of Hildesheim) (CER, 1933–35, p. 28). The events are intertwined with the changes in Seem abbey and the negotiations with the Herrisvad monks. Only recently, in 1145, the Flemish Bishop of Ribe, Elias, had organized the prebends and given the cathedral canons the right to administer the school and to appoint new canons (*DD 1,2*, no. 87), but the matter had not calmed down. It must have been during Eskil's exile from Denmark that Archbishop Stephen of Uppsala, the previous Alvastra monk, threatened the chapter with excommunication because it had 'apostacized' from its promise to adopt the Rule of St Augustine. He is said to have obtained in Benevent the papal letter of 8 November 1169 quoted in CER (*DD 1,2*, no. 191), where the Pope states that he had heard that:

> *cum vos habitum regularem professi secundum beati Augustini regulam vivere elegissetis ... ad vomitum postea remeastis nec professionem promissam in modico servastis*
> (you, after you had pronounced your vows in the regular habit and had chosen to live according to the Rule of St Augustine ... have then returned to your vomit and for a while do not observe the vows you have promised.)

The conflict leading up to the papal letter seems to have lasted for several years in the mid-1160s. Bishop Radulf is mentioned as the one who wanted the chapter to become regular, but the chronicle states that a vote was taken and *plurima pars iuvenum* (the greater part of the young [canons]) were against the regular state of the chapter. An effort to initiate a public discussion on the matter at the great meeting of king, lords and bishops in Ringsted in June 1170 came to nothing, since Bishop Radulf died soon afterwards. As we have seen earlier, his successor, Bishop Stephen, the former abbot of Herrisvad, was apparently not interested in making the canons stick to their vows. To him, Seem and Løgum were more important. Thus the Augustinian community life became restricted to Northern Jutland, whereas in the diocese of Ribe, and elsewhere, the Rule of St Benedict became the landmark for the monastic interpretation of Christianity.

Northern Jutland: diocese of Børglum

The foundation in the diocese of Børglum of a community of Augustinian canons who counted Steinfeld in the Rhineland as its mother abbey has been treated above. This community apparently followed Steinfeld in the gradual acceptance of the statutes of the French abbey of Prémontré in the period 1150–80 (Nyberg, 1986, p. 96). These statutes were observed in the four Scanian abbeys as well, where they had not been implanted from Steinfeld but, as it seems, directly from Prémontré. Therefore, the Scanian Norbertines may have differed from those in the diocese of Børglum and its derivations.

It is against this background we have to understand the exemplary letters of Abbot William of Æbelholt on Zealand concerning monastic observance among some non-specified regular communities in the diocese of Børglum (Nyberg, 1986, pp. 90–93, 102). The community must have enjoyed a certain tolerance on the part of Bishop Tyge (1145/46–76/77), the founder of Ø Kloster for nuns in an island in Limfjorden. The same may have been the case under Bishop Omer, who participated in the Lateran Council of 1179, but was transferred to Ribe 1183/85, where he died in 1204. That there was a shift after Omer, and that this was expected by Abbot William to happen, is evident from the words he addressed to his successor, Bishop Turgot, who came to office at the latest in July 1187 (*DD 1,3*, pp. 531–3, Lib. II, p. 41):

> You ought to know, Father, that we congratulated ourselves to hear of your happy promotion, and still more devotedly so, the more we expected that the Church of God by your efforts would carry its fruits more abundantly ... But now, Father, the fresh colour has changed, cither and choir are replaced by sorrow and, as we hear, the organ by the voice of those who weep, for our expectations are gone ... Does it not seem to you, Father, to be an injustice not to follow the rules of the old, not to obey those in charge, and thus annihilate the Rule of our Father Augustine?

The collection of Abbot William's letters contains two versions of this letter, Lib. II, 41 and 66, of which the latter (*DD 1,3*, pp. 558–60) is longer and more explicit, amongst other things accusing the members of an unspecified community of leaving their dormitory at night to visit prostitutes. William refers to the good relations which formerly existed between this community and Turgot and what the observant members in its midst expected the bishop would do with the negligent ones.

In the context of twelfth-century monastic movements, the harsh words of Abbot William must not be taken too literally. We know nothing of the sources he had in his assessment of a corrupt state of affairs in the unnamed Augustinian community of the diocese of Bishop Turgot. His words fit too well into the general pattern of condemnation of 'non-reformed' monasteries. Another letter (Lib. II, p. 42, in *DD 1,3*, pp. 533–4) is addressed to a persecuted religious superior who is recommended to seek refuge in Esrum. In the collection it is presented as *Ad praepositum sancti Theodegarii* (To the provost of St Thøger's [church]) (Vestervig, cf. Chapter 10 in this volume). But there is nothing in the text of the letter to refer to Vestervig, Børglum or St Augustine. It is not certain that the rubrics are assigned to the right letters; in the course of copyists' work they may have been derived from an index (Boserup, 1992). It also seems strange that a provost in North Jutland should be advised to flee to Zealand seeking refuge from sufferings which are hardly possible to define. There may well have been a crisis in regular community life at some place or other in the diocese of Børglum in the 1180s. Vestervig is not the only alternative; Vrejlev, Børglum and a possible community at the St Thøger's church in Vrensted are discussed by Hviid (1993). Abbot William may have used a crisis to demonstrate his ability to get involved in what must have seemed to him to be a case of urgent necessity.

Zealand

Augustinian monasticism in Zealand is intimately linked to Abbot William (1127–1202), a canon of the Abbey of Ste-Geneviève in Paris, whose biography is known from his *Vita*, written in preparation for his canonization in 1224 (*VSD*, pp. 287–386). The intervention in his abbey resulting from an incident in June 1147, when Pope Eugenius III, preparing to celebrate mass in the presence of the king and the queen, became witness to a violent fight between his own and the canons' servants, was decisive for William's future. After William, among others, had opted to do so, canons from St Victor were transferred there to implant the better observance of rule and statutes (cf. Bautier, 1991).

Personal contacts with Absalon, who studied in Paris in 1146–56, may have led to his involvement in Denmark, which began in 1165, upon the call of then Bishop Absalon. By way of Ringsted, William was brought to the small Augustinian community in Eskilsø in Roskilde Bay, of which we know nothing else other than what his *Vita* tells us, except for the death notice of its former canon, Bishop Asser of Roskilde, in *NL* (see Chapter 10 in this volume). After a decade, the canons, whom William had re-educated or attracted to Eskilsø, moved to Æbelholt in the parish of Tjæreby, not far from the great Lake Arresø further north, between Roskilde Bay and Lake Esrum. The first church must have been built during 1175–78 (Abbot William Lib. II, p. 14, *DD 1,3*, pp. 493–4; cf. Møller-Christensen, 1958, p. 85), its earliest property was confirmed by Bishop Absalon *c.* 1175 and by Pope Alexander III in 1179 (*DD 1,3*, nos. 51, 78, 79).

From 1178 Absalon was also archbishop; his successor in 1191 on the chair of Roskilde, Peder, a son of his cousin Sune, had gone to school in Æbelholt. The abbey church took over the dedication to St Thomas from Eskilsø but the place was also called *Paraclitus* 'the Consoler', perhaps in remembrance of the refuge by this name of Abelard in Champagne after the sentence against him procured by Bernard (*DD 1,3*, no. 51, p. 75). Abbot William's involvement in state affairs kept him away from his abbey time and again, and for several years in the 1190s, especially because of the unhappy fate of the Queen of France, the Danish princess, Ingeborg, who had been married to King Philip August (1180–1223), but repudiated by him after the wedding night (Damsholt, 1996). The abbey developed into a unique centre of knowledge and skill, not least in the medical field: its function as a hospital became known to scholars by the excavation of its cemetery and the classification of deaths observable on the skeletons, the first research project of this kind in Denmark (Møller-Christensen, 1958).

Æbelholt meant primarily an opening to a regular community life with an emphasis on the social duties to be practised on the way to perfection. In that sense, it brought to Zealand the essence of Augustinian monasticism in a way neatly corresponding to that which the canons of Viberg did for Jutland. There was no fundamental difference between the attitude of these canons to their surrounding world, and that of the canons who followed the Prémontré statutes and visited its general chapter. The institutionalized corrective power among the Premonstratensians corresponded well to the charismatic flair of Abbot William, so strongly felt through all his letters.

Norway and Iceland

The sequence of monasteries following the Rule of St Augustine in Norway is striking in the way they were evenly distributed all along the rocky coast.

St Olav's Augustine monastery in Stavanger, generally assumed to have been the first of its kind in Norway (Gunnes, 1987, p. 57; Lunde, 1987, p. 100), seems to have been above all an asset to the episcopal see (see Chapter 8 in this volume).

The next Augustinian monastic foundation, tentatively dated to *c.* 1150, may have been St John the Baptist's monastery, Jonsklostret, across Strandgaten up to Tårnplass in Bergen (Lunde, 1987, p. 103). Its central position in the urban layout, matching that of St Olav's in Stavanger, might indicate a comparable role in relation to pastoral tasks, the cathedral clergy and urban growth (Helle, 1995, pp. 141–2).

An important mediator of cultural impulses was the most famous Icelandic bishop of the twelfth century, Þórlákr Þórhallsson (1133–93), venerated as a saint immediately after his death. During his years of study, 1153–59, he had been influenced by St Victor in Paris. But he had also studied in Lincoln. Upon his return to Iceland he founded, in 1168, the first Augustinian monastery of his island, Þykkvabœr, and became its first abbot. This was the first male regular religious community in Iceland's principal diocese, Skálholt, an area covering the eastern, southern and western quarters of the island, and it became a counterpart to the Benedictines of Þingeyrar in the northern diocese of Hólar. In 1172, an Augustinian daughter abbey was founded from Þykkvabœr on the island of Flatey in the western quarter, and transferred to Helgafell closer inland in 1184. By the hand of its abbot, Ögmundr Kálfsson, a *Skrá um kanoka setr og staðar forráð að Helgafelli* (statutes for the canonry and its administration at Helgafell) from *c.* 1186 has been preserved (*Diplomatarium Islandicum*, I, no. 69). As bishop of Skálholt, Þórlákr kept the newly founded monasteries in strict obedience.

It must have been from these surroundings – hardly from Norway – that the urge for a realization of the monastic alternative in the remote Norse settlements in Greenland was awakened. In the southernmost corner of Greenland, the so-called Eastern settlement on Greenland's west side, in the Ketilsfjord/Tasermiut Bay, an Augustinian abbey or priory dedicated to St Olav existed which may have been founded during this period (Jansen, 1972, p. 118).

Male Benedictine monasticism on Iceland was now confined to the northern diocese of Hólar, where it developed further with the foundation of Munkaþverá in 1155. Here, the first Icelandic Marian poetry was composed during these years by Einarr Skúlasson and Abbot Nikulás Bergsson (died 1159 or 1160), the latter also the author of *Leiðarvísir*, a complete guide for the road to Jerusalem (Wilkinson, Hill and Ryan, 1988).

On the other hand, female Benedictine monasticism was given its first and only Icelandic site in the Skálholt diocese under Þórlákr: according to the Icelandic annals, a convent of nuns was founded in 1168 in Kirkjubœr in the eastern quarter, on the melting water of the glacier Vatnajökull. Since we find a Benedictine nuns' convent also in Greenland, said to have been situated in Sigurdfjord/Unartoq Bay still in the

Eastern Settlement, one may reasonably assume that it was founded in the same period under inspiration from Kirkjubœr.

But in 1164, in the presence of the Austin Abbot of Wellow by Grimsby (Gunnes, 1987, p. 58), a Norwegian magnate, Erling Skakke, the father of the boy king, Magnus Erlingsson, who had been crowned in 1163, founded the Augustinian Holy Spirit monastery on the island of Halsnøy in the diocese of Bergen between Bergen and Stavanger (Lidén, 1967; Lunde, 1987, pp. 107–8), centrally placed in the communication system along the coast. Documentary evidence from later centuries shows that the agrarian, richly endowed Halsnøy depended heavily upon the bishop for most of its transactions. The foundations of the earliest church of Halsnøy have been uncovered, measuring 28.5 × 9 m on the outside. Halsnøy seems to have been a kind of completion to the urban Jonsklostret in Bergen and was in any case the first Augustinian monastery in Norway to represent the life of regular canons in a wholly agrarian setting – thereby certainly rendering the model for Utstein, the island monastery to which the St Olav canons of Stavanger moved *c.* 1263/80.

The higher Norwegian clergy under Archbishop Eystein supported the kingdom of Magnus, which it had brought to life and patronized from the beginning. This, together with the Victorine inspiration from Paris, may partly explain the Norwegian archbishop's share in further Augustinian monastic foundations such as (H)Elgeseter outside Trondheim (Lunde, 1987, p. 114) and Kastelle monastery on the north-western outskirt of the harbour town of Konghelle or Kungahälla on the Göta Älv, the south-eastern Norwegian border to Sweden, in present-day Bohuslän, Sweden (cf. Schück, 1983–84, pp. 152–8). Both were certainly younger than Halsnøy. On the other hand, Archbishop Eystein had a personal reason for choosing Konghelle far away from his bishopric and from central areas of Norwegian power and administration: in this important harbour and border town he had served as a priest in 1157, when he was nominated by King Inge to the archbishopric, as stated by Pope Alexander III in the 1160s (Vandvik, 1959, no. 14; cf. pp. 21–3):

> *Ad audientiam nostram iam pridem peruenit, quod tu in ecclesia de Conongellia, de qua in episcopum uocatus et electus fuisti, regulares uelis canonicos ordinare et eorum sustentationem de bonis a Deo tibi collatis congrue providere.*
> (Already long ago it has come to our knowledge that you wish to institute regular canons in the church of Konghelle, from which you were called and chosen to the bishopric, and that you wish adequately to provide for their living by property which God has given to you.)

The Pope allows this, provided the Bishop of Oslo has nothing against it, but he does not want to confirm the foundation yet, before the canons have been installed. The name Kastelle indicates a fortress, and the site of the monastery has been identified on functionally transformed foundations on the northern outskirts of the town, which does not exist today (Andersson, 1981). Schück (1983–84) believes that the Konghelle monastery, on account of its peripheral position in Norway, was more important as a mediator of teachings from St Victor to the neighbouring Swedish diocese of Skara by way of Æbelholt. Abbot William addressed one of his letters to this convent (Lib. II, p. 39, in *DD 1,3* pp. 529f.) and mentioned it indirectly in a letter to the Bishop of Skara (Lib. II, p. 16, in *DD 1,3*, pp. 495f.). Treating moves in the thirteenth century to introduce the Rule of St Augustine in the cathedral chapter of Skara, Schück discusses influences from Augustinian monasticism in the surroundings. There were close contacts between the Swedish harbour town Lödöse further upstream Göta Älv and Denmark, as evidenced by the runic calendar found in Lödöse but displaying saints' feasts according to Danish calendars (Nyberg, 1993b).

The most important inspiration for these Norwegian Augustinian foundations has been sought in St Victor in Paris. During their studies, the higher Norwegian clergy had established contacts with the St Victor canons – some may even have been living in the abbey. Arne Odd Johnsen states in an English summary (1943–46, p. 431; cf. Johnsen, 1955, pp. 113–17):

> In an earlier work the author has proved that three successive Norwegian archbishops, Øystein (1160–88), Eirik (1189–1205) and Tore (1206–14) have all stayed in the convent of St Victor in Paris ... In this connection it is of interest to mark that the convent which must have given so vital impulses to the Norwegian archbishops, managed very well to reconcile marked reforming tendencies with loyalty to the royal house ... no doubt at least two or three of the Augustinian convents that were founded at the time of Archbishop Øystein were organized on the model of St Victor's ... It is not only Theodoricus's 'History of Norway' that is influenced by the spiritual activity at the convent of St Victor, but that is demonstrably also the case with Norwegian liturgical works of the latter half of the 12th century.

That influences from Iceland reached Norway and Theodoricus – possibly identical with Archbishop Þórir of Trondheim (1205–14) – for the composition of his *Historia Norwegiae* and *Historia de antiquitate regum Norwagiensium* is beyond doubt (Cormack, 1993), and a Victorine inspiration must be assumed. But there is no direct evidence for placing the cultural milieu in which this historical writing originated in a specific monastery like, for example, the Augustinian monastery of Elgeseter in Trondheim or Benedictine Nidarholm.

Among Augustinian foundations of the twelfth century in Norway we count, last but not least, St Olav's Premonstratensian abbey in Tønsberg. It is mentioned in the *Historia de profectione Danorum in Hierosolymam* (*SM*, II, pp. 444–92), which was composed at the latest in 1191, probably in the Premonstratensian cathedral monastery of Børglum (Backmund, 1972, pp. 244–51; Johnsen, 1976). It was favoured by income from the 'beautifully built' St Michael's church on the hill above the settlement. By 1180, Børglum had followed its mother abbey, Steinfeld, on its way to full participation in the community of abbots around Prémontré. The mention of a planned daughter foundation in an unnamed kingdom in the letters of the prior of Steinfeld, Ulrich (1152–70), may possibly refer to Norway (Nyberg, 1986, p. 110, n. 481). It has been assumed that St Olav's abbey in Tønsberg was strictly oriented towards promoting the cult of St Olav; the monastic church, finished in 1207, a circular construction – the only one of its kind in Norway – with an interior diameter of 23 m, recalling the octagon of the cathedral of Trondheim which housed the tomb of St Olav (Lunde, 1987, p. 98; 1993). Lunde proposes that the good political relations between King Valdemar the Great (1157–82) and Erling Skakke, which in 1170 led to the nomination of Erling as earl of the Viken area, facilitated the spread of these canons to Norway. Earl and archbishop were the main protagonists of the kingdom of young Magnus Erlingsson, who can be shown to have stayed in Tønsberg on several occasions between 1176 and 1180. The monastery was situated at the eastern end of the urban settlement along the shore of Tønsberg and had its own anchorage.

Børglum and Tønsberg have been given their early profile in the monastic history of Scandinavia by the circumstances of their foundation stories and by the history of the pilgrimage to Jerusalem planned to be a common Danish–Norwegian project by sea through the Mediterranean (Johnsen, 1976). It is quite clear that the origin of both abbeys was intimately linked to political developments of the Valdemarian age. Also commercial links with export of surplus production are possible: in the thirteenth century, contacts with the isolated Scottish abbey of Fearn are suggested by one of the abbey lists which places Fearn between the Jutish–Norwegian and the Scanian abbeys of Prémontré (Nyberg, 1993a).

Hospitallers of St John

The Rule of St Augustine was also adopted by such knights, sergeants, brothers and priests who became organized in the 1130s and 1140s with the common religious purpose of protecting a holy area in Jerusalem – the Temple, the Hospital. The fundamental intention of these brethren, to care for pilgrims who stayed in the Hospital of St John in Old Jerusalem, was not suppressed as other, more striking and more sensational features, related to this monastic movement as well as to that of the Templars, emerged: the spectacular, institutional integration of the virtues of knightly warriors in a monastic setting of self-denial and action for God. As the knights of the Hospital began defending the frontier of the Kingdom of Jerusalem against the hostile hordes who threatened Frankish supremacy, they appeared to be, and to all intents and purposes they were, the leaders of their organization, fulfilling the roles of religious superiors although without clerical ordination, and making themselves indispensable in matters requiring decisions. The peaceful charitable work of sergeants, brothers and priests remained the stable factor, however, so it was soon made clear that a house of Hospitallers could very properly exist without knights. The door was open for them to establish houses over all Europe.

In Scandinavia there is no conclusive evidence for any presence of the Hospitallers prior to Archbishop Eskil's visit to Jerusalem, which is generally dated to 1164.[1] Among the subscriptions of *prepositus* Isak's foundation for the nuns of Our Lady's in Roskilde (*DD 1,2*, no. 163) we find *Fratres de hospitali in Hierusalem subscripserunt*, but this undated charter, from 1164 at the earliest, may have been given as late as 1178.

We have no information about gifts to the Hospitallers prior to their arrival, in the way we know of gifts to the Holy Sepulcre in, among other countries, *Datia*, as can be seen from papal letters to the Austin canons of the Holy Sepulchre in 1170, 1182 and 1196 (*DD 1,3*, nos 16, 105, 214). While we have no trace of these canons in Scandinavia and do not know who received these gifts and how they were administered – according to Kaspar Elm, the canons of the Holy Sepulchre created an organization capable of administering goods given to the Holy Sepulchre in several European countries (Elm, 1980) – the Hospitallers may have received gifts addressed to the Hospital and started to administer them and to send the revenues through Europe as a contribution to the struggle against the infidel.

Certainly the Hospital and the Hospitallers were known to Scandinavians who had visited the Holy Land. Sometime during the

1160s they must have arrived in Zealand and received the compound on the western outskirts of Slagelse which developed into Antvorskov monastery. The knightly way of combining warrior virtues with monastic self-denial had an appeal to King Valdemar the Great, who granted the Hospitallers the right to collect a special tax from every *familia* in Denmark (known from *DD 1*,7, no. 156, from 1244). The Hospitallers, with their background in St Bernard's ideas of a life in knightly and monastic order, were certainly to Archbishop Eskil's taste as well (Reitzel-Nielsen, 1984, pp. 142–50), so Antvorskov may well have been a mutual project of Valdemar and Eskil and an expression of their reconciliation after Eskil's return from exile in 1167 (Nyberg, 1990).

It is less clear who invited the Hospitallers to Norway and Sweden, only that it happened in the same generation as Antvorskov. We may assume that the pioneer settlers all came from or by way of Antvorskov.

Norwegian Varne or Varna south of the town of Moss in Østfold, on the eastern shore of Viken in the diocese of Oslo (Lunde, 1987, p. 92), must have been functioning before Sverre became king in 1177. It was in charge of the care of aged members of the royal retinue, according to the Norwegian *hirdskrá* 'Statutes for the retinue' (Norges gamle Love, 2, 1848, p. 410; Nyberg, 1990). The popular rebel king could hardly have taken such an initiative. Varna is therefore assumed to be Erling Skakke's family foundation.

The Swedish Eskilstuna house of the Hospitallers near the episcopal see of Strängnäs on the southern shore of Lake Mälar (Hellberg, 1935, pp. 74–90) was entrusted with the cult of the Anglo-Saxon missionary St Eskil, mentioned by Aelnoth as *pie memorie Eskillinus episcopus ex nobilissimo Anglorum orbe deueniens* (*VSD*, 83). He had been killed under that very Sven who was the last Swedish king to perform public sacrifice in Uppsala, which – according to Henriksson's sequence of sacrificial years – would have been in 1084. Since then Eskil had been venerated as a saint in Tuna, a royal manor near Strängnäs. According to the papal confirmation of 6 September 1231 (*DS*, I, no. 839), the church was under the patronage of the earl, Birger Brosa (cf. Hellberg, 1935, pp. 92–4), and the monastery had been founded by Bishop William of Strängnäs (cf. *DS*, I, no. 58) and the Archbishop of Uppsala, who must have been Stephen, who died in 1185. In the same years, probably the 1170s, the Viby monks, who had lived on ground donated by Doter in the Uppsala diocese on the northern side of Lake Mälar since *c.* 1160 (see Chapter 12 in this volume), moved to Saba/Säby, or Julita, on the southern shore not far from Strängnäs and Eskilstuna. The king's charter to that effect (*DS*, I, no. 64) has been quoted in Chapter 12 in this volume.

Earlier scholars identified Eskilstuna with a supposed Swedish diocese of Tuna, one of the names in the list of Swedish diocesan places from *c.* 1104 (Nyberg, 1991). The monastery would then have been a compensation for the loss of Tuna's episcopal status, in a way similar to Dalby in Scania. Hellström (1971, pp. 60–63) noted, however, that there are several other Tuna places to choose from if one wants to identify the Tuna of the 1104 list worthy of a bishop.

From the religious point of view, the Hospitallers as well as the Cistercian monks would give spiritual strength to the rather small diocese of Strängnäs, which Pope Alexander III confirmed, stating that it also comprised the inland western neighbouring province of Närke (*DS*, I, no. 58). From a pastoral point of view, Archbishop Stephen may have appreciated the Hospitallers – the way of life of these Augustinian priests and brothers in many respects came close to that of Augustinian canons with their share in pastoral responsibilities. By its attachment to the crusading idea and the knightly virtues of nobility, they had a strong appeal among Swedish noblemen and women, as is illustrated by the many renowned names entered later in their necrology (Collijn, 1929).

A papal mandate, the text of which is known only from the Vatican archives (*DD 1,3*, no. 245), permits an inside look into the early world of the Scandinavian Hospitallers. Apparently, soon after the nomination of Pope Innocent III, Archbishop Absalon had complained about the Hospitallers' methods of collecting alms. The Pope's answer of 9 December 1198 and his summary of Absalon's petition makes the issue a question of lay or clerical authority, stating that he has understood from the petition

> that lay brethren of the Hospital of St John, who have not studied (*laici et illiterati*), are being sent out in these countries in order to collect the alms which people out of devotion are accustomed to give to that place to support the poor. But since they are not numerous enough to reach all around, they engage clerics, priests and lay people, even such who are uneducated and not bound by vows (*etiam rudes non religiosos*) but trained in evil deeds, and attach the sign of the Cross on their breasts.

The 'place' to which the money was being sent can hardly be the motherhouse in Jerusalem, but from the context it must refer to Antvorskov, for the benefit of which begging and alms-collecting hordes mentioned here had been engaged on behalf of the 'poor' (of that place). Furthermore, 'these lay people are invested with the office of a prior and are at the head of clerics as well as priests', writes Pope Innocent III, criticizing their lack of respect for the interdict and other acts of episcopal jurisdiction. Archbishop Absalon is entitled to excommunicate such people if they are lay, and to suspend priests and clerics.

The Antvorskov Hospitallers after three decades of existence seem to have made radical use of their exemption from episcopal authority, relying upon permanent papal support in any type of problem. Their structural hierarchy, with knights and sergeants in high offices even making decisions over clerics and priests, could of course not be rejected, since it was written into the statutes. Disregarding episcopal interdict was certainly audacious, however. The Antvorskov Hospitallers had apparently collected alms and the special tax afforded to them since they arrived in Denmark, and thereby from time to time they may have moved on the fringe of law and ecclesiastical order.

What the mandate does not say, is that alms-collecting presupposes some kind of preaching or announcement with a Christian content – therefore the double stress on the two expressions *laici et illitterati* and *etiam rudes non religiosos* quoted above. These first wandering preachers in Denmark institutionally approved of by the highest ecclesiastical authority could not easily find enough educated people to fulfil the task of alms-collecting in a decent manner, hence the complaint and the mandate.

Augustinian monasticism made a deep impact upon Danish and Old Norse culture in the twelfth century. Its influence grew as the Dominicans – who structurally are Augustinian canons, dressed in the habit of Mendicants – spread over the whole of Scandinavia and gained their dominating influence in Finland. Numerous men and women, either young or mature after married life, found their way to the monastic alternative under the guidance of St Augustine's short rule in combination with the customary performance of liturgical, intellectual, pastoral and spiritual tasks. Augustinian monasticism generally did not bear the mark of exclusive group identity feelings, and if it did – as in the case of the Premonstratensians – its adherents acted more peacefully than some monks did. They were willing to accept, to a higher degree than most monks, their duties towards bishops and secular authority, so their striving for perfection clearly included the words of the Gospel: 'Give unto Caesar what belongs to Caesar, and to God what belongs to God.' The Icelandic poem Harmsól (The Sun of Sorrow), composed in the Augustinian monastery of Þykkvabœr by an otherwise unknown canon, Gamli, is the most outstanding early example of this type of piety in an Old Norse setting. The key role of notions like repentence and conversion in the monastic movement of the eleventh and twelfth centuries has left visible traces in Harmsól. The poem mediates the overwhelming impression of man as a sinner, and of God as sole King, the Sun and the

Lord, incarnate in order to approach mankind and lead it to peace and happiness, but without any special Trinitarian notion of God who is equal with Christ, and who is Lord of all the heavens.

Note

1. Skyum-Nielsen (1971, p. 128) took the presence of one *domino Girardo priore de Valle sancti Johannis* in an undated royal letter for Esrum as an indication that the Hospitallers were already in Denmark at the time of this gift; on diplomatic considerations he dated the letter (*DD 1,2*, no. 129) not later than 1160.

CHAPTER FOURTEEN

The Valdemarian age 4: peripheria and conclusion

I Among the Obodrites and Pomeranians

In the lands east of the *limes Saxoniae*, the north–south dividing frontier between the Saxons and the Slavs through the present German land of Schleswig-Holstein, the archbishops of Hamburg-Bremen had been able to keep control of the Christian mission. After the Slav rebellions in 983, however, it took two generations before anyone could again consider establishing a diocesan structure for the eastern areas. But the effort made *c.* 1062 to divide the primary diocese of Oldenburg into three, with Oldenburg, Ratzeburg and Mecklenburg as episcopal sees, went down in the blood of martyrs during the Slav rebellion of 1066, so again until the time of the Saxon Duke Henry the Lion there was no organized episcopal authority in these areas.

Helmold of Bosau is our source for the new beginning of mission among the Wagrians with Vicelin. He had studied in Paderborn in the early 1120s in Adalbero's times as Archbishop of Hamburg-Bremen, then went to Laon, the diocese where Norbert of Xanten founded Prémontré, and was ordained priest by Norbert in Magdeburg in 1126. Extremely well acquainted with the community life of regular Augustinian canons, as he must have been, he gave to the community which he founded at the church of Faldera or Wippersdorf in Holsten in the Hamburg archdiocese a similar monastic structure under the head of a *prepositus* (in 1127) (Pelc, 1998, p. 68). Helmold von Bosau (1973, chs 55–6) speaks of *Falderensis portus* (harbour) as well as *pagus* (county). After long years of priestly missionary work among the Slavs, Vicelin was made bishop of the now reduced, only Wagrian diocese of Oldenburg (1149–54) (*SE V: II*, 55, pp. 63f.), a place where practically no Christians were living (Petersohn, 1979, p. 79). The dioceses of Ratzeburg and Mecklenburg were also formally revitalized at the same time (Petersohn, 1979, pp. 58–96), but all three lacked economic resources, so the Faldera community outside Vicelin's own diocese remained the basis for his activities. In 1160 its episcopal see, Oldenburg, was transferred to Lübeck, a new German town just founded and privileged by Henry the Lion.

In 1163, Bishop Gerold (1154–63) consecrated the church of Faldera, giving it the new name of Novum Monasterium (Neumünster). It is evident from Helmold von Bosau's (1973, ch. 47) account that the *cives*, the citizens of Faldera who came to Vicelin in Meldorf shortly after his ordination in the late 1120s asking for a priest, in reality received a priestly community at their church of Our Lady, from where, even within a few years, some went to Lübeck to serve at the new church there (ibid., ch. 49). They were confronted with resistance against Christian mission in the same way as that reported for Bishop Henrik of Sigtuna during these same years (see Chapter 9 in this volume). An earlier daughter foundation from Faldera in Segeberg (in 1134) (Pelc, 1998, p. 68) had been re-established while Gerold tried to make Eutin his residence (Petersohn, 1979, p. 79). Vows are not mentioned in the community of Faldera, and after Vicelin's death, the monastery loosened its ties with the Oldenburg-Lübeck bishopric's Wagrian mission. The new name Neumünster may indicate a community of regular Augustinian canons, but considering the use of the term *monasterium* in Adam of Bremen, we cannot be sure the canons were not secular after all. The inspiration Vicelin received from Norbert of Xanten had in any case not been sufficient to make Faldera a community of Prémontré canons, although these were the decades when such canons arrived in Danish Scania directly from Prémontré.

The access to the monastic option for Christians in the Wagrian diocese went through monasteries in neighbouring dioceses belonging to the Saxon Benedictine tradition, like Lüneburg, Harsefeld or St Egidius in Braunschweig. Benedictines had settled in Stolpe, Western Pomerania, already in 1153 (Grabkowsky, 1995; Pelc, 1998, p. 68). A great step forwards was taken when the Abbot of St Egidius in Braunschweig, Henry, became Bishop of Lübeck (1173–82). He came from Brussels, had studied in Paris and worked in Hildesheim and Braunschweig before he became a monk. Inaugurating a new era, he founded Our Lady's, St John the Baptist's and St Egidius's Benedictine abbey in Lübeck, consecrated its church in 1177 and made Arnold from Braunschweig its first abbot. Arnold procured papal confirmation in 1191 and 1198 and wrote the continuation of Helmold's chronicle covering the years 1171–1209 (*Germania Benedictina VI*, p. 321). Within a few years refounded German and Christian Lübeck had become a cultural centre of the Wagrian land on its way to becoming the leading commercial magnet of the Baltic (Nyberg, 1976). This great development, perhaps also the attached nuns' convent, caused problems to the monks, however, and *c.* 1240 they moved to Cismar, where the Benedictine monastic option of the diocese was to be found from that time onwards.

In 1186/89, however, Cistercians from Loccum of the Morimond line had arrived and settled in Reinfeld, in a forest area north of the River Trave, invited there and endowed by Count Adolf III of Holsten and for the future held as the 'family monastery' of the counts (*Germania Benedictina XII*, p. 586).

The diocese of Slesvig was one of the neighbours. This would therefore be the opportunity to mention Guldholm, the *Aurea Insula* in Strukstrup hundred, 7 km north of Slesvig, which in 1191 became the successor of St Michael's in Slesvig after the abolition of the latter and the transition of some of its monks to the Cîteaux interpretation of the Rule of St Benedict. Deeply involved in this process, which reached a temporary end in King Cnut VI's confirmation of Guldholm Abbey in 1196 (*DD 1,3*, no. 216), was Abbot William of Æbelholt, as can be seen from two often quoted versions of one of his letters (Lib II, pp. 11 and 12, in *DD 1,3*, pp. 489–91; cf. ibid., nos 110, 169). William's language has been adopted in the royal letter:

> We wish that it be known ... that we approve of the change of order, carried out by the Apostolic Lord, of the black monks of the church of St Michael in Slesvig to the white order which was motivated by the unbearable licentiousness and misconduct of the blacks, who in altogether unrestricted ways shamefully trod the paths of their life there.

The move to Guldholm in Strukstrup hundred may have been motivated by the concentration of some of the abbey's property there, as evidenced by King Cnut VI's letter of 1196. Besides 38 ground plots in the city of Slesvig, the abbey owned Husby, Rosager and parts of Skovby and Bojbøl in Arns hundred, where Slesvig is situated, but also Klensby and a number of shares in Isted, Nybøl and Bregling in Strukstrup hundred, where also the parish churches of Kalleby, Nybøl and Tolk were situated, from which the abbey drew the tithe. The abbey unquestionably belonged to, and oriented itself towards, the Danish realm. After moving in 1209 further south to Ryd in Husby hundred, the *Rus Regius*, the community contributed heavily to Danish history writing by its *Annales Ryenses* (*DMA*, 1980, pp. 148–76 in Latin, followed by several medieval Danish translations). Because of its position in a bilingual and bicultural region, it offered the monastic alternative to different groups in a vast region otherwise entirely lacking cradles of monastic life.

Most startling, the complete necrology of Løgum has been handed down to our time. In 1518, under the auspices of Lord Henrik *abbate et commissario* – Sorø's Abbot Henrik Christensen Tornekrans, 1508–38 – but at the cost of Abbot Henichinus *huius domus abbatis*, a copy was produced of the complete necrologue of Løgum abbey, says the introductory text of the Ms. AM 868 4° in Copenhagen ('Necrologium Monasterii Loci Dei', 1776). According to this preface, the book contained the names of all founders, close adherents and benefactors of 'our house' (= Løgum), as well as of all its abbots, monks and lay brothers who had served the Lord in this place 'from its first foundation until the present day'. Since palaeographical criteria cannot be applied upon this 1518 copy to unravel the time layers through the more than three centuries during which the original necrology was in use, it is not possible to achieve a statistical survey of the number of monks for the limited period *c.* 1170–*c.* 1200 only. A closer analysis with the application of other methods will possibly lead to some results of a more general character for the whole period of more than three centuries.

It may be added here that the development of monasticism in the archdiocese of Hamburg-Bremen took a step forwards in the same period, but mainly in the city of Bremen and its immediate surroundings. Besides the two Stade monasteries as well as Rastede, Harsefeld and the nunnery of Heeslingen (under the inspiration of the missionary work of Vicelin, the latter had been moved to Zeven in 1141 [*Germania Benedictina*, XI, p. 553]), we find here three Benedictine houses. From St Paul in Bremen *c.* 1138/39 (ibid., VI, p. 57), one of the monks, from the family of the counts of Strotel, went out and founded a priory at Osterholz north of Bremen in 1182/85 (ibid., VI, p. 401; XI, p. 487); south of Bremen arose Heiligenrode for monks and nuns in 1181/83, mainly recruited from ministerial families, especially in Bremen. Furthermore, in 1172, a convent for Benedictine nuns arose in Lüne south of Lüneburg (ibid., XI, p. 377). The pattern is definitely more restrained than that of the intense monastic movement in Scandinavia or in Frisian lands in these decades.

In the east, the centre of the Polabians south of the Wagrians was Ratzeburg. There, things turned out differently. When Vicelin had been severly ill for more than a year, in 1154 Henry the Lion negotiated the revitalization of a diocese to the south of Oldenburg for the Polabians with Wichmann, the Archbishop of Magdeburg. In the archdiocese, the Premonstratensians had a very strong position since Norbert had been its archbishop 1126–34. The first bishop, Evermod, Norbert's disciple, a canon in famous early Norbertine monasteries like Cappenberg and Gottesgnaden and finally *prepositus* in Our Lady's in Magdeburg, became the first Bishop of restored Ratzeburg (1154–78); he was afterwards venerated as a saint (*SE V: I*, p. 73). The cathedral chapter became the Premonstratensian monastery. The chapter had the same voting rights at the election of a bishop as we have found in Odense and Viberg (Nyberg, 1986, pp. 132–40).

This, however, was not the first effort of Norbert's Augustinian canons of Prémontré to settle further north on the Slav side of the Baltic Sea. The abbey of Grobe on the island of Usedom, in some abbey lists called Usnam, may have been founded already in 1148; it was in existence at the latest in 1155 (Pelc, 1998, p. 68). According to Jürgen Petersohn (1979, pp. 507–12) its canons came partly from Our Lady's in Magdeburg, where Evermod was the *prepositus*, partly from Pardwin outside Brandenburg. Grobe's *prepositus* Walter witnessed to donations made by Prince Kasimir I and Bishop Benno of Schwerin to Dargun in the mid-1170s (*DD 1,3*, nos 58, 59). Experiences from here may have contributed to the decision to have regular canons constitute the cathedral chapter of Ratzeburg.

Grobe at the mouth of the River Peene, mentioned above, was under Pomeranian ecclesiastical jurisdiction, as was also the earliest monastic site in this area, Stolpe a little further upstream on the Peene, founded around 1153, as we learn from a notification issued 1155/64 by *Adelbertus Dei gratia primus Pomeranorum episcopus* (Pommersches Urkundenbuch, I, no. 43). The foundation was made under Duke Ratibor I, who died on 7 May 1155 or 1156, in memory of Duke Wartislav I, killed in 1147/48 (Helmold von Bosau, 1973, ch. 100; Petersohn, 1979, pp. 356–9). The monastic tradition was implanted from the Abbey of Berge near Magdeburg under its abbot, Arnold, known under the author name of Annalista Saxo. It is quite obvious that it was the concern of Bishop Adelbert that monastic life should flourish in his diocese by this foundation near the church built on the spot where Duke Wartislaw had been killed:

> Since therefore, as our office demands from us, we have a main concern for the improvement of this new plantation, and are burning with the desire of the monks who were our collaborators, after we had got brothers from the most prominent monastery of the church of Magdeburg, we located these brothers on the River Peene in a place called Stolpe ...

Stolpe was the important site of Hirsau Benedictine monasticism in Pomerania in the first generations after the conversion of the country's leaders.

At the time the Premonstratensians arrived in Ratzeburg, the four Prémontré abbeys in Scania must have had a strong appeal and recruited promising members in the course of the 1160s, judging from the series of foundations in Tommarp, Öved and Vä. Duke Kasimir I's positive attitude towards the Danes in the 1170s, since he needed to be backed up by a third power between Polish and German interests (Szacherska, 1988, p. 149), found an echo in the oldest of the four, St Saviour's or Holy Trinity in Lund. In 1177, its canons, some of whom may have been there already, accepted the site of Belbuk on an island in the estuary of the River Rega between Kamień/Kammin and Kołobrzeg/Kolberg, downstream from the city of Trzebiatowo/Treptow. The foundation of Belbuk was supported by Slav noblemen, characterized by Szacherska (1977) as pro-Danish. The foundations of two pagan sanctuaries in the region have been uncovered, so there was without doubt a missionary task linked to the decision of the Lund canons to settle in this new country. The political situation out of which Belbuk was conceived soon changed, however, says Szacherska, for after Kasimir I had fallen in battle in 1180, his brother Boguslav I found it inopportune to support two Premonstratensian foundations so close to each other. The paternity was transferred from Lund to Mariëngaarde in the Frisian lands (Nyberg, 1975–76, p. 35), but the canons from Denmark must have returned to Lund some time in the 1180s, where a crisis hinted at in a letter of Abbot William of Æbelholt to the Abbot of Prémontré (Lib. II, p. 50, in *DD 1,3*, pp. 542–4) may indicate that Lund had overestimated its capacities:

> In case of our brother and co-abbot John from the house of the Holy Trinity in Lund we have heard that he has presented his cause to your mildness ... He is a straightforward and just man, keeping himself away from evil ... There is one thing, however, most dear Father, that I ask of you, that I beseech you to do: that in your care for the honour of your Order you will remove from its midst the evil things on account of which that house has earned a bad reputation, by which, as I have heard, the property of the house is getting lost and the order is upset.

We may reasonably assume that the Pomeranian adventure has tapped the house for some of its resources. It is striking that in later abbey lists, Lund figures only as a priory under Öved.

Finally, for the Cessins and Circipans, two more Obodrite groups further north-east, the bishopric of Mecklenburg had been renewed together with a reduced Oldenburg. Both Vicelin and Mecklenburg's first new bishop, Emmehard, had been consecrated on 25 September 1149 in the abbey church of Harsefeld. Like Vicelin, Emmehard had no resources at his disposal but stayed in the entourage of Henry the Lion until his death in 1155. For the monastic development it must have been rather decisive in this area that his successor was a German Cistercian, Berno, from Amelungsborn in the diocese of Hildesheim (1155–90/91). Unlike Vicelin, who first refused to receive his diocese as a fief from Henry the Lion, out of the conviction that it was an imperial prerogative to enfeoff someone with a bishopric (Helmold von Bosau, 1973, chs 69–70), Berno, who had got papal licence to preach among the Obodrites, immediately after his nomination swore the feudal oath to the duke. His see was transferred to Schwerin in 1160, a new German urban foundation; here, the cathedral was consecrated in 1177.

It is by the introduction of monasticism in this diocese that we become aware of the synchronism between Danish and German developments. That Berno would try to introduce his own abbey's interpretation of monasticism in his diocese is most natural: Doberan, in a lonely part of the Rostock region near the coast, was founded in 1171 by the Slav prince, Pribislaw, and the monks that settled there came from Amelungsborn. But in the same year, Danish monks from Esrum were on the march, settling in Dargun further inland in an area not far from where the diocese of Kammin began. This diocese covered the land of the Pomoranians on both sides of the Oder estuary including parts of the eastern Obodrites, especially the old city of Demmin, the centre of the Circipanians, whereby this region south of Rügen was taken out of the diocese of Schwerin.

The monks counted 25 June 1172 as their beginning in Dargun, the second anniversary of the canonization of Cnut Lavard, the father of Valdemar the Great who, as well as being a Danish Duke, previously had been King of the Obodrites. According to Saxo (Lib. 14, XLVII, pp. 497–9), King Valdemar and Bishop Absalon, on an expedition in the autumn of 1170, had vanquished the Slav Prince Otimar, to be identified with the founder, Chotimar, who confirmed the property of Dargun in the earliest charters (Szacherska, 1977, p. 129): 'The hypothesis that Otimar bought his life at the price of the foundation of the Cistercian monastery known as Dargun abbey has been generally accepted.' Since the marshy land destined to the abbey belonged to Henry the Lion's Saxon duchy, it could not be claimed from the Danish side, but possibly could develop into a Danish sphere of interest in the function of a monastery, argues Stella Szacherska. Apparently King Valdemar wanted to have a share in colonizing and Christianizing the Slav country. Stella Maria Szacherska (1977, p. 131) observes: 'The domain assigned to the abbey of Dargun comprised a territory claimed by three bishoprics, Kamień, Havelberg and Schwerin, but neglected by all of them because of its peripheral situation. It seems in consequence to have been only superficially Christian.' In 1173, Bishop Berno consecrated the new chapel with its altar of Our Lady in the presence of Duke Kasimir I of Pomerania, who also wanted to be counted among the founders. The monks started missionary work in the area.

Dargun did not long contribute to the monastic culture in the land of the Obodrites. Danish controversies with the Pomeranian Duke Kasimir I brought the monks into trouble and in 1199 they moved to Eldena on the *Dänische Wiek*, which belonged to the diocese of Kammin and the Duke of Rügen, where they felt more secure, and where a monastic foundation from Denmark already had been inaugurated. After Rügen had been sieged and finally conquered by the Danes in 1169, its aggregation to Denmark had been acknowledged by the Pope (*DD 1,2*, no. 189). Thus, Danish power was not far away and it resulted in the aggregation of Rügen to the diocese of Roskilde in 1180 (*DD 1,3*, no. 91).

This is the reason why the foundation of a nuns' convent on Rügen is mostly being dealt with under Danish monastic expansion. As Prince Jaromar of Rügen's charter of 1193 for a convent in Bergen on Rügen makes clear, however (*DD 1,3*, no. 196), his foundation of an Our Lady's and St Peter's convent on the island was meant to be an act of gratitude for conversion *de ydolorum cultura* (from the cult system of the idols), if we may translate *cultura* in this way here, in fresh remembrance of past pagan liturgies. The first nuns were Danish, arriving from Our Lady's in Roskilde.

In 1173, a Danish war expedition to the eastern shore of the Oder estuary brought Szczecin/Stettin into Danish hands and forced another Pomeranian prince, Wartislav of Stettin, into collaboration. This led to the foundation of a second Danish Cistercian abbey, in Kołbacz south of Stettin (Petersohn, 1979, pp. 448, 501; Szacherska, 1977, p. 144), renowned among Danish historians because of the earliest known version of the Lund Annals which came there from Belbuk, the *Annales Colbazenses* (*DMA*, pp. 1–11). This foundation was made on cultivated soil on the river Płonia/Plöne, a tributary of Oder. It not only had a long history later on, but was also flourishing enough to be able to send, *c.* 1186, under its first abbot, Everard (died 1195), a group of monks to settle in Pomerelia, west of the Wisła/Weichsel estuary, creating Oliva Abbey (Petersohn, 1979, p. 449; Szacherska, 1988), a future Polish cultural and religious centre.

The Pomeranian adventure gives evidence of Esrum's great potentialities. Under Abbot Valbert or Walbert, from his first appearance as a witness at Eskil's final confirmation of the foundation of Vä *c.* 1170 (*DD 1,3*, no. 13) to his last subscription in the papal protection letter for his abbey in 1193 (*DD 1,3*, no. 193), Esrum became the principal Danish abbey of the observance of Cîteaux, although it was not the oldest one. This development without doubt is due to Zealand's central place in the Danish political structure, to the frequent interference of

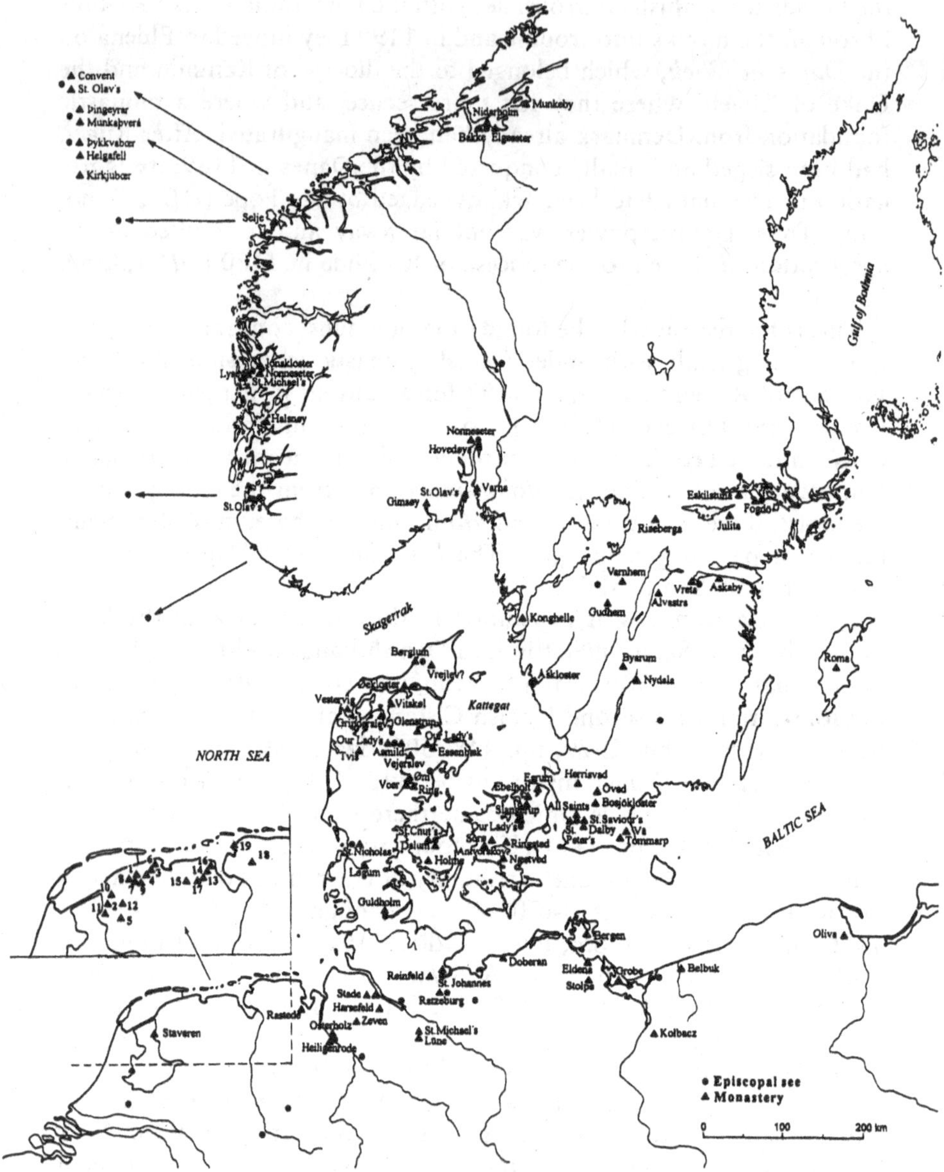

Map IV Monasteries and episcopal sees in North-Western Europe, *c.* 1200. (Drawn by Inger Bjerg Poulsen.)

Note to Map IV: numbers indicate the Frisian monasteries founded after Staveren:

1 Foswerd OSB, 1109?–1200
2 Ludingakerk OSA, 1158
3 Dokkum OPraem, prior to 1170
4 Klaarkamp OCist, 1163
5 Bloemkamp OCist, 1191
6 Sion OCistMon, 1191
7 Genezareth OCistMon, 1191
8 Mariëngaarde OPraem, 1163
9 Bethlehem OPraemCan, 1170
10 Lidlum OPraem, 1182
11 Pingjum OPraem, prior to 1200
12 Monnikebajum OPraemCan, 1186
13 Wittewierum OPraem
14 Roozenkamp OPraemCan
15 Aduard OSB, 1192
16 Feldwerd OSB, 1183
17 Thesinge OSBMon, 1182
18 Meerhusen OSB, prior to 1198
19 Marien Dale, prior to 1198

Absalon in the affairs of Esrum and Sorø (McGuire, 1982, pp. 90f.), to the personal abilities of Abbot Walbert, and perhaps also to the zeal of Abbot William of the neighbouring Æbelholt abbey. As mother of Sorø, of the Dargun community now moving to Eldena, and of Kołbacz, Esrum abbey, probably still under Walbert, in 1194 took the decision to use its Halland property for the creation of a regular abbey, called Ås or Åskloster, Latinized Asilum, on the mouth of Viskan, the northernmost river estuary of Halland before one arrives at Göta Älv. The spot was well adapted for keeping up communications between Varnhem in Västergötland and Vitskøl abbey on the Limfjorden (Nyberg, 1993b).

Six of William of Æbelholt's letters are addressed to 'the abbot of Esrum', giving evidence to the close relations between the two (Lib. I, pp. 36–8; Lib. II, pp. 27, 31, 72, in *DD 1,3*). Esrum was sure of the intercessory prayer of the cathedral chapter of Lund for its first abbot, Folmar, for a certain Count Nicholas, a relative of Eskil's, who had become a monk in Esrum, and for a *Iohannes presbiter et monacus* (*NL*). Further entries for deceased members of the Esrum community are found in the *Liber daticus Lundensis*, among which, however, an entry for Abbot Walbert himself is lacking. From the decades around 1200, we find as deceased from Esrum one Tholf priest and monk, Fromaldus, Johannes (twice) and Godefridus styled *monacus*, and as *conversus* Thorstanus (twice), Sicfridus, Ako, Eggibertus, Thorth. If this is a complete list of deceased members of Esrum from the decades around 1200, it can only be explained by the settlement in Åskloster and by the Pomeranian adventure, keeping monks abroad in a colonizing country where some may have stayed for the rest of their days.

II Among the Frisians

The first great development of Frisian monasticism moves on the time-scale of Valdemarian Denmark. Monasticism was at first nothing but monastic property owned by great abbeys abroad and, as such, without roots among the Frisians themselves. As monasticism finally entered into Frisian lands (Mol, 1979), it came from the west and, characteristically enough, as a result of pastoral efforts of the Bishops of Utrecht (Ehbrecht, 1974, p. 62). St Odulphus abbey in Staveren, situated in the *comitatus* Zuidergo which lost much of its land through floods and storm surges in the twelfth and thirteenth centuries, was Benedictine in 1132 and later (first mentioned in 1245) settled monks at St Nicholas in Hemelum further inland. Benedictine monks and nuns were established in Foswerd in Ostergo, west of Dokkum and not far from the sea (see Map IV), *c.* 1200 at the latest (probably not as early as 1109, under the Bavarian Bishop Burchard 1100–12, [*SE V: I*, p. 194; Mol]). Augustinian canons settled in Ludingakerk in Westergo near present-day Harlingen in 1158 under Bishop Godefrid (1156–78), previously dean of the cathedral chapter of Utrecht. Little is known of the community life which probably existed in Dokkum prior to the renewal which took place there in 1170.

As pointed out earlier, in Frisian lands a monastery could only exist as a settlement on one of the *terpen*. Monasteries were thereby physically limited to a restrained area and were distinguished from other *terpen* only by their more impressive building constructions. As for property, there was no limit to what they could acquire of the easily inundated lowlands.

The breakthrough came with the new movements of the twelfth century: the 'white' orders of Augustinian canons of Prémontré and Benedictine monks of Cîteaux. In the same year, 1163, they both arrived and settled in Ostergo (Mol, 1979, pp. 11–17).

Cistercians from Clairvaux made Klaarkamp between Foswerd and Dokkum their first and most influential abbey in the Frisian lands (Mol, 1996), a mother abbey and model for several other great and influential abbeys, like the well-protected inland abbey of Bloemkamp near Hartwerd in Westergo in 1191. They may have supervised two Cistercian nunneries founded in Ostergo in the same year 1191, Sion north of Dokkum and Genezareth south of Foswerd.

On one of the *terpen* west of Foswerd near the sea, at the mouth of the River Boorne, directly north of present-day Leeuwarden, the rector of the parish, Frederik, who died in 1175, had founded Mariëngaarde and got it approved by Bishop Godefrid. Frederik established the bonds with Prémontré by going personally to Steinfeld, requesting of *prepositus* Ulrich that Steinfeld take on the function of a mother abbey towards Mariëngaarde (Ehbrecht, 1974, p. 61). Like the Danish bishops, among them the Flemish Bishop of Ribe, Elias, Godefrid in the early 1160s also adhered to Frederik Barbarossa's Pope Victor IV, afterwards returning to Alexander III like the others. The Frisians shared the Steinfeld filiation with the Premonstratensian cathedral canons of Børglum who must also have followed their Bishop Tyge in support of the king, the Emperor and Pope Victor. As pointed out earlier, the Norwegian foundation in Tønsberg probably emerged from the same net of connections. Being situated very near the sea, Mariëngaarde had easy access to the ship connections. The canons could easily get in touch with the canons of Børglum and Tønsberg and, for that matter, also with their brethren in Belbuk in Pomerania, over whom they exerted paternity rights as long as it existed, as they did later over Grobe on Usedom (abbey lists, Nyberg, 1975–76; Wallin, 1955–91, VI, p. 7). In 1170, while Frederik was still alive and still under Bishop Godefrid, a convent for canonesses called Bethlehem was established inland between Mariëngaarde and Klaarkamp, and the canons in the same year also proceded to Dokkum, where they implanted their observance of the Rule of St Augustine in the existing community of St Boniface (Mol, 1979, p. 10).

In the 1180s the canons sent settlers westwards from Ostergo to Westergo. In 1182 they founded the Abbey of Mariendal in Lidlum, whereas its priory of Vinea Domini in Pingjum probably came later. Both were situated in exposed situations close to the sea, Lidlum north of, Pingjum south of the Augustinian canons in Ludingakerk. Further inland in Westergo, well protected, a priory of canonesses was established in 1186 at the *Mons Sancti Michaelis* in Bajum or Monnikebajum.

Not until the next generation did the Premonstratensian canons move eastwards from Dokkum. Here, they were in the area of the Bishops of Münster, who according to Wilfred Ehbrecht (1974, pp. 70–93) exercised another policy towards monastic foundations than the bishops of Utrecht in their diocese: they supported those among the Frisian nobility who did not cherish great monastic foundations. Most renowned is the somewhat younger Emo, the founder of *Floridus Hortus* in Wittewierum and *Campus Rosarum*, or Roozenkamp, for canonesses in the area north of Groningen. Prior to Emo, the abbey of Aduard in the same region had been founded by Cistercian monks in 1192. Benedictine monks and nuns had established themselves in Feldwerd, west of the Ems estuary, in 1183 (the nuns moved in 1204 to a new site called Nijeklooster), in Thesinge, west of the Ems, *c.* 1182 and, under the guidance of the holy Abbot Hatebrand, in Meerhusen, east of the Ems estuary near the present-day German town of Aurich, in 1183/98. The foundation of Marien Dale for Benedictine monks and nuns, further north-west of Aurich, on the extreme tip of land west of the later town of Norden on the eastern shore of the Ems estuary, is also said to have taken place under Abbot Hatebrand (Streich, 1986, p. 96).

Frisian monasticism became important to Scandinavia especially because of Mariëngaarde and its northern network of contacts. But in itself it offers striking evidence of the birth of monastic institutions in a culture which, like Scandinavia and the Slav regions south of the Baltic, for long periods stubbornly resisted these influences. The spread of monasticism is intimately linked to the development of a class of nobles and better-off farmers who were the first to open their eyes to monasticism. Among the Frisians as well as among the Scandinavians, urban culture was still a foreign and generally unknown phenomenon. The monastic alternative was accessible to members of the land-owning class as soon as monasteries could adjust to the conditions of this class and establish themselves in institutions adapting themselves to the manor structure they had become accustomed to. In Frisian lands and in Scandinavia, this land-owning class was bred of the same population that had lived there for generations. Only in the Slav regions of the southern Baltic were these groups to some extent overturned by the German immigrants, and perished or became Germanized.

III Conclusion

Monasticism in maritime North-Western Europe until *c.* 1200 was limited to one part of the population, the same social layer that filled ecclesiastical offices at higher and medium levels. The structure of monastic life was bound up with the agrarian manorial system. Urban life was not foreign to the existing monasteries, but it was an urbanity of secular and ecclesiastical administrators and their men, merchants, artisans and servants. If growing city life surrounded a monastery, it was generally something the abbey or convent itself had generated. But as a rule monasteries neither sought nor were burdened by urban surroundings. Instead, much of their living depended upon the keen administration of landed property with the help of lay brothers and other officials. Here, then, monastic superiors got their training in the 'worldly' skill.

Culturally, monasteries in maritime North-Western Europe until *c.* 1200 saw themselves as centres for the spread of the Christian message and way of life. Monks and nuns knew that their interpretation of the Gospel could not be transferred to other groups in society. But they participated in the general conviction of churchmen that they were there to serve the Christian people by whatever means they had at their disposal, in the beneficial effects of which they placed their confidence. On some occasions we also find, or may suppose, a more disinterested attitude as to the effects of their way of life on the surrounding world, especially in Augustinian houses that participated in active pastoral work and therefore by their direct confrontation with daily life acquired a more detached attitude. The preceding contribution has not been able to uncover texts that would totally upset our previous understanding of the extent to which monks and canons shared the worldly life of their surroundings. But it is a fair conjecture that monks and nuns in maritime North-Western Europe until *c.* 1200 had an unreflecting contact with the surrounding world, and that different observances fundamentally meant nothing but degrees of physical and mental confrontation of monks and nuns with their surroundings.

From the preceding chapters it has become clear that the rhythm and various waves of monastic foundations in Scandinavia and adjacent areas on the Continent show similarities and parallels, clearly distinguishing these regions from the pattern of monastic developments prevalent in those countries that were the inheritors of the Roman empire. We lack, for example, eremiticism as an initial stage of monasticism. Monasteries are from the moment of their foundation always institutions, protected by a system of Canon Law which already exists. They may be small, consisting only of a handful of monks, but as such, they are part of the institutionalized church, as were those abroad when Christianity was adopted in maritime North-Western Europe. It is characteristic that efforts around 1161–62 to introduce the eremitical Carthusian monks in Denmark (*DD 1,2*, nos 142, 148) – they were assigned Asserbo in Zealand, later part of Esrum's property – did not materialize. To the French monks who inspected the place, it must have been evident that there was no tradition in Scandinavia of a community life which tried to imitate that of the hermits of the Egyptian desert. Community meant being a member of an institution practising a communal, not a solitary, life.

Another result of the preceding research, I think, is the necessity we are faced with of looking at the Cistercian reform with eyes other than was often the case in previous scholarship on monasticism. The 'Religious Orders' are no 'Orders' yet. An 'order' in this epoch is a way of interpreting one of the fundamental monastic rules of Western Christianity – and there are only two here, those of St Benedict and of St Augustine. To interpret both rule and statutes, it is necessary to meet and discuss how to apply them in daily conflicts. Therefore, the two most famous discussion fora of the epoch, Cîteaux and Prémontré, invested as they were with the right to supervise and punish, deeply influenced the still inexperienced monastic world of maritime North-Western Europe as they began to exert their influence there in the 1150s. In addition to secular problems of worldly administration, from 1157 onwards King Valdemar the Great saw himself faced with the task of integrating the new phenomenon of foreign religious authority with his political system. Realizing that such institutions as the general chapter of these two groups ultimately received their authority from the Pope, the king initially was strongly motivated to counteract growing papal influence – hence his decision in the 1160s, as the most potent ruler of maritime North-Western Europe at that moment, to support the emperor's pope and counteract the hierarchical ecclesiology of Archbishop Eskil. In a few years, however, his administrators acquired the skill of integrating even aggressive movements among different groups of monks with his state church system. This explains how the transition of royal abbeys from one to another interpretation of the Rule of St Benedict, which included even the abolition of monastic life in some places, could be tolerated within the established system. As a guarantee for the stabilization phase of this system, the king forced the election of Absalon as Eskil's successor, so that the monastic option from now on got its place in the system without endangering its inner balance.

All in all, the monastic option in maritime North-Western Europe, as seen from the point of view of an applicant pondering the embrace of monastic life, opened up free perspectives into the spiritual and intellectual world of Christian religion in its Roman setting. But it was also bound up with the agrarian manorial system, and practically unthinkable in any other social context, since in this situation only the agrarian basis could secure the necessary material background for spiritual development. Maybe one may interpret the crisis in 1198 around the Hospitallers of St John concerning their preaching, the object of Absalon's complaint to the Pope (see Chapter 13 in this volume), as a signal that new factors such as the money economy began to influence, and threatened to change, the established system. But the tremendous efforts to stabilize the system had long-lasting effects, and in spite of urbanization, led to the stabilization of already existing monasteries and a continued stream of new agrarian monastic foundations within the framework of the same system from where resources were available. Very often the foundation of nuns' convents was easier and recruitment more stable, there being less competition between the chances offered to women. So the number of agrarian monasteries grew in maritime North-Western Europe throughout the thirteenth century – thanks to the stability reached in the integrative system during the decades treated in the preceding chapters.

One main result of the investigation is that the activity of bishops nearly always permeates the process of a monastic foundation. The bishop was not just formally obliged to have monastic life cultivated within the borders of his diocese, but very often he apparently found it a pressing need for himself and his diocese to do so. Bishops took an interest in all forms of monastic life, and exemption privileges do not seem to have been decisive for the attitude of bishops towards the monasteries within their jurisdiction. Perhaps the idea of exemption has been exaggerated among scholars, especially since the extent of exemption varies highly and depends upon what is written into the foundation documents and in customary law in every single case. This topic could not be treated here, but the constant participation of bishops in monastic foundations suggests that exemption cannot have been such a horror to them, as it might sometimes appear to be in the literature on monastic history.

Finally, liturgical practice and spiritual reading in the monasteries of maritime North-Western Europe were at this stage probably totally dependent upon what had been inherited from the mainstream of monastic tradition in Europe. But at the same time, as the Icelandic example teaches us, monks and nuns were remarkably independent in their way of remodelling and reformulating this heritage. Not only the passages from foundation charters and chronicles quoted above witness to this independent way of reading and combining; we must also assume that the basic content of liturgical and biblical texts was independently transformed to fit the mental horizon of a recently Christianized population. Such a dynamic transformation of mental entities can alone explain the strength and survival of this monastic culture in the same institutions for the many hundreds of years that followed.

APPENDIX

Development of Cistercian foundations in Denmark

Periods	*Cîteaux line*	*Clairvaux line*	*Clairvaux line via Sweden*
Geographical expansion	Scania South-west Jutland Funen	Zealand Pomerania South-east Jutland	Northern Jutland Middle Jutland
First move: Eskil and king	Herrevad, 1144	Replacing black monks Esrum, 1151	Vitskøl, 1157/58
Second move: bishops and earl	Tvis, 1163	Replacing black monks Sorø, 1161	Sminge, 1165
Third move: bishops	Replacing black monks Seem, 1166/71 (→ Løgum, 1175)	Dargun, 1171 (→ Eldena, 1199)	Replacing black monks Veng, 1165 Kalvø, 1168
Fourth move: monks' design	Holme, 1172/74	Kołbacz, 1174 Oliva, 1186	Øm, 1172
Fifth move: bishops, monks, abbot William of Æbelholt		Replacing black monks Guldholm, 1192 (→ Ryd, 1209) Ås, 1194	
Result:	Four abbeys until Reformation	Seven abbeys until Reformation	Two abbeys until Reformation

Bibliography

Abrams, L. (1995), 'The Anglo-Saxons and the Christianization of Scandinavia', *Anglo-Saxon England*, 24, 213–49.

Adam von Bremen, Hamburgische Kirchengeschichte (1917), ed. B. Schmeidler (Scriptores Rerum Germanicarum in usum scholarum), Hannover and Leipzig: Hahnsche Buchhandlung, 3rd edition.

Ahlkvist, H. B. and Tollin, C. (1994), *Kring Stång. En kulturgeografisk utvärdering byggd på äldre lantmäterikartor och historiska kartöverlägg* (Arkeologiska undersökningar, Skrifter No. 7), Stockholm: Riksantikvarieämbetet.

Ahnlund, N. (1945), 'Vreta klosters äldsta donatorer', *Historisk tidskrift*, 65, 301–51.

Andersen, A. (1987), *Middelalderbyen Næstved* (Projekt Middelalderbyen 3), Copenhagen: Centrum.

Andersen, P. S. (1977), *Samlingen av Norge og kristningen av landet 800–1130* (Haandbok i Norges historie, 2), Oslo: Universitetsforlaget.

Andersson, H. (1981), *Kungahälla* (Medeltidsstaden 29), Stockholm: Riksantikvarieämbetet.

Andrén, A. (1980), *Lund* (Medeltidsstaden 26), Stockholm: Riksantikvarieämbetet.

Andresen, J. K. (1990), 'Odense Skt. Knuds Klosters gårde', Odense: Center for Historie, Odense Universitet.

Annell, G. (1983), 'Bidrag till Vårfruberga klosters äldsta historia', *Kyrkohistorisk årsskrift*, 83, 78–90.

Arentoft, E., e.a. (1985), *Albani kirke & torv* (Fynske Studier XIV), Odense: Odense Bys Museer.

Arhnung, J. O. (1937), *Roskilde Domkapitels Historie I: Tiden indtil 1416*, Roskilde: Erh. Flensborg.

Backmund, N. (1972), *Die mittelalterlichen Geschichtsschreiber des Prämonstratenserordens* (Bibliotheca Analectorum Praemonstratensium 10), Averbode.

Balle, S. (1983), 'Ulf Jarl og drabet i Roskilde', *Historisk årbog fra Roskilde amt*, 23–59.

Bartholdy, O. (1973), *Munkeliv i Løgum Kloster*, Løgumkloster.

Bautier, R.-H. (1991), 'Les origines et les premiers développements de l'abbaye Saint-Victor de Paris', *L'Abbaye parisienne de Saint-Victor au Moyen Age*, ed. J. Longère (Biblioteca Victorina, 1), Paris: Brepols, 23–52.

Biskupa sögur (1858), vol. I, ed. Hiðíslenzka bókmentafélag, Copenhagen: S. L. Møller.

Bleiber, W. (1965), 'Fränkisch-karolingische Klöster als Grundherren in Friesland', *Jahrbuch für Wirtschaftsgeschichte*, Teil III, Akademie-Verlag Berlin, 127–75.

Blomkvist, N. (1978), 'De äldsta urkunderna om Kalmar', *Historisk tidskrift*, Stockholm, 98, 129–55.

Blomqvist, R. (1951), *Lunds historia, 1. Medeltiden*, Lund: C. W. K. Gleerup.

Bolton, B. (1973), 'Mulieres sanctae', *Sanctity and Secularity. The Church and the World*, ed. D. Baker (Studies in Church History, 10), Oxford: Blackwell, 77–95.

Boureau, A. (1993), 'Hypothèses sur l'émergence lexicale et théorique de la catégorie de séculier au XIIe siècle', *Le Clerc séculier au Moyen Age*, ed. M. Balard, Paris: Publications de la Sorbonne, 35–43.

Breengaard, C. (1982), *Muren om Israels hus. Regnum og sacerdotium i Danmark 1050–1170*, Copenhagen: G. E. C. Gad.

Burton, J. (1994), 'The Monastic Revival in Yorkshire: Whitby and St Mary's, York', *Anglo-Norman Durham 1093–1193*, ed. D. Rollason e.a., Woodbridge: Boydell, 41–51.

'Chronicon Roskildense', *SM*, I, 3–33.

Cinthio, E. (1947), 'Remains of the Cloister of the Monastery of Dalby', *Meddelanden från Lunds universitets historiska museum*, ed. H. Arbman, Lund: C. W. K. Gleerup, 92–7.

Cinthio, E. (1968), 'The churches of St. Clemens in Scandinavia', *Res medievales R. Blomqvist oblatae* (Archaeologia Lundensia III), Lund, 103–114.

Cinthio, E. (1983), 'Dalby kungsgård', *Kungl. Vitterhets Historie och Antikvitets Akademiens Årsbok*, Stockholm: Almqvist & Wiksell, 89–100.

Cinthio, E. (1989), 'Benediktiner, augustiner och korherrar', *Skånska kloster*, ed. E. Cinthio (Skånes Hembygdsförbunds Årsbok 1987/88), Lund: Skånes Hembygdsförbund, 19–45.

Claesson, E. (1989), *Cuius ecclesiam fecit. Romanska kyrkor i Västergötland*, Lunds Universitet: Medeltidsarkeologiska institutionen.

Collijn, I. (1929), *Ett nekrologium från johanniterklostret i Eskilstuna*, *Nordisk tidskrift för bok- och biblioteksväsen*, 16, 1–21.

Consuetudines canonicorum regularium Springirsbacenses-Rodenses (1978), ed. S. Weinfurter (Corpus Christianorum, continuatio Mediaeualis 48), Turhout: Brepols.

Consuetudines Lundenses. Statutter for kannikesamfundet i Lund c. 1123 (1978), ed. E. Buus. Copenhagen: C. A. Reitzel.

Cormack, M. (1993), 'Theodoricus: Historia de antiquitate regum Norwagiensium', *Medieval Scandinavia. An Encyclopedia*, ed. P. Pulsiano, New York and London: Garland, 643.

Cronica Ecclesiae Ripensis: Ellen Jørgensen (1933–35), 'Ribe Bispekrønike', *Kirkehistoriske Samlinger* 6, 1, Copenhagen, 23–33.

Curman, S. and Lundberg, E. (1935), *Vreta klosters kyrka* (Sveriges kyrkor [43]: Östergötland II), Stockholm.

Dahlerup, T. (1968), *Det danske sysselprovsti i middelalderen*, Copenhagen: G. E. C. Gad.

Damsholt, N. (1985), *Kvindebilledet i dansk højmiddelalder*, Copenhagen: Borgen.

Damsholt, N. (1996), 'Medieval Women's Identity in a Postmodern Light. The Example of Queen Ingeborg', *The Birth of Identities. Denmark and Europe in the Middle Ages*, ed. B. Patrick McGuire, Copenhagen: C. A. Reitzel, 225–41.

Danmarks Kirker (1933), ed. Nationalmuseet, Copenhagen.

Danmarks middelalderlige annaler (1980), ed. E. Kroman, Copenhagen: Selskabet for udgivelse af kilder til dansk historie.

Dansk Biografisk Leksikon (1979–84), 3rd edn, 1–16, Copenhagen: Gyldendal.

Daugaard, J. B. (1830), *Om de danske Klostre i Middelalderen*, Copenhagen.

Davidsen, H. G. and Møller-Christensen, V. (1971), *Liden Kirsten og Buris*, Copenhagen: Fremad.

Der Bremer Dom. Baugeschichte, Ausgrabungen, Kunstschätze. Handbuch und Katalog zur Sonderausstellung vom 17. Juni bis 30. Sept. 1979 (1979), ed. A. Löhr, Bremen: Bremer Landesmuseum für Kunst und Kulturgeschichte.

Diplomatarium Danicum 1,2: 1053–1169 (1963), eds L. Weibull and N. Skyum-Nielsen, Copenhagen: Munksgaard.

Diplomatarium Danicum 1,3: Diplomer 1170–1199 & Epistolæ abbatis Willelmi de Paraclito (1976–77), eds C. A. Christensen, H. Nielsen and L. Weibull, Copenhagen: C. A. Reitzel.

Diplomatarium Danicum 1,4: 1200–1210 (1958), ed. N. Skyum-Nielsen, Copenhagen: Munksgaard.

Diplomatarium Danicum 1,7: 1238–1249 (1990), eds N. Skyum-Nielsen and H. Nielsen, Copenhagen: C. A. Reitzel.

Diplomatarium Danicum 2,8: 1318–1322 (1953), eds A. Afzelius, F. Blatt, C. A. Christensen, G. Hermansen and K. Olsen, Copenhagen: Munksgaard.

Diplomatarium Islandicum = Islenzkt fornbréfasafn (1857–76), I, 834–1264, ed. Islenzka bókmentafélagi, Copenhagen: S. L. Möller.

Diplomatarium Suecanum (1829–37), I–II, ed. J. G. Liljegren, Stockholm: P. A. Norstedt.

Drögereit, R. (1978), *Sachsen, Angelsachsen, Niedersachsen. Ausgewählte Aufsätze in einem dreibändigen Werk*, Hamburg: Commercium.

Edenheim, R. and Rosell, I. (1982), *Varnhems klosterkyrka* (Sveriges kyrkor 190), Stockholm: Almqvist & Wiksell.

Ehbrecht, W. (1974), *Landesherrschaft und Klosterwesen im ostfriesischen Fivelgo (970–1290)* (Geschichtliche Arbeiten zur westfälischen Landesforschung 13), Münster: Aschendorff.

Elm, K. (1980), 'Kanoniker und Ritter vom Heiligen Grab', *Die geistlichen Ritterorden Europas* (Vorträge und Forschungen XXVI, eds J. Fleckenstein and M. Hellmann, Sigmaringen: Thorbecke, 141–69.

'Erik den heliges Legend' (1954), ed. T. Schmid, *Erik den helige. Historia – kult – reliker*, ed. B. Thordeman, Stockholm: Nordisk Rotogravyr, pp. xi–xx.

Eriksson, J. E. G. (1994), 'Å forvalte sitt pund – om klostre og næringer', *Fra hammer til kors. 1000 år med kristendom. Brytningstid i Viken*, utg. av Borre Historielag, red. J. I. Hansen and K. G. Bjerva, Oslo: Schibsted, 215–32.

France, J. (1992), *The Cistercians in Scandinavia* (Cistercian Studies Series, 131), Kalamazoo: Cistercian Publications.

Freytag, E. (1977), 'Die Klöster als Zentren kirchlichen Lebens', *Schleswig-Holsteinische Kirchengeschichte I: Anfänge und Ausbau*, Neumünster: Karl Wachholtz, 147–202.

Gad, T. (1974), 'Seem-relikviernes pergamentstrimler', *Hikuin*, 1, 64–7, also as extract together with Vellev (1974), pr. 1975.

Gallén, J. (1976), 'De engelska munkarna i Uppsala – ett katedralkloster på 1100–talet', *Historisk Tidskrift för Finland*, 61, 1–21.

Gallén, J. (1985), 'Knut den helige och Adela av Flandern. Europeiska kontakter och genealogiska konsekvenser', *Studier i äldre historia tillägnade Herman Schück 5/4 1985*, ed. R. Sandberg, Stockholm: Författarna, 49–66.

Gallén, J. (1993), *Det 'Danska itinerariet'. Franciskansk expansionsstrategi i Östersjön*, ed. J. Lind (Skrifter utgivna av Svenska Litteratursällskapet i Finland, 579), Helsingfors: Svenska Litteratursällskapet i Finland.

Garner, H. N. (1993), 'Gudenåens klostre', *Hikuin*, 20, 17–32.

Gejrot, C. (1992), *Diplomata Novevallensia. The Nydala Charters 1172–1280. A Critical Edition with an Introduction, a Commentary and Indices* (Acta Universitatis Stockholmiensis, Studia Latina Stockholmiensia XXXVII), Stockholm: Almqvist & Wiksell International.

(*Germania Benedictina VI=*), *Die Benediktinerklöster in Niedersachsen, Schleswig-Holstein und Bremen* (1979), ed. U. Faust, St Ottilien: Eos Verlag.

(*Germania Benedictina XI=*) *Die Männer- und Frauenklöster der Zisterzienser in Niedersachsen, Schleswig-Holstein und Hamburg* (1994), ed. U. Faust, St Ottilien: Eos Verlag.

(*Germania Benedictina XII=*) *Die Frauenklöster in Niedersachsen, Schleswig-Holstein und Bremen* (1984), ed. U. Faust, St Ottilien: Eos Verlag.

Gjerløw, L. (1961), 'Hallvard', *Kulturhistorisk leksikon for nordisk middelalder* 6, 63–6.

Grabkowsky, A.-T. (1995), 'Die Errichtung von Bistümern und die Gründung geistlicher Gemeinschaften im 12. und 13. Jahrhundert in Mecklenburg und Vorpommern', *Ein Jahrtausend Mecklenburg und Vorpommern*, utg. W. Karge, P.-J. Rakow, R. Wendt, Rostock, 50–60.

Green-Pedersen, S. E. (1981), 'De danske cistercienserklostres grundlæggelse og den politiske magtkamp i det 12. årh.', *Middelalder, metode og medier. Festskrift til Niels Skyüm-Nielsen på 60–årsdagen den 17. oktober 1981*, ed. K. Fledelius e.a., Copenhagen: Museum Tusculanum, 41–65.

Gunnes, E. (1987), 'Klosterlivet i Norge. Tilblivelse – økonomi – avvikling', *Foreningen til norske fortidsminnesmerkers bevaring, Årbok*, 141, 49–84.

Gustavi, P. (1983), *Birka och Vreta kloster* (Vreta klosters hembygdsförenings skriftserie 7), Linköping: Sahlströms.

Hald, K. (1963), 'The Cult of Odin in Danish Place Names', *Early English and Norse Studies presented to Hugh Smith*, eds A. Brown and P. Foote, London: Methuen, 99–109.

Hassø, A. G. (1922), *Bidrag til Randers Købstads Historie indtil Aar 1600*, Ringsted: Eget Forlag.

Hellberg, K. (1935), *Eskilstuna genom tiderna. En svensk märkesstads historia*, Katrineholm: Författarens förlag.

Helle, K. (1975), *Stavanger fra våg til by*, Stavanger: Stabenfeldt.

Helle, K. (1995), *Bergen Bys Historie I: Kongssete og kjøpstad. Fra opphavet til 1536*, 2nd edn, Bergen: Alma Mater Forlag.

Helle, K. and Nedkvitne, A. (1977), 'Sentrumsdannelser og byutvikling i norsk middelalder', *Urbaniseringsprosessen i Norden 1: Middelaldersteder. Det XVII. nordiske historikermøte Trondheim 1977*, ed. G. A. Blom, Oslo: Universitetsforlaget, 189–286.

Hellström, J. A. (1971), *Biskop och landskapssamhälle i tidig svensk medeltid* (Rättshistoriskt bibliotek 16), Stockholm: Nordiska Bokhandeln.

Hellström, J. A. (1979), 'Reflexioner kring de tidigaste biskoparna i Skara stift', *Svensk Teologisk Kvartalskrift*, 55, 67–71.

Helmold von Bosau (1973), *Slawenchronik*, ed. H. Stoob, Darmstadt: Wissenschaftliche Buchgesellschaft.

Helms, H. J. (1940), *Næstved St. Peders Kloster (Skovkloster)*, Næstved: P. Haase and Søn.

Henriksson, G. (1995), 'Riksbloten och Uppsala högar', *Tor*, 27, 337–94.

Herzog, E. (1964), *Die ottonische Stadt*, Berlin: Gebr. Mann.

Hill, T. (1992), *Könige, Fürsten und Klöster* (Kieler Werkstücke A:4), Frankfurt: Peter Lang.

'Historia de antiquitate regum Norwagiensium' (1880), *Monumenta historica Norvegiae. Latinske Kildeskrifter til Norges Historie i Middelalderen*, ed. G. Storm, Kristiania, 1–68.

'Historia Fundationis Monasterii Lysensis in Norvegia' (1776), *Scriptores Rerum Danicarum Medii Aevi*, IV, ed. J. Langebek, Copenhagen: Godiche, reprint Kraus, 1969, 406–9.

'Historia Monasterii Rastedensis' (1880), *MGH SS*, XXV, Hannover, reprint Hiersemann, 1964, 495–511.

Hoffmann, E. (1975), *Die heiligen Könige bei den Angelsachsen und den skandinavischen Völkern. Königsheiliger und Königshaus* (Quellen und Forschungen zur Geschichte Schleswig-Holsteins 69), Neumünster: Karl Wachholtz.

Hoffmann, E. (1976), *Königserhebung und Thronfolgeordnung in Dänemark bis zum Ausgang des Mittelalters* (Beiträge zur Geschichte und Quellenkunde des Mittelalters 5), Berlin: Walter de Gruyter.

Hoffmann, E. (1980), 'Beiträge zur Geschichte der Stadt Schleswig und des westlichen Ostseeraums im 12. und 13. Jahrhundert', *Zeitschrift der Gesellschaft für Schleswig-Holsteinische Geschichte*, 105, 27–76.

Hoffmann, E. (1986), 'Sachsen, Abodriten und Dänen im westlichen Ostseeraum von der Mitte des 10. bis zur Mitte des 12. Jahrhunderts', *Schiffe und Seefahrt in der südlichen Ostsee*, ed. H. Bei Der Wieden, Köln: Böhlau, 1–40.

Hohler, C. (1963–64), 'Remarks on the Early Cathedral of Stavanger and Related Buildings', *Universitetets Oldsakssamling, Årbok*, Oslo: Universitetets Oldsaksamling, 8–52.

Hohler, C. (1964), 'The Cathedral of St Swithun at Stavanger in the Twelfth Century', *Journal of the British Archaeological Association*, Third Series, 27, 92–118.

Holmström, M. and Tollin, C. (1990), 'Alvastra klosters äldre godsinnehav. Framväxt och rumslig struktur samt jämförelser med kontinentala förhållanden', *I Heliga Birgittas trakter. Nitton uppsatser om medeltida samhälle och kultur i Östergötland 'västanstång'*, ed. G. Dahlbäck, Uppsala: Swedish Science Press, 301–27.

Hommedal, A. T. (1993), 'Selja i Nordfjord. Eit forskningsprosjekt rundt eit kyrkjesenter på Vestlandet i tidleg mellomalder', *Hikuin*, 20, 93–104.

Hviid, P. (1993), 'Den tidlige Klostertid i Børglum og Vrejlev', *Seminaret 'Kloster og by' 11.–13. november 1992 – omkring Olavsklosteret, premonstratenserordenen og klostervesenet i middelalderen*, eds J. E. G. Eriksson and K. Schei, Tønsberg: Tønsberg bibliotek og Riksantikvaren, 55–66.

Hyenstrand, Å. (1996), *Lejonet, draken och korset. Sverige 500–1000*, Lund: Studentlitteratur.

Ingvordsen, J. (1990), 'Asgarth og broder Martins kanal; bidrag til Øm klosters topografi', *Århus Stifts Årbøger*, 75, 45–79.

Ingvordsen, J. (1991), *'De gode nonners konvent i Ring'. Ring klosters middelalderlige bygningshistorie belyst primært ud fra de arkæologiske levn*, Århus: Aarhus Universitet.

Jansen, H. M. (1972), *A Critical Account of the Written and Archaeological Sources' Evidence Concerning the Norse Settlements in Greenland* (Meddelelser om Grønland 182, 4), Copenhagen: C. A. Reitzel.

Janson, H. (1998), *Templum nobilissimum. Adam av Bremen, Uppsalatemplet och konfliktlinjerna i Europa kring år 1075* (Avhandlingar från Historiska institutionen i Göteborg 21.) Göteborg: Göteborgs Universitet.

Jensen, J. S. (1995), see *Tusindtallets Danske Mønter ...* (1995).

Johansen, P. (1951), *Nordische Mission, Revals Gründung und die Schwedensiedlung in Estland* (Kungl. Vitterhets Historie och Antikvitets Akademiens Handlingar 74), Stockholm: Wahlström & Widstrand.

Johansson, H. (1964), *Ritus Cisterciensis. Studier i de svenska cisterciensklostrens liturgi* (Bibliotheca theologiae practicae 18), Lund: Gleerups.

Johansson, H. (1985), 'Skara som stiftsstad', *Skara I. Före 1700. Staden i stiftet*, ed. A. Sträng, Skara: Skara historiekommitté, 387–542.

Johnsen, A. O. (1943–46), 'Om St. Victorklosteret og nordmennene', *Historisk Tidsskrift*, Oslo, 33, 405–32.

Johnsen, A. O. (1955), 'Fra den eldste tid til 1252', *Nidaros erkebispestol og bispesete 1153–1953*, ed. A. Fjellbu e.a., Oslo: Land og Kirke.

Johnsen, A. O. (1965), *Om pave Eugenius III's vernebrev for Munkeliv kloster av 7. januar 1146* (Avhandlinger utgitt av Det Norske Videnskaps-Akademi i Oslo II, Ny serie 7), Oslo: Universitetsforlaget.

Johnsen, A. O. (1968), 'Biskop Bjarnhard og kirkeforholdene i Norge under Harald Hardråde og Olav Kyrre', *Bjørgvin bispestol. Frå Selja til Bjørgvin*, ed. P. Juvkam, Oslo: Universitetsforlaget, 11–31.

Johnsen, A. O. (1970), *Kong Sverre og England 1199–1202* (Avhandlinger utgitt av Det Norske Videnskaps-Akademi i Oslo II, Ny serie 13), Oslo: Universitetsforlaget.

Johnsen, A. O. (1974), 'Omkring grunnleggingen av klostret på Hovedøya', *Oslo bispedømme 900 år. Historiske studier*, ed. F. Birkeli e.a., Oslo: Universitetsforlaget, 37–49.

Johnsen, A. O. (1976), 'Ny tolkning av Historia de Profectione Danorum in Hierosolymam', *Från medeltid till välfärdssamhälle. Nordiska historikermötet i Uppsala 1974. Föredrag och mötesförhandlingar*, Uppsala: Almqvist & Wiksell, 507–27.

Jørgensen, J. O. (1989), 'Esrum klosters godsdrift fra klostrets grundlæggelse til o. 1400', *Fra Frederiksborg Amt. Årbog 1989*, Frederiksborg Amts Historiske Samfund, 1–99.

Jørgensen, O. (1985), *Alfred den Store. Danmarks geografi* (North-Western European Language Evolution = NOWELE, Supplement vol. 1), Odense: Odense Universitetsforlag.

Jørgensen, O. and Nyberg, T. (1992), *Sejlruter i Adam af Bremens danske øverden* (Antikvariskt arkiv 74), Stockholm: Kungl. Vitterhets Historie och Antikvitets Akademien.

Karlsson, J. O. M. and Sigsjö, R. (1987), *Varnhems kloster*, Varnhem: Varnhems församling.

Karlsson, J. O. M. (1999), *Viby romanska gårdskyrkas arkitektur och arkitekturhistoriska ställning* (Sigtuna Museums Skrifter), Sigtuna: Sigtuna Museum.

Kleberg, T. (1968), *Medeltida Uppsalabibliotek I. Biskop Siward av Uppsala och hans bibliotek* (Acta Universitatis Upsaliensis C:15), Uppsala: Almqvist & Wiksell.

Kletler, P. (1924), *Nordwesteuropas Verkehr, Handel und Gewerbe im frühen Mittelalter*, Wien: Österreichischer Schulbuchverlag.

Knudsen, B. M. and Kock, J. (1992), 'Anden del. Fra 975 til 1534', *Aalborgs historie I: Fra Aalborgs fødsel til Grevens Fejde 1534*, Aalborg: Aalborg Kommune, 108–458.

Knytlinga Saga (1986), translated by H. Pálsson and P. Edwards, Odense: Odense University Press.

Koch, H. (1936), 'De ældste danske Klostres Stilling i Kirke og Samfund indtil 1221', *Historisk Tidsskrift* (Copenhagen), **10. R., 3. B.**, 511–82.

Krins, H. (1968), *Die frühen Steinkirchen Dänemarks*, Hamburg: Philosophische Fakultät der Universität Hamburg.

Kristensen, A. K. G. (1969), *Danmarks ældste annalistik. Studier over lundensisk Annalskrivning i 12. og 13. Århundrede*. København: Historisk Institut.

Kumlien, K. (1962), 'Sveriges kristnande i slutskedet – spörsmål om vittnesbörd och verklighet', *Historisk tidskrift*, Stockholm, 82, 249–97.

Kvalheim, W. (1949), *Heilagdomane på Selja*, Volda: Aarflot.

Lafrenz, D. (1985), *Die Kunstdenkmäler der Stadt Schleswig III: Kirchen, Klöster und Hospitäler*. Berlin: Deutscher Kunstverlag.

Lambert, A. M. (1985), *The Making of the Dutch Landscape. An Historical Geography of the Netherlands*, 2nd edn, Orlando: Academic Press.

Lange, C. C. A. (1847), *De norske Klostres Historie i Middelalderen*, Christiania; 2nd edn, 1856.

'Liber daticus Lundensis vetustior' (1884–89/1973), *Libri memoriales capituli Lundensis. Lunde Domkapitels Gavebøger*, ed. C. Weeke, Copenhagen: Rudolph Klein, 1–324.

Lidén, H.-E. (1961), *Mariakirken. Romansk kirkebygningskunst i Bergen. En undersøkelse av kirkebygningsvirksomheten i Bergen i 1100–årene med utgangspunkt i Mariakirken* (Det Hanseatiske Museums Skrifter 18), Bergen: Universitetsforlaget.

Lidén, H.-E. (1967), *Halsnøy kloster* (Fortidsminner 54), Oslo: Foreningen til norske fortidsminnesmerkers bevaring.

Lidén, H.-E. (1970), 'Domkirken i Bergen og utviklingen av de norske domkirketypene i 1000–1100 årene', *Bjørgvin bispestol. Byen og bispedømmet*, ed. P. Juvkam, Oslo: Universitetsforlaget, 11–40.

Lobbedey, U. (1977), 'Northern Germany', *European Towns: Their Archaeology and Early History*, ed. M. W. Barley, London: Academic Press.

Lorenzen, V. (1933), *De danske Benediktinerklostres Bygningshistorie* (De danske Klostres Bygningshistorie X), Copenhagen: G. E. C. Gad.

Lund, N. (1996), *Lið, Leding og Landeværn. Hær og samfund i Danmark i ældre middelalder*, Roskilde: Vikingeskibshallen.

Lunde, Ø. (1977), *Trondheims fortid i bygrunnen* (Riksantikvarens skrifter 2), Trondheim: Riksantikvaren.

Lunde, Ø. (1987), 'Klosteranleggene', *Foreningen til norske fortidsminnesmerkers bevaring, Årbok*, 141, 85–128.

Lunde, Ø. (1993), 'Premonstratensernes kloster i Tunsberg – kirken og klosteranlegget', *Seminaret 'Kloster og by' 11.–13. november 1992 – omkring Olavsklosteret, premonstratenserordenen og klostervesenet i middelalderen*, eds J. E. G. Eriksson and K. Schei, Tønsberg: Tønsberg bibliotek og Riksantikvaren, 9–22.

Mason, E. (1990), *St Wulfstan of Worcester c.1008–1095*, Oxford: Blackwell.

McGuire, B. P. (1974), 'Patrons, Privileges, Property – Sorø Abbey's First Half Century', *Kirkehistoriske samlinger*, 5–39.

McGuire, B. P. (1982), *The Cistercians in Denmark: Their Attitudes, Roles, and Functions in Medieval Society* (Cistercian Studies Series 35), Kalamazoo: Cistercian Publications.

McGuire, B. P. (1985), 'Why Scandinavia? Bernard, Eskil and Cistercian expansion in the North, 1140–1180', *Goad and Nail*, ed. E. R. Elder (Cistercian Studies Series, 84), 251–81.

McGuire, B. P. (1988), *Friendship and Community. The Monastic Experience 350–1250* (Cistercian Studies Series, 95), Kalamazoo: Cistercian Publications.

McLees, C. (1988–89), *The Ruin Speaks ... The Church of the Benedictine Abbey of Nidarholm. Report from excavations on the island of Munkholmen* (= Arkeologiske undersøkelser i Trondheim 5), Trondheim: Riksantikvarens utgravningskontor for Trondheim.

Mol, J. A. (1979), 'Grootgrondbezit van Friese kloosters in de middeleeuwen', Doctoraalscriptie Mediaevistiek en Historische Geografie, Vrije Universitetit te Amsterdam.

Mol, J. A. (1996), 'De stichting fan it Cistersiënzer kleaster Klaarkamp by Rinsumageast', *It Beaken*, 58, 1, 1–13.

Møller-Christensen, V. (1958), *Bogen om Æbelholt kloster*, Copenhagen: Dansk Videnskabs forlag.

'Narratiuncula de fundatione monasterii Vitaescholae in Cimbria', *Scriptores minores historiæ Danicæ medii ævi* (1918–22/1970), ed. M. C. Gertz, I–II, Copenhagen: Selskabet for udgivelse af kilder til dansk historie, II, 134–51.

Necrologium Lundense. Lunds domkyrkas nekrologium (1923), ed. L. Weibull, Lund: Berlingska.

'Necrologium Monasterii Loci Dei in Sora 1518 scribi coeptum' (1776), *Scriptores Rerum Danicarum Medii Aevi*, ed. J. Langebek, IV, Copenhagen: Godiche, reprint Kraus, 1969, 575–87.

Newman, M. G. (1995), *The Boundaries of Charity. Cistercian Culture and Ecclesiastical Reform, 1098–1180*, Stanford: Stanford University Press.

Nicolaysen, N. M. (1892), 'Om ruinerne paa Selje', *Foreningen til norske fortidsmindesmærkers bevaring, bilaga til aarsberetning 1891*, Kristiania.

Nielsen, I. (1985), *Middelalderbyen Ribe*, Viby Jylland: Centrum.

Nielsen, Y. (1905), 'De gamle Helligdomme paa Selja', *Historiske Afhandlinger tilegnet Professor Dr. J. E. Sars paa hans syttiende*

Fødselsdag den ellevte Oktober 1905 af Venner og Disciple, Kristiania: Aschehoug, 164–81.

Nilsson, T. (1989), 'De arkeologiska vittnesbörden om premonstratensklostret i Lund', *Skånska kloster*, ed. Erik Cinthio (Skånes Hembygdsförbunds Årsbok 1987/88), Lund, 82–83.

Norbert von Xanten. Adliger – Ordensstifter – Kirchenfürst (1984), ed. Kaspar Elm, Köln: Wienand.

Norges gamle Love indtil 1387, 2 (1848), eds R. Keyser and P. A. Munch, Christiania: Gröndahl.

Norsk Biografisk Leksikon (1923–83), I–XIX, Oslo: H. Aschehoug.

Nyberg, T. (1975–76), 'De nordiska premonstratenserklostrens ställning i ordensorganisationen', in C. Wallin, *Tommarps Urkundsbok*, II, 7–22.

Nyberg, T. (1976), 'Kreuzzug und Handel in der Ostsee zur dänischen Zeit Lübecks', *Lübeck 1226. Reichsfreiheit und frühe Stadt*, ed. O. Ahlers e.a., Lübeck: Hansisches Verlagskontor H. Scheffler, 207–25.

Nyberg, T. (1978), 'Die skandinavische Zirkarie der Prämonstratenserchorherren', *Secundum regulam vivere. Festschrift P. Norbert Backmund O.Praem.*, ed. G. Melville, Windberg: Poppe-Verlag, 265–79.

Nyberg, T. (1981a), 'Die "Ottonische Stadt" als Forschungsproblem', lecture for the degree of Dr.phil.habil., Augsburg.

Nyberg, T. (1981b), 'St Knud and St Knud's Church', *Hagiography and Medieval Literature. A Symposium*, Odense: Odense University Press, 100–110.

Nyberg, T. (1982), 'Grenzen erzählen Geschichte. Zum Konzept der frühen Mission in den Ländern und Gebieten Skandinaviens', *Zeitschrift der Gesellschaft für Schleswig-Holsteinische Geschichte*, 107, 15–36.

Nyberg, T. (1984), 'Stad, skrift och stift. Några historiska inledningsfrågor', *Adam av Bremen. Historien om Hamburgstiftet och dess biskopar*, translated [into Swedish] by E. Svenberg, Stockholm: Proprius, 295–339.

Nyberg, T. (1985), 'König Knut der heilige, Teuzo und der Peterspfennig aus Dänemark', *Archivum historiae pontificiae*, **23**, 359–65.

Nyberg, T. (1986), *Die Kirche in Skandinavien. Mitteleuropäischer und englischer Einfluss im 11. und 12. Jahrhundert. Anfänge der Domkapitel Børglum und Odense in Dänemark* (Beiträge zur Geschichte und Quellenkunde des Mittelalters 10), Sigmaringen: Thorbecke.

Nyberg, T. (1990), 'Skandinavisches Königtum, Papsttum und Johanniter: Versuch einer Charakterisierung', *Die Ritterorden zwischen geistlicher und weltlicher Macht im Mittelalter* (Ordines militares – Colloquia Torunensia Historica V), ed. Z. H. Nowak, Toruń: Uniwersytet Milołaja Kopernika, 127–42.

Nyberg, T. (1991), 'Adam av Bremen och Florenslistan', *Scandia*, 57, 153–89, 347–8.

Nyberg, T. (1993a), 'Børglum, Tønsberg, Dragsmark', *Seminaret 'Kloster og by' 11.–13. november 1992 – omkring Olavsklosteret, premonstratenserordenen og klostervesenet i middelalderen*, eds J. E. G. Eriksson and K. Schei, Tønsberg: Tønsberg bibliotek og Riksantikvaren, 67–77.

Nyberg, T. (1993b), 'Saints and Place-Names around Kattegat', *Twenty-Eight Papers Presented to Hans Bekker-Nielsen on the Occasion of his Sixtieth Birthday 28 April 1993* (NOWELE 21/22), Odense: Odense University Press, 181–204.

Nyberg, T. (1995), 'Odense im 12. und 13. Jahrhundert', *Die Stadt im westlichen Ostseeraum. Vorträge zur Stadtgründung und Stadtverwaltung im Hohen Mittelalter* I, ed. E. Hoffmann and F. Lubowitz (Kieler Werkstücke A:14), Frankfurt: Peter Lang, 177–94.

Nyberg, T. (1995/96), 'Autour de la Sacralité Royale en Scandinavie', *Annuarium historiae conciliorum*, 27/28, 177–92.

Nyborg, E. (1979), 'Enkeltmænd og fællesskaber i organiseringen af det romanske sognekirkebyggeri', *Strejflys over Danmarks bygningskultur. Festskrift til Harald Langberg*, ed. R. Egevang, Copenhagen: Nationalmuseet, 37–64.

Odense bys historie [I]: Fra boplads til bispeby. Odense til 1559, (1982), ed. T. Kaarsted e.a., Odense: Odense Universitetsforlag.

Olsen, O. (1972), 'Sankt Mikkel i Slagelse. Om en nyfunden 1000–talskirke og dens forhistorie', *Nationalmuseets Arbejdsmark*, 131–52.

Olsson, H. (1947), 'Cistercienserklostret i Herrevad', *Sæasæ. Skånsk samling*, 5, Glumslöv, 15–27.

Ortved, E. (1927), *Cistercieordenen og dens Klostre i Norden*, I, Cistercieordenen Overhovedet, Copenhagen.

Ortved, E. (1933), *Cistercieordenen og dens Klostre i Norden*, II, Sveriger Klostre, Copenhagen.

Østergaard, B. (1994), 'Sven Estridsens danmarkshistorie. Danmarks politiske historie ca. 890–965', *Historie Jyske Samlinger*, 3–32.

Østvedt, E. (1971), *Nonneklosteret på Gimsøy*, Skien: Oluf Rasmussens forlag.

Ottar og Wulfstan, to rejsebeskrivelser fra vikingetiden (1983), ed. N. Lund, Roskilde: Vikingeskibshallen.

Parikh, K. [Drar] (1991), *Kvinnoklostren på Östgötaslätten under medeltiden. Asketiskt ideal – politisk realitet* (Biblioteheca Historico-Ecclesiastica Lundensis 26), Lund.

Paulsson, G. (1974), *Annales suecici medii aevi. Svensk medeltidsannalistik* (Bibliotheca historica Lundensis XXXII), Lund: C. W. K. Gleerup.

Pelc, O. (1998), 'Feldkloster und Stadt im Wendischen Quartier der Hanse', *Hansische Geschichtsblätter*, 116, 65–82.

Pernler, S.-E. (1977), *Gotlands medeltida kyrkoliv – biskop och prostar. En kyrkorättslig studie*, Visby: Barry Press.

Persson, E. (1999), 'Vad ägde Kristi fattiga nunnor i Byarum?', *Byarums Hembygdsförening, Årsskrift*, Vaggeryd, 4–16.

Petersohn, J. (1979), *Der südliche Ostseeraum im kirchlich-politischen Kräftespiel des Reichs, Polens und Dänemarks vom 10. bis 13. Jahrhundert. Mission – Kirchenorganisation – Kultpolitik* (Ostmitteleuropa in Vergangenheit und Gegenwart 17), Köln: Böhlau.

Platelle, H. (1993), 'Le ministère pastoral dans une paroisse de Frise au XIIe siècle, d'apres *La vie de Frédéric de Hallum* (+1175), prêtre séculier, puis chanoine prémontré, *Le clerc séculier au moyen âge* (Série Histoire Ancienne et Médiévale 27), Paris: Publications de la Sorbonne, 81–98.

Pommersches Urkundenbuch (1958), I, 2nd edn, Cologne: Böhlau.

Radtke, C. (1984), 'Anfänge und erste Entwicklung des Bistums Schleswig im 10. und 11. Jahrhundert', *850 Jahre St.-Petri-Dom zu Schleswig 1134–1984*, eds C. Radtke and W. Körber, Schleswig: Schleswiger Druck- und Verlagshaus, 133–60.

Radtke, C. (1992), 'König Magnus der Gute und Haithabu/Schleswig', *Mare Balticum. Beiträge zur Geschichte des Ostseeraums in Mittelalter und Neuzeit. Festschrift zum 65. Geburtstag von Erich Hoffmann* (Kieler Historische Studien 36), Sigmaringen: Thorbecke, 67–91.

Radtke, C. (1995), 'Die Entwicklung der Stadt Schleswig: Funktionen, Strukturen und die Anfänge der Gemeindebildung', *Die Stadt im westlichen Ostseeraum*, eds E. Hoffmann and F. Lubowitz (Kieler Werkstücke A:14), Teil 1, Frankfurt: Peter Lang, 47–91.

Rahmqvist, S. (1986), 'Gamla Uppsala by – Upplands största', *Från Östra Aros till Uppsala. En samling uppsatser kring det medeltida Uppsala* (Uppsala stads historia VII), Uppsala: Riksantikvarieämbetet, 254–71, 285–6.

Randers købstads historie (1952), I, ed. Povl v. Spreckelsen, Randers: Randers byråd.

Randsborg, K. (1980), *The Viking Age in Denmark. The Formation of a State*, London: Duckworth.

Rasmussen, P. (1956), 'Alling klosters jordegods (1536)–1586', *Østjydsk Hjemstavn*, 21, 71–80.

Die Rasteder Chronik 1059–1477 (1976), ed. H. Lübbing, Oldenburg: Heinz Holzberg.

Reitzel-Nielsen, E. (1984), *Johanniterordenens historie med særligt henblik på de nordiske lande*, I, Copenhagen: C. A. Reitzel.

Rhyzelius, A. (1740), *Monasteriologia Sviogothica eller Kloster-Beskrifning*, Linköping

Ribe Excavations 1970–76, (1981–90), ed. M. Bencard, I–IV, Esbjerg: Sydjysk Universitetsforlag.

Ridyard, S. J. (1988), *The Royal Saints of Anglo-Saxon England*, Cambridge: Cambridge University Press.

Riis, T. (1975), 'Bruddet mellem Valdemar den Store og Eskil 1161. Søborg, diplomerne og Saxo', *Saxostudier*, ed. I. Boserup, Copenhagen: Museum Tusculanum, 156–66.

Rollason, D. (1989), *Saints and Relics in Anglo-Saxon England*, Oxford: Blackwell.

Roth, S. (1973), *Gudhems klosterruin* (Acta Regiae Societatis Scientiarum et Litterarum Gothoburgensis, Humaniora 8), Göteborg: Kungl. Vetenskaps- och Vitterhets-Samhället.

Saga Óláfs Tryggvasonar (1932), ed. F. Jónsson, Copenhagen: Gad.

Sandnes, J. (1993), 'Middelalderens Trøndelag. Den kirkelige organisasjon i landsdelen, fylkeskirker, sognekirker, klostre', *Hikuin*, 20, 105–12.

Sawyer, P. (1991), *När Sverige blev Sverige*, Alingsås: Viktoria (Swedish version of *The Making of Sweden*, 1989).

Saxonis Gesta Danorum (1931), eds J. Olrik and H. Ræder, I–II, Copenhagen: Levin and Munksgaard.

Schelde-Jensen, B. G. and Juhl, F. A. (1991), *Et irreligiøst forsøg på en forståelse af de danske nonneklostres grundlæggelse og placering*, Odense. Speciale i historie, Historisk Institut.

Schmid, T. (1934), *Sveriges kristnande. Från verklighet till dikt*, Stockholm: Svenska Kyrkans Diakonistyrelse.

Schück, H. (1959), *Ecclesia Lincopensis. Studier om Linköpingskyrkan under medeltiden och Gustav Vasa* (Acta Universitatis Stockholmiensis, Stockholm Studies in History 4), Stockholm: Almqvist & Wiksell.

Schück, H. (1983–84), 'Det augustinska kanikesamfundet vid Skara domkyrka', *Västergötlands Fornminnesförenings Tidskrift* [Skara?]: Västergötlands Fornminnesförening, 136–93.

Scriptores minores historiæ Danicæ medii ævi (1918–22/1970), ed. M. C. Gertz, I–II, Copenhagen: Selskabet for udgivelse af kilder til dansk historie.

Seegrün, W. (1967), *Das Papsttum und Skandinavien bis zur Vollendung der nordischen Kirchenorganisation (1164)* (Quellen und Forschungen zur Geschichte Schleswig-Holsteins 51), Neumünster: Karl Wachholtz.

Seegrün, W. (1976), *Das Erzbistum Hamburg in seinen älteren Papsturkunden*, Köln: Böhlau.

Selja. Heilag stad I 1000 år (1997), ed. M. Rindal, Oslo: Universitetsforlaget.

Series Episcoporum Ecclesiae Catholicae Occidentalis ab initio usque ad annum MCXCVIII: Series V: Germania I: Archiepiscopatus Coloniensis (1982), eds S. Weinfurter and O. Engels, Stuttgart: Hiersemann.

Series Episcoporum Ecclesiae Catholicae Occidentalis ab initio usque ad annum MCXCVIII: Series V: Germania II: Archiepiscopatus Hammaburgensis sive Bremensis (1984), eds S. Weinfurter and O. Engels, Stuttgart: Hiersemann.

Series Episcoporum Ecclesiae Catholicae Occidentalis ab initio usque ad annum MCXCVIII: Series VI: Britannia II: Archiepiscopatus Lundensis (1992), ed. H. Kluger, Stuttgart: Hiersemann.

Severinsen P. (1932), *Viborg Domkirke med Stad og Stift i 800 Aar*, Copenhagen: O. Lohse.

Sigsjö, R. (1979–80), 'Klosterstaden Varnhem', *Västergötlands Fornminnesförenings Tidskrift* [Skara?]: Västergötlands Fornminnesförening, 103–56.

Sigsjö, R. (1990), 'Kyrkan på Lurö – Västsveriges första kloster?', *Fornvännen*, 85, 55–6.

Skovgaard-Petersen, I. (1977), 'Oldtid og vikingetid', *Danmarks historie, 1: Tiden indtil 1340*, eds A. E. Christensen, H. P. Clausen, S. Ellehøj and S. Mørch, Copenhagen: Gyldendal, 15–209.

Skyum-Nielsen, N. (1969), 'Das dänische Erzbistum vor 1250', *Kirche und Gesellschaft im Ostseeraum und im Norden vor der Mitte des 13. Jahrhunderts* (Acta Visbyensia III), Visby: Gotlands Fornsal, 113–38.

Skyum-Nielsen, N. (1971), *Kvinde og Slave. Danmarkshistorie uden retouche*, Copenhagen: Munksgaard.

Smith, G. G. (1973), 'De danske nonneklostre indtil ca. 1250', *Kirkehistoriske Samlinger*, 1–45.

Streich, G. (1986), *Klöster, Stifte und Kommenden in Niedersachsen vor der Reformation* (Studien und Vorarbeiten zum Historischen Atlas Niedersachsens 30), Hildesheim: August Lax.

Svenskt biografiskt lexikon (1918–), I– , Stockholm: Bonniers.

Swartling, I. (1959), '"... det dyrbaraste fähus i riket"', *Gotländskt arkiv*, 31, 35–48.

Swartling, I. (1967), *Nydala Abbey. An Outline of its Architecture from Foundation to Dissolution* (Stockholm Studies in History of Art 11), Stockholm: Almqvist & Wiksell.

Szacherska, S. M. (1977), 'The Political Role of the Danish Monasteries in Pomerania 1171–1223', *Mediaeval Scandinavia*, 10, 122–55.

Szacherska, S. M. (1988), 'Valdemar II's Expeditions to Pruthenia and the Mission of Bishop Christian', *Mediaeval Scandinavia*, 12, 44–75.

Thun, E. and Anglert, M. (1984), *Vä* (Medeltidsstaden 57), Stockholm: Riksantikvarieämbetet.

Tollin, C. (1998), 'Nydala klosters grundläggning och jordegendomar under äldre tid', *Nydala kloster*, ed. L. Aldén (Växjö Stiftshistoriska Sällskap, Meddelande, 20), Tingsryd: Växjö Stiftshistoriska Sällskap, 35–58.

Tunberg, S. (1926), *Sveriges historia till våra dagar 2: Äldre medeltiden*, Stockholm: P. A. Norstedt.

Tusindtallets Danske Mønter fra Den kongelige Mønt- og Medaillesamling. Danish Coins from the 11th century in The Royal Collection of Coins and Medals (1995), ed. J. S. Jensen, København: Nationalmuseet.

Vandvik, E. (1959), *Latinske dokument til norsk historie fram til år 1204*, Oslo: Det Norske Samlaget.

Vellev, J. (1974), 'Relikvierne fra Seem kirke', *Hikuin*, 1, 55–64, also as extract, 1975.

Vellev, J. (1977), 'Arkæologiske undersøgelser i Randers 1873–1977', *Hikuin*, 3, 101–22.

Vellev, J. (1990), *Asmild Klosterkirke i 900 år*, Aarhus: Hikuin.

Vellev, J. (1991), 'Biskop Gunners domkirke', *Jydske Lov 750 år*, eds O. Fenger and C. R. Jansen, Viborg: Landsarkivet, 209–17.

Vita Anskarii auctore Rimberto (1884), ed. G. Waitz (Scriptores rerum Germanicarum in usum scholarum), Hannover: MGH.

'Vita Sancti Botvidi maryris' (1828), *Scriptores Rerum Suecicarum Medii Aevi*, II, ed. E. M. Fant, Uppsala: Palmblad, 377–82.

Vitae Sanctorum Danorum (1908–12), ed. M. C. Gertz, Copenhagen: G. E. C. Gad.

Walbran, J. R. (ed.) (1862), *Memorials of the Abbey of St. Mary of Fountains* (The Publications of the Surtes Society 42), London.

Wallin, C. (1955–91), *Tommarps Urkundsbok 1085–1600*, I–VI, Tomelilla: Författarens förlag.

Wallin, C. (1961), 'Ärkebiskop Eskil som klosterstiftare', *Scandia*, 27, 217–34.

Wallin, C. (1989), 'Premonstratenserna och deras kloster i Skåne', *Skånska kloster*, ed. E. Cinthio (Skånes Hembygdsförbunds Årsbok 1987/88), Lund: Skånes Hembygdsförbund, 63–81.

Wavra, B. (1991), *Salzburg und Hamburg. Erzbistumsgründung und Missionspolitik in karolingischer Zeit* (Giessener Abhandlungen zur Agrar- und Wirtschaftsforschung des europäischen Ostens 179), Berlin: Duncker and Humblot.

Weinfurter, S. (1975), *Salzburger Bischofsreform und Bischofspolitik im 12. Jahrhundert. Der Erzbischof Konrad I. von Salzburg (1106–1147) und die Regularkanoniker* (Kölner Historische Abhandlungen 24), Köln and Wien: Böhlau.

Westman, K. B. (1915), *Den svenska kyrkans utveckling från S:t Bernhards tidevarv till Innocentius III:s*, Stockholm: Norstedts.

Westman, K. B. (1954), 'Erik den Helige och hans tid', *Erik den helige. Historia – kult – reliker*, ed. B. Thordeman, Stockholm: Nordisk Rotogravyr, 1–108.

Widéen, H. (1949), 'Klostret på ön. Från en sommarexpedition till Lurö i Vänern', *Julhälsningar till församlingarna i Skara stift*, 44, 24–31.

Wilkinson, J., Hill, J. and Ryan, W. (1988), *Jerusalem Pilgrimage 1099–1185* (The Hakluyt Society Second Series 167), London: Hakluyt Society.

Yrlid, I. A. (1976), *Och i hopp om det eviga livet. Studier i Skånes romanska muralmåleri*, Lund: Corpus Iuris Förlag.

Yrwing, H. (1978), *Gotlands medeltid*, Visby: Gotlandskonst.

Ziese, J. (1982), *Wibert von Ravenna, der Gegenpapst Clemens III. (1084–1100)* (Päpste und Papsttum 20), Stuttgart: Hiersemann.

Index

Note on the order of the alphabet:

1. Swedish Å/å counts as Aa/aa. Pronounced: like *a* in b*a*ll, f*a*ll.
2. Swedish Ä/ä counts as A/a. Pronounced: like *a* in h*a*ppy. Inversely, however, Danish and Norwegian Æ/æ count as Ae/ae. Pronounced: similar but more closed.
3. Swedish Ö/ö and Danish and Norwegian Ø/ø count as O/o. Pronounced: in Swedish like *i* in f*i*rst, in Danish and Norwegian more closed.

/ indicates alternative forms of the same name.
There is no index for Denmark, Norway, Sweden.